SPEAKING AMERICAN

Race and Culture in the American West
Quintard Taylor, Series Editor

SPEAKING AMERICAN

LANGUAGE EDUCATION
AND CITIZENSHIP IN
TWENTIETH-CENTURY
LOS ANGELES

ZEVI GUTFREUND

UNIVERSITY OF OKLAHOMA PRESS : NORMAN

This book is published with the generous assistance
of the McCasland Foundation, Duncan, Oklahoma.

Portions of this book appeared, in a version since revised, in "Immigrant Education and Race: Alternative Approached to 'Americanization' in Los Angeles, 1910–1940," *History of Education Quarterly* 57, No. 1 (February 2017): 1–38, and are published here with permission.

Library of Congress Cataloging-in-Publication Data

Names: Gutfreund, Zevi (Zevi Moses), author.

Title: Speaking American : language education and citizenship in twentieth-century
    Los Angeles / Zevi Gutfreund.

Other titles: Language education, race, and the remaking of American citizenship in
    Los Angeles, 1900–1968

Description: Norman : University of Oklahoma Press, [2019] | Series: Race and culture in
    the American West series ; volume 15 | Revised and expanded version of the author's
    thesis (doctoral)—University of California, Los Angeles, 2013, titled Language
    education, race, and the remaking of American citizenship in Los Angeles, 1900–1968. |
    Includes bibliographical references and index.

Identifiers: LCCN 2018030004 | ISBN 978-0-8061-6186-0 (hardcover : alk. paper)

Subjects: LCSH: Education, Bilingual—California—Los Angeles—History—20th century. |
    Ethnic schools—California—Los Angeles—History—20th century. | Mexican
    Americans—Education—California—Los Angeles—History—20th century. | Japanese
    Americans—Education—California—Los Angeles—History—20th century. | Los
    Angeles (Calif.)—Ethnic relations.

Classification: LCC LC3733.L7 G87 2019 | DDC 370.1170979494—dc23

LC record available at https://lccn.loc.gov/2018030004

Speaking American: Language Education and Citizenship in Twentieth-Century Los Angeles is Volume 15 in the Race and Culture in the American West series.

The paper in this book meets the guidelines for permanence and durability of the Committee on Production Guidelines for Book Longevity of the Council on Library Resources, Inc. ∞

To my parents, Isac and Minette Gutfreund

CONTENTS

ILLUSTRATIONS

ACKNOWLEDGMENTS

One of the many rewards of writing about the history of education is that it has allowed me to tell the fascinating stories of teachers. Not only did teachers whom I had never met become the most colorful characters in my research, but this project would not have been possible without a long list of teachers who have enriched my life. My second-grade teacher, Mrs. Hilda Burness, recognized my interest in history when she encouraged me to write a letter to the publisher about an error in a biography of George Washington. At Harvard, William Gienapp inspired me to major in history with his brilliant lectures about the Civil War and baseball in American society. Most importantly for this book, at UCLA I was fortunate to learn from a master teacher, Stephen Aron. He patiently answered my countless questions, encouraged me to think about why my project was original and significant, and always left me more eager to return to my research and writing. Steve's interest in "convergence" at the Autry Museum of the American West inspired my own approach to this book, which is better off because of his suggestion to include all three ethnic groups (Japanese American, Mexican American, and Anglo-American) in every chapter. Although I now live in the "Other LA" (Louisiana), Steve continues to be an invaluable advisor, and I aspire to the example he has set as a teacher, writer, and public historian.

I benefited from other model teachers at UCLA as well. Patricia Gándara is not only an expert in the field of language education, she is actively participating in the uphill battle to protect what remains of bilingual education in the United States today. Her work at the UCLA Civil Rights Project/

Proyecto Derechos Civiles is worthy of a history of its own, and I have always appreciated her enthusiasm for my study of a more extended history of civil rights. Kelly Lytle Hernández has conducted groundbreaking research on immigration, and I am fortunate to have worked with her as a student and as a teaching fellow. My interest in bilingual education originated from a research paper I wrote for her seminar, and her comments pushed me to find more sources and tell more stories in this project. Other UCLA professors who did not sit on my dissertation committee have also been generous with their time, experience, and interest in my career. Many thanks to Eric Avila, Caroline Ford, Toby Higbie, Ben Madley, David Myers, Gary Nash, Marian Olivas, Jan Reiff, Brenda Stevenson, Joan Waugh, and Craig Yirush.

Many people helped me through the twists and turns of archival research. Some of them may not have expected to hear from an academic historian. In particular, I want to thank Mr. Joseph Zanki Sr., a teacher who retired from Roosevelt High School in Los Angeles. Mr. Zanki invited me into his home to read old student newspapers and yearbooks at his dining room table. I visited so many times that I got to know many members of the Zanki family, all of whom made me feel welcome. Thanks also to Los Angeles–area teachers Olga Stara at San Fernando High School, Pamela Bailey at Jefferson High School, and especially Sherri Whitham at Hollywood High School, all of whom shared primary sources from their campus libraries. Many librarians and archivists at academic and public institutions were just as helpful in the research process. I am grateful for the guidance I received from the staffs of the Japanese American National Museum in Los Angeles; the Department of Special Collections and the Chicano Studies Research Center, UCLA; the Grand Avenue Library & Book Depository, the University of Southern California; the Honnold/Mudd Library, Claremont Colleges; the Department of Special Collections and the Hoover Institution, Stanford University; the Bancroft Library, UC Berkeley; and the Foreign Language Center, Defense Language Institute.

This work was supported by generous fellowships and grants I received from the John Randolph Haynes and Dora Haynes Foundation, UCLA Department of History, UCLA Graduate Division, UCLA Institute for Research on Labor and Employment, LSU Department of History, and LSU Office of Research and Economic Development.

A myriad of scholars read or heard previous versions of individual chapters at academic conferences, and their comments and suggestions improved the quality of writing and depth of research in this book. I am indebted to Thomas Andrews, Laura Barraclough, John Bezis-Selfa, Geraldo Cadava, Jon Christensen, Lawrence Culver, William Deverell, John Mack Faragher,

Matt Garcia, Steven Hackel, Todd Holmes, David Igler, Sarah Keyes, Jessica Kim, David Labaree, Farina Mir, Robert "Roy" Ritchie, Virginia Scharff, Josh Sides, Rachel St. John, Eric Steiger, Alan Taylor, Louis Warren, Mark Wild, and Richard White. Rosina Lozano and Natalia Mehlman Petrzela graciously shared their recent research about language education in New Mexico and California, respectively. Thanks also to Nancy Beadie and Kathy Nicholas at *History of Education Quarterly* for helping to clarify some of the larger arguments about education and citizenship in this book. A portion of chapter 2 is adapted from my article "Immigrant Education and Race: Alternative Approaches to 'Americanization' in Los Angeles, 1910–1940," *History of Education Quarterly* 57, no. 1 (February 2017), 1–38.

I have also learned a lot from fellow students, to whom I owe many thanks. As they finished their own doctoral degrees, Erik Greenberg, Joshua Paddison, Erika Pérez, and Karen Wilson each advised me on my own writing process. In addition, I appreciate the many attendees who heard several presentations of mine at the UCLA History Department graduate colloquium, including Max Baumgarten, Alfred Flores, Matthew Luckett, Daniel Lynch, Devin McCutchen, Michael Slaughter, Devon Van Dyne, and JoAnna Wall. Most of all, I extend deep gratitude to the members of my dissertation writing group, Lauren Acker, Jean-Paul deGuzman, Caroline Luce, and Laura Redford. They read long rough drafts of each chapter, and their thoughtful comments over lengthy lunches, and occasionally heated debates during dinner, improved my dissertation. I especially appreciate that Caroline and Laura took the time to read revised chapters long after we had all completed our dissertations. Finally, I thank Beth Carmichael for reading the final version of the manuscript.

I am indebted to my editors at the University of Oklahoma Press, Kathleen Kelly and Steven Baker. Kathleen was enthusiastic about this book when we first met to talk about it at a UCLA coffee shop. With patient support for a first-time author, Kathleen guided me through the feedback of three anonymous reviewers. Thanks also to Kirsteen Anderson for copyediting and to Bethany Mowry for leading me through the process of acquiring permissions for photographs and illustrations. Any errors that remain are my own.

The final manuscript benefited greatly from the input of my current colleagues in the History Department at Louisiana State University. Victor Stater has been an incredibly supportive chair, and I am especially grateful to Charles Shindo and Aaron Sheehan-Dean for reading multiple chapters and helping me navigate the process of turning my dissertation into a book manuscript. Thanks also to Catherine Jacquet for organizing our department's junior faculty writing group, where I received thoughtful feedback on several chapters from Asiya Alam, Stephen Andes, Sherri Johnson, Brendan Karch, and Kodi Roberts. It is a privilege to work with so many wonderful teachers here in Baton Rouge.

At the same time, I am very lucky that the greatest teachers in my life happen to be close relatives. I am grateful to my family for giving me the gift of a lifelong love of learning. My parents, Minette and Isac Gutfreund, hooked me on history as soon as I could read by buying a set of childhood biographies of famous Americans. I thank my mother for suggesting I study the history of education in the first place, and my father for making many sacrifices so that I could receive the best education, even if that meant my moving to San Francisco's rival city to the south for graduate school, then moving to the Deep South as a professor. My own thinking about this book improved as I answered numerous questions from my parents, my sister Mia Gutfreund, and my grandparents, Ken and Esther Trigger. I cannot thank enough all of the family members who have always supported me. Finally, I could not have written this book without Rosalyn Won, who has helped me through this process in countless ways. In addition to being my best friend, an indispensable companion, and a great sports fan, Roz is one of the best elementary schoolteachers I know. In the last six years, both of us have learned even more about the art of teaching as we have watched Milo develop his own curiosities about how the world works. I am grateful to Roz, Milo, and the Gutfreund family for bringing love and joy to my life. I owe this book to all of you.

SPEAKING AMERICAN

INTRODUCTION

THE RACIAL POLITICS OF LANGUAGE IN LOS ANGELES

When Lyndon Johnson signed the controversial Bilingual Education Act (BEA) in 1968, language learning became a focal point in the culture wars of the late twentieth century. Perhaps ironically, the most disruptive protests occurred in Los Angeles, the same city where elected officials from both parties had played pivotal roles in lobbying the president to authorize federal funding to teach immigrant students in their native languages. Despite bipartisan support for the legislation, the curricula in Los Angeles schools did not follow the language reforms that local members of Congress, senators, and school board members had proposed. Two months after the president signed the law, thousands of Mexican American students walked out of seven high schools in East Los Angeles, protesting the school board ban on Spanish-language instruction. These contradictory events represented the multiple levels at which Americans debated bilingual education. At a policy level, the BEA reignited questions about whether immigrants were better served by learning English only or by maintaining their heritage language in conjunction with English. At a local level, the East LA "Blowouts" indicated that students were willing to challenge authorities and demand language instruction that reflected their dual identities as immigrants and Americans. This book tells the story of how immigrants in Los Angeles used language learning as a vehicle to influence American politics, society, and culture throughout the twentieth century. Issues and policies related to language learning helped Angelino newcomers identify competing concepts of US citizenship that were tied to their actions and deeds rather than the English language itself.[1]

The Blowouts and the BEA are both part of a tradition that for more than a century has brought national attention to language innovations launched in LA schools. These advances occurred in a wide range of formats, including foreign-language courses, in which students learned to communicate in an unfamiliar idiom, and bilingual education classes in which non-English speakers studied academic subjects in their native languages. Yet the purpose of such instruction went beyond simply improving the mechanics of language acquisition. This book is titled *Speaking American* because disparate communities used all of these instructional methods—from English-only classes to heritage-language schools—to engage in the continuous project of remaking American citizenship. Each of these experiments demonstrates that deciding which language (or languages) an immigrant should learn is necessarily a political act that influences one's attitude about American values such as racial diversity and civic participation.

The federal government used the mobilization for World War II to promote a national citizenship in which social rights came to be protected by the state. From a local perspective, different approaches to immigrant education revealed competing conceptions of citizenship. Anglo (meaning white, English-speaking) reformers wanted to require that foreign-born students complete English-only curricula to become eligible for civic membership. On the other hand, immigrant instructors organized community schools to teach the second generation the heritage language, encouraging their children to maintain an ethnic identity as they sought dual citizenship. It is difficult to compare immigrant community schools with public school language programs because the latter had far more students and financial resources. However, by examining all these schools' language curricula as competing proposals, *Speaking American* puts the voices of ethnic minorities on a level playing field with those of the Anglo-American mainstream. Despite a state-sanctioned Americanization agenda that used language to limit access to citizenship before the war, many immigrant educators eagerly embedded democratic values in vocabulary lessons in their native languages. From this diverse array of language instruction before and after the war, generations of children in the nation's fastest-growing, most diverse metropolis learned to "speak American" in many different ways.[2]

Scholars have found it difficult to discuss the overarching debate over immigrant citizenship because the arguments are often isolated within distinct ethnic and racial groups. This book puts these disputes in dialogue with one another by comparing the language agendas of the school districts that served the two largest non-Anglo, nonnative populations in the city and county of Los Angeles—Mexican and Japanese—with the language schools that first-generation immigrants established to teach their American-born offspring the heritage language. As many language projects competed and coexisted, they empowered immigrants and their children to think of citizenship as a process of negotiation within a multiethnic community. The range of programs proposed by Angelinos (a term that includes everyone who lived in Los Angeles County) reflected the centrality of language in civic discourse about assimilation, immigration, and what it means to be an American.[3]

Language instruction had long offered a forum in which Angelino educators could articulate their responses to federal and local policies that racialized access to citizenship. In the Progressive Era, the LA city schools and some school districts across LA County designed English-only courses to reinforce federal legislation that used "national origins" quotas to restrict immigration. When Congress removed race from its immigration quotas in 1965, LA schools instituted bilingual education programs that reflected a more expansive vision of citizenship. Meanwhile, immigrant communities pushed back against local efforts to limit their civil liberties. Discrimination against Japanese Angelinos included two alien land laws that restricted their rights to own property, and subsequently their forced removal and internment during World War II. Mexican Americans endured repatriation raids during the Depression, the Zoot Suit Riots in 1943, and increasing threats from Border Patrol inspections after 1965. At each moment of crisis, Mexican and Japanese educators crafted new methods of language learning that challenged the discrimination they faced. Acting alone, ethnic minorities could not change their unequal access to civil liberties, but they created language-learning experiments that questioned the prejudiced assumptions of citizenship restrictions imposed upon them. Through studying English and their heritage languages at the same time, Mexican and Japanese Angelinos learned to advocate for themselves as Americans and as children of immigrants.

The many language experiments in Los Angeles County produced a plethora of documents written by Mexican and Japanese educators, students they taught, and Anglo-American administrators. Through these writings, neglected communities injected their own agendas into national debates about education and citizenship. As US Supreme Court rulings and federal legislation set immigration policy during the Progressive Era, some Anglo-American women published journal articles and lesson plans that determined how school district language courses would reflect quota restrictions. As diplomats and military officers coordinated international affairs before World

War II, immigrant educators planned study abroad trips to Mexico and Japan to introduce their students to their cultural heritage. As public schools braced for war in the 1930s (and during the civil rights reforms afterward), young people used student clubs, newspapers, and protests to demand changes in language instruction. Curriculum guides and summer camp proposals illustrate what judicial rulings and US Senate resolutions do not: that Mexican and Japanese Angelinos used language learning as a vehicle to take control of their Americanization experiences in spite of the racialized constraints they faced.[4]

Until World War II, many Americans assumed that the public school system was the country's primary instrument of assimilation or, as Woodrow Wilson put it, "the great melting-pot of America, the place where we are all made Americans of."[5] Scholars today often refer to "programs of forced Americanization" in the context of nativism and the immigration restriction acts of the 1920s. At the time, however, public and private institutions joined the president in romanticizing Americanization. At Henry Ford's Model T assembly plant, for example, immigrant auto workers celebrated their graduation from the Ford English School's language and civics program by dressing in their ethnic garb, then marching into a physical "melting pot," and finally emerging in identical suits waving American flags. The ceremony represented Wilson's Americanization model, reflecting the notion that all immigrants (especially those from Europe) absorbed Anglo-American values and norms simply by showing up at school. In multiracial Los Angeles, however, the dynamics of Americanization were not as linear or absolute as Henry Ford's symbolic melting pot. Rather than representing total integration, Americanization in Los Angeles became a contested cultural ideal that was shaped by ethnic differences as much as it was defined by processes of assimilation.[6]

Although graduations resembling Ford's melting-pot ceremony did occur in Los Angeles, the city's Mexican and Japanese communities also created alternative rituals that reimagined Americanization as a socially inclusive celebration of ethnic traditions and heritage languages. Angelinos active in these Americanization debates have largely been forgotten, but recent scholarship has challenged the assumption that Americanization was a simple effort to assimilate immigrants by obliterating children's previous ethnic cultures and replacing them with social and moral attitudes acceptable to mainstream Americans. Instead, many immigrants embraced key aspects of Americanization, including learning English, because they believed American democracy protected their ethnic heritages. Such studies shift the focus of Americanization from forced assimilation to cultural negotiation, but their narratives are often limited to European immigrants in the Midwest and on the Atlantic Seaboard, or to single-group studies of Asian or Latin American newcomers in the West. This book builds on that literature by comparing how Mexican and Japanese educators in Los Angeles designed language instruction programs to complement and compete with the city's Americanization agenda. While the school district insisted on English-only classrooms, racialized groups in Los Angeles promoted immigrant education as an antidote to nativist calls for forced assimilation.[7]

Americanization became less controversial after Congress enacted national origins quotas in 1924, causing immigration rates to slow down. The National Origins Act limited the annual number of immigration visas by country to 2 percent of the number of people of each nationality living in America as of the 1890 census. Subsequently, the national education debate shifted from the assimilation of foreigners to the integration of racial minorities. Language reforms in Los Angeles after World War II influenced this transition. Like earlier citizenship fights, this precursor to the civil rights movement concerned issues of social and political inclusion. Inclusion meant many things in a multiethnic state like California, where the injustices suffered by immigrants of Asian and Hispanic descent rivaled those of African Americans in other regions. Angelinos continued to propose language innovations after the war, but immigrant education experiments carried new political implications in the early civil rights period.[8]

Recent political historians have made a convincing case that California was central to the "long civil rights movement" at mid-century and to the rise of modern conservatism since the 1960s, and some have used the history of language education to support these assertions. Some have also factored language education into their analyses of California liberals and conservatives, respectively. According to Mark Brilliant's comprehensive history of civil rights litigation and legislation, language instruction played a vital role in the school desegregation lawsuit *Mendez v. Westminster* and in Governor Earl Warren's effort to write integration into the California Education Code. Natalia Mehlman Petrzela explains how California officials such as Governor Ronald Reagan and Superintendent of Public Instruction Max Rafferty, both advocates of the New Right in the 1960s, proposed bilingual education bills to recruit Spanish speakers to the Republican Party. These works expand the story of the civil rights movement from World War II to the 1978 California tax revolt that limited government spending and contributed to Reagan's election as president. Focusing specifically on language education, however, offers an even longer period in which to evaluate the civil rights struggle in Los Angeles.[9] Considering the continuities between language experiments in 1915 and Proposition 227, the 1998 referendum that banned bilingual education, allows us to examine the influence of immigrant activism on interracial reform movements in California. As attention turned from Americanization to integration, immigrant educators in Los Angeles became civil rights advocates and community leaders.

Los Angeles offers unique possibilities for local study because students left behind abundant evidence about their attitudes toward Americanization, language learning, and civic participation. Their voices turned traditional debates about assimilation and cultural maintenance into discussions of broader issues of political inclusion. In the Progressive Era, Angelino adolescents did not sit by as educators of Anglo, Mexican, and Japanese descent struggled to shape the LA city schools' approach to Americanization. Rather, they reconciled the lessons of Progressive reformers who taught English-only classes with the ethnocentric lessons they received after school from teachers who argued that learning Spanish was a central component of full Americanization. They observed the paradoxes of wartime policies that prohibited Japanese instruction in internment camps but permitted it in the army. After World War II, in court testimony and street protests, immigrant teachers and students advocated for bilingual education to become a key component of school integration. From the turn of the twentieth century to the protests against Proposition 227 in 1998, language learning served as a vehicle for student activism even as school districts used it as a mechanism of control. The participation of young people in debates that included Anglo-American administrators, Progressive educators, and immigrant parents turned LA schools into forums in which local authorities could not prevent powerless communities from voicing alternative visions of citizenship and race relations.[10]

Student voices add a new dimension to recent scholarship that has analyzed immigrant education to explain the relationship between race and politics in American life. This is a departure from the traditional narrative of European history, in which language instruction played a central role in nation-state formation. European historians used the consolidation of language groups as one example of nineteenth-century nationalism, citing the old quip that "a language is simply a dialect with an army and a navy." In America, in contrast, public education was attached less to nation-building than to the social construction of concepts like race and culture. Laws from the Home Teacher Act of 1915 to the Bilingual Education Act of 1968 generated thoughtful debates about the relationship between public schools and foreign-born students who lacked citizenship and English literacy. By analyzing all types of instruction from English-only programs to bilingual education courses under the umbrella of "speaking American," I explore how each method promoted a specific vision of American citizenship. School officials pioneered many language programs throughout the century, selling their English instruction ideas as assimilation models for other cities. At the same time, Spanish- and Japanese-language schools opened across the county, and students showed ethnic pride by using their heritage languages in speeches and protests. Language operated under different dynamics in Los Angeles, a city that stood apart for its multiracial makeup and one whose residents launched experiments that devised uniquely American ways to incorporate immigrants into civic life.[11]

Even before World War II, students in Los Angeles simply looked different than the European newcomers who had entered Woodrow Wilson's public school melting pots. In 1930, racial minorities composed 14 percent of the population. The only city with more nonwhites was Baltimore, but most of those minorities were African American. Few blacks lived in Los Angeles in 1930, but together the 97,000 Mexican residents and 21,000 people of Japanese descent constituted 10 percent of the city's 1.2 million inhabitants. This demographic reality was not lost on Angelino educators. In 1923, the superintendent of the LA schools observed that Los Angeles had become "the third largest Mexican city in the world." Others noted that more than one-third of the Japanese students in California schools lived in LA County. This multiethnic population became the backdrop for high-profile language learning lawsuits in Los Angeles that aimed to influence legal decisions in the 1920s over the Fourteenth Amendment (which guarantees all citizens equal protection under the law) and judicial rulings in the 1940s over school integration. The close proximity of many races also triggered the East LA walkouts in 1968 and the subsequent backlash against the Chicano civil rights movement. The disproportionately large numbers of Spanish and Japanese speakers, along with the history of innovative language experiments, make Los Angeles a prime location to examine how immigrant communities used language education to stake a claim to American citizenship.[12]

Previous scholars have celebrated the city's rich diversity by examining multiple ethnic groups in LA schools. In their accounts of working-class neighborhoods like Boyle Heights in East Los Angeles, Allison Varzally and Mark Wild both argue that adolescent Angelinos created new cultural identities simply through interacting with neighbors and classmates of other races. At Roosevelt High School in Boyle Heights, students organized "international dress-up days" to honor their parents' diverse traditions, helping Angelinos overcome ethnic differences to forge lasting personal and political bonds. Other historians have examined how LA educators designed curricula to accommodate the region's unique student population, a process which began in 1903 when Anglo women operating settlement houses in industrial neighborhoods organized English classes for immigrant mothers. From then on, women have continued to propose innovations in English instruction that have raised the school district's demand for female administrators with experience teaching the growing immigrant population of Los Angeles. A recent biography of Helen Heffernan, for example, tells the story of a principal who supervised instruction of Spanish-speaking children during World War II until Douglas MacArthur invited her to Tokyo to revamp the Japanese school system during the American occupation. As ambitious educators and assimilated students collaborated (and clashed) on language curricula from the Progressive Era through the Cold War, they created new meanings of citizenship and Americanization. Whereas past scholarship has established that public schools were the original sites of multiethnic mixing in Los Angeles, in this book I emphasize debates over language learning to challenge the romantic model of interracial harmony in LA schools.[13]

At the same time, the city's ethnic diversity reconstructed language education into a racial project. Immigrant educators created community language schools to teach the American-born second generation that embracing their ethnic heritage made America a stronger nation. Language instruction was one of several challenges to the melting-pot myth in the Progressive Era. In 1916, Randolph Bourne questioned the assimilation emphasis of Americanization advocates. Bourne praised universities for defying Henry Ford's melting-pot ceremony and allowing students of every ethnicity to intermingle on campus while "weaving back and forth" between their ethnic heritage and their American surroundings. Yet evidence suggests that language instruction occurred in isolation, allowing each immigrant community to forge its own attitudes toward studying English and preserving ethnic traditions. This made language learning a messy business in diverse neighborhoods like Boyle Heights, where speakers of Spanish and Japanese (and Yiddish and Russian) would spill onto the street in simultaneous yet separate conversations. As multiple language projects progressed side by side, they provided alternative means to immigrant education in a cosmopolitan city. Language experiments reflected an unspoken dialogue between the LA school district and the city's two largest nonwhite immigrant communities. As they faced challenges like immigration restrictions, cultural assimilation, wartime internment, racial segregation, and measures banning bilingual education, both communities created language curricula to respond to their specific political conditions.[14]

This dual examination of Mexican American and Japanese American history engages multiple interpretations of past limits on citizenship for people of color. Scholars of LA's two largest non-Anglo groups have found language schools useful sources because they enabled distinct ethnic cultures to coexist in an era of burgeoning "internationalism." Community schools helped immigrants of color to create inroads to assimilation even as they navigated a system with racialized restrictions on the privileges of citizenship. The historian George J. Sánchez emphasized language learning to give agency to Spanish speakers, noting that immigrants "became Mexican American" by combining these two national identities into a new culture. Sánchez argued that Mexican Angelinos experienced "ambivalent Americanization" as they used schools to expand civic membership while maintaining Spanish-language organizing traditions from the Mexican Revolution of 1910. Other scholars have suggested that Mexicans (LA's largest non-Anglo community) used Spanish-language schools to shape an approach to assimilation that the school district rejected. In *Speaking American*, I compare the Mexican-origin community's "ambivalent Americanization" with studies of Japanese Angelinos to explore how language instruction allowed alternative approaches to citizenship education in the same city.[15]

In contrast, scholars of individual groups have focused on immigrants' relationships with their countries of origin. This is especially true for Japanese Americans, who developed labels that distinguished between first-generation immigrants, the Issei, and their US-born offspring, the Nisei. Eiichiro Azuma's analysis of the "Issei frontier thesis," captured in Japanese-language textbooks that described California as a future extension of Japanese imperialism, implies that some immigrants flipped the onus of assimilation from the Issei to Anglo-Americans. Language acquisition was so important that many Issei sent their school-age children back to Japan to learn the heritage language. Whereas Azuma interpreted this language curriculum as Japan's "racialized ideology of self-empowerment," other historians have viewed the frontier thesis and community-based language instruction as elements of a broader project to turn the Nisei into "bridges of understanding" between Japan and America. Such stories of binational bridge-building overlook the fact that Japanese schools taught the concept of "Issei internationalism" to the same students who took "internationalism studies" classes at Roosevelt High School. It is not surprising that Issei educators maintained closer contact with the Japanese government than with their LA neighbors who taught in public schools or in Mexican consulate schools. Heritage learning represented a racialized strategy of national belonging in a transnational community, but the "bridges of understanding" concept demonstrates that language projects influenced diplomatic circles as well as working-class areas like Boyle Heights.[16]

Perhaps the purest expression of Woodrow Wilson's melting-pot ideal was the California Home Teacher Act of 1915. Written by an Angelino reformer, the state law authorized school districts to hire social workers to Americanize immigrant mothers by teaching them to speak English and to keep clean, orderly homes. By 1923, the LA school district led all school districts in the state with more than one hundred home teachers. Anglo-American reformers were not the only ones who used language to sway citizenship in Los Angeles. In 1926 the Mexican consul general opened a school in the East LA barrio of Belvedere. With financial backing from the Mexican Office of Public Education, ten consulate schools pledged to help immigrant children become dual citizens by teaching them Mexican history and maintaining their Spanish language ability. Although Japanese-language schools lacked official ties to Tokyo, more than one hundred belonged to the Southern California Japanese Language Association by 1930. Unfortunately, the association's president was one of the first Japanese citizens arrested on the day of the Pearl Harbor bombing, December 7, 1941. These efforts were more than just a series of language experiments that paralleled increasing immigration levels in Los Angeles. Rather, the city's language programs shaped national debates about citizenship and transnational identities at key moments of the twentieth century.

Telling these stories together amplifies the significance of language learning as a racial and national project. In examining numerous innovations in immigrant education, both inside and outside the LA schools, I document how different communities used language learning to articulate alternative approaches to controversial national debates over race, immigration, and education. The first two chapters compare and contrast the school district's language experiments in Americanization and citizenship courses with Mexican immigrant approaches to "ambivalent Americanization" and the Japanese community's ideal of "bridges of understanding." Angelinos used language learning to articulate competing responses to the racialized citizenship restrictions imposed by the federal government before World War II. Chapters 3 and 4 explore how Mexican and Japanese Angelinos responded to discriminatory wartime policies by introducing language learning goals that became linked to the fight for racial integration after the war. While the federal government banned language schools from Japanese internment camps and juvenile detention centers, efforts to revive instruction in Japanese and Spanish became key legal arguments for desegregating schools before *Brown v. Board of Education*. Chapters 5 and 6 focus on the 1960s, when bilingual education became one of the first demands of the budding Chicano civil rights movement. The Bilingual Education Act and the East

LA Blowouts of 1968 marked a climax of student activism and legislative achievement. The following decades, however, saw the return of English-only politics from new sources, namely S. I. Hayakawa, California's first Japanese American US senator. The final chapter compares the 1998 decision to ban bilingual education in California with the latest experiment in Los Angeles, language immersion schools. Today, given the coexistence of English-only and language immersion advocates, students and teachers in Los Angeles continue to use language instruction as a vehicle to remake citizenship policies in the twenty-first century.

Tracking these language experiments over the course of the twentieth century illustrates how LA schools served as a laboratory for ideas about immigration, assimilation, and exclusion. School officials offered a number of creative approaches to English-language instruction in the hopes of Americanizing immigrants. While most immigrants were eager to learn English, many were just as adamant about preserving the languages they had spoken in the old country. Just as passionately as Progressives promoted Americanization courses, non-English-speaking newcomers argued that studying their native language (and embracing an identity that made them distinct from other Americans) was also a pure expression of their commitment to US citizenship. Anglo-American superintendents, Japanese American educators, and Mexican American students all struggled to shape the dynamics of American democracy by proposing their own language programs in the Progressive Era, in the years between the two world wars, and in the postwar civil rights era. These debates about assimilation and school desegregation have deep roots in language experiments dating back to 1900, when students and teachers in Los Angeles believed that Spanish and Japanese classes were racial and national projects as important as learning English. Instruction in multiple languages taught immigrants and citizens alike to "speak American."

1 | MAKING AMERICANIZATION MORE THAN ENGLISH INSTRUCTION, 1900–1930

In June 1926, the graduation ceremony for the 28th Street School's Americanization class featured the pomp and circumstance that characterized many immigrant education commencements during the Progressive Era. The Anglo-American women who taught these classes stressed their professionalism by staging the event in a room lined with portraits of the nation's leading citizens and inviting dignitaries like the state superintendent of public instruction and the former mayor of Mazatlán, Mexico. Everyone had come to celebrate the six foreign women who had completed LA's rigorous Americanization class. The six honorees who sat behind a polished wooden table in their best dresses, one of them carrying a baby, were the only graduates in a class that began with sixty-seven immigrants. Mrs. Portillo, the Mazatlán official's sister-in-law, articulated her classmates' struggles and aspirations: "You don't realize how sad I was because I couldn't understand any word in English. I thought I was the most ignorant person in the world. I am in the middle way of my ambitions. . . . My aim is to be a Spanish teacher in the schools here. Today is the happiest day of my life because I am going to have my certificate."[1]

Language learning in Los Angeles complicated national debates about Americanization during the Progressive Era. Mrs. Portillo's goals did not reflect the original intent of the LA Americanization classes. To be sure, she credited the 28th Street School instructors for teaching her to speak English and enabling her to advance in the city's social hierarchy as a professional, but she took the class in order to get a job teaching Spanish. Whereas in later culture wars lines were drawn between English-only advocates and those who wanted to teach immigrants in their native language, Mrs. Portillo believed in both types of language instruction. For this privileged mother with ties to Mexican officials, English and Spanish were both central to her sense of Americanization.

This chapter explores how three language experiments in Los Angeles overturned the national paradigm that Americanization was an English-only experience. Mass immigration in the decades before the National Origins Act of 1924 brought an abundance of non-English speakers to the United States, many of whom wanted to learn English and assimilate. Progressives who proposed Americanization courses assumed that learning English would help the distinctive ethnic traits of immigrants disappear into the mythical melting pot. In Los Angeles, sociologists and social reformers believed the lack of English learning among two of the city's largest racial minority groups was central to what they dubbed the "Mexican Problem" and the "Oriental Problem." Many Mexican and Japanese immigrants agreed that learning English would help them adapt, though some grew ambivalent as they struggled to assimilate. From 1903 to 1930, Mexican-origin, Japanese-origin, and Anglo-American groups proposed new ideas about immigrant education to the state legislature, in school district publications, and at community meetings. These innovative proposals helped foreign-born newcomers and their native-born children navigate their own paths toward the elusive goal of Americanization. They empowered immigrants like Mrs. Portillo to learn English in order to become a Spanish teacher. Not all LA educators approved of speaking multiple languages, but they agreed that the languages Mrs. Portillo learned and taught were central to her civic identity.

Angelinos also agreed that they were changing the national debate over Americanization. Elected officials across the country promoted

The graduation ceremony for the 28th Street School's Americanization class. *From* The Survey, *June 1926.*

Americanization as an assimilation effort that meant eliminating immigrants' previous ethnic culture and replacing it with social and political attitudes acceptable to mainstream Americans. However, leading LA reformers insisted that the movement was not simply a radical reaction to new immigration patterns. Teachers tried to draw a line between themselves and nativists, introducing a series of experiments in the schooling of foreign-born students that made Los Angeles a laboratory for questions about language and citizenship in an age of mass immigration. They believed that Progressives across the nation looked to their city for the latest innovations. In 1926, *The Survey* published three articles on the "California Plan." The Progressive journal praised the Golden State for questioning the use of "Americanization" in the context of xenophobic efforts like the National Origins Act or the Palmer Raids of the 1920 Red Scare. California reformers rejected reactionary politics and remade the term, as described in *The Survey*: "'Americanization,' a smug and patronizing word at best, means in many communities a waning war-time enthusiasm, now expressed through a few classes in English for Foreigners. But in California it has been translated into something vital.... This far reaching innovation in the public school system is California's unique contribution to the 'new education.'"[2]

In negotiating between postwar extremism and participatory democracy, LA reformers captured the contradictions of Americanization. They developed lessons that taught immigrants to adopt middle-class Protestant values but also took pride in their efforts to implement culturally sensitive social reform. Like Progressive settlement workers, Mexican- and Japanese-origin educators designed new language programs to suit their particular community's attitudes toward Americanization.

Although there were many voices in the LA language debate, white reformers were able to promote their vision for language education to the largest audience. Their chief advocate was Amanda Mathews Chase, who began her career teaching English to immigrants like Mrs. Portillo in a settlement house, a community center run by affluent Anglo-American women in one of LA's poor Mexican neighborhoods. Chase chronicled her settlement house classes in the form of short stories, using fiction to describe English instruction in romantic terms. She later incorporated volunteer women into the school system by authoring the 1915 Home Teacher Act, which linked Americanization to the Progressive idea of "city housekeeping." Home teachers argued that Americanizing immigrant mothers would encourage them to create "American" homes and assimilate their families. They also hoped that women who became home teachers would gain recognition from the city's school bureaucracy. Anglo-American reformers congratulated themselves for romanticizing and professionalizing immigrant education. Progressive Angelinos also viewed Americanization courses as a path to personal advancement for women willing to work with immigrants who could not speak English.[3]

The women who inaugurated the Los Angeles immigrant education division in 1916 believed that they could redefine the Americanization debate at a national level. Long before she attracted attention for writing statewide legislation and pedagogical curricula for immigrant instruction, Chase articulated her vision of Americanization in a short story. This work of fiction drew upon her experience as one of the original evening schoolteachers at the College Settlement in 1903. This settlement house, run by college-educated women near the Pueblo de Los Angeles, a historic area where new immigrants were settling, recruited volunteers to teach foreigners to read and write English. These classes became so popular that three years later, the clubwomen persuaded the school board to take charge of the program and hire an assistant superintendent to oversee immigrant education and evening schools. Those three years had inspired enough ideas for Chase to publish a book of short stories in 1906, *The Hieroglyphics of Love: Stories of Sonora Town and Old Mexico.* One of these stories depicted the mundane routines of English instruction as romantic episodes of love and heartbreak. This founding myth helped Progressive reformers link language acquisition to Americanization as they promoted immigrant education from its pioneering days in LA to a statewide campaign a decade later.[4]

In "Cupid and the First Reader," Chase's character Ramon Morales treated his English-language primer like a "Lover's Manual of Correspondence." Although he and Guadalupe Puentes were teenagers, their long absences and illiteracy had placed them in the foreign first-grade class. Ramon wanted to express his instant attraction to Guadalupe on paper. Since he did not know how to write in Spanish, he flipped through his first reader for a pick-up line and wrote, "The duck runs to the hen." After she wrote back, "The hen can run to the duck," they were officially in love with each other—and with foreign first grade. The young lovers began coming to school every day, and in the final scene, they embraced at their desks.[5]

As the story developed, the racial undertones of Chase's descriptions suggested that the tale's true hero was not Ramon, or even Guadalupe, but their teacher. The author used this romance to encourage regular school attendance and a new interest in English vocabulary. In the final scene, the teacher separates Ramon and Guadalupe when an Italian boy complains, "I no can study when Greasers all the time hug themselves." So she "punishes" the lovers by making them skip recess and copy "The little hen flew to the duck" twenty times. In Chase's imagination, two Mexican immigrant teenagers could not fall in love without the aid of a white teacher and, of course, her English first reader. The fictional teacher did more than sympathize with her students; by providing them the skills to learn English, she had given them the keys to happiness. In the end, when that happiness aroused reproach from a European immigrant student, the settlement woman believed she was the only character equipped to resolve the racialized conflict.[6]

Chase's attitude about language instruction grew more romantic after she left to teach English at a private girls' school in Mexico City for four years. When she returned, she became the first volunteer in LA's second immigrant education experiment. On top of publishing new language curricula, Chase wrote the first draft of the California Home Teacher Act. The legislature approved this new Americanization approach in 1915, authorizing local school districts to hire home teachers to work with schools in immigrant neighborhoods. Many school boards resisted the idea, and the Los Angeles city schools only "hired" Chase when the Daughters of the American Revolution offered to pay her salary. By 1921, Los Angeles had 108 home teachers, more than twice the number in any other California city. Home teachers were like traveling settlement house workers: they made home visits during the day and held evening classes to teach immigrant mothers how to make "American" homes. "We have ignored the natural home-maker and yet tried to Americanize the home," Chase explained. "The home teacher, like the family doctor and the family pastor, is to be a real and intimate possession of the family." She wanted Progressive women to serve as home teachers because, whereas immigrant children acculturated at school and their fathers adapted at work, there was no institution to assimilate mothers. In Chase's model of Americanization, settlement workers would teach immigrant mothers how to meet the gendered and racialized expectations of white womanhood.[7]

Chase's most innovative ideas merged her expertise in English language instruction with the ideals of Americanization. She proposed that all schools in immigrant neighborhoods acquire a "school cottage" to serve as "a model American home, small but complete, attractive, but simple and inexpensive." These cottages would supply immigrants with tangible images of American values such as hygiene and sanitation. Chase advised home teachers to visit pupils' homes on Friday field trips: under the guise of a social call, teachers would discreetly inspect the homes and compare their upkeep with that of

A home teacher visits a pupil and her children. *From* The Survey, *June 1926.*

the school cottage. More persuasively, Chase proposed English lessons that would teach immigrant mothers the vocabulary of the Americanized life they were meant to live. Drawing on her experiences teaching English to illiterate adults at the College Settlement and to privileged girls in Mexico City, Chase urged instructors to "be lively, practical, interesting, even dramatic" as they led language lessons about groceries, household activities, and clothing. Reasoning that immigrant mothers would want to learn English vocabulary that they could apply in their daily activities, she encouraged home teachers to focus on the practical homemaking aspects of Americanization.[8]

Chase's curriculum conveyed the type of Americanization that she wanted home teachers to model, and it reflected her assumptions about race and gender. In her ninth English lesson, for example, mothers learned to say, "I cook the eggs. I wash the dress. I iron the dress. I sweep the floor. I mop the floor. I dust the chairs." This vocational approach to English instruction was not always successful. In 1921 Chase complained that, even if home teachers "talked cleanliness, hygiene, school attendance, thrift, and adult education 'up one street and down another,'" immigrant mothers resisted most efforts to change their routines. Many immigrant women were eager to learn English when they arrived in Los Angeles, but they did not share Chase's vision of language classes as domestic service training. Chase's racial assumptions influenced her curriculum because the first home teachers worked at one of the city's most diverse campuses, Amelia Street School. The student population was "one-half Mexican, a third Japanese, while the remaining one-sixth compris[ed] Italians, Arabians, Syrians, Poles, Spaniards and Negroes." Although Chase enrolled almost ninety mothers for her courses in English, singing, patriotism, sewing, and cooking, she was lucky if fifteen people came to the classes, which met twice a week for Mexican mothers and once a week for Japanese women. These mothers were not interested in Americanization lessons limited to words they needed only for unskilled or domestic work.[9]

Although the mission of the Home Teacher Act was Americanization, its advocates also hoped to create professional titles for Progressive women. Amanda Chase's mentor, who co-authored the assembly bill in 1915, joined the California Commission on Immigration and Housing (CCIH), and another home teacher became an assistant superintendent at the State Department of Education. The CCIH hired Ruby Baughman and Carol Aronovici, a pair of PhDs, to train home teachers in LA County. These experts each approved of Amanda Chase's decision to place language instruction at the center of Americanization classes, but they disagreed about whether to include immigrants' native languages in the Home Teacher program. This debate turned into a public argument among LA administrators about the role of language learning in Americanization curricula.

Baughman mixed Amanda Chase's romantic enthusiasm for immigrant instruction with scholarly skepticism when she arrived as a professor at the Los Angeles State Normal School. When the LA city school board converted Chase's home teacher status from volunteer to regular employee in 1916, it hired Dr. Baughman to direct its newly established Department of Immigrant Education. Baughman augmented her part-time position (and half salary) by offering a Saturday class called "The Teaching of English to Foreigners," and was able to expand her staff to twelve home teachers by 1918. Aware that many immigrant mothers worked outside the home, she ordered teachers to hold "factory classes" in paper mills, laundries, car barns, canneries, Pullman cleaning departments, and labor camps. Baughman compiled a textbook of lessons in "industrial English" published by the California Fruit Growers Exchange, an organization that later lobbied the legislature to add Americanization classes. She worked with the fruit growers because she hoped agribusiness would integrate immigrants into society. However, these commercial interests also colored her views about the role of language learning in immigrant education.[10]

Baughman believed that Americanization meant learning English. In a 1921 article, she justified English-only education for immigrant adults by arguing that "concerning the need of a common national language there can be no debate." Baughman went beyond Woodrow Wilson's description of public schools as the nation's melting pots: she argued that English instruction itself was essential to Americanization. "For the illiterate our schools are responsible directly; for the non-English-speaking citizen, only indirectly. They are both the task of the public school," she explained, "not as afterthoughts, but as a large constituent part of the huge plan by which we make over our concept of the business of education." Baughman's business model worked: with funds from the fruit growers, she quadrupled the home teacher faculty by 1921. Yet emphasizing instruction for foreign laborers limited her home teacher lessons. She argued that Mexican-origin orange pickers "must be taught not only the English vernacular of their own familiar process but they do well also to learn the existence of other related processes of growing, cultivating, pruning, picking, and irrigating." Operating in the context of racialized assumptions about which ethnic groups were capable of skilled professional work, Baughman focused on "industrial English," thereby hindering immigrants from learning other vocabulary and limiting their upward mobility.[11]

As LA schools were expanding their home teacher programs and promoting them across the country, Angelinos debated Baughman's proposed language limitations before a national audience in 1921. Baughman's article "Elementary Education for Adults" appeared in the *Annals of the American Academy of Political and Social Science*, which devoted an entire issue to "Present-Day Immigration" after California passed its second Alien Land Law, which denied landownership to "aliens ineligible for citizenship." Five of the twenty-eight articles in this special issue came from Angelino reformers. In addition to Baughman's English-only piece, two pieces discussed Japanese immigrants, the primary target of the Alien Land Law because Asian immigrants remained prohibited from citizenship under the Chinese Exclusion Act. A third article addressed Mexicans in Los Angeles. Contrasting with these four articles was one by the final LA author, Carol Aronovici, who argued that immigrants learning their heritage languages was a vital part of the Americanization process.[12]

By the time Baughman's article was published, she had left Los Angeles to join the Anthropology Department at the University of Minnesota. The CCIH tried to improve her home teacher program by offering courses for

Americanization instructors at the University of California Extension School. Once it had approval to organize the course (contingent on finding funding), the commission identified two intriguing teacher trainers. One of the finalists was Carol Aronovici, a Romanian immigrant who had studied city planning at Cornell and Brown before coming to California. He had already served the CCIH as housing director in Belvedere, an unincorporated area adjacent to the Pueblo de Los Angeles where Amanda Chase had taught her first college settlement classes. In the end the CCIH hired the other candidate, John Collier, a prominent Progressive who would later become the longest-serving director of the Bureau of Indian Affairs under Franklin Roosevelt. However, its executive officer told the board that "Dr. Aronovici's essay on Americanization reads more harmoniously with our ideas on the matter than anything I have ever seen." Paradoxically, that essay may have cost him the job. Its opposition to English-only education may have been too progressive for the political realities in which the statewide commission operated.[13]

Aronovici argued that educators should respect immigrants' emotional attachments to their native languages. His perspective countered Ruby Baughman's self-declared practical approach, which faulted adult evening schools that "neglected the education in a common language so essential in a democracy." Instead, Aronovici lamented the laws that had suppressed foreign-language newspapers during World War I. Preaching that tolerance led to loyalty, Aronovici said he "would rather the immigrant would love America in German than hate America in English." He argued that Americans could never understand the struggles of immigrants unless they tried to learn a new language themselves. The CCIH settled this dispute by electing not to hire him as an instructor in 1921. Even though Baughman's English-only emphasis prevailed that year, Aronovici had articulated a new approach to immigrant education. In urging native-born citizens to empathize with their newly arrived neighbors, he declared that "the weaving of national and racial characters of the alien into the fabric of American civilization is the real task of Americanization." Different approaches to language learning shaped the Americanization debate among Progressive Angelinos like Baughman and Aronovici. They also allowed Mexican and Japanese immigrants to forge their own interpretations of Americanization as they established new community language schools in Los Angeles.[14]

Students in Progressive Era Los Angeles left few written documents, and those that remain rarely mention Americanization curricula. While it is likely that most foreign-born Angelinos found many aspects of Americanization desirable, few non-Anglo immigrants said so in their own words. Yet other records demonstrated immigrant Angelinos' academic achievement and their eagerness to assimilate. The blue book exams of home teachers and quantitative analysis from administrators indicate how Mexican and Japanese immigrants performed in school. Analyzing these evaluations captures how LA teachers exoticized ethnic groups in different ways. The blue book exams were written for home teacher training courses taught by John Collier. In 1920, he taught Americanization courses across the state, certifying hundreds of white women as home teachers, and the CCIH proudly kept Collier's files. His student-teachers wrote exam essays describing organizations they worked for and immigrants they taught, explaining their efforts to Americanize non-English speakers in their individual classrooms.[15]

The blue books reveal the range of opinions Progressive reformers held about non-Anglo immigrants. The essays suggest that these women took professional pride in their efforts to assimilate immigrants in 1920. However, in reading past the biases of these Progressive reformers, their essays reveal glimpses into how students negotiated home teachers' idealistic ambitions with their own attitudes on Americanization.[16]

One LA teacher, Annie Callaghan, expressed a blend of sympathy and low expectations for her students. She taught at Brownson House, whose mission mixed the development of immigrant leadership from the bottom up with a Progressive skepticism of working-class ingenuity. The settlement house aimed "to develop in the people a self-respect, to encourage initiative," she explained, "to make the people feel they have a relation to society and a place in the community and to have them understand [that] the problem of the neighborhood is their problem, and that this is an agency to which they can appeal in any trouble." Arguing that hosting "properly supervised" dances would help Mexican immigrants "solve some of the problem of juvenile delinquency," Callaghan captured the paradox of self-reliance and social welfare that motivated home teachers and shaped the experiences of the immigrants they taught.[17]

Some home teachers were more open to learning from their students. Druzilla Mackey's career was informed by her early experiences in Boyle Heights in East LA, the city's most diverse district. "Since our neighborhood is composed of Mexicans, Italians, Germans, Armenians, Syrians, Japanese, and Negroes," her blue book began, "the process of community organization must be slow." Before her first class, Mackey met with representatives of other agencies in Boyle Heights and asked how she could "plan English lessons which would teach the people the use of all the agencies." She quickly learned that students themselves wanted to create the curriculum, noting that "young people asked repeatedly for classes of their own." Mackey's limited funds meant that she "could offer only classes in Elementary English for adults," but she helped immigrant teens organize a local boys' club and girls' club. She was impressed when the girls' club took "leadership in community singing and dramatic entertainments" to raise money for extra classes. Her exam illustrates that Mexican students were not passive vessels, but rather active participants in their own education. Mackey moved to rural Orange County shortly after writing this essay in 1920, but her two years in Boyle Heights taught her to trust the immigrants she worked with.[18]

Mackey's career after Collier's class reflects the contradictions Americanization teachers faced. The California Fruit Growers Exchange recruited Mackey to organize classes for migrant camps in the orange groves of La Habra and Fullerton. Although her work served the agriculture industry's economic interest, Mackey "chose to live in one of the houses supplied by the fruit growers," turning it into the "neighborhood model" with flowers and a vegetable garden. She persuaded the fruit growers to pay for evening classes, establish a well-baby clinic, and build a meeting hall, where migrant workers gave musical performances that impressed Progressive reformers with the "unusual talent among the Mexican people." Mackey was so moved by her teaching experiences that she visited Mexico City in the summer of 1925. There she met a university-trained Spanish instructor who elected to leave the capital to work in "the mountains where nobody could read or write." Mackey described this teacher to her LA colleagues as "Mexico's Amanda Chase." Even the harshest critics of Orange County's migrant labor camps have praised Mackey, who supervised six Americanization centers by 1930. Although the Fruit Growers Exchange curriculum taught men the words for menial tasks ("to prune," "to snip"), she made the centers safe spaces where Mexican migrants could speak in Spanish about leaders like Benito Juárez and Abraham Lincoln. Mackey's myriad teaching strategies reflected respect for Mexican migrants and their culture while also accepting the reality that her job was to teach English to manual laborers. Although she taught students who faced discrimination at work and elsewhere, Mackey developed a range of Americanization approaches to assimilate Mexican migrants to localized conditions.[19]

While Mackey celebrated her students' culture, other home teachers stressed students' failures. Many blue books described immigrants who dropped out of school for various reasons. One teacher wrote about Kiyoshi Miyato, a twenty-five-year-old truck farmer from San Pedro who left school to sell berries despite enjoying draftsmanship classes in which he had developed "rather remarkable" landscaping skills. Satsuki, another Japanese young man from El Monte with "an aptitude for drawing and painting," planned to stop school after he had mastered conversational English in order to support his family as a vegetable farmer. A survey of Mexican American youths reported other reasons for leaving school, such as struggles in arithmetic, need to care for siblings, and marriage. For both ethnicities, economic necessity was the primary cause for leaving school. Manuel had to stop after the tenth grade because, "We went to the fruit two years. The first year I tried to make my grade and I did, but when the same thing happened again the next year I quit." One eighteen-year-old girl wanted to stay in school because, "My teachers all gave me a regular lecture and told me it was wrong to quit, but my father said it is bad enough to worry about something to eat without worrying about school." The home teachers may have cast these young people as failures, but the students' words suggest that they made the most of their schooling while negotiating the needs of their families.[20]

Other Angelinos were more impressed at the initiative immigrants took to learn English. At the Mission Road Camp School, the boxcar instructor enticed Mexican women to learn English by providing badly needed quilting materials and teaching "simple stories" and English "rhyme songs" as the group sewed. In Los Angeles, the Americanization director who replaced Ruby Baughman boasted about a 1926 program that encouraged interethnic cooperation:

> One group of women was very much interested in stenciling curtains for the school bungalow, and it developed that a Mexican woman knew a "stitch" which a Japanese woman wished to learn. A restless baby was making it practically impossible for the Japanese mother to be taught the desired new "stitch." To the rescue came a Jewish woman, who cared for the Japanese baby while the Mexican woman taught the Japanese mother.

When this class began, "ninety percent of our Mexican applicants were unable to talk or understand English. However," the supervisor wrote, "a decided improvement has been noted in the sixteen weeks in the class. It is now possible to talk with them in English without difficulty."[21] Among both Mexican- and Japanese-origin students in adult English classes, the majority were women. One home teacher opined that "the Japanese perhaps more than any other racial group within our midst are anxious to learn English," noting that they organized classes at three churches and hired Anglo instructors to teach groups of various ability levels. Separating classes by English ability pleased Progressives because it made language learning the focus of instruction. Japanese immigrants' emphasis on language ability may have been a more direct display of assimilation than the Mexican immigrant mothers' interest in quilting, but still women from both ethnic groups made every effort to learn English.[22]

Despite these similarities, Progressives promoted opposite narratives about Mexican versus Japanese students. Citing poor test results and the failure to advance in grade levels, reformers argued that Mexican immigrants could not succeed in school. On the other hand, Japanese pupils often earned higher grades than their Anglo-American peers, prompting Progressives to believe they possessed natural academic instincts that gave them an unfair advantage. Home teachers solidified these storylines by comparing the classrooms in which they taught each ethnic group. Although they lived in isolated districts, Japanese Angelinos were less peripatetic than Mexican immigrants because many of them worked as gardeners and produce vendors rather than as migrant laborers. With more stable employment, Japanese immigrants were able to offer language classes in local churches, settlement houses, and public schools. Mexican communities were more segregated, and their class schedules more erratic. In rural Huntington Park, a home teacher started the Mission Road Camp School in a boxcar to Americanize the Spanish-speaking women in nearby shacks. In neighboring San Bernardino County, rural schools taught women in "La Escuelita," an old school bus that rolled from one Mexican camp to another, holding English classes for orange pickers' wives. These conditions likely made it more difficult for Mexican migrant families to succeed in school compared to Japanese pupils. In ignoring such structural inequality, home teachers writing blue book exams hid the lived experiences of immigrant students.[23]

––––––––––––––

To substantiate their interpretations, administrators published statistical data that quantified immigrants' academic performance. They praised many Japanese immigrants for eagerly assimilating while questioning the language ability of many Mexican Americans. Such reports exoticized ethnicity, dismissing Mexican-origin students as incapable and claiming that Japanese superiority, even over Anglo children, justified "Oriental otherness." Statistical studies of school achievement seem to confirm those stereotypes, but a closer reading suggests that academic outcomes were not racially determined. The data did, however, influence how Mexican and Japanese educators approached their individual Americanization proposals.[24]

Anglos assumed that racial differences explained why Japanese students assimilated more fully. Miss James was an enthusiastic LA teacher who played favorites. "If I assign a topic to a Japanese boy he will work it out, and not only that . . . he will do more than he is asked to do," she said. "If a topic is assigned to a Mexican, he will try to get by as easily as possible." Teachers tried to turn these intuitions into scientific fact during the Progressive Era, when Stanford psychologists devised a standard measure of intelligence that Paula Fass called the "Americanization of mental testing." The Stanford-Binet test had critics from the start, but most Progressives accepted that testing could demonstrate a link between mental ability and race. While the tests confirmed Miss James's observation that the Japanese-origin students were more successful students than their Mexican counterparts, they also indicated that both groups had less intelligence than their Anglo-American peers. The bias of IQ tests aside, the data analysis suggested the broader challenges, and successes, that immigrant students experienced in school. These tests showed that Mexican-origin students always seemed to exceed very low Anglo expectations in academic achievement and that Japanese-origin students were the only racial group that consistently outperformed native-born whites.[25]

Data on dropout rates, advancement, and academic grades reveal the discriminatory conditions that perpetuated these stereotypes. Merton Hill drew on contradictory assumptions about ethnic intelligence in his 1928 survey of hundreds of Mexican immigrant families in the Chaffey Union High School District of Ontario, just east of LA County. As the Americanization director in the district where home teachers visited Mexican camps in "La Escuelita," the bus-turned-classroom, he hoped to document why Ontario needed to expand its immigrant education program. Hill assured readers that he was not trying "to prove the children or adults of any nation inferior in native capacity." Rather, he found that Mexican-origin students did "not have advantages equal to those of American children." Thus, he "corrected" Mexican "index of ability" scores that were at least 60 percent of white scores in vocabulary, arithmetic, and language memorization in Spanish and English to conclude that Mexicans' overall "index of ability" was only 52 percent of whites. While this logic seems flawed, Hill included other statistics that explained Mexican education more plainly. In particular, he noted that 78 percent of Mexican children were "over-aged," or older than their assigned grade levels, compared to only 33 percent of white pupils. Whereas the average Anglo fourteen-year-old was in ninth grade, his typical Mexican counterpart was in fifth grade. Hill believed this discrepancy went beyond "index of ability" and even language handicap. Finding that more than 40 percent of all "Mexican peon parents" had never gone to school (in Mexico or California) and that more than a third of them were illiterate (in both Spanish and English), he concluded that "home conditions make the Mexican child under-nourished" in the skills needed to avoid the "retardation and elimination of Mexican pupils." Hill's survey of "home conditions" and "over-aged" (or "retarded") students seemed more persuasive than his manipulation of Mexicans' "index of ability" scores. Simply by reporting the rate at which Mexican immigrant students advanced (or failed to advance) to the next grade, Hill demonstrated that public schools were not properly serving the Mexican community.[26]

Because ethnic Japanese students were more likely to stay in school, scholars had more data to study. Stanford's director of citizenship, Reginald Bell, measured the achievement of LA high school students using teachers' marks by grade level and by academic subject. Teachers' subjectivity influenced the accuracy of the data, but the numbers indicated that second-generation Japanese students (Nisei) were successful in school. Using the grades of Nisei Angelinos in 1927–28, Bell corrected his earlier conclusion that language caused an "educational retardation" of Japanese children. As ninth graders, Nisei students were far more likely to receive A and B grades than their white peers (74 percent to 41 percent) and less likely to receive D and E marks (5 percent to 25 percent). The statistical significance of this academic superiority dissipated over time, until Nisei and Anglo twelfth graders had nearly identical grade distributions, causing Bell to question Nisei "mental development." Bell's bias led him to claim that, although the Nisei earned higher grades in every class, they mostly excelled in "non-academic" subjects. It was true that the greatest disparities came in shorthand and mechanical drawing classes, but the Nisei still earned 25 percent more A and B marks in science, 23 percent more in Spanish, and 22 percent more in math. Although a limited look at language courses did not show statistical significance, the Nisei scored at least 8 percent higher than whites in English, French, and German. Despite Bell's belief that the Japanese were unlikely to excel in relatively advanced classes, their superior marks in almost every subject suggested that, if they could afford to stay in school, the Nisei could succeed there.[27]

Rather than reading the data to understand the needs of immigrant Angelinos, administrators like Reginald Bell and Merton Hill used it to reinforce Anglo-Americans' stereotypes of each ethnic group. Bell brushed aside the Nisei's superior course scores as biased grading, arguing that the Japanese students received good grades not for their intelligence, but because "other factors such as liking for hard work, interest in school subjects, persistence, docility, and likability all seem to affect teachers' marks greatly." In Hill's survey, eighty teachers in his district ranked only Japanese and Germans as having a higher "capacity to do academic work" than native-born whites. These findings were early iterations of the "model minority myth"—sociologist William Petersen's claim that Japanese Americans heroically overcame racial discrimination more successfully than other immigrant groups did.

In contrast, Hill reported educators thought black students were the only group with less potential than Mexicans, who ranked at 68.5 percent as much academic "capacity" as whites. Moreover, they assigned Mexican Americans even less "capacity" than Anglo-Americans in subjective qualities like initiative, dependability, determination, and energy. The Anglo teachers also opined that Japanese and Mexicans shared the highest "capacity to do manual work." In measuring student success by race, administrators used statistics to extend the narratives that Amanda Chase had introduced in her short stories two decades earlier. Like the blue books from John Collier's home teacher classes, these studies also provide glimpses into the immigrant experience in LA city schools. These statistics projected stereotypes that Mexican and Japanese Angelinos attempted to refute by designing their own Americanization curricula.[28]

Ethnic minorities did not share the Progressives' passion for home teachers. The records of Mexican and Japanese Angelinos suggest that the school district's immigrant education experiments were not as central to their lives as reformers believed. When immigrants did discuss language learning and assimilation—in ethnic newspapers, sociological surveys, and life history interviews—they often spoke about their own efforts to teach the second generation their heritage languages, not English. Just as Woodrow Wilson believed the public school was the primary place for Americanization, Mexican and Japanese immigrants insisted that their new language schools could become educational pillars in their respective communities. Some immigrants supported these instructors' language preservation projects, but others thought schools should help their children assimilate and learn English. These contradictory impulses were evident in Los Angeles's two largest foreign-language programs. Japanese-language schools were able to incorporate Americanization concepts and become influential institutions, while Mexican consulate schools rejected assimilation efforts and rapidly dissolved.

The Mexican consulate schools probably failed to gain traction because they lacked grassroots leadership in the eastside barrios but, like the home teacher program, they received positive coverage in print media. In 1926, the Mexican consul to Los Angeles proposed the establishment of fifty schools in southern California funded by the Mexican Department of Education. He was endorsed by the new newspaper *La Opinión*, already America's largest Spanish-language daily, which covered the schools' progress for the next four years. The consul and his backers opened eight schools across LA County by 1929, offering free textbooks and a curriculum that included Spanish language and Mexican history (*lengua castellana y historia patria*). In patriotic vernacular that emphasized Mexico's European (Castilian) ties, consulate schools sponsored the Mexicanization of American-born children. They did not last long. After only three consulate schools remained open in 1930, with a total enrollment of 200 students in a city of 97,000 Mexican-origin residents, *La Opinión* stopped reporting on them.[29]

Anthropologist Manuel Gamio revealed a more complex relationship between language and assimilation in his 1931 book, *The Life Story of the Mexican Immigrant*. Gamio, who had emigrated from Mexico City to the United States in 1925 after denouncing corruption in the Mexican Ministry of Education, interviewed Mexican immigrants across the Southwest. In Los Angeles, he found particular interest in the consulate's school campaign. One immigrant Gamio interviewed was Anastacio Cortés, a Belvedere business-man who formed El Pensador Mexicano, an organization to help children develop Mexican patriotism. An undertaker and Methodist minister, Cortés paid to build the first Mexican consulate school and hire its first teacher in 1926. Despite his efforts to instill pride in their Mexican heritage in his children, they had all learned English and Cortés became angry when they did not speak Spanish at home. Gamio interviewed ten other Angelinos who refused to surrender their Mexican citizenship and wanted their children to learn Spanish; two of Cortés's neighbors joined El Pensador Mexicano, but the others dreamed of sending their offspring to the Mexican school system that Gamio had criticized. In contrast, only four of Gamio's LA interviewees were happy their children had learned English. All fifteen immigrants had seen their children and siblings assimilate quickly. Two of them observed that the Mexican community in Los Angeles was more likely to speak English than counterpart communities in El Paso, Phoenix, and other parts of the Southwest, despite the presence of consulate schools in LA.[30]

Mexican Angelinos experienced Americanization as a paradox—the first generation resisted the benefits of citizenship while their children embraced the local language and culture. Maybe this marked the triumph of LA's home teachers and the school district superintendent, who in 1923 complained that it was "unfair for Los Angeles, the third largest Mexican city in the world, to bear the burden alone of taking care educationally of this enormous group.... We have these immigrants to live with, and if we can Americanize them we can live with them." Perhaps it proved that El Pensador Mexicano had backfired by rejecting English-language education and favoring Spanish textbooks from the Mexican consulate instead of the LA city schools.[31]

In contrast to Mexican families who wanted their students to return south of the border, Japanese immigrants eagerly established their own language schools to put students on a pathway to Americanization. Mindful that exclusionary sentiments had led the California legislature to restrict Japanese farm ownership through the Alien Land Laws of 1913 and 1921, officials at Japanese-language schools were careful to avoid the impression that they despised the customs of their Anglo neighbors. This accommodation helped make such schools a community institution in Los Angeles until internment began in 1942. Comparing the longer-lasting Japanese schools with the brief Mexican consulate school experiment shows that these heritage-language educators believed they were just as responsible for the Americanization of their community's children as were Anglo instructors like Amanda Chase.

Whereas Mexican consulate schools had dwindled to three campuses in 1930, the number of Japanese language schools in LA County had grown to thirty-five. While only 0.2 percent of Mexican Angelinos attended consulate schools, more than 40 percent of Nisei attending the 36th Street Elementary School spent their afternoons in language school. A Nisei born in Little Tokyo in 1923 remembered the language school and the public school, along with the Japanese grocery, barbershop, and mortuary, as pillars of her neighborhood. By 1930, Japanese schools stretched across the LA basin from San Pedro to San Fernando, but this expansion came with some legal controversy. Facilities were opening so rapidly that the Japanese Chamber of Commerce proposed consolidation because the schools were expensive to operate. Although most schools remained separate institutions, they united to form the Southern California Japanese Language School Association (SCJLSA). Unlike Mexican consulate schools, which had full-day schedules, SCJLSA schools gathered the Nisei for a few hours every evening after public school "to instruct children in reading and the writing of the language, to make them understand daily conversations . . . and to furnish the American-born children with a Japanese background."[32]

For political purposes, instructors left the meaning of "Japanese background" open to interpretation. The president of the SCJLSA was Kohei Shimano, who had founded the city's first language school in 1911. Shimano's Rafu Daiichi Gakuen (Los Angeles First Campus) was close to the Amelia Street School, where Amanda Chase would become LA's first home teacher five years later. Shimano always tried to work with the Amelia Street principal, especially after passage of the second Alien Land Law in 1921. That year, the same state legislature that had endorsed home teachers passed the Private School Control Law, requiring all language schools to hire only teachers proficient in English and to use only textbooks approved by the State Board of Education. Shimano led the effort to publish a series of texts that expressed the Nisei's dual allegiance as Beishu Nichijû (primary emphasis on America and secondary on Japan). However, after the US Supreme Court overturned the Private School Control Law in 1927, two-thirds of SCJLSA schools abandoned Beishu Nichijû and returned to the Japanese-approved textbooks that discussed loyalty to the emperor. Shimano disapproved, warning that, "although the moral training of the children can be greatly accomplished by the presentation of good Japanese racial traits, we must not forget that we are educating American citizens."[33]

Many principals did not share Shimano's sympathy for Beishu Nichijû, but the SCJLSA balanced Americanization and cultural preservation more carefully than the Mexican consulate schools did. Unlike El Pensador Mexicano, which sought to have children return to Mexico for their education, the SCJLSA policy was that "Japanese children are Americans and are going to spend all their years here, and our whole educational system must be founded upon the spirit of the public instruction of America." Whereas the Mexican consulate created all-day schools as substitutes for public schools, Japanese educators offered supplementary instruction on afternoons and weekends that would not compete with the public school schedule. These efforts may have been another reason that Nisei students excelled academically in LA city schools while Mexican children struggled.[34]

Despite different policies, language assimilation had a similar impact on each community. Just as Anastacio Cortés's children angered him by speaking English at home, one Nisei teenager spoke English with her siblings but warily switched to Japanese "the minute when my father or mother should enter our presence." Although Japanese schools were more popular and enduring than Mexican consulate schools, most Nisei never became proficient in conversational Japanese. However, just as consulate schools reflected the Mexican government's position on repatriation, Japanese educators designed curricula to avoid further Supreme Court cases. In these two transnational models of language instruction, federal policies influenced different approaches toward Americanization from Mexican and Japanese immigrants.[35]

In the spring of 1926, as Mrs. Portillo declared her intention to become a Spanish teacher upon receiving her diploma from the 28th Street School's Americanization class, a sixteen-year-old Nisei at Hollywood High School was preparing his graduation speech. John Aiso was Hollywood's first Nisei salutatorian, but this was one of many bittersweet honors in his school career. Three years earlier, when Aiso had been elected student body president at his middle school, Hollywood's Anglo-American parents complained so loudly that the principal urged him to leave student government. The middle school

POINSETTIA

COMMENCEMENT SPEAKERS

John Aiso was one of two commencement speakers in 1926. *Courtesy of Hollywood High School Library.*

election was a less complex situation than Hollywood High's oratorical contest on the US Constitution, which Aiso won as a junior and senior. After his 1926 victory, the *Los Angeles Times* stated that the "Japanese silver tongue" would not compete in the national contest in Washington, D.C., due to illness. The *Times* did not report that Hollywood High's principal had encouraged Aiso to withdraw, but the newspaper later added that his performances had "inspired his fellow students at Hollywood" to pay for part of his travel to Washington so that he could coach the school's runner-up, Herbert Wenig. Aiso arrived at the train station in a bow tie and fedora and smiled as he stood behind Wenig, who was six inches taller but dressed the same. Aiso watched Wenig win the national championship on Capitol Hill in front of eight thousand spectators, including President Coolidge. As the new national president of the Constitution Club, Wenig was invited to speak to the Daughters of the American Revolution and the Better America Federation back in Los Angeles.

Even though Wenig was in demand at LA's social clubs, the Hollywood High faculty still selected Aiso as the male commencement speaker.[36]

John Aiso and Mrs. Portillo did not represent the average Mexican-origin or Japanese-origin student, but their transnational ties influenced the range of experiences available to immigrant Angelinos during the age of Americanization. The city schools offered pathways to civic participation for adult immigrants like Portillo, a mother of five who had gone to college in Mexico before the 1910 revolution, as well as to American-born teenagers like Aiso and other Nisei students. The graduation speakers were determined to overcome educational challenges, although Portillo's language barrier was different than the discrimination that denied Aiso his title as oratorical champion. While they both used school success to propel their future careers in America, they never abandoned their native languages. In the fall of 1926, Portillo became a Spanish teacher and Aiso spent a year in Japan, where he continued the language study he had begun in Los Angeles. John Aiso and Mrs. Portillo may have been in the minority of non-Anglo Angelinos who completed their diplomas in LA schools, but their efforts reflected the majority of Mexican and Japanese immigrants who actively sought Americanization while struggling to maintain their native languages.[37]

2 | LANGUAGE AND CITIZENSHIP RESTRICTIONS, 1910–1940

The Amelia Street School had tested language learning as a tool for Americanization in 1915, when Amanda Chase launched her home teacher curriculum there. In the following decade, Amelia Street became a laboratory for competing visions of citizenship. While Americanization advocates like Chase focused on assimilating immigrants into daily life at work and at home, other Progressives debated the roles that English and other languages played in citizenship education, or courses that prepared foreign-born students to participate in civic life. For example, the Los Angeles Diploma Plan was a fifteen-week civics class culminating with a naturalization exam. In 1919, a local judge came to Amelia Street to naturalize Diploma Plan graduates at a ceremony in which the "children of foreign parents appeared in drills in which they carried flags of different nations and also recited selections of a patriotic nature." The spectacle concluded when an immigrant boy read a statement by Theodore Roosevelt that revealed the Diploma Plan's position on the role of language instruction in citizenship programs: "We have room but for one flag, the American flag. . . . We have room but for one language here and that is the English language, for we intend to see that the crucible turns our people out as Americans and of American nationality, and not as dwellers in a polyglot boarding house."[1] The Diploma Plan was desirable because it brought naturalization judges from the federal courthouse to the neighborhood school. However, administrators were uneasy about naturalizing parents from schools like Amelia Street that served, according to the *Los Angeles Times*, "Mexicans who removed their silver-laced sombreros to bow to their principal, Russian women in gaudy head-dress, dark-eyed Slavs and Italians, and eager, slant-eyed Japs." Although they worked with different ethnic populations, home teachers and Diploma Plan advocates agreed that learning English was essential to American naturalization.[2]

At the same time, those immigrants also used Amelia Street School to introduce alternative views of American citizenship. Kohei Shimano started the city's first Japanese language school, Rafu Daiichi Gakuen, a few blocks from Amelia Street. He reached out to the principal, Nora Sterry, to build "bridges of understanding" between educators from Japan and Los Angeles. Shimano hoped this partnership would assimilate students into civic life beyond Little Tokyo. In 1915, he said that Japanese language teachers intended to serve "the Nisei who will live and work permanently here, not to those who will return to Japan." He even conveyed this message to colleagues across the Pacific. In 1917, seven teachers from Japan visited Amelia Street School to inquire about the education of the Nisei. Shimano asked Sterry to host a reception for the Japanese educators at Amelia Street, rather than his campus, because he wanted the guests to know he was serious about Americanization. Mexican immigrants initiated similar exchanges in the 1920s. Fifty years later, one Nisei student from Amelia Street School recalled: "People say that things like Chicano studies or black studies are innovations in education. We had all that. . . . On May 5 there was Cinco de Mayo and Japanese Boys' Day, and they used to have people come in from the community or have kids from the school to do these programs. We actually had a cultural program all year round." The two holidays on May 5 fit the bridges of understanding format in that it used ceremonies to study other nations. In contrast to the Diploma Plan ceremony's celebration of Roosevelt's statement, Amelia Street had room for many flags and multiple forms of language instruction.[3]

Alternative approaches to language and citizenship programs reflected foreigners' racialized access to federal naturalization between the two world wars. The LA Diploma Plan was an innovative naturalization experiment for white immigrants from European countries, and it influenced a national effort to exclude immigrants racialized as nonwhite in the 1920s. Mae Ngai and others have shown how the Immigration Act of 1924 designed national origin quotas to classify immigrants from outside of Europe and Latin America as illegal aliens. In *Ozawa v. United States* (1922) and *United States v. Bhagat Singh Thind* (1923), the Supreme Court ruled that immigrants from groups considered neither black nor white were ineligible for citizenship. These rulings reaffirmed previous exclusionary acts originally aimed at the Chinese and extended them to other Asians. As Natalia Molina has argued, in the decade after the National Origins Act, federal immigration officials tried to use the precedent of Asian exclusion, or "racial script," to nullify Mexican immigrants' access to citizenship as well. The racialization of naturalization policy informed Progressive Era Angelinos as they designed curricula like the Diploma Plan. Yet it also encouraged Japanese and Mexican teachers to propose other immigrant education programs that challenged this racialized restriction of citizenship. The politics of exclusion shaped the development of four new language learning models in Los Angeles.[4]

––––––––––––––––––

Naturalization ceremonies were not the only occasions when Nora Sterry deployed the flag with a missionary zeal. Sterry, who posed for a portrait in the *Los Angeles Times* wearing a white headdress with a red cross, believed that the flag could link language instruction to her larger goal of preparing citizens to participate in a democratic society. From 1910 to 1934, she headed both the Amelia Street and Macy Street Schools, which were near the historic Pueblo de Los Angeles, an area the *Los Angeles Times* labeled "Little Mexico" in 1924. When city officials quarantined the Macy Street district due to an outbreak of the pneumonic plague that year, Sterry insisted on opening her school during the two-week epidemic. One thousand residents in the "district of suffering" had "saved their pennies" to buy a medal for Sterry, but she was even prouder that Macy Street students "hoisted the American flag at full staff" every day of the quarantine. In 1927, Sterry's students wrote prize-winning essays that they performed for the LA chapter of the Daughters of the American Revolution. Sterry accompanied a Macy Street home teacher, fourth grader Daniel Wong, and sixth grader Ampara Macias to celebrate their awards for "The Story of Our Flag" and "How I Can Be a Good Citizen of the United States," respectively. These essays about the flag by children of non-English-speakers showed how Angelino educators designed language learning for immigrants to fit an idealized vision of American citizenship.[5]

Sterry's stunts during the 1924 epidemic extended the home teacher model by turning Americanization curricula into broader nation-building projects that promoted civic participation. Other bureaucrats disagreed about which immigrants should take part in those projects. Sterry believed citizenship training belonged in the city's poorest districts, such as her schools in Little Mexico, where white women could teach foreign mothers and children the refined language of domestic life. However, another teacher who had been a missionary in Asia, Charles Kelso, confined his outlook on immigrant education to a few classrooms close to the school district's downtown office. The father of LA's Diploma Plan for Naturalization of the Alien, Kelso promised naturalization to all immigrants who passed his evening civics class, if they could speak English. The two most innovative projects of the Progressive Era reveal the range of attitudes toward citizenship education. While neighborhood schools invited all foreigners willing to learn English into their classrooms, the L.A. Diploma Plan used language to limit access to naturalization.[6]

In particular, the role language instruction played in each program indicated how Progressive teachers distinguished between Americanization and citizenship. Americanization belonged in less desirable neighborhood schools—where white women saw a position as a home teacher working to assimilate poor immigrants as their only path to school leadership positions. The more prestigious Diploma Plan, in contrast, required white men to explain the principles of democracy to educated immigrants from Europe who already spoke English and needed only a crash course on the Constitution to qualify for citizenship. Although it has received little analysis from historians, the Diploma Plan attracted national attention to immigrant education in Los Angeles. The women who taught in neighborhood schools were more prolific writers who reached more of LA's foreign-born population, but the school district did not compensate them in salary or title. Conceived at the same time, the home teacher program and Diploma Plan both used language instruction to put Americanization and citizenship courses on separate tracks in LA schools after World War I.

Even though Sterry was aligned with the ranks of home teachers, she mentored the man who revamped the school district's fledgling Citizenship Department. Charles Kelso shared Sterry's missionary background. He began his career in India, where a Methodist bishop asked him to teach at the Calcutta Boys' School. From there, he moved to Singapore to head the Anglo-Chinese school for four years. This experience abroad led him to graduate studies in comparative religion and education. Then Kelso came to Los Angeles, where Sterry trained him to become the city's first citizenship instructor in 1912. Fifteen years later, he had created his own bureaucracy while Sterry was still fighting for funding. Both teachers believed it was their duty to teach foreigners how to benefit from American society, but whereas Sterry started neighborhood schools in LA's majority Mexican communities, Kelso catered his Diploma Plan to English speakers only. This contrast became clear at the Amelia Street graduation in 1919, when Sterry's students staged elaborate flag displays while Kelso quietly conferred citizenship on their parents. The women who ran neighborhood schools celebrated the diversity of foreign-born youth with symbols like flags, but foreign languages had no place in the citizenship curriculum designed by Kelso's male colleagues. The collaboration between Kelso and Sterry turned to competition as English-language citizenship classes superseded foreign-language lessons after World War I. As Congress created quotas to restrict immigration by national origin, LA's citizenship ceremonies found room for but one language.[7]

Male administrators adored Sterry's flag activities, and they outright co-opted her vision of citizenship training. Before moving to her neighborhood schools, she had devised the experiment that ultimately became the Diploma Plan. In 1910, Sterry revived LA's latent immigrant education classes when she sought citizenship papers for the parents of her foreign-born students. With little support from the superintendent, Sterry recruited allies for adult education. She asked the city's naturalization director if he would work with an evening class to assist immigrants applying for citizenship. He agreed, but Sterry could find only one willing adult, an Italian, to attend her first class in February 1910. By March, she had recruited twenty-seven immigrants, but the superintendent refused to let her use the Amelia Street campus. When allies in women's social circles expressed concerns about the "educational lack" of immigrant workers in the *Los Angeles Times*, they pressured the school board to open a school for foreign-born adults, though it did not fund teacher salaries. City officials did not support Sterry's efforts to turn LA's first two neighborhood schools into naturalization facilities, so women like Sterry made language learning central to their "social center work" at the Amelia Street and Macy Street Schools.[8]

Sterry recruited students by stressing language lessons over citizenship. She opened the evening school at Macy Street in 1911 because that facility had a large hall where she planned to stage concerts and show moving pictures. When Sterry saw that the parents of her daytime students were most interested in learning English, she shelved the citizenship classes that the director of naturalization had endorsed and offered English classes taught by bilinguals who could speak Italian and Spanish, urging immigrants who spoke other languages to bring their children as interpreters. Nearly three hundred adults arrived the first night. Only one classroom had electricity, but by the end of the first week the language learners had brought enough lanterns and candles to light every room. The *Los Angeles Times* described Sterry's students as a "motley and cosmopolitan" crowd that included Mexicans with "silver-laced sombreros" and "slant-eyed Japs," among others. Sterry made English classes accessible to adults and offered the music and dance classes they requested—but not naturalization.[9]

The following year the city's first citizenship class opened at Amelia Street School. Sterry persuaded the naturalization director to make Los Angeles the nation's "first city to have her evening work accepted in the courts in lieu of an examination for citizenship papers." This alternative was so popular that enrollment in evening schools had nearly tripled by 1914. The school board's opinion of Sterry's actions became clear in 1915, when they restricted her duties to daytime principal at Macy Street School, shaving $600 off her salary. However, a parent petition persuaded the school board to let her continue supervising both day and night schools. By listening to immigrants' requests, Sterry had made herself, and her neighborhood schools, integral to the communities she served.[10]

Paradoxically, she also set the groundwork for the Los Angeles Diploma Plan, which revised Sterry's citizenship program by removing Americanization classes. In 1912, Charles Kelso was teaching at Los Angeles High School by day while overseeing the "social center work" at the campus by night. When the immigrants at Sterry's neighborhood schools became fairly proficient in English, she asked Kelso to teach them about American government in order to prepare them for the naturalization exam in federal court. Kelso's initial lessons merely tutored to the test, but gradually he became more attached to the citizenship classes than to his day job. In 1915, despite the pay cut the school board had handed her, Sterry helped Kelso create the Diploma Plan. She went to the regional naturalization director to describe immigrant parents at her schools and asked him to oversee Kelso's instruction of "those who already knew English but needed teaching in preparation for citizenship." Although Kelso later argued that his citizenship work belonged in a different department than Sterry's neighborhood schools, his agenda came from collaborating with LA's most prominent Americanization advocates—white women.[11]

Kelso's influence elevated the Diploma Plan's emphasis on citizenship above Sterry's stress on Americanization in three ways. First, whereas Sterry focused on language instead of naturalization, Kelso created a fifteen-lesson curriculum that fulfilled the city's citizenship requirements. Second, by 1915 he had convinced the school district to create a new Citizenship Department, under his leadership, with the authority to naturalize immigrants. Third, in 1928 he converted an old elementary school building into a new School of Citizenship for Naturalization. In making citizenship classes a direct path to naturalization, the Diploma Plan also redefined the primary purpose of Americanization classes as English-language instruction at a time when citizenship status and nation of origin were under close scrutiny. Requiring English literacy segregated the two models of immigrant education by race. Whereas the Home Teacher Act of 1915 had offered a variety of services to women classified as nonwhite and non-American at the height of the Progressive Era immigration wave, Kelso's school made citizenship courses more racially exclusive by 1928, four years after Congress passed the restrictive National Origins Act of 1924.[12]

———————

Having watched men like Kelso assume control over immigrant education by 1915, Sterry started a new Americanization agenda. Comparing the two administrators' policies from the late 1920s indicates that the LA city schools valued citizenship over assimilation. This shift becomes clear if we examine how neighborhood schools and the Diploma Plan approached language instruction and campus location. Gender differences influenced these decisions. In multiple articles, female faculty insisted that the key to Americanizing foreigners was to work in the poorest parts of the city. Sterry praised the school district's efforts to serve "an extensive slum area filled with a foreign population," but other women used less subtle language. When the *Los Angeles School Journal* published a "Neighborhood Schools" issue in 1927, one principal wrote that these schools were often in "the dumps" near old railroad cars, adding that the foreign children who attended them were "mostly poor . . . probably dirty and unkempt." She reported that one class from "the back-wash of a feverishly growing city" won a blue ribbon banner for learning about bathing, brushing teeth, and eating vegetables. Some women who saw the poor conditions of these neighborhoods placed cleanliness above language and academics.[13]

Sterry's 1927 article "The Neighborhood School" conveyed her goal of creating a community center where immigrants could come for full assimilation. The Macy Street School served immigrants from three continents (although 70 percent were Mexican) and offered showers and "penny lunches" to children who came to school "dirty, ragged, underfed . . . with little or no medical care." It also provided playgrounds for kids and evening lectures for adults to counter the area's "cheap picture houses, dance halls, and pool rooms of more than doubtful propriety." Sterry expected her teachers to have an "intimate knowledge of the neighborhood," from housing conditions to the "streets and alleys and vacant lots" their students navigated en route to school. The community center concept carried over into the classroom, where teachers required all fourth graders to get library cards for regular field trips and assigned students to duties such as sweeping the streets and interpreting foreign languages for nurses who made home visits. Macy Street's language program aimed to serve the entire community. Stressing that immigrants' language barriers prevented standardized tests from "properly classifying children," Sterry set up her own grade placement system, and she offered "English classes for grown people at any hour or place advisable." The LA

A group of young women sewing at Macy Street School in 1938. *Courtesy of Los Angeles Daily News Negatives, Negative #16875, Department of Special Collections, Charles E. Young Research Library, University of California, Los Angeles.*

neighborhood schools offered immigrants many activities, but language education was a central service because it fulfilled Sterry's mission of assimilating foreign-born students in both academic and social circles.[14]

The home-front experience during World War I persuaded Progressive women that foreign-language instruction could play a positive role in immigrant assimilation. One convert was Ruby Baughman, the city's first Americanization director, who had previously advocated for a "common national language." As the war wound down in September 1918, she laid out her department's agenda for the new school year. Baughman admitted that the war had caused a "kaleidoscopic rearrangement of ideas" causing her to shift away from her personal priority that all immigrants "learn English—the language of America." Despite her belief that English was the only acceptable language in Los Angeles, Baughman proposed "Americanization propaganda in English and foreign language press." While she compiled a textbook of "industrial English" lessons for the California Fruit Growers Exchange, she also recruited "foreign societies" and volunteers who spoke other languages to spread news of the school district's war effort. In asking non-English speakers to stress the "absolute democracy of the draft," Baughman brought foreign languages into an Americanization campaign that she would have preferred to be English-only.[15]

Most Americanization teachers accepted Baughman's idea that newcomers needed English-language instruction despite "race prejudice" against them, but many opposed her plans for a common national language. In 1919, Central Intermediate Evening School teacher Mary Cox speculated in print about the relationship between Americanization and foreign languages in postwar Los Angeles. Whereas the war had shown Baughman how many immigrants lacked literacy in English, it had convinced Cox of Anglo-Americans' "lack of ability to use foreign tongues." Cox called the war a catastrophe—not just for the tragic loss of life, but also because it had disrupted the nation's reluctant acceptance of non-English languages that had grown over four decades of mass immigration. For Cox, Americanization was a "counter-current" to her ultimate goal of seeing foreign languages studied in every school. She rejected English-only education by arguing that immigrants were more likely to assimilate if Americans could talk to them "sympathetically, with an appreciation of all they have left behind." Cox's desire for Angelinos to acquire other languages was one example of some women's efforts to create a more inclusive Americanization agenda in LA's neighborhood schools.[16]

Meanwhile, men enforced more restrictive language and location policies for participation in the Diploma Plan. In contrast to the women who opened neighborhood schools across the city, Kelso concentrated his courses at the single facility that became the Citizenship School in 1928. The two-story, wood-frame structure on a tree-lined street represented the triumph of Progressive Era bureaucracy. With its chain-link fence, picture windows, and open air on all four sides, the school enjoyed the kinds of amenities that middle-class Americans wanted for their own homes. The architecture and style of the school suggested that Diploma Plan graduates did not simply wave flags and read speeches; they were active citizens steeped in the nation's history and prepared to vote on election day. Male educators awarded more pomp and circumstance to the Citizenship School's inauguration than they did to the event honoring 350 graduates who had taken the oath of naturalization in federal court a few weeks earlier. The 1928 ceremony marked the school district's shift in emphasis from the Americanization of children from Mexico and Japan to the naturalization of adult migrants from European, English-speaking nations.[17]

While women wrote many articles about neighborhood schools, the Diploma Plan's only records were written by a biased source, Asbury Bagwell. A citizenship teacher himself when he wrote a master's thesis on the naturalization program in 1929, Bagwell brushed over female contributions to the school district's success. He credited Sterry for the initial idea, but called Kelso the "Father of the Diploma Plan." Excepting the female Americanization director, he referred to most women by their husbands' names (e.g., Mrs. Frank Gibson). Although he did not report data, every Diploma Plan teacher in Bagwell's thesis was male—women were Americanization teachers.[18]

Bagwell boasted about the exclusivity of the male-dominated Diploma Plan. He surveyed teachers in sixty cities, concluding that LA's policy was superior because of its strict requirements for naturalization and English-language ability. No other city empowered its teachers to decide whether or not immigrant adults were worthy of the right to vote. Bagwell bragged that more than 20,000 immigrants had earned citizenship in the program's first twelve years, but he added that LA had nearly 150,000 "foreign born white men and women of voting age." This low naturalization rate was a point of pride for Bagwell, who said, "No effort is made to 'drum up' students for the citizenship classes. . . . Indeed, the entire enrollment is made up of those who have applied for naturalization and have been sent by the naturalization director to the citizenship school [Kelso]." The idea of "aliens studying their way into citizenship" stressed that the Diploma Plan limited citizenship to an elite group of immigrants, almost all of whom were financially independent white Europeans. Bagwell's boast of low enrollment was opposite to the approach of Americanization director Ruby Baughman, who creatively recruited immigrant students during World War I, even if she had to find bilingual volunteers to promote her programs in non-English languages.[19]

Bagwell used Mexican students to demonstrate the differences between LA's Americanization and Citizenship Departments. He noted that more than six thousand Mexican adults attended Americanization classes in 1926–27, making up 53 percent of the evening school population. In contrast, there were only eight Mexicans enrolled in the Diploma Plan, a ratio of one Mexican for every 173 citizenship students. Another Diploma Plan teacher argued that Mexicans were unlikely to seek citizenship because "their easy going habits preclude the industry necessary to become a factor in the government under which they are living." Thus, the Diploma Plan appealed to federal officials who were looking for ways to make Mexican immigrants ineligible for citizenship. Republican James Davis, US Secretary of Labor from 1921 to 1930, approved Kelso's proposal to promote the plan on a national scale. Natalia Molina has shown that Davis had wanted to include Western Hemisphere immigrants in the quota restrictions of the 1924 National Origins Act when he oversaw the Bureaus of Immigration and Naturalization. The labor secretary saw that the Los Angeles model of immigrant education could

Immigrants attend a Diploma Plan class at the School of Citizenship for Naturalization in 1929. *From Bagwell, "Los Angeles Diploma Plan of Naturalizing the Alien."*

serve a broader, nationwide effort to deny Mexican immigrants access to naturalization through language restrictions.[20]

———————————

Comparing the publicity for the Diploma Plan and the Home Teacher Act reveals two different possibilities for advancement for white teachers who created immigrant education policies in Los Angeles. Kelso and his male faculty wrote few public statements promoting the Diploma Plan, but they won private audiences with the US Secretary of Labor and with congressmen far from California who supported their vision of restricting naturalization. Meanwhile, the neighborhood school women defended their cause in countless publications. Sterry served as the longtime editor of the *Los Angeles School Journal,* which devoted an entire issue to neighborhood schools in 1927, and Amanda Chase wrote several volumes of curriculum guides after authoring the Home Teacher Act. Though Diploma Plan teachers published only one article between 1917 and 1930, Kelso's Citizenship Department was flush with funds while Sterry's wages were cut. Kelso quietly mimeographed outlines for fifteen lessons on US government and history for his salaried citizenship teachers while some women worked at neighborhood schools without pay. By 1931, the year of the repatriation raids, Sterry had left the Macy Street School and evening Americanization classes at five schools in the Mexican district had been canceled. In contrast, 1928 marked the dedication of the nation's first School of Citizenship for Naturalization, where students from seven branch schools would come to take citizenship exams every semester. At the ceremony, the new US congressman from Los Angeles congratulated Kelso and pledged to expand his program across the country.[21]

Kelso promoted the Diploma Plan as a means to enforce the nation's new national origins quotas. He won endorsements from local judges and from University of Southern California sociologist Emory Bogardus, who in his 1919 book, *Essentials of Americanization*, declared that the Diploma Plan's three-month course gave immigrants "a heart and content to citizenship." One supporter introduced Kelso to a friend of Labor Secretary Davis, who in turn brought Kelso to the secretary's attention. In 1928, Kelso carried the secretary's endorsement to Washington, where he persuaded a Pennsylvania Republican to author a bill calling for "higher standards for admission to American citizenship." Democrats from immigrant strongholds in the Northeast killed the bill, but still the legislation illustrated the influence of immigrant education models that authorized local school districts to restrict access to citizenship. In his campaign to take his city's Diploma Plan nationwide, Kelso boasted that a citizenship school would streamline the naturalization process—skirting the fact that white European immigrants would disproportionately benefit. This discrimination against foreigners deemed nonwhite (including Mexicans) weakened the ability of neighborhood school women to Americanize the very immigrant students who were barred from the Diploma Plan on the basis of race.[22]

Whereas Kelso restricted immigrant education to recitations of the Bill of Rights, Sterry stayed away from political lessons and focused on her fellow Progressives' interest in food. She was so proud of the meals in the Macy Street district that she invited a *School Journal* writer to visit several Mexican homes with a teacher. Although the instructor reported poor housing conditions (a family of seven ate dinner on a surface "the size of a card table"), she remarked that "the American people have yet to learn a great deal about the chili and its possibilities as a flavoring." She was also struck by the idea of food as a teaching tool. "The women were eager to teach me how to cook," the teacher wrote. "One of them asked me when I was going to bring a class of American women down to learn how to cook." Sterry's teachers Americanized mothers by having students share family recipes.[23]

In urging immigrant women to embrace their ethnic identity in the kitchen, Sterry sought to use food to celebrate the diverse population of her Americanization classes. In 1930, she published *The International Cook Book of the Elementary Principals' Club of Los Angeles*, an organization of which she was president. Sterry said the principals contributed the recipes, but the majority of dishes likely came from the parents (and evening students) she had taught over two decades. The cookbook featured recipes from thirty-seven different cultures, primarily from Russian (thirteen), Mexican (eleven), and Jewish (seven) families. Interestingly, Sterry intended to share these dishes with female teachers only. Instead of celebrating the cookbook's ethnic diversity, she wrote the foreign recipes would spice up the next principals' bridge luncheon: "These recipes have been secured by principals of Los Angeles schools from the people of various foreign groups living within their respective districts. . . . Only those have been chosen for publication which are suited to American tastes. . . . [We] hope that the teachers and their friends will enjoy the novelty of these strange dishes and will thereby in some small measure gain in sympathetic understanding of our foreign people." By balancing empathy for immigrants with a desire for foods "suited to American tastes," Sterry highlighted the double meaning of Americanization in LA schools. Like her cookbook, immigrant education mixed concern for the foreign-born with American tastes for sanitation, capitalism, free labor, and of course, the English language. Her neighborhood schools shared some assimilation goals with the Diploma Plan, but foreign recipes were a far cry from naturalization exams. Although women wrote recipe books to promote assimilation, their publications could not match the political clout of Kelso's Diploma Plan to enforce citizenship restrictions.[24]

———————————

The Diploma Plan and neighborhood schools reinforced the citizenship restrictions of federal national origins quotas for noncitizen immigrants, but simultaneously immigrant educators were teaching their children to participate actively in American society and world affairs. Between the world wars, Japanese and Mexican communities in Los Angeles created their own citizenship curricula based on a foreign diplomacy model of "building bridges." This concept called for immigrant children to represent the best of both America and their ethnic heritages. These programs mixed study of history and government with instruction in language and culture. Like their Anglo-American counterparts, Mexican and Japanese educators traveled overseas, worked with foreign diplomats in Los Angeles, taught students about rhetoric, and used symbols like flags to represent their communities.

Nisei study tours, "Friends of the Mexicans" conferences, and oratory contests were all organized collaboratively between ethnic educators and Progressive Anglos. However, these events also allowed immigrants to develop their own independent notions about citizenship in school settings beyond the control of federal naturalization officers or local administrators like Kelso and Sterry.

The Issei (first-generation immigrants) debated whether their children would become better bridges of understanding if they went to school in Japan or America. Some wanted Nisei youngsters to stay in California so that they could learn English in the mornings at public schools and study their ethnic language and culture in the evenings at Japanese community schools. Other Issei created a Nisei subset, the Kibei, or American-born Japanese who left their families and went to Japan for school. In the interwar years, the relative popularity of US-based language schools versus Japan-based programs for Kibei fluctuated with the diplomatic relationship between the two Pacific powers. Ironically, while community leaders avoided taking a stance, the Nisei themselves came up with their own compromise. In the mid-1920s, they started summer study tours to Japan to learn about their parents' origins and make sense of their ties to each country. Up until the bombing of Pearl Harbor, these study tours reflected Japanese immigrants' struggles to participate in the civic life of both nations. Whereas Kelso used his overseas experience to influence his restrictive citizenship curriculum, Kohei Shimano, like other foreign-born Issei, took his students abroad as young bridges of understanding to secure peaceful relations between the two nations he loved.[25]

Shimano had hoped that Japanese-language schools could help assimilate the Nisei when he opened the city's first *gakuen* in 1911. His faith in Americanization was not simply an expedient response to the Private School Control Law. Even after the Supreme Court ruled that the California Board of Education could not regulate language textbooks in private schools, Shimano urged Issei educators to teach Beishu Nichijū, "primary emphasis on America and secondary on Japan." Shimano showed his patriotism by emulating Nora Sterry at the nearby Amelia Street School. Just as Sterry's school had unfurled the Stars and Stripes during the pneumonic plague outbreak in 1924, Shimano displayed the American flag alongside the Rising Sun of Japan at Rafu Daiichi Gakuen. When both flags were defaced, one of his students later recalled that Shimano called a special assembly to give a "stern lecture about the care of a flag and the respect that we owed to the flag because it was a symbol of a country." In drawing on the expertise of educators from Japan and Los Angeles, Shimano coordinated a transnational effort to turn students into upstanding American citizens. This collaboration colored his approach to the Nisei study tours of the 1920s.[26]

After the National Origins Act of 1924 restricted Asian immigration, Issei leaders believed that sending the Nisei on study tours of Japan was the best way to improve diplomacy. Each trip was organized in a different way. When Shimano took fifteen students to Japan in 1925, he also invited sixty-four-year-old Nellie Oliver, who had taught Earl Warren at the Amelia Street School in the 1890s, to accompany them. By 1925, Oliver was superintendent of Stimson Lafayette Industrial Institute, a charity that shared a building with Rafu Daiichi Gakuen. She held Americanization classes in cooking and sewing on the second floor while Shimano taught his Japanese classes downstairs. Shimano hoped Oliver's voyage would persuade Angelino educators that Japan study tours enhanced the Americanization of Nisei students and helped them become bridges of understanding with Anglos.[27]

However, the same year that Shimano invited an Anglo Americanization teacher to accompany him to Japan, a more publicized study tour recruited Nisei who demonstrated the greatest loyalty to Japan. In 1925, *Nichibei Shimbun*, the largest Japanese-language newspaper in the United States, with editions in San Francisco and Los Angeles, sponsored an essay contest offering an all-expenses-paid trip to Japan for students who were fluent in Japanese. Three of the eleven winning entrants came from LA, including Grace Umezawa, who finished in first place. When they returned to California, Umezawa and her fellow Nisei tourists made speeches describing their activities in Japan and their efforts to shed some of their Americanization, learn their parents' culture, and as the tour leader put it, "act as bridges of peace and understanding between our two countries as only they could have done." While the Japanese newspaper and Shimano shared the hope that Nisei study tours would help pupils promote diplomatic relations, they used opposite methods, muddling the manner in which Nisei would become world citizens ("bridges"). When Japan invaded Manchuria in 1931, political events affected Japanese-language education in Los Angeles. Shimano's alliances with Anglo administrators diminished and Issei educators looked to Japan instead for guidance in citizenship instruction.[28]

The Manchurian invasion challenged the concept of the Nisei as bridges of understanding. The League of Nations branded Japan a military aggressor and refused to recognize Manchuria as a satellite state. In Los Angeles, the Japanese consul looked to the Nisei to explain Japan's political culture to their American peers. In 1933, the consul sponsored an essay contest on the theme "The Pacific Era and Japanese Americans." One of Shimano's students won the contest, and the second prize went to a pupil from the Compton gakuen who wrote that, as Nisei bridges, "we must study the Manchurian question in depth in order to dispel the misunderstandings Americans have and to preserve peace between the United States and Japan." As the consulate planned new study tours encompassing Japan, Manchuria, and Korea, the Japanese Ministry of Home Affairs encouraged Nisei to become full-time students in Japan. Indeed, the Kibei enrollment in Tokyo and Kyoto rose from fewer than one hundred in 1930 to some 1,700 by 1935. Thus, diplomatic fallout from the Manchurian Incident forced the Japanese consul to reframe Nisei duties as bridges of understanding and to restrict the Americanization agenda that Shimano had developed with his study tours in the 1920s.[29]

However, Nisei students had their own approach to Americanization. One of the most ambitious study tours turned into a trans-Pacific adventure for John Aiso (Hollywood High's controversial salutatorian when he graduated in 1926 at age sixteen). When he was unable to compete in a national oratorical contest after winning the local finals, the *Los Angeles Times* helped underwrite his trip to Washington to coach his classmate. Aiso used his speaking success to build relationships with influential adults in Los Angeles, Tokyo, and Washington. The Japanese consul in LA advised Aiso to call on the Japanese ambassador in Washington, who sent him to meet the president of Brown University. The college had worked with the Japanese embassy when a Brown alumnus, Secretary of State Charles Evans Hughes, tried to repair US-Japanese diplomacy after Congress passed immigration restrictions in 1924. Brown did not reject Aiso outright, but asked to see his transcript before admitting him.[30]

Aiso leveraged his consular connections to improve his personal status and build bridges of understanding. After giving the salutatorian address at Hollywood High, he also spoke to the local Japanese vice-consul, who offered a year of room and board in Tokyo. There, Aiso attended a special class at Seijo Gakuen for children of Japanese diplomats returning from overseas service. Once he arrived in Japan, he learned that Brown had admitted him with a sizable scholarship. The Japanese ambassador in Washington sent Aiso's parents a stern letter asking, "What is your son doing when I have gone to the trouble of obtaining a scholarship to Brown University for him? Get him back and have him enroll promptly." Instead, Aiso stayed in Tokyo for ten months. He likely earned the ambassador's appreciation later that year when the *Los Angeles Times* asked him to write a series of articles from Tokyo, "Impressions of Japan." Aiso's assertion in a 1927 article that "now is the dawn of a new Pacific era destined by Providence to engage the attention of the whole civilized world" articulated the same messages that consuls were conveying to Japanese-language teachers. Even before he enrolled at Brown in 1927, Aiso had pleased senior diplomats in Washington and Tokyo, the capitals of the two nations with which he identified. Significantly, it was the eloquent essays about citizenship he wrote in Los Angeles that had first brought him to the attention of the consuls who made his travel and education possible. Aiso's fluency in Japanese and English made him an ideal "bridge of understanding."[31]

The Mexican consul also worked with Progressive Angelinos to frame the "problem" of immigration in the context of schooling. Although the effort to establish consular schools in Los Angeles failed in the 1920s, Mexican Subsecretary of Public Education Moisés Sáenz, contributed to a successful initiative at Pomona College, a small college in eastern LA County. Starting in 1921, Pomona hosted nine Friends of the Mexicans conferences where Mexican diplomats and Anglo educators discussed controversial issues of the decade such as immigration, labor, and education. These conferences gained popularity over the years, drawing more than five hundred participants in 1929. These were adult-oriented events where Mexican-origin students had minimal influence, in contrast to the similar gatherings in the Japanese community where John Aiso was able to form diplomatic connections. While the Friends of the Mexicans conferences led to a more coordinated educational program on both sides of the border, they left students with little say in citizenship instruction and less hope of becoming bridges of understanding than the Japanese programs had provided for the Nisei.[32]

These conferences were part of the Mexican government's efforts to collaborate with southern California government officials on language education for Mexican nationals in Los Angeles. In 1926, the same diplomat who launched the consulate school in East LA arranged for a group of Mexican teachers to attend a summer school at Pomona for "special study of the English language and American educational methods." The consul also asked Subsecretary Sáenz to invite a Pomona administrator to Mexico. By 1928, the exchange had extended to Los Angeles schools. Angelino teachers toured schools in Mexico City and rural areas, and visited the National Autonomous University of Mexico. That spring, twenty-eight Mexican educators spent a week in LA schools, where "Spanish speaking teachers" served as hostesses. The Mexican contingent, composed of fourteen male professors and administrators along with fourteen female primary school principals, mixed business with pleasure. After touring LA public schools and observing Spanish classes at the National Automotive, Electric, and Aviation School, they visited Hollywood movie studios and attended the San Gabriel Mission Play, a pastoral imagining of California under Spanish colonial rule. Pomona's summer program and the LA visit gave more attention to teachers from Mexico than most neighborhood schools gave to immigrants who lived in the city's poorest communities. The

Friends of the Mexicans conference reflected a transnational effort to define Americanization as a class-based concept catering to educators on both sides of the border, not the masses they taught.[33]

The annual pilgrimages to Pomona allowed Angelino educators to reevaluate their positions on Mexican immigration law, citizenship, and labor status. At the 1929 conference, Nora Sterry represented LA teachers and defended Mexican workers against exploitation from organizations like the Western Growers Protective Association. Though lamenting the ways that migrant labor disrupted Mexican family life, Sterry stressed the social cost of starting "foreign district" schools and hospitals instead of the poverty of low-wage seasonal work. She mixed sympathy with low expectations, noting that "Mexican children have as fair intellect as other children but they are stunted mentally as well as physically by the spiritual and mental paucity of their homes." In her lecture the principal opined that Congress should extend the National Origins Act quotas to restrict future Mexican migration. Sterry's strong defense of the quota system stood out at the Pomona conference because Mexican speakers who followed her took the opposing position.[34]

Sterry was not the only US educator to endorse immigration restrictions. At the 1928 conference, the assistant superintendent of the LA city schools asserted that Californians were concerned about the nations with which they shared a border or an ocean, mentioning both Mexico and America's "Pan-Pacific policies and prospects" with Japan. Compared to Issei study tour guides, this administrator had a more measured outlook on building bridges of understanding, noting that from World War I to the National Origins Act, "periods of fairly friendly feeling have on a few occasions been interrupted by more hostile attitudes." This statement could describe the relationship along the Mexican border as well, but the superintendent was interested in hearing Spanish speakers' views about US citizenship. He persuaded the Friends of the Mexicans conference participants to discuss the topic by asking them "why so few Mexicans have any desire to become American citizens." Emphasizing that migrant workers lacked interest in citizenship programs like the Diploma Plan, he accepted the conference consensus that "Mexicans entered the United States for economic reasons, but nationally and racially remain Mexican in most cases." Such statements detracted from the agenda of immigrant educators who argued that Mexican students, who made up a majority of LA's Americanization classes, should not be excluded from the city's naturalization classes due simply to language ability. Rather than focusing on cultural assimilation, the Friends of the Mexicans conference participants stressed class differences that reinforced racial stereotypes among Anglo-American administrators. Perhaps this outcome was a result of inviting teachers, diplomats, and politicians from Mexico. The elite educators who came to Pomona could not articulate the attitudes of most Mexican immigrants.[35]

In their Pomona speeches, Mexican Progressives deployed language instruction to debate the relative merits of Americanization versus Mexicanization and competing national loyalties. At the 1925 conference, Mexican public education subsecretary Moisés Sáenz explained his goal of Americanizing rural children in his country. Historian Mary Kay Vaughan has described Sáenz's educational agenda as the "real cultural revolution" of Mexico in the 1920s, an era when schools served as sites of negotiation between the national modernizing project and the campesino traditions of the rural masses. For a Progressive like Sáenz who studied at Columbia Teachers College, US economic and cultural might after World War I stood as an ideal for his teachers to emulate. Sáenz appointed a committee of teachers and journalists "to direct a movement in the [Mexican] public schools to teach Mexican children love of the United States." This proposal impressed LA educators. After Sáenz's 1925 lecture, the Friends of the Mexicans conference director wrote that "Mr. Sáenz not only uses English fluently but has a fund of wit, humor and irony, which makes him a very interesting speaker." Sáenz's speeches in LA, delivered in English, and his Spanish-language curriculum in Mexico, suggested that the bureaucrat from Mexico City was more interested in Americanization than was the Mexican consul who lived in the LA barrio.[36]

Not all educated Mexicans shared Sáenz's enthusiasm for Americanization and learning English. One critic was Alberto Rembao, who had graduated from Pomona in 1921. After four years directing an international school in Guadalajara, he became head of the Spanish Bureau of the US Foreign Language Information Service. Rembao was skeptical of Sáenz's innovations and critiqued groups like the Friends of the Mexicans—"our flying and joking and educational ambassadors of good-will"— for their "noble gesture." At the 1928 conference, Rembao advocated for a new form of Americanization, one with "less flag-waving and less anthem-singing" and more emphasis on teaching children to be global citizens. While admitting that Mexicans' main barrier to American education was their "ignorance of our language, laws and customs," he added that impatient Americans did not give them time to assimilate. Rembao's Foreign Language Information Service borrowed from the Japanese bridges of understanding idea but put the onus of understanding on Anglo-Americans rather than second-generation Mexican immigrants. He urged Californians to visit Mexico, meet Sáenz and, most importantly, "learn Spanish, that sweet dialect that seems to sound as the chants of the Castilian books." In advising Angelino educators to study Spanish, Rembao reversed the premise that Americanization was an English-only exercise.

Such statements changed the Friends of the Mexicans conference from a pedagogical dialogue among teachers to a political debate about Mexican immigration.[37]

Whereas the Friends of the Mexicans conferences were venues where adults articulated their views on citizenship and language learning, Japanese events were outlets where Nisei students could voice their opinions. In addition to the Japan study tours, Nisei competed in oratorical contests where "world friendship" was a frequent theme. The best speeches were printed in *Orations and Essays by the Japanese Second Generation of America*, a book self-published by Issei Paul Hirohata in 1932 and expanded in 1935. A journalist for the Los Angeles daily *Rafu Shimpo,* Hirohata expressed his generation's dreams by compiling the commencement addresses of forty-nine Nisei students who graduated from California schools during the Depression. While the students' speeches reflected the academic accomplishments of many Japanese Americans, their oratory often reflected the political agendas of the adults who had taught them. In fact, the most insightful descriptions of world friendship and bridges of understanding appeared in several introductory statements by Angelino educators and Japanese diplomats in the foreword to Hirohata's book.[38]

The forewords by Japanese officials stationed in Los Angeles couched citizenship in a geopolitical framework. The secretary of the LA Japanese Association wrote a message in Japanese characters that addressed the National Origins Act of 1924, stating that since the quotas had halted Japanese immigration, Nisei bore the burden of "promoting goodwill between Japan and the United States." Not only were the Nisei cultural "bridges," the secretary said, but "the future development of our race in North America fell solely upon activity of the Nisei." As the historian Eiichiro Azuma has argued, this passage reflects an image the Issei had created of themselves as laying claim to the "Eastern" frontier and settling California as Japanese territory. In 1935, Kay Sugahara, a former oratorical champion from Polytechnic High who was president of the LA chapter of the Japanese American Citizens League, advanced this "Issei pioneer thesis." He praised the "gifted Nisei trailblazers" whose speeches were printed in the book, urging them to "never lose sight of . . . the indomitable courage of our pioneer forefathers." Noting the turmoil of the Great Depression, Sugahara suggested that his generation could improve diplomatic relations because, as American citizens of Japanese descent, the Nisei were "a blend of two great cultural forces, play[ing] a prominent role in the molding of a more pacific relationship between two great powers." In his expanded 1935 edition, Hirohata printed the speeches by Sugahara and the secretary in both Japanese and English, perhaps to emphasize the "bridge" and "pioneer" themes to readers in both nations.[39]

In contrast to Issei contributors' emphasis on bridges of understanding, other forewords in the book were written only in English and focused on the California schools' world friendship theme. Toshito Satow, the Japanese consul in Los Angeles, argued that oratory contests had made the Nisei "skilled in the art of self-expression," enabling them to "promote understanding and friendship between America and Japan." Whereas the consul combined the "bridge" and "friendship" themes to describe dialogue across nations, the state superintendent of public instruction explained "friendship" and "language" in the context of a California classroom. Vierling Kersey, who later became superintendent of the LA school district, wrote that "where there is a desire for understanding and an aim to promote friendship . . . we may be assured that no mere barrier of race or language can stand in the way." Like the Issei educators, Kersey commented on students' capacity to interact with peers of different ethnicities. However, rather than using these relationships to promote international diplomacy he wanted to create harmony in California. He cited the Olympic Games, which Los Angeles had hosted in the summer of 1932, as an example. Just like the LA schools, the Olympics had united people from various nations. Kersey called for the Olympic spirit to continue in California's classrooms where, with "students working together, there is the greatest opportunity of appreciating . . . the customs, the temperament and the problems of other countries." His remarks echoed the bridges of understanding theme that Issei officials had articulated, but shifted the focus from the Pacific Rim to California. While the superintendent focused on civic participation within the Golden State, the Japanese consul wanted to teach the Nisei to be transpacific citizens.[40]

Orations and Essays also emphasized how the Nisei themselves envisioned citizenship in America and Japan. Based on their speeches, Nisei adolescents expressed their ideas about assimilation as immigrant children who were interested in the Olympics, government, economic justice, and ethnic holidays. A close reading of two statements by the city's most accomplished orator reveals several ways in which children of nonwhite immigrants used language learning to gain access to American civic life. John Aiso's first oratorical contest came in 1923, when the sophomore "silver tongue" gave a speech about "Lincoln's Devotion to the Constitution" that would have made any Diploma Plan teacher proud. In 1927, the *Los Angeles Times* published one of his editorials under the headline "As Japan Sees America." The two titles reflect the range of geopolitical influences on a second-generation youth coming to terms with how to participate in American civic discourse without abandoning the ethnic identity he inherited from his parents. Aiso aimed these declarations at different audiences, but the settings in which he delivered them defied expectations. He spoke about Abraham Lincoln at a contest run by the Federated Japanese Young Men's Association of Southern California, an organization affiliated with the transnational language instructors who argued that learning Japanese would make the Nisei better American citizens. Four years later, Aiso opined about Japan to the largely white readership of the *Los Angeles Times*.[41]

These speeches show how Aiso became a bridge of understanding. Aiso was a talented orator who articulated the interwar ideals of both Japan and America and appeared most assimilated when surrounded by fellow Nisei. His eloquent explanation of Abraham Lincoln's "God-like" ability to preserve the Constitution's integrity showcased his "loyal devotion" to American law. Aiso's interest in Lincoln's political path from saving the Union to abolishing slavery may have reflected his struggle to square American ideals with the racial prejudice he had experienced. After all, in 1922 he had quoted Lincoln in the speech that temporarily earned him election as the student body president. Ironically, the same patriotism that had led his junior high school to suspend student government rather than honor his election as president won first prize at the Federated Japanese Young Men's Association the next year. The same speech that the school district had used to exclude a nonwhite student from civic participation became a symbol of Nisei loyalty to the US when delivered to LA's Japanese American community.[42]

Aiso was proud to be both Japanese and American. During his postgraduate year in Japan, when he wrote the *Los Angeles Times* essay, Aiso stressed Japan's "admiration for and devotion to the United States." Pointing out Theodore Roosevelt's role in resolving the Russo-Japanese War of 1907, he declared that the twentieth century would be the "dawn of a new Pacific era." Although some Anglo-Americans suspected Japanese immigrants of harboring "imperial ambitions" to colonize America, Aiso believed Nisei like him could clear up such "misunderstandings" and persuade citizens stateside that "the hearts of the Pan-Pacific countries are attuned to friendship." As an American citizen of Japanese descent studying in the land of his parents' birth, the John Aiso of 1927 admired the balance of "international understanding and friendship" just as he had venerated "Lincoln's devotion to the Constitution" at Hollywood's LeConte Junior High School four years earlier. The essay Aiso wrote in Tokyo represented the efforts of other Nisei Angelinos who took Japan study tours, as well as of Spanish-speaking students who attended Mexican Consulate schools in Los Angeles, to foster allegiance to both of their nations.[43]

———————————

While educators from Japan, Mexico, and LA city schools struggled over citizenship curricula, students embraced the idea of world friendship. By forming World Friendship Clubs after World War I, diverse groups of students used concepts like bridges of understanding to bring global events to neighborhood schools. During the Depression, oratory contests and student clubs at Roosevelt High School allowed students to engage with "internationalism studies." Just as Nisei like John Aiso viewed their Japan study tours as diplomatic missions, Anglo teachers used their own experiences abroad to experiment with anti-prejudice education during the buildup to World War II. The rise of World Friendship Clubs reflected the transition in immigrant education from the reforms of Progressive Anglos like Sterry and Kelso to a New Deal liberalism that developed in multiethnic districts like Boyle Heights in East LA.[44]

In the 1920s, world friendship references forced the *Los Angeles School Journal* to consider transnational content. The *Journal* linked world friendship to the overseas experiences of Angelino educators in a 1925 issue entitled "Education for World Relationships." One writer reframed Americanization as "brotherhood making or brotherization," suggesting that after international travel, teachers now looked at immigrant students as representatives of their parents' homeland rather than as young Americans, which turned their classrooms into international summits. Another article, "Teaching Brotherhoodness," promoted the Pan Pacific Association for Mutual Understanding, a new group that hosted "monthly travel dinners" and arranged lectures with LA consuls from Pacific Rim countries including Mexico and Japan. The Pan Pacific Association wanted schools to have "ample provision for the teaching of the Oriental languages, training for diplomatic service and commercial leadership." A story on the next page reported about the most recent League of Nations meeting, where a world peace curriculum was endorsed. World Friendship courses were not unique to Los Angeles, or even to the United States, but LA teachers used these internationalist ideas to endorse language and social studies content that addressed the city's larger immigrant populations.[45]

It was ironic that World Friendship Clubs became more popular in LA schools in the Progressive Era. The idea that students could form a miniature League of Nations presupposed that schools in immigrant districts were integrated. In fact, during the interwar period Mexican students across southern California were sent to segregated schools. Yet Anglo educators emphasized the few racially diverse schools in Central and East Los Angeles.

One of these exceptions, John Aiso's alma mater Hollywood High School, founded the Cosmopolitan Club in 1915, "the first club of that nature in any high school of the country." The History Department chair arranged evenings at Japanese, Chinese, Italian, and French restaurants, where Hollywood students dined and debated with the consuls from the corresponding countries. This experience was not typical for Mexican students in the 1920s, but some Americanization advocates argued that world friendship was an important alternative to segregation. The author of the "Brotherization" article in the *Los Angeles School Journal* lamented the presence of "so-called Mexican schools" in LA. Focusing on world relations led teachers to discuss the cultures of other countries, prompting the contributor of the article to ask, "Are we educating Mexicans to be Mexicans, or are we educating them to be Americans?" The world friendship model offered teachers an international construct to include Mexican students in conversations about citizenship, even as Diploma Plan instructors were adhering to a curriculum designed to make them ineligible for naturalization.[46]

By the 1930s, immigrant students had reinvented World Friendship Clubs in light of recent events that were leading the world closer to global war. When Roosevelt High opened the city's sixteenth chapter in 1931, students saw their Peace Club as a symbol of the school's eastside neighborhood of Boyle Heights, LA's most diverse district. Roosevelt High's Peace Club in 1931 was different than the first Cosmopolitan Club founded at Hollywood High in 1915. Unlike the school whose principal once told John Aiso to drop out of the national oratorical contest, Roosevelt opened its doors to successful students of color. Throughout the 1930s, several student body presidents demonstrated their civic participation in times of economic and diplomatic crisis. Nisei Arthur Takemoto, the president in 1939, called his weekly column in the *Rough Rider* newspaper the "Fireside Chat," borrowing the title of Franklin Roosevelt's radio addresses. Hugh Acevedo, the vice president in 1935, joined the school's Reserve Officer Training Corps. Acevedo was also the only Mexican or Japanese officer of the World Friendship Club, which had mostly Anglo-Christian and Jewish students during the Depression. A 1936 survey estimated that 28 percent of Roosevelt's students were "American," 26 percent were Jewish, 24 percent were Mexican, and 6 percent were Japanese. The school's multiethnic makeup shaped the Peace Club in other ways during the 1930s, when multiple members won the annual Los Angeles Federation of World Friendship Clubs Oratorical Contest.[47]

By emphasizing international diplomacy over ethnic identity, the Peace Club borrowed Japanese immigrants' bridges of understanding idea. It worked with the Spanish Club on two projects. In 1932, members corresponded with a school in Barcelona, sending a portfolio that included images of Hollywood, beaches, and the 1932 Summer Olympics in Los Angeles. When the Catalonian school sent a similar portfolio in 1933, with photos of Gaudí architecture and the city's soccer stadium, the Peace Club asked member Eddie Roybal, also president of the Spanish Club, to translate the letter. Roybal later became California's first Latino congressman since 1879. Roybal joined the New Deal's Civilian Conservation Corps after graduating from Roosevelt, but returned in 1934 to help his old club celebrate Pan American Day, playing a Chilean song on guitar. In 1935, the Peace and Spanish Clubs partnered to present Pan American Day, winning praise in the *Rough Rider* for promoting "world peace and international goodwill." Through songs, dances, and speeches, the Peace Club president expected Pan American Day to "establish even closer relations between races in this school."[48]

Although it was popular in the 1930s, the Peace Club did not have many minority members to participate in its international diplomacy discussions. Yet the sizable immigrant population of Boyle Heights made Mexican and Japanese students impossible to ignore. Victoria Holguin, the oratory champion who extolled Columbus during Día de la Raza, was elected secretary of the 1935 Peace Club, and honors student Masako Fukumoto was a member. The 1940 yearbook allotted two pages to school assemblies, culminating in a nine-picture montage of the Peace Club's "Peace Day Costume Parade," featuring photos of Mexican boys in sombreros and Japanese girls in kimonos. The caption listed twenty-nine minority groups represented in the ceremonies, starting with Jewish, Mexican, and Japanese. Ethnic minorities also played smaller roles in more serious events that did not include costumes. At the 1934 Armistice Day assembly, the only Mexican American participant was Viela Espinoza, who sang after the salute to the flag. Although several Japanese students represented Roosevelt High in the *Los Angeles Herald* oratorical contest during the Depression, the only Nisei mentioned at the 1939 Los Angeles World Friendship Federation oratory contest was a "Japanese girl [who] gave two tap dances." Although the Roosevelt High Peace Club celebrated diversity more than other organizations did, the more obviously diverse students struggled to be included in activities of citywide importance.[49]

When the World Friendship Federation did discuss world peace, it referenced Japan and Mexico as military threats, not as sending countries of immigrants to California. Isolationism was an issue that dominated the federation's speech competitions, which resembled the oratorical contest on the Constitution John Aiso had won a decade earlier. In 1934, "Peaceful Relations in the Pacific" and "Latin American Contributions to Peace" were two of the seven debate topics, and one year later, the contest's main theme was "Pan-American

Peace." When the war in Europe began, keynote speakers grew more isolationist. In 1939, two months after Germany had invaded Poland, Roosevelt's Peace Club addressed five resolutions of the World Friendship Federation that neglected other nations, stressing that "participation in a war would destroy American Democracy." The planned speaker at that year's citywide contest was a socialist actor who later became one of nineteen Hollywood artists blacklisted by the House Un-American Activities Committee. Instead, as Russia was invading Finland, the club invited California's lieutenant governor, who equated isolationism with democracy. "War is essentially murder," he told the Roosevelt assembly. "We have freedom of speech, freedom of press, freedom of liberties, freedom of religion which we want to keep by staying out of international problems and solving our own problems." If Japanese and Mexican students were willing to embrace the ideals of "brotherization" and world friendship, the Peace Club offered them the opportunity to state their views on war and democracy at a time when many Anglos were questioning minorities' American citizenship and promoting isolationism.[50]

The four models of language and naturalization education implemented in Los Angeles schools between the world wars illustrated the changing ideals of Americanization and citizenship. In the first two models, neighborhood school women and Diploma Plan teachers created curricula that enabled them to carry out federal policies that restricted future immigration by race, such as the National Origins Act of 1924 and two Supreme Court cases that ruled Asian immigrants were ineligible for citizenship. These racialized restrictions constrained the Americanization experience for non-European immigrants on the West Coast. In response, the Mexican and Japanese communities in Los Angeles launched a variety of language-instruction experiments that demonstrated their many contributions to American society as engaged citizens able to leverage access to transnational networks. They engaged in a process of cultural negotiation between progressive reformers and immigrants eager to assimilate. Japanese and Mexican Angelinos designed their own citizenship models based on the ideals of bridges of understanding and world friendship, respectively. These models were, like neighborhood schools, forms of negotiation, but they also helped students and teachers of color take control of their own Americanization experience in spite of the racialized constraints they faced.[51]

Roosevelt High School encapsulated the interwar negotiation over language instruction and citizenship, as Anglo teachers supported minority students' isolationist views while urging them to think globally. Students recruited teachers to participate in Peace Club events by inviting them to speak about their travels around the world. The club's first sponsor in 1931 was Mrs. Helen Bailey, a social science teacher who summered in South America. She left the faculty after she married, but returned to address the Peace Club in 1934, when she told students about her experiences in Mexico. Bailey brought paintings to her talks and wore "a Mexican national costume which was made for her by her Mexican friends." She compared urban and rural living conditions and hinted at her own urban bias by explaining "how the Mexican federal government is starting a plan to educate the Aztec Indians who still speak the Aztec Indian language and are many years behind times." By arguing that indigenous Mexicans could (and should) learn other modern languages like Spanish, Bailey implied confidence in the ability of immigrant students in Roosevelt's Peace Club to assimilate into American society and become productive citizens of the United States and the world.[52]

Language learning had a different political context when a Latin teacher, Miss Ida Eby, addressed the World Friendship Club in 1935 and shared her experiences teaching English in Japan. After visiting a Nisei student at college and touring Tokyo, Eby decided that Japan's "scenery was very interesting and like that of England." Concluding that "the English language was quite common in Japan," Eby informed the Japanese Club that learning English was important for Nisei no matter where they lived. It was notable that Eby made language a priority when she spoke to the Japanese Club but drifted to cultural diplomacy when she told the Peace Club about her summer in Europe four years later. In 1939, on the eve of war, Eby shared her observations of Fascist Italy, where the trains were overcrowded, the hotels were in bad condition, and Mussolini was hiring "cheering squads" for public parades. Roosevelt's lone Latin teacher suggested that the war had changed her ideas about Americaniza-tion and citizenship curricula. When she addressed the Japanese Club in 1935, Eby emphasized that Nisei students needed to learn English before they could participate in advanced discussions of democracy like the ones she had held about Italy. Her remarks sent a message that, while Nisei students might be able to learn English and assimilate into American life, they did not yet deserve the same access to civic participation that white students enjoyed. Faculty like Bailey and Eby brought their individual assumptions of Americanization and civic membership to their meetings with the Peace Club.[53]

Students also shaped how Roosevelt teachers came to understand the world friendship model of citizenship education and the difficult process of naturalization. The faculty expert on citizenship was Asbury Bagwell, who had written his master's thesis on the history of the Diploma Plan in 1928. Upon arriving at Roosevelt, Bagwell started oratory competitions in his economics classes, which the *Rough Rider* called "an unusual and effective method of teaching." In 1933, Bagwell's students (mostly Jewish and Nisei) debated an early New Deal program, the controversial National Recovery Administration. This activity was consistent with the Diploma Plan's dedication to curriculum about the Constitution and the branches of government. As Bagwell got to know his new students at Roosevelt High, however, he began to address topics other than domestic politics. In 1933, he delivered a lecture entitled the "Economic Situation in Cuba before and after the Revolution" to the honors society and to Roosevelt's new Latin American History class. In 1935, he was the guest speaker at two Peace Club meetings, where he addressed World Friendship Club resolutions about international disarmament. This indicates that the economics teacher considered Cuba and peace treaties to be as important as the New Deal or the naturalization policies he had helped to change through implementation of the Diploma Plan the previous decade. While teaching in the most diverse high school in 1930s Los Angeles, Bagwell began to see his students as global citizens.[54]

Bagwell's transition from Charles Kelso's Citizenship Department to the Roosevelt Peace Club demonstrates the shift in LA's immigrant instruction experiments. Bagwell began teaching white immigrants in evening naturalization classes in the 1920s to supplement his job at Manual Arts High School, where he had judged the oratorical contest on the Constitution in 1927, a year after the John Aiso controversy. Transferring to Boyle Heights, he joined a new generation of Angelino educators. These New Deal teachers were not like Kelso, the missionary who naturalized only white, English-speaking students, or Nora Sterry, the devout principal who marched into a quarantine zone to unfurl the American flag. They were secular savants who explored the Pacific Rim. Roosevelt High teachers summered in Asia and the Americas and shared travel stories with their students.

In comparison to Sterry's stern portrait in 1924 wearing a white headdress emblazoned with a cross, Mrs. Bailey made her 1932 lecture fun, organizing personal photos into "a motion picture [to] depict the customs, life, and habits of the Mexican people." She loved the kids of East LA, she admired their nations of origin, and she empowered them to take charge of their own education. The rise of World Friendship Clubs in the 1930s signaled that students were altering the direction of LA citizenship curricula. By moving to the city's most ethnically diverse high school, Bagwell, the chief advocate of the Diploma Plan's approach to restrict naturalization, placed citizenship in a more global context. Angelino educators like Bailey and Bagwell often mediated tensions between American ideals and the actual treatment of their immigrant students during a period of Mexican deportation and imperial competition with Japan.[55]

3 | WARTIME PATRIOTISM TESTS FOR JAPANESE AND SPANISH SPEAKERS, 1941–1945

World War II abruptly changed the structures of language instruction in Los Angeles. Kohei Shimano's Japanese school closed on December 7, 1941, the day he was arrested. Shimano had opened LA's first language school in 1911, a few blocks from Nora Sterry's Amelia Street School, which Earl Warren had once attended. By 1941, Warren had become California's attorney general and its chief advocate of Japanese removal. Warren was unaware of Shimano's efforts to prove Japanese immigrants' American patriotism. Shimano had long insisted that Issei educators write Japanese-language textbooks for Nisei that stressed Beishu Nichijū, the "primary emphasis on America and secondary on Japan," even after the Supreme Court ruled that California had no jurisdiction to impose such a requirement on his private school curriculum. Regardless of his dedication to Americanization, Shimano was arrested hours after the bombing of Pearl Harbor. The Federal Bureau of Investigation (FBI) sent him to detention facilities in Montana, Louisiana, and finally New Mexico, where he died in 1943 at age sixty-nine. He never returned to the city where he had spent three decades teaching Nisei to be proud of their allegiance to America as well as Japan.[1]

The state's oldest Japanese-language school lost its Anglo advocates during the war. After Shimano's arrest, Sterry's successor as principal of the Amelia Street School, who had shared many of Shimano's students, refused to write him a recommendation because she "just couldn't say that he was not a spy or a saboteur." Her failure to act haunted her later, but at the time it enabled the government to label Shimano a "Japanese male alien enemy." FBI notes filed on Pearl Harbor Day indicated that investigators used Shimano's language school to question his loyalty to the United States. Rather than reporting that the principal's five trips to Japan were for Nisei study tours, often accompanied by Anglo educators, the notes stressed that Shimano had received a wooden cup from the emperor, met with a "nationalistic leader," and enjoyed "the warm reception that his party was given by the army." Such gifts, the FBI report implied, had influenced Shimano to reverse course from his Beishu Nichijû curriculum of the 1920s. Citing unnamed sources, the report alleged that many Japanese schools stored two sets of textbooks and that the "primary emphasis on America" set was merely for show to "curious Occidentals," whereas "practically every page of the other set pledges loyalty to Japan and treason against the American government."[2]

Accusations such as these led the federal War Relocation Authority (WRA) to ban Japanese-language schools from internment camps. At the same time, however, many Nisei Angelinos were using language learning to demonstrate their American patriotism. Weeks before Pearl Harbor, the army opened the Military Intelligence Service (MIS) Language School. By 1945, six thousand Nisei volunteers had left internment camps, where they were banned from studying their heritage language, and had enlisted in the US Army for more rigorous instruction in Japanese history, geography, and military language than Kohei Shimano ever gave in Los Angeles. The MIS Language School's founding teacher was none other than John Aiso. The "Nisei silver tongue" was aware of the irony of his situation—that fifteen years after Hollywood High School would not let him compete in an oratorical contest because of his ancestry, his Japanese proficiency now made him invaluable to the army. Language learning became a paradoxical test of patriotism for Nisei Angelinos during the war. Aiso rose to lieutenant colonel, becoming the army's highest-ranking Nisei officer, for teaching Japanese, while Kohei Shimano was arrested for performing the same job.[3]

Wartime events removed Japanese Angelinos from LA County and also relocated the debate over language education for both Japanese and Mexican Americans. Before the war, Shimano had designed language curricula to counter local efforts to restrict Japanese Angelinos' access to citizenship rights. During the war, language instructors set aside citizenship status and focused on questions of national loyalty. After the Zoot Suit Riots, a series of attacks by white sailors against Mexican Americans that resulted in the mass arrests of Mexican American youths, public outrage pushed Los Angeles authorities to prohibit Spanish-language schools just as internment camp officials banned Japanese-language instruction after Pearl Harbor. Despite this discrimination, racial minorities viewed language learning as an opportunity to prove their patriotism in the midst of crisis. Nisei enrolled in Japanese courses to study the language of their new enemies, not their parents. Similarly, Mexican American educators who had articulated "ambivalent Americanization" in the 1920s now urged Spanish-speaking youths to join the US Army. Spanish speakers promoted Pan-Americanism as a wartime military strategy to encourage cooperation among nations in the Americas through diplomatic and educational means. By teaching Spanish language and culture, Pan-American schools aimed to calm Mexican children, reduce juvenile delinquency, and increase loyalty to the United States. If immigrants could prove their patriotism through military service and the MIS Language School, Japanese and Mexican Angelinos argued, then Americanization was no longer a valid reason not to learn Spanish or Japanese. By shifting the local emphasis from citizenship to national loyalties during World War II, LA educators formulated the emotional and political arguments that made language instruction central to national debates about school integration after the war.[4]

After Franklin Roosevelt declared war against Japan, the military mobilization transformed the entire home front. Changes in education included a new approach to citizenship and language learning called tolerance education. Zoë Burkholder argues that by 1941, "teachers understood tolerance education as a new, better form of Americanization to cultivate the democratic ideal of tolerance while forging a unified, patriotic citizenry." Anglo educators across the country believed the Americanization ideas they had emphasized before the war could help mobilize a new generation of soldiers and factory workers to spread democratic values to fascist states overseas. Burkholder also makes clear that racial minorities were often excluded from the wartime vision of tolerance education. This was especially true in Los Angeles, where Nisei relocation and fears of Mexican juvenile delinquency drove the school district to ban Japanese instruction and restrict its Spanish offerings. Mexican and Japanese Angelinos responded by framing language instruction as part of the trend in tolerance education that teachers used to contrast American pluralism with the evils of Nazi racial ideology. The minority educators were joined by a few Anglo administrators who identified language instruction as a cure to the crises of 1942. While the government was closing language schools, some Angelinos were arguing that ethnic Japanese and Mexican youth needed to learn their heritage languages. These opposing visions forced a reconsideration of the role of language education. As domestic hostilities continued during the war, these passionate advocates shifted the Americanization debate from citizenship status to wartime loyalty.[5]

Some Nisei leaders ceased arguing that Japanese-language institutions were effective Americanization tools. When LA's largest Japanese-language newspaper, *Rafu Shimpo*, hired Togo Tanaka to edit its English section, he encouraged fellow Nisei to be patriotic Americans. Tanaka was the principal interviewee for a 1939 *Saturday Evening Post* article, "Between Two Flags," which argued that Nisei were fully Americanized. To defend his generation's loyalty, Tanaka was quoted as calling language schools an example of assimilation, describing them merely as "an overdose of school" imposed by Issei parents on their children, not "hotbeds of Japanese propaganda" as many Anglos feared. Tanaka insisted that most Nisei were not interested in the afternoon schools because they "refused to think in Japanese; they thought in English." He responded to concerns about Nisei disloyalty with a satire about "the great Japanese-American map-remaking plot." In this silly conspiracy, Issei would reassign all American cities Japanese names; for example, LA would become Rafu because in Japanese Ls sound like Rs and *fu* means "city." Many Americans did not appreciate this kind of humor. In 1942, Tanaka was relocated to a camp that banned Japanese-language schools. Tanaka's interview in the *Saturday Evening Post* article articulated the nuanced ways that Nisei used language to prove their patriotism.[6]

When Japanese removal began in 1942, all LA teachers and students had to confront the question of wartime loyalty. Statements in the Roosevelt High School *Rough Rider* newspaper show how the war upended Progressive visions of public education. In the spring of 1942 the student editors replaced stories about citizenship classes and World Friendship Clubs with a four-month discussion of the eminent departure of their Nisei classmates. Importantly, they no longer linked language to Americanization. Their silence on language clubs and classes belied the patriotic optimism of their "melting pot" rhetoric. Japanese and Mexican students alike avoided speaking their heritage languages at school because they feared seeming sympathetic to foreign nations. Internment also caused chaos in student government at Roosevelt High, because four student council officers and the senior class president were Japanese. Yet Nisei leaders not only agreed with the Roosevelt administration that internment was necessary, they embraced it as a chance to prove their loyalty. Since Mexican students were not forced to relocate, they viewed joining the military as the best way to demonstrate their allegiance to the United States. This paradoxical patriotism in a time of rising prejudice reveals how students struggled to sustain their citizenship status during the war.

Roosevelt High's non-Nisei students were slow to accept Americanization as a military necessity. Initially, the *Rough Rider* opposed Japanese removal. Eleven days after Pearl Harbor, an editorial preached tolerance for the school's four hundred Nisei. The Nisei "not only equaled but in many cases surpassed, other racial groups on the campus in service to the school, in academic achievement and in all around good citizenship," the editors insisted, and "there is no sane reason why they should not continue to do so."[7] By March, however, the *Rough Rider* reframed evacuation as inevitable and patriotic. "There is nothing that can be done to remedy this situation," an editor admitted. "I'm sure that our Japanese students realize the necessity of this action."[8] Two months later, the student staff reversed its position again and opposed evacuation. These rapidly changing opinions reflected the reporters' struggles to reconcile their wartime loyalties with their memories of the relocated Nisei as "some of my most worthy friends" who starred at assemblies, on varsity sports, and in student government.[9]

Teachers tried language "tricks" to make internment more palatable to Japanese students. The principal proposed a "bazaar-type sale day" when Nisei could sell their belongings before leaving Los Angeles. When this garage sale depressed morale, he invited families under evacuation orders to meet with a teacher who had learned about "the Japanese people, language, and customs" over three years in Japan. The teacher also helped his Roosevelt High colleagues buy radios, refrigerators, and even houses at discounted prices from Japanese families rushing to vacate their homes. The World Friendship Club was more compassionate, asking members to write letters to their soon-to-be-interned Nisei classmates. Teachers hoped language and citizenship skills would ease the internment process. Yet Nisei student leaders stuck to Americanization as they awaited evacuation in the spring of 1942.[10]

As relocation became reality, most Japanese leaders hid their fears behind the language of Americanization. Echoing the feelings of many ethnic Japanese, George Maruki, who was elected senior class president days after the government announced internment, could not state his forthcoming relocation directly. "I am rather confused as to what will become of me when I leave school," he told the *Rough Rider*.[11] Three Nisei student council members said evacuation was "justified . . . all believe it is an exceptional way to prove their loyalty." Some Nisei hoped demonstrations of loyalty, such as avoiding Japanese clubs and language schools while participating in student government, would delay their internment indefinitely. Student body vice president Kazumi "Choo-Choo" Tsukimoto tried not to think about internment, advising all Japanese to "keep on working as usual till the actual time comes." Japanese students stressed Americanization activities to prove their patriotism as they faced the uncertainties of internment.[12]

The distance between Americanization rhetoric and reality was even greater at the Santa Anita and Pomona assembly centers in Los Angeles County. Education was not the first priority of the WRA after internment began in February 1942. Within three months, 18,000 Japanese Angelinos had been moved to the Santa Anita Racetrack, and the famous horseracing grounds held California's thirty-second largest population. The Army Corps of Engineers spent four weeks converting horse stalls into housing at assembly centers along the Pacific coast to temporarily contain 118,000 evacuees while ten larger camps were built farther inland. Being focused on providing shelter and food, the WRA did not set up formal schooling for the internees until the end of May. Those makeshift classes met in grandstand lobbies facing the racetrack betting windows. The WRA outlawed Japanese-language instruction, claiming that Santa Anita's crude classrooms could acculturate Nisei students.[13]

In fact, visits by two LA school administrators signaled that the language-learning ban had made it harder to inspire Japanese American patriotism. Los Angeles City Superintendent of Schools Vierling Kersey came to Santa Anita on June 26, 1942, to give the keynote address at an all-purpose graduation ceremony, thereby fulfilling a promise from Roosevelt High's principal to hold "some type of graduation" for the Nisei. Kersey allowed the students to transfer credits from their former schools, but Santa Anita set up so few classes that only 250 students graduated. Adult evacuees offered to teach additional courses, and an Issei history professor from Stanford formed a parent teacher association. By June, 2,470 Japanese Americans had enrolled in courses taught by 130 volunteer teachers. These volunteers carried on the education of Nisei children as best as they could in a camp enclosed by barbed wire and with living quarters that lacked toilet facilities.[14]

School administrators continued to apply language learning to their assimilation agenda within the camps. Assembly center schools articulated an ironic view of Americanization in both languages. Adults signed up for English classes in conversation, reading, writing, and pronunciation, along with advanced classes that stressed assimilation. By summer, 220 Issei had enrolled in Democracy Training, a course offered in both English and Japanese. Underscoring the paradox of preaching patriotism to incarcerated people, this bilingual class was Santa Anita's only non-English instruction option. The WRA had banned "Japanese print of any kind," even translation dictionaries, and announced its intention to seize all Japanese publications except Bibles. This came as welcome news to the younger generation. An evacuee at another assembly center noted that "Nisei as a whole rejoice that they no longer have to attend Japanese language school." Internment initially succeeded in driving Nisei away from learning Japanese. However, the poor quality of the classes that were offered discouraged them from pursuing an American education, allowing the allure of Japanese culture classes to linger as the war progressed.[15]

Afton Nance noticed the inadequate conditions that Vierling Kersey had overlooked because she had a deeper relationship with Nisei students than the LA superintendent did. Kersey's contact with the Japanese community was limited to English-language journalists like Paul Hirohata, who had compiled a book of Nisei commencement addresses in the 1930s. As state superintendent of public instruction, Kersey had written a foreword to that book, referencing the general role of the Nisei speeches as "bridges of understanding." In contrast, Afton Nance knew several dozen Nisei students very well from her eighth-grade classes at Malaga Cove School in Palos Verdes Estates, a rural seaside community in southwestern LA County. An English teacher who was passionate about rural schools, Nance could not tolerate her students' forced relocation. She joined a Quaker group, the American Friends Service Committee, to protest internment. She also kept in touch with many of her former students, sending hundreds of letters and care packages and traveling across LA County to visit its two assembly centers. Through these letters and visits, Nance observed a much different school system than the one Kersey described in his Santa Anita speech.[16]

Tomi Matsumoto, for example, almost failed to graduate. At Nance's urging, the sixteen-year-old enrolled in English and science classes as soon as they opened. Matsumoto wrote her former teacher that Santa Anita had a good English teacher, but that her dishwashing job left little study time. When Kersey visited two weeks later, Matsumoto ignored Nance's advice and skipped the ceremony. This meant she had to get her diploma at the assembly center office, where she learned the WRA did not have her graduation records. Stuck at Santa Anita, she asked Nance to talk to the school board. Matsumoto's mistrust of assembly center schools deepened the next week when the WRA closed classes for all Nisei older than fifteen, who instead were assigned to make military camouflage. The diploma mix-up dampened Matsumoto's interest in Kersey's Americanization agenda.[17]

In fact, Matsumoto was still learning more from her former teacher than she did from Santa Anita's volunteer teachers. Her evening school instructor taught English by having students transcribe radio newscasts and correcting their mistakes. Matsumoto admitted that rewriting war reports only "made me understand I must study English harder." In response, Nance urged her to keep writing her own stories on the side. Nance also brought candy, clothes, and letters from old classmates when she visited in May. Matsumoto enjoyed hearing about her friends' graduation plans, and her response to them highlighted the stark differences in not just their education, but their living conditions and circumstances. Rather than writing about future plans, she told them she was lucky to have a job washing 3,200 dishes after every meal because the alternative was to handle chemicals in camouflage production. This response motivated Nance to send more baked goods, books, and teaching tips to former students. Tomi thanked her for the language instruction when she wrote, "I feel guilty to trouble you some more on my English, but I learn so much the way you stuck those study in me I cannot decline your kindness offer" [sic]. Matsumoto continued writing out nightly newscasts for her Santa Anita classes, but her progress stalled without Nance's language assistance. The rural teacher realized that the prewar Americanization process had changed dramatically after Pearl Harbor. Nance continued to support her Nisei students' assimilation and education, but she had to do so from outside the classroom.[18]

That summer, Nance left Palos Verdes Estates to become a school administrator five miles up the coast in Manhattan Beach. She soon met Helen Heffernan, who had just arrived in Los Angeles to direct the California Department of Education's Inter-American Demonstration Center Project. This meeting began a twenty-year partnership dedicated to bilingual education initiatives for the children of migrant workers. Decades before writing California's first program in English as a second language in 1966, the two women devoted their wartime discourse to international relations. They talked to teachers who wrote about Pan-American summers in Mexico, Peru, or Brazil to "awaken the interest of our own people" and strengthen ties while the world was at war. Like tolerance education, Pan-Americanism framed Spanish-language learning in the context of a racially inclusive curriculum that appealed to LA educators more than the Mexicanization programs of the 1920s had done. Liberal rhetoric about tolerance and language instruction also informed Mexican American responses to two wartime tragedies in Los Angeles: the Sleepy Lagoon "murder" and the Zoot Suit Riots. Nance and Heffernan promoted Pan-Americanism after the Sleepy Lagoon murder of 1942. After the Zoot Suit Riots one year later, the East LA attorney Manuel Ruiz tried to tie language learning to civil rights reforms. The language reforms of Nance, Heffernan, and Ruiz illustrate how Angelinos used Pan-Americanism to demonstrate that Mexican Americans were patriotic.[19]

Helen Heffernan helped form the Pan-Americanism movement in 1930 after speaking at several Friends of the Mexicans conferences at Pomona College. In the spring of 1942, she was chief of California's elementary school division when the Department of Education asked her to open a new Office of Inter-American Affairs in Los Angeles. Just months later, an act of violence in East LA spawned a national debate about "juvenile delinquency." In August, José Díaz was found dying of traumatic injuries at the Sleepy Lagoon reservoir, five miles south of Boyle Heights, days before he was to begin army boot camp. Rather than writing about a Mexican Angelino joining the war effort, the mainstream media focused on the provocative zoot suits worn by his accused killers. The LA police rounded up hundreds of young Mexican American men who wore draped pants, oversized coats, and ducktail haircuts. The district attorney brought twenty-two of these defiantly dressed youths to trial, where nine were convicted of second-degree murder. A year later the convictions were overturned on appeal due to bias in the court proceedings and lack of evidence. While photos of zoot-suiters smiling behind bars fueled the national narrative that Mexican American teenagers were dangerous criminals, Angelino activists used the incident to demand better education. If city schools offered more services to Spanish-speaking students, they insisted, then juvenile delinquency would be less of a problem. This was nearly the opposite of the Mexicanization approach in the 1920s, when the Mexican consulate created schools to teach students in Spanish-only classes. In 1942, top students also supported Heffernan's Pan-Americanism program to counter charges of Mexican delinquency.[20]

Once Heffernan moved to Los Angeles, she began to persuade Anglo educators to abandon traditional language instruction. As editor of the *California Journal of Elementary Education*, she published the article, "The Teaching of Speech to Mexican Children," by Alma Wedberg, the speech supervisor in San Bernardino County, east of LA County. Referring to Heffernan's Inter-American project and "the enormous program of defense-training education in California," Wedberg urged teachers to preach patriotism and citizenship. She called southland schools "the first line of defense" in training loyal Americans. Despite declaring that Mexican children should learn the "history, customs, and language" of their families, she insisted that "the greatest factor for bringing about this understanding [of loyalty] is the mastery of the English language." Wedberg wanted to learn other languages because "we do not mean to belittle the use of the mother's tongue. Instead these children should be taught to speak both languages equally well." However, the speech supervisor used a teaching technique that demeaned Mexican students.[21]

After noting advances in language and cultural sensitivity, Wedberg endorsed teaching English with an approach called the "direct method." She described the practice in detail, diagramming sentences and listing "speech errors" Mexican children made in pronouncing consonants and vowels. Focusing on accent erasure, she advised instructors to teach students that "in English the tongue is placed above the teeth on the gum ridge" to say words beginning with the "dental consonants" *t, d, n, l,* and *r.* Any teacher could "gather the children around her in the reading circle and show them with her own mechanism where to place the tongue on those sounds," she explained. By using traditional speech drills in segregated schools, Wedberg treated Mexican children as if they had a disability that was preventing them from speaking English clearly. Yet Heffernan published Wedberg's article in May 1942, tacitly endorsing the direct method. After the Sleepy Lagoon murder one month later, however, Heffernan adopted a more inclusive curriculum that used language learning to combat the Mexican delinquency trope.[22]

At the LA Office of Inter-American Affairs, Heffernan used Pan-Americanism to foster the acceptance of Spanish speakers. In 1941 she attended the Inter-American conference at the University of Southern California, where teachers talked about improving hemispheric relations during the war. The next year, Heffernan hosted her own conference, Unifying the Americas through Education, at the LA Biltmore Hotel. The *Los Angeles School Journal* noted that teachers who toured South America could offer "a wholesome contradiction to the impression left by Hollywood movies and radio comedians that all Latin Americans are either gigolos or bandits or peons." Rather than dismissing language instruction, teachers argued that learning Spanish was integral to Pan-Americanism. They called for Latin American history courses and travel opportunities so that students and teachers could collect radio programs and films, along with course catalogs in Spanish, to help Anglo and Latin American students "stimulate understanding through languages, sympathy, personal contacts, and trade." LA educators who attended Heffernan's Inter-American conferences were aware of, and appalled by, Anglo stereotypes of Spanish speakers, which were disproven by their own Mexican-origin students.[23]

At Roosevelt High School, the highest-achieving students used the war effort to dismiss the delinquency debate. Ruben Holquin was president of Los Caballeros, a club of eighteen boys who "aim to raise the morale and ideals of Mexican students." This prestige helped him win the election in

March 1942 to complete the term of vice president Choo-Choo Tsukimoto, one of several Nisei class officers who had just been interned. Like *Rough Rider* reporters, Holquin had to navigate the meaning of the government relocating student leaders simply because of actions by a foreign country. As leadership positions transferred from Nisei to Mexican American students, Holquin appealed to Spanish speakers by endorsing wartime service.[24]

Holquin also used the language of loyalty to respond to Anglo fears about gang violence. In March 1942, he tried to prove his patriotism with a clever play on words. As internment loomed (before he was elected as vice president), he urged classmates to consider a different form of early departure. In his advertising class, Holquin created an honor roll to celebrate students who "walked out" of Roosevelt and "walked right into the United States Army." The same issue of the *Rough Rider* where Holquin's honor roll was published also ran a front-page story called "East L.A. Educational Problems Discussed by School Leaders." LA Superintendent of Schools Vierling Kersey came to Roosevelt High to hear Boyle Heights business leaders declare an "urgent need for educational facilities made necessary by the present emergency and other changes in the social, civic, and industrial life of the community." These leaders wanted to attract burgeoning defense contracts to East LA, but they did not trust either the students or the schools to supply the workforce they would need. This lack of faith did not match Holquin's portrait of Roosevelt students eager to join the war effort. The ongoing delinquency debate drove reformers to discuss language learning as a civil rights issue after World War II.[25]

———————

Manuel Ruiz tried to use the delinquency hysteria to win reforms for Mexican Angelinos. Echoing Heffernan's rhetoric, he promoted several Pan-Americanist projects by arguing that bilingual instruction in English and Spanish would keep scary zoot-suiters off the streets. In 1942, Ruiz proposed two Pan-American schools that stressed language learning, but he failed to secure funding. After the Zoot Suit Riots of 1943, he founded the Coordinating Council for Latin American Youth. By continuing to laud language instruction as a form of delinquency prevention, Ruiz carved a niche as a Mexican American leader who worked with local agencies. His access to officials from city hall to Capitol Hill enabled Ruiz to develop political connections that he could leverage to make language education a reasonable civil rights demand after the war.

Ruiz drew on Helen Heffernan's Pan-American diplomacy to promote two language schools that departed from the "direct method." He had attended her 1941 Inter-American Affairs conference at USC, his alma mater. The idea of teaching Spanish through travel, radio, and film inspired Ruiz to reshape Pan-American curricula in several entrepreneurial adventures, all unsuccessful. He created a corporation, Cultura Panamericano, Inc., in hopes of establishing a Spanish-language library, school, and industrial training program in East LA. After the Zoot Suit Riots, Ruiz revised his proposals and tried again. From these initial failures he realized that segregated language schools would not succeed. Even when Ruiz recruited elites to support his Pan-Americanist projects, funding still did not follow. In 1940, his corporation pitched a "Spanish-American library in this largest American center of Spanish-speaking population." In a grant proposal to the World Peace Foundation, he said that a library "supervised by persons who do not only speak the Spanish language, but . . . are imbued with the spirit of Spanish-American culture . . . would indeed be a boon to the Pan-American ideal." When the foundation did not fund the library, Ruiz researched other ways to promote his brand of Pan-Americanism.[26]

Military mobilization in 1942 stalled Ruiz's proposed Pan-American School for Anglo educators, intended to teach evening courses in Spanish. After Pearl Harbor, helping teachers learn Spanish lacked urgency. Yet Cultura Panamericano advertised aggressively, and by August seven Latino instructors and one hundred teachers had pledged to attend weekly Spanish classes. Ruiz wrote a course catalog and planned to open the school by October, but his plan imploded. Lacking school district support, he had to charge learners $1.50 for each Spanish-language lecture. He also struggled to find a suitable space for the school. Ruiz made a preliminary deal with the coveted Black-Foxe Military Institute, located next to the Wilshire Country Club, a private school where celebrities sent their children. However, after announcing the agreement, Black-Foxe backed out of the deal. The registrar wrote to Ruiz that the war had increased interest in the military institute and it could not spare any classrooms, day or night. Ruiz realized that linking language instruction to the war effort might help start his school.[27]

In reality, Black-Foxe was wary of the Pan-American School's language program. Its classes clashed with the curriculum Helen Heffernan had just endorsed. Ruiz's language professor taught Spanish using the "direct progressive method," which was nothing like the traditional "direct method" Heffernan had endorsed in the *California Journal of Elementary Education* in 1938. Far from adjusting jaws and lips, the professor explained, "the student is permitted to take an active part in each lesson . . . this method compels him to think in the new language." Ruiz supplemented this instruction with classes in Spanish art, literature, and his own course, History and the Future of Inter-American Relations. This seemed to bother Black-Foxe officers, who broke the contract despite Ruiz's pledge that teachers would not "do or say anything inimical to the established American constitutional form of government." Seeing the same prejudice that Japanese-language schools had faced in the 1920s, Ruiz tried to promote language instruction as a patriotic enterprise.[28]

The lawyer learned that public schools like Roosevelt High were more open than Black-Foxe Military Institute to promoting language instruction and Mexican American wartime contributions. Eduardo Quevedo, a Democratic Party organizer in Boyle Heights, got permission to offer adult education and citizenship classes with a "verbal picture of Mexican history" in 1942. Although the recent Japanese evacuation had moved Mexican American youth into Roosevelt's highest positions in student government, few of their parents were mobilizing for war or taking night courses. Roosevelt's evening-school principal did not mind sparse attendance in Quevedo's citizenship classes so long as able-bodied Mexicans enrolled in vocational classes and proved their "willingness to cooperate fully with our defense efforts." Roosevelt High's war effort began by inviting Quevedo to "sum up the important points in the Mexican language." The principal promised to distribute Spanish-language handbills about Roosevelt's industrial education program to all parents of daytime students. With this bilingual promotion, Quevedo urged Ruiz to recast his language-school campaign as a facility for "training in war industries on the east side." In November 1942, the school board considered "war training for the Mexican colony," and the East LA leaders tried to link language learning to this project.[29]

When the city sought funding for vocational training in war-related manufacturing, Ruiz proposed a Pan-American Trade School. Aware of the growing LA defense industry, he incorporated earlier language appeals into a new economic vision. He wrote letters in English and Spanish inviting dignitaries across California and Mexico to celebrate the school's opening on Pan-American Day in April 1943. Although Governor Warren sent his regrets, the ceremony included speeches from Superintendent Vierling Kersey, the principal of a vocational trade school, the mayor, and the Mexican ambassador to the United States, who spoke via live radio broadcast from Washington, D.C. In a dual-language letter to *parientes y amigos*, the vocational school principal assured Mexican parents that all Spanish speakers older than sixteen could enroll in the trade school, "whether they are American citizens or not." Ruiz promised that classes would "fit workers into immediate jobs in war industries—where they will receive the same pay as anyone else." He used both languages to tell all Mexican Angelinos that the sacrifices of war also offered opportunities to integrate themselves into the city's schools and workplaces.[30]

During its short lifespan the Pan-American Trade School shifted Ruiz's efforts from language learning to school integration. When the school opened on Pan-American Day, the vocational classes resembled those at many segregated Mexican schools offering such courses as auto repair that taught "greasing, washing, oiling, polishing." The training courses for LA's large aircraft industry were still waiting for supplies, which may have discouraged many Mexican Americans from signing up. In July 1943, the school board closed the trade school because enrollment was too low to qualify for federal defense funds. This convinced Quevedo and Ruiz that separate schools would not succeed, regardless of whether they focused on language or wartime work. Yet they decided not to make school integration a campaign issue when Quevedo ran to represent Boyle Heights in the state assembly. His election defeat in the summer of 1943 was overshadowed by the Zoot Suit Riots, which had erupted a month before the Pan-American Trade School closed.[31]

In June 1943, approximately fifty white sailors attacked a group of Mexican American youths, tearing off their baggy zoot suits and clubbing boys as young as thirteen. This set off a week of riots in eastside barrios like Boyle Heights, and the LA Police Department decided to "protect" Mexican teens by arresting more than five hundred of them. Naming the event the Zoot Suit Riots, newspapers blamed the boys behind bars for the violence, making Mexican-origin youths the face of wartime fears about juvenile delinquency. As they had done in earlier debates about naturalization and repatriation, Mexican Angelinos used the Spanish language to respond to this crisis in creative ways. Manuel Ruiz led the Coordinating Council for Latin American Youth (CCLAY), which explicitly linked language learning with reducing juvenile delinquency. Meanwhile, the zoot-suiters themselves developed an internal Spanish argot called caló that expressed their defiance against the prejudice they faced from LA cops and teachers. These opposing views of language and youth show how the Zoot Suit Riots pushed language experiments beyond wartime tests of patriotism. After 1943, the demand for a decent education in both Spanish and English became central to Mexican Americans' civil rights plans.[32]

Language shaped public perceptions on both sides of LA's delinquency debate. Edward Escobar's study of the LA police and press proves that officials exaggerated concerns about Mexican youth criminality. The words "Mexican" and "delinquency" became nearly inseparable in newspapers, even as the felony rate fell in 1942 and 1943. Manuel Ruiz relied on his bilingualism to state the CCLAY's stance after Sleepy Lagoon and the Zoot Suit Riots. His

Local newspapers influenced public opinion about the Zoot Suit Riots by printing photographs of Mexican American youths in zoot suits detained for questioning in a Los Angeles jail following a brawl. *Courtesy of Los Angeles Daily News Negatives, Negative #28789, Department of Special Collections, Charles E. Young Research Library, University of California, Los Angeles.*

dual-language ability allowed him to navigate between the calls for compromise by Spanish speakers in the federal government and the defiant dialect of caló, an underground language that captured the youthful rebellion of zoot-suiters, or pachucos. Caló politicized Spanish in new ways. Before the 1943 riots, Ruiz had wanted to extend wartime work to Spanish speakers who studied English and "proper Spanish" at the Pan-American Trade School. As media coverage emphasized Mexican delinquency and portrayed caló as a deviant dialect, the CCLAY broadened its demands from language learning to parks, community centers, and schools.[33]

To outsiders, caló was a slang that symbolized juvenile delinquency, or *pachuquismo*. Many Mexican teens who behaved as model citizens were proud of the "pachuco" label, despite (or perhaps because of) its derogatory stereotypes. An Anglo observer named Beatrice Griffith pointed out that two-thirds of poor Mexican boys wore zoot suits during the war, but less than 5 percent of them were classified as delinquent. Despite being empa-thetic, Griffith criticized zoot-suiters for using caló, which she described as "a jargon spoken among gypsies, ruffians, and prisoners" in Mexico City. She emphasized the influence of LA car culture on caló by noting Hispanicized English words like *los laites* (headlights) and *las brecas* (brakes), and wrote that "Pachuco talk represents a degeneration of the Spanish language which has resulted from an inadequate Spanish vocabulary and the inability to write in the tongue that is spoken in the home." Griffith compared caló to "Negro jive, such as *'slick chick'*" and "*he's sharp, man!*" She concluded that caló was a language handicap to the average pachuco "because he cannot adequately explain his thoughts in Spanish to his parents, nor in English to his teacher, employer, or the court." Griffith, who used statistics to disprove the stereotype of Mexican delinquency, blamed an idiom with no written form for causing public misperceptions. She did not see that caló appealed to pachucos because it was a rebellious dialect, whether or not they were delinquent.[34]

While zoot-suiters used language defiantly, the CCLAY tried to turn bilingualism into a means through which the state could "solve" juvenile delinquency. When they cofounded the council in 1941, Quevedo and Ruiz made language central to its articles of incorporation, which were written in both English and Spanish: "It is not our purpose to make language a barrier but instead [to] unite the various modes of expression," the document declared. They invited everyone to weigh in on "the problem of juvenile delinquency, whether they be parents or offspring, and irrespective of creed or tongue." They were skeptical of past Progressive methods for curtailing criminal behavior, claiming that the CCLAY "can no more indulge in a program of Americanization than it can Mexicanization or Cubanization." Yet the council aligned itself with law enforcement agencies and adopted their positions on juvenile delinquency. Although its members included "72 civic, fraternal, religious, and other organizations of Spanish-speaking people," the council concentrated on public safety projects with the LA Police Department and the District Attorney's Office. Ruiz recruited the chief of LA County's Juvenile Delinquency Prevention Division to serve as the CCLAY's vice president. If neither Americanization nor Mexicanization could stop juvenile delinquency, Ruiz was content to pass the problem on to local probation officers.[35]

The CCLAY used Spanish and English in its campaign against delinquency. Days after the Sleepy Lagoon murder, Ruiz requested airtime for Spanish-language radio broadcasts. He told the Southern California Broadcasting Association that "gang forays on the east side [were] a partial symptom of the present war and a problem which will become more vital." Ruiz recommended a Mexican social worker with experience "lecturing by radio to the parents of potentially delinquent minors" in their native language. Six weeks after the Zoot Suit Riots, the CCLAY held its 1943 annual meeting. The dual-language agenda included speeches by the Mexican consul as well as the LA county sheriff and LA city police chief. The council cemented its standing by blaming pachuco gangs for Sleepy Lagoon and the Zoot Suit Riots. His Spanish and English denunciations of uneducated youth earned Ruiz respect from Anglo Angelinos who viewed delinquency as the essential "Mexican Problem."[36]

LA educators asked Ruiz to help resolve the problem. A month after the riots, Ruiz accepted Superintendent Kersey's invitation to a ten-day event at eastside's Lincoln High School on the Education of Mexican and Spanish-speaking Pupils. Some reformers, like the Anglo lawyer who defended the pachucos wrongly convicted of the Sleepy Lagoon murder, criticized LA schools for building a "papier-mâché façade of 'Inter-American Good Will.'" The workshops welcomed educators and artists from Mexico through Heffernan's Office of Inter-American Affairs, but they also provided a platform for Ignacio López, who had just resigned as Heffernan's Spanish-speaking director to protest underfunding. López and Ruiz jointly moderated a discussion about delinquency, but other panels featured law-enforcement and probation officers. The agenda also included study groups in which educators examined "problems of adjustment" and inadequate guidance counseling for Mexican-origin students in LA schools in the run-up to the riots.[37]

Language education set this wartime workshop apart from the 1920s Friends of the Mexicans meetings. Language held a prominent place in both conferences, but the earlier emphasis on English and Americanization was replaced by a focus on Spanish-language education after the Zoot Suit Riots. Each morning, instructors taught "sentences and phrases which are of special help to a teacher in registering children and greeting parents who speak only Spanish." This focus on bilingualism made Anglo educators more open to learning Spanish after the war and turned Spanish teachers into key advocates for shifting the educational focus from earlier Americanization agendas to postwar plans for integrated classrooms. For example, the executive committee of the Lincoln High workshop included Marie Hughes, LA County's specialist in minority group education, and one study group was led by Ruth Ginsburg, a county Spanish teacher. Two years after the Zoot Suit Riots, Ginsburg and Hughes would be instrumental in the discussions about desegregation and bilingual education in LA schools.[38]

While the school district emphasized language instruction by Anglo educators, Mexican leaders insisted that Spanish speakers could prevent future violence on their own. A month after the Zoot Suit Riots, the CCLAY seemingly abandoned its cooperation with local law enforcement and argued that the only way to stop Mexican delinquency was "a program of direct action within the community group itself." Bypassing the school board, it asked the board of supervisors to approve a $12,000 budget with which the CCLAY would support its own youth reform efforts. Although this resolution did not refer to the role of Spanish-language instruction, the council's statement seemed to stem from Ignacio López's frustrations over lack of funding for the Office of Inter-American Affairs. The introduction to the council's resolution included this controversial statement: "Juvenile delinquency among American youngsters of Latin-American extraction has inspired Nazi and Fascist sources to adversely exploit Inter-American relations, and emphasis has been made of the fact that persons of Latin-American extraction are victims of American persecution and racial bigotry, giving aid and comfort to the enemy." This alarming reference to racial prejudice indicated that the CCLAY had problems with the city's response to the Zoot Suit Riots. Los Angeles officials were willing to host summer workshops that studied juvenile delinquency as a long-term trend. Mexican Angelinos like Manuel Ruiz were willing to participate in these studies only if they saw significant progress in the self-improvement project. The direct comparison between LA's Inter-American relations campaign and totalitarian regimes revealed that Ruiz was ready to fight for more than a Pan-American Trade School by the war's end. His rhetoric warned that, if opposition to Pan-Americanism came from "Fascist sources," Mexican Americans might end up in internment camps like their former Japanese neighbors.[39]

Despite Ruiz's rhetoric, Spanish speakers avoided relocation. Unfortunately, Japanese Americans endured more oppressive wartime treatment. It took a year for the government to plan the mass incarceration of 118,000 people. With the WRA ban on use of the Japanese language, Nisei Angelinos discussed how they could use language instruction to articulate their attitudes about evacuation. The range of language projects during World War II reveals the ways in which Nisei students and Anglo educators used Japanese to express different loyalties. State emphasis on schools as sites of citizenship training caused what the historian Thomas James called a "political dilemma" for internment camp curricula. Ideas about language education led to programs that provided hope to Japanese Angelinos who were evacuated in 1942. Just as Manuel Ruiz turned the delinquency debate into a campaign for Spanish classes in East LA, Nisei like Paul Kusuda tried to use his forced removal from Los Angeles City College as an opportunity to teach interned students. The historian Richard Drinnon has argued that "incarceration had unintended

Schoolchildren work at a bench at Manzanar Relocation Center in 1942. The photographer Dorothea Lange documented schoolchildren to demonstrate the inadequate services that Japanese Americans received at Manzanar. Her full caption read, "An elementary school with voluntary attendance has been established with volunteer evacuee teachers, most of whom are college graduates. No school equipment is as yet obtainable and available tables and benches are used." *Courtesy of War Relocation Authority, Department of the Interior, Number 537964.*

consequences and by-products, not all of which were negative." Internment made many evacuees engaged citizens—both the vast majority that supported the war effort and the minority that opposed it. This political participation culminated in the Manzanar Riot. The debate leading up to that incident indicated how Nisei Angelinos used language learning to protect their civil rights during internment.[40]

Manzanar was a windswept town in the eastern Sierra Nevada with breathtaking views of Mount Whitney. When the WRA built an internment camp there in 1942, Manzanar became the largest community between Los Angeles and Reno. That summer, ten thousand Japanese internees made the two-hundred-mile journey from Los Angeles, taking buses or cars up the dusty mountain roads. When elementary schools opened in September, 1,001 students entered facilities that lacked chairs, tables, books, and playground equipment. When 1,376 high school students started their semester on October 15, there were no heaters against the cold air or linoleum to block the sand that filtered through cracks in the floorboards during storms. These conditions encouraged Nisei teens to apply to college, the army, or any institution that would enable them to leave the relocation camp. Many left before Manzanar schools were fully furnished in 1943. Those who stayed struggled to succeed under the outdated curricula that their Anglo teachers used. In segregated schools where instruction in Japanese language and culture was banned, it was difficult to construct the patriotic classrooms that progressive Angelinos like Nora Sterry and Kohei Shimano had promoted before the war. The absence of foreign languages made Americanization look different in internment camp schools.[41]

Yet many students and teachers tried to re-create the culture, activities, and values of the public schools they had left behind in Los Angeles. The emphasis on citizenship and democracy in Manzanar High School newspapers and yearbooks suggests that faith in progressive education helped some students adjust to the harsh realities of incarceration. Nisei who had held leadership positions in clubs and on athletic teams in Los Angeles were the most likely to graduate from Manzanar. Just as Sterry had braved the barrio quarantine to teach immigrant classes at Macy Street School in 1924, Angelino teachers came to internment schools with missionary attitudes. All children and faculty were aware of the awful facilities, but star students and teachers ignored those conditions in the official records of Manzanar High School. Instead, they produced publications that celebrated Sterry's traditional Americanization agenda to conceal the shame of studying in segregated schools behind barbed wire. As a result, they said little about the language learning ban.

Ironically, internment enabled educated Nisei to take jobs that had not been available to Japanese Americans before the war. High school graduates like Paul Kusuda had opportunities to work as teachers for the first time. Nisei volunteers played an integral role in Manzanar schools because there was little incentive for Anglo teachers to relocate to the remote mountains above Death Valley in order to teach children in cold classrooms or outside on the dirt. The WRA offered only $1,620 per year, which was lower than teacher salaries in Los Angeles. Most of Manzanar's credentialed teachers came from states that paid less than California did. Yet many educators who stayed in LA still tried to help their former students start a fledgling school district. A professor from Los Angeles City College drove two hundred miles through the Sierra Nevada to bring two thousand books, sports equipment, a phonograph, and records to the camp. The principal of UCLA's elementary school, a friend of Helen Heffernan's, asked parents at her school to send toys and books.[42]

The compassion of a few Angelino educators could not improve the curriculum in relocation schools, however. Thinking in the prewar context of

In the caption for this 1942 photograph of students with a Nisei assistant teacher, Dorothea Lange noted that, as parents worked to finish building school furniture, classes were often "held in the shade of the barrack building." *Courtesy of War Relocation Authority, Department of the Interior, Number 537962.*

progressive education, WRA Superintendent Lucy Adams saw these schools as agents of Americanization. Eager to re-create traditional classrooms, Adams failed to consider the differences between established schools and the temporary institutions starting from scratch behind barbed wire. The WRA allowed instruction in English only—Japanese-language schools were not permitted. Adams did not consult with the Nisei volunteers who had started schools at the assembly centers. She merely hired fifty evacuees who had teaching certificates along with about six hundred white teachers and four hundred Nisei assistants. The student-teacher ratio was forty-eight to one in WRA elementary schools and thirty-five to one in high schools, compared to the national average ratio for all public schools of twenty-eight to one. The combination of inadequate facilities and overcrowded classrooms made successful instruction virtually impossible in the internment camps.[43]

Many evacuated students embraced the Americanization agenda, but they described key differences between LA and WRA schools. The Manzanar High yearbook stressed all-American achievements by the class of 1943, but it also acknowledged the absence of language learning. Every Manzanar senior that year had previously attended school in LA County, the majority at Roosevelt High in Boyle Heights and many others at either Jefferson High near Little Tokyo or University High on the Westside. The yearbook could not conceal Nisei ambivalence about graduating from high school behind barbed wire. Seniors listed extracurricular activities at their old schools in Los Angeles alongside the few clubs at Manzanar High. Many Nisei had participated in World Friendship Clubs, Latin Clubs, or Japanese Clubs at Roosevelt and other city schools. As evacuees, some even studied a foreign language. Manzanar High offered classes in Spanish, French, and Latin in 1943, but the WRA refused to teach Japanese. Students strove to make Manzanar High as similar as possible to the schools they had attended two hundred miles to the west in Los Angeles. In the absence of World Friendship and Japanese clubs however, they could hardly forget that they were spending their senior year at a relocation center where the language their parents had grown up speaking was prohibited.[44]

While the internment camp administration did not dispute the yearbook's facts, it offered its own narrative to explain them. In a 1945 report, WRA staffers said the camp's subpar schools were a result of the Nisei's poor language abilities, not the hasty relocation project. The report insisted that the schools had some success despite these language deficiencies. Ignoring the lack of heaters or chairs when classes began in 1942, the report stressed that "in the fundamentals of the English language our students were about one year retarded as late as 1943." It credited Anglo teachers, rather than improved facilities, for a slight rise in test scores, noting that "in spoken language [the students] have made significant progress but are still retarded in enunciation, pronunciation, stage presence, etc." The WRA targeted language learning at an early age, hiring Nisei women who were mostly "young English-speaking mothers" as preschool instructors and starting a nursery school program focused on "parent education, the speaking of English, and basic democratic principles." The educators speculated that Manzanar's elementary students had fewer Japanese-educated Kibei than Manzanar High did, as well as a few third-generation Sansei, "which gives them a better advantage on English performance." They were shocked that Manzanar students tested at the statewide average intelligence level "in spite of their reading and language handicap." The report revealed a crucial difference between internees and the WRA: both sought Americanization of the Nisei, but Issei educators considered Japanese classes a resource toward that end, whereas the WRA considered learning Japanese a sign of disloyalty. This tension made language learning a key topic in the loyalty debates after the Manzanar Riot of 1942.[45]

On December 5, 1942, six Nisei cooks beat up the former president of the Los Angeles chapter of the Japanese American Citizens League (JACL), who had supported forced relocation. When the WRA arrested the lead cook for showing "contempt for the authorities," hundreds of Nisei protested. This "December Incident," one year after Pearl Harbor, was the peak of internee anger at both the government and the JACL. In response to the attack, the WRA required all Japanese Americans to vow loyalty to the country that had incarcerated them. The "riot" and the subsequent loyalty oath altered the language education situation in internment. Just as Manuel Ruiz proposed new Spanish-language programs after the Zoot Suit Riots, Nisei activists used the Manzanar Riot to insist on reinstating Japanese-language schools at the camps. Paul Kusuda, like many educated Nisei at Manzanar, questioned the WRA's Americanization agenda but was equally dubious about his peers' proposals to teach Japanese to younger Nisei and their Anglo instructors. Despite his skepticism, the many responses to the Manzanar Riot suggest that some Japanese Angelinos viewed language learning as a civil rights question by 1943.[46]

The riot devastated Manzanar's adult language program. A WRA report praised camp officials for promptly organizing adult education in September 1942, when an educated Nisei organized eighteen adult English classes while Manzanar "was still being settled." English and history instruction fit the WRA's Americanization approach, but the teacher recruited more than three thousand Issei students by offering courses in commerce, science, and *ikebana* (Japanese flower arrangement). After the Manzanar Riot, however, evacuees were afraid to attend evening classes. Instruction shut down for two weeks, and adult enrollment decreased after the army issued its loyalty oath. Five Nisei teachers who refused to sign the oath lost their jobs. This forced the WRA to reconsider the role of language learning in its adult education program.[47]

In 1943, the WRA Adult Education Department defined two goals: to "stimulate relocation" and to keep students attending classes in the camps. That summer, Manzanar opened an "Adult English Hall" featuring cooking demonstrations "by both evacuees and Caucasians." The WRA was proud to offer more than thirty English classes in 1945. It also recruited interned instructors by offering junior college credit for teaching. Whereas five adult language educators were sent to Tule Lake internment center for refusing to sign the loyalty oath, in 1945 the WRA boasted that eleven other teachers had relocated out of the internment camps by enlisting in the US Army or getting admitted to colleges east of California. On the basis of relocations and college credits the WRA called the adult education program successful, but the downside was that only six Nisei educators were left to teach 1,500 non-English-speaking adults in Manzanar's final year.[48]

Paul Kusuda was one of the Nisei instructors who relocated before 1945. Kusuda's letters to his former English teacher, Afton Nance, challenged the WRA narrative about education at Manzanar. Kusuda came to the camp in 1942 as a bright but shiftless high school graduate. He had attended LA City College before internment and, in the camp, he read liberal publications like *The Nation* when Nance sent them. He did not think highly of standardized tests or establishment groups like the JACL. Kusuda grew more critical when eastern colleges rejected his student relocation applications, extending his internment by eighteen months. The tone of his letters to Nance changed after he witnessed the Manzanar Riot, however. That incident forced Kusuda to consider language learning more seriously than he had before.

Kusuda used Americanization to advocate for his tutoring work. In a 1942 letter, he asked the US Commissioner of Education to set up schools at Santa Anita to instill "American ideas and ideals among the children." Kusuda favored hiring white teachers to "establish closer relations between Nisei and fellow Americans." Yet he insisted educated evacuees like himself should tutor students "eager to continue their education which was so abruptly cut-off." He offered to teach any subject, including Spanish and Latin. Kusuda's eclectic language interests led to the most playful aspects of his letters to Afton Nance. He thought like an Americanized adolescent, sending Nance a Beetle Bailey cartoon of a GI dreaming of exotic women, surrounded by pamphlets in Spanish, Hawaiian, Arabic, Chinese, Russian, and French. "I'm prepared to go anywhere they send me," read the caption. "I can say 'Hi Babe' in half a dozen languages!"[49]

Kusuda scoffed at the WRA's early efforts at preparing white teachers to work with the Japanese community. He attended the first Adult Education Department meeting in the Caucasian Mess Hall in September 1942 to inspect the new teachers. Some were fresh out of college, he told Nance, while others were "attracted by wages which were just a little better than those offered by small communities," and some simply wanted to offer the internees "as much help as possible." The adult education supervisor invited evacuees to the initial staff meeting because he assumed "few of the teachers had ever come in contact with the Japanese except on an exceedingly casual basis."[50]

The supervisor may have been surprised at the level of concern about language learning among the internees. Two Nisei Angelinos addressed the WRA faculty that night, and both speakers stressed the significance of heritage-language instruction. The first speaker outlined the history of Japanese immigration, from the Chinese Exclusion Act of 1882 to the "era of Americanization" after 1924. He explained that language school did not make Nisei fluent in their ethnic idiom, but it made them familiar with their family's culture. The second speaker was Frank Chuman, whose 1934 address at LA High School had appeared in Paul Hirohata's *Orations and Essays*. His salutatorian speech, "Persistent Idealism," had declared that Nisei could succeed in Los Angeles despite the racial discrimination they faced in America. Chuman's optimism continued during World War II. While admitting that internment was "disillusioning," he was confident that Manzanar's Anglo educators could "revive the spark of the idea of American democracy." He argued that employment was the biggest problem for Nisei Angelinos, lamenting that many high school graduates had to settle for "fruit stand jobs." Chuman said that "one way out is for the Nisei to learn the usage of the Japanese language so that he may work with the Japanese here or go to Japan to work there." This suggestion recast learning Japanese as an economic strategy rather than an ethnic tradition. Speaking to white teachers in Manzanar's segregated dining hall, Chuman limited his advocacy for language learning to economic interests to prove his generation's loyalty to the United States.[51]

As Paul Kusuda listened to the two speakers, his impressions focused on how they represented Japanese-language instruction. Kusuda admired the first talk about immigration because it was given by a "Nisei of high caliber" who went to school in LA but "learned to speak and write Japanese and he is fluent with its usage." He had less respect for Frank Chuman, although they were both alumni of Los Angeles High. He noted, perhaps jealously, that Chuman's academic success allowed him to attend UCLA and become one of the few Nisei hired by the LA County civil service. Kusuda criticized the former salutatorian's speaking skills, calling him "rather wordy, but he doesn't say very much." He may have resented Chuman's appointment as supervisor of Manzanar's 250-bed hospital. After the war, Chuman would become the JACL's lead counsel and its national president. Paul Kusuda frequently criticized the JACL for cooperating with the WRA and endorsing internment. JACL officers worked "only for personal gains and glories,"

Kusuda told Nance, alleging that members had "turned in the lists of former Japanese school teachers" before the arrests on December 7, 1941. Whether Kusuda was praising one internee for speaking Japanese fluently or charging another with unfair attacks on language-school teachers, the language question made him more passionate about adult education. These emotions boiled over when he witnessed the Manzanar Riot.[52]

Kusuda's attitudes colored his experiences during the December riot. He supported the cooks who had beaten the former JACL president. Kusuda noted linguistic pride in the crowd that gathered to protest the cook's arrest. He heard some evacuees shout "Banzai! . . . Others whistled or sang Japanese airs." At the same time Kusuda was concerned that the Adult Education Department had organized an open forum with the Anglo director for that evening. He and a friend walked to WRA staff housing to warn the administrator not to come out during the riot, risking a hostile interrogation by soldiers in the cold night. Kusuda showed interest in internment camp politics, but his actions during the Manzanar Riot revealed a deeper commitment to adult education as well as a fascination with the Japanese language.[53]

The aftermath of the riot caused Kusuda to reconsider his position on evacuee classrooms as well as camp politics. Kusuda had criticized the JACL for its ties to the white establishment. After the beating, however, he was eager to return to work at the Adult Education Department. The violence closed down the WRA offices, but Kusuda joined the staff that was assisting at Manzanar High School. He developed respect for the education director, who waited tables in the mess hall, and some of the white "male teachers [who] helped with the dish-washing." Before the riot, Kusuda felt insulted by the JACL's decision to defend the government that incarcerated him; but he was even more outraged by disloyal evacuees when he heard that "foul words were said to a few teachers" after school reopened. He abandoned his vision of Nisei rebellion in the camps and focused on life after Manzanar. When Kusuda wrote to Nance in January, he explained his New Year's goal: "to get free in '43." By the end of the year, he relocated to Illinois after gaining admission to the University of Chicago.[54]

Similarly, the riot complicated Kusuda's views about language education. This is evident in two responses he wrote to Nance when she confessed that she had considered leaving her new job as principal in Manhattan Beach to teach at Manzanar. In November, he warned her, "it won't be a picnic," citing the small salary as "a chisel for all the hard work done by teachers." After the Manzanar Riot Kusuda learned that police had torn down posters written "in Japanese, calling for self-government." A few weeks later, in January, he urged Nance not to learn Japanese. Kusuda's new critiques indicated that language policies made evacuees more fearful of the conditions of their internment.[55]

Nance asked Kusuda why he disapproved of her teaching at the camp and learning Japanese. Why wouldn't he welcome his favorite English teacher? And why would he dissuade a woman who displayed more compassion than most of Manzanar's teachers? Kusuda responded with his own question, "Just how much luck do none-too-bright (but earnest) adult Caucasians have in learning acceptable (non-funny) Japanese?" Seeming intimidated by the language he called himself an illiterate who could "converse rather poorly. . . . In Japanese, there are the basic vowel sounds, but consonant sounds are combined in tongue-twisting, brain-battling ways," he wrote. He cited his own Japanese name, Haruo, which whites pronounced "Ha-Roo-Oh" when the correct intonation was "Ha-RLU-Oh." Kusuda claimed that fluency was only possible after years "among people who speak Japanese and only Japanese . . . even then, there will be a noticeable trace of 'Caucasian accent.'" He was more skeptical when WRA teachers stopped taking Japanese classes after the Manzanar Riot. "Many dropped out," Kusuda told Nance. "Others did not attend classes regularly. No kidding, the language is extremely difficult to master." Japanese-language instruction never succeeded at Manzanar, but it did become important later at Tule Lake Segregation Center.[56]

Weeks after the Manzanar Riot, the WRA distributed a loyalty questionnaire to 118,000 Japanese internees throughout the internment system. Two questions were controversial. Question 27 asked draft-age Nisei men if they would join the US Army, which would require them to "swear unqualified allegiance to . . . and faithfully defend the United States from any or all attack." Question 28 asked all evacuees if they would forswear "obedience to the Japanese emperor" and pledge loyalty to the United States, whether or not they were citizens. Most internees answered "yes" to at least one of these questions, but a little over 10 percent answered "no" to both. The WRA decided to relocate those twelve thousand internees, yet again, to a segregated camp of Japanese loyalists at Tule Lake near the Oregon-California border, where their US citizenship was revoked. The segregated Japanese included half of the draft-eligible Nisei from Manzanar, by far the highest percentage of young men who refused to serve from any WRA camp. The Manzanar Riot and the WRA questionnaire forced interned Angelinos to declare their loyalty unequivocally for either Japan or America. Whichever they decided, Nisei used language education to express their views about America's role in World War II. To preserve order at Tule Lake, the WRA allowed "disloyal" evacuees to open all-day Japanese-language schools. At the same time, many other

Nisei left Manzanar by volunteering to study Japanese at the new Military Intelligence Service (MIS) Language School.[57]

Once they left Manzanar, Japanese Angelinos opened many language schools far from the City of Angels. Nisei who refused to sign the loyalty oath set up ten Japanese schools at Tule Lake. Together they taught more than four thousand children, instilling pride in a Japanese identity behind barbed wire. Meanwhile, more than six thousand Nisei who swore allegiance to the United States enrolled at the MIS Language School in Minnesota. They studied Japanese under the tutelage of Hollywood High alumnus John Aiso before sailing to the South Pacific, where they used their language skills to interrogate prisoners and translate stolen documents. The language schools at Tule Lake and at the MIS represented opposite loyalties during the war. Yet both sides rejected the WRA's initial decision to prevent US citizens from learning an enemy language after the bombing of Pearl Harbor. Comparing their curricula and student experiences explains how questions of loyalty changed the politics of language learning during World War II.

In his *Exile Within: The Schooling of Japanese Americans, 1942–1945* (1987), a thorough history of internment education, Thomas James addresses Japanese-language schools only in the final chapter about evacuee resistance to white bureaucracy. Language restrictions lessened at all internment camps after the Manzanar Riot, but Japanese instruction flourished at Tule Lake Segregation Center. In addition to the camp's WRA-sanctioned schools, James identified at least ten underground language schools at Tule Lake Segregation Center, which housed nearly all Japanese "disloyals" by late 1943. The most popular Japanese schools adopted the Americanization curriculum that Kohei Shimano had developed in the 1930s, but vocal evacuees also started rival language schools that embraced the "disloyalty" label. James's research on the rapid rise of Japanese schools at Tule Lake illustrates increasing tensions about the relationship between language and loyalty. After decades of insisting that learning Japanese could help Nisei become active US. citizens, some segregated evacuees embraced language schools as symbols of resistance to the US government that had interned them.[58]

Education debates at Tule Lake differed from those at other camps. At Manzanar, Nisei like Paul Kusuda worked with the WRA to improve schools. At Tule Lake, the WRA's education classes drew little interest from a population that had already rejected the loyalty oath. WRA schools did not open until 1944, and then attendance was not compulsory. James notes that the Japanese-language school population was nearly twice as large (4,300 students) as the Tule Lake public school total (2,300 students). James argues that the rise of private schools reflected "a spectrum of belief and disbelief in the collective symbols being forged" at Tule Lake. Recognizing that its public schools were unpopular, the WRA allowed evacuees to form a Japanese Language School Board. The board included accommodationists who worked with the WRA to provide facilities (but not supplies) for Japanese schools. Like LA language schools before the war, Tule Lake's officially recognized schools urged students to attend public schools by scheduling classes after school hours and on weekends. Even after two relocations, most families who refused to sign the loyalty oath still shared Kohei Shimano's belief that Japanese cultural training improved US public schools.[59]

As the officially condoned language schools became more popular, they also drew criticism. Many Japanese who had refused to declare loyalty to the United States were skeptical of any ties to the WRA establishment. While the Japanese Language School Board was unique to Tule Lake, many Nisei dismissed board members as "loyals" because they coordinated their calendar with WRA school schedules. Such critics showed resistance, James wrote, by creating their own language curricula in eight "underground 'school republics' operating as self-contained systems against WRA regulations." These schools denounced the accommodations of the Japanese Language School Board and used language instruction to express dissent in the final year of internment. Many parents found the rhetoric at these language schools too radical, but they were also grateful to see fellow evacuees finally protesting their incarceration.[60]

The underground schools at Tule Lake opposed the WRA and its Japanese Language School Board whenever possible. Unlike the voluntary WRA schools, the camp's subversive schools made attendance mandatory and held classes at times that conflicted with the public school schedule. Whereas officially condoned schools used Americanization curricula, protest schools designed language instruction to train a new Kibei generation that would "return" to Japan immediately after their release from internment. Ward 7, Tule Lake's center of WRA resistance, organized a language school that copied the curriculum of Kokumin Gakko, Japan's elementary school system, which taught martial arts and stressed "discipline, conformity, and respect to superiors." Even if families did not favor such dogmatic nationalism, many believed renegade schools should have the freedom to teach this curriculum.[61]

Most language schools fell somewhere between the extremes of Ward 7's nationalism and the accommodationist Japanese Language School Board. When one school assigned students to recite patriotic Japanese songs, one girl asked to sing a Bing Crosby wartime hit, "Pistol Packing Mama," in English. Other language schools offered less divisive subjects and appealed to Nisei interested in Japanese rituals like the tea ceremony and flower arrangement.

These linguistic expressions of nationalism, for Japan and America, were not new in language schools. Yet they had heightened significance in the context of an internment camp for evacuees who refused to sign the loyalty oath. Tule Lake Segregation Center celebrated the return of Japanese schools by offering ten different environments for language learning. While two worked with the camp's public schools, the eight underground schools enabled some segregated Japanese to turn language learning into a symbol of protest by the end of World War II.[62]

Refusing to pledge loyalty and winding up at Tule Lake was not the only way for Nisei to escape Manzanar. A few educated students resettled in college towns outside the militarized zone, as Paul Kusuda did when he enrolled at the University of Chicago after a year of incarceration. Additionally, more than six thousand interned Nisei moved to a Minnesota army camp to study Japanese for six months before graduating as noncommissioned officers in the US Army. Many had responded to an army flyer posted in the Manzanar mess hall recruiting students to be trained "as interrogators and translators, [who] shortly after graduation will be sent out to the combat areas" in the Pacific. The fledgling MIS Language School offered more than a ticket out of Manzanar. This language learning allowed Japanese American citizens to prove their patriotism.[63]

The MIS Language School was founded by John Aiso and Colonel John Weckerling, two Americans who had lived in Japan. Weckerling wanted the chief instructor to be Aiso, Hollywood High's 1926 oratory champion who was denied a chance to compete nationally. By the time he began the first MIS class in November 1941, Aiso had two Ivy League degrees and five years of work experience in Japan, where he had practiced law and taught English. Weckerling had also studied and worked in Japan, but he did not share Aiso's language proficiency. By 1941, he was worried about America's intelligence capability because he believed that "the complexities of the Japanese language are almost beyond occidental comprehension." In Japan, he had spoken to military officers who "boasted that the Japanese language was so difficult that it constituted a code itself not susceptible of solution by foreigners." Weckerling wrote to the War Department explaining that linguists had to learn two written syllabaries, *katakana* and *hiragana*, along with some eight thousand Chinese ideographs. Describing the four distinct steps in writing each character as "the ultimate in confusion," he urged the army to recruit Japanese Americans. "Looked upon with great suspicion before and immediately after the outbreak of war," Weckerling recalled, "the Nisei

Nisei linguists attend a class at the MIS Language School. *Courtesy of Park Archives and Records Center, Golden Gate National Recreation Area, National Park Service.*

justified the confidence of those who knew them and supplied the answer to one of our most vital war problems—the need for efficient interpreters and translators of the Japanese language."[64]

The MIS Language School expanded rapidly throughout the war. Aiso planned his first class at the Presidio military base in San Francisco with a $2,000 budget and orange crates as desks. On November 1, 1941, he began instructing forty-five Nisei and fifteen other students. Six months later, after the military had evacuated the Pacific coast, the MIS Language School moved to Camp Savage in Minnesota. The Midwest was more welcoming to Nisei students, but the camp had been a center for homeless men during the Depression and, "in some respects, the facilities were poorer" than those in the internment camps. Yet former Manzanar evacuees not only graduated from the MIS Language School, they also became instructors under the supervision of Aiso, whom students called *kocho-sensei,* "director of academic training." By 1944, the school had outgrown Camp Savage and moved to Fort Snelling, near St. Paul, a permanent facility with more than 125 classrooms. The original class of sixty language learners was only 1 percent of the six thousand students who graduated from the MIS Language School by the end of the war. In terms of attendance, the MIS taught more Nisei students than all of Tule Lake's Japanese-language schools combined.[65]

At its peak, Aiso's outfit operated with military precision. By 1945, the MIS had 1,836 students taking classes five days a week from 8:00 A.M. to 4:30 P.M. and resuming from 7:00 to 9:00 P.M. Japanese instruction only paused on Wednesday afternoons for military training and on Saturdays for language exams. The curriculum included lessons using stolen documents, maps of the Pacific, and radio monitoring. With these written, visual, and audio sources, Aiso's instructors taught reading, writing, interrogation, translation, and interpretation of Japanese politics and culture. Nisei linguists were then embedded in army units, bringing all of these skills to "every major unit in every engagement from Guadalcanal . . . to the march into Tokyo."[66]

Aiso did not create this curriculum until after the army realized it was necessary. In 1941, Colonel Weckerling assumed that "there would be sufficient Japanese-speaking Nisei so that only a few weeks' review in general Japanese vocabulary . . . military terminology and combat intelligence would be required." However, a survey of the first 3,700 Nisei to attend the MIS Language School found that only 3 percent were "accomplished linguists," 4 percent were "proficient," and 3 percent spoke "fair" Japanese. This proved that the Nisei generation had truly been Americanized, despite the fears about disloyal language-school principals. Still, the military was selective in its admissions, leaning on the loyalty tests administered to all internees to admit the most patriotic students. Even John Aiso underwent screening before the army appointed him to train Nisei evacuees as interrogators, translators, propaganda writers, and radio broadcasters.[67]

The very opening of the MIS Language School signaled that the concept of Americanization had evolved. Despite language restrictions at WRA camps, the federal government now recognized that Nisei could demonstrate their loyalty by learning Japanese in service to the US Army. This job offer was a new experience for Aiso, whose election as student body president of a junior high school in Hollywood had caused such outrage that parents demanded a student council shutdown in 1923. After graduating from Brown University and Harvard Law School, Aiso went to Japan, where he received better treatment from bankers and diplomats than he had from New York law firms. Aiso was one of many Nisei who worked in Japan in the 1930s. He moved back to Los Angeles in 1940, planning to practice law and get married. Instead he enlisted in the army, where he met Weckerling one month before Pearl Harbor.

Aiso was modest, but his assistants saw him as a model of Nisei assimilation. They celebrated his job offer by contrasting it with the discrimination

Major John Fujio Aiso. *Courtesy of the Defense Language Institute Foreign Language Center.*

he had faced in Hollywood schools. "John had never been told by anyone that America was his country," one aide recalled. "John had been told again and again that America did not need him." He could have turned down the job. If thousands of Tule Lake internees could refuse to sign a loyalty oath in the heat of war, why could a faithful Nisei not refuse a military post before Pearl Harbor? According to his aide, Aiso accepted the job to show the country that Japanese Americans were vital to the national interest: "Colonel Weckerling was saying to all Japanese Americans, 'We consider you to be loyal American citizens. We respect you. . . . We ask that you perform a vital task in national defense that no other American can do. Your country needs you.'"[68] By agreeing to teach Nisei soldiers, Aiso demonstrated that Japanese-language instruction did not have to translate into the message of rebellion and disloyalty that some Tule Lake schools embraced. Instead, the MIS Language School was the ultimate symbol that American citizens could protect the homeland by learning their heritage language.

Just as John Aiso used his Japanese language skills to serve his country, Manuel Ruiz applied his expertise in delinquency to prove his patriotism. As the only Spanish-speaking representative on Governor Warren's Citizens Committee on Youth in Wartime (CCYW), he tried to make education of Mexican Americans a priority. Whereas the war meant Aiso received military funds to found a language institute, for Ruiz the CCYW curtailed his ambitions for a Spanish-language school. After Earl Warren and the LA school district rejected his Pan-American language schools during the war, Ruiz shifted his reform agenda from language learning to more controversial issues of desegregation and civil rights. By 1945, the attorney was arguing that California's segregated schools had led to Mexican delinquency.[69]

Spanish-speaking leaders leapt at every chance to involve Mexican American youth in the war effort. When Governor Warren appointed him to the CCYW three months after the Zoot Suit Riots, Ruiz promptly wrote a bilingual pamphlet to recruit Mexican Angelinos into the US Army (and away from a life of delinquency). He brought Eduardo Quevedo to Garfield Elementary School, a segregated Mexican school in eastern LA County. Quevedo addressed the Parent Teacher Association in Spanish before Ruiz gave a lecture in English entitled "Allegiance to America through Service to Youth." He also screened a motion picture about military training for Mexican youths who enlisted in the army. Parents may have sensed hypocrisy in a program that asked students to sacrifice their lives for a nation that sent them to segregated schools, but Ruiz hoped dual-language loyalty campaigns in schools situated in Spanish-speaking areas would prove Mexican American patriotism—and create a foundation to demand language learning and other youth programs after the war.[70]

Concerns about delinquency dominated the discussions of the CCYW. When Ruiz attended his first meeting in Sacramento, he called for reforms and improvements in all areas of Mexican American life, from probation officers to community centers to schools. Instead, California's attorney general and superintendent of public instruction focused on law enforcement. The committee listened to an LA Police Department deputy chief who said, "Los Angeles picks up children during school hours who are not in school and either turns them over to the school if they are regularly enrolled or gives them special treatment if they are not." Ruiz responded by advocating for alliances among the Office of Inter-American Affairs, the LA Probation Department, and the LA Mexican Chamber of Commerce, which would have created connections among law enforcement, East LA business leaders, and the Spanish-speaking director at Helen Heffernan's office. Unfortunately, this promising program never proceeded.[71]

Rather than a balance between law enforcement and education, punishment became the CCYW's central focus. Karl Holton, director of the California Youth Authority and secretary of the CCYW, expanded a youth farm labor experiment he had started in Los Angeles in 1942. The legislature gave him control of three youth correctional schools, including camps in eastern LA County and neighboring Ventura County. In 1944, Holton started another wartime work program in collaboration with the Pasadena school district. The San Gabriel Valley Citrus Association hired the Pasadena YMCA to bring transient teen boys to rural LA County for "harvest camp," where they slept on cots in Covina High School after picking and packing oranges. The San Diego school superintendent, a fellow CCYW member, informed Ruiz this was not child exploitation because "in wartime youth accept more responsibility." Ruiz took pains to divert Mexican American adolescents who got into trouble from such labor camps. After three years of courting the establishment, the lawyer began to clash with officials about which juveniles were delinquent and how they should be reformed. He did not support the CCYW's plan to deter delinquency with forced labor.[72]

To deemphasize probation, Ruiz petitioned the CCYW with familiar language proposals. He invited eleven Mexican Americans to join CCYW members like Karl Holton on the Committee for the Betterment of the Welfare of Los Angeles County Youth of Latin American Ancestry. Ruiz requested $100,000 for cultural and athletic activities, leadership training, social work services, and bilingual programs. His proposal set aside $5,000 for an English-Spanish youth newspaper and $10,000 for a Spanish-language radio program. As he had done with the Pan-American Trade School, Ruiz couched his language ideals in wartime rhetoric, arguing that the Zoot Suit Riots gave "aid and comfort to the enemies of the United States." Despite this appeal, the CCYW declined to spend $15,000 on Ruiz's language proposals.[73]

Ruiz was also frustrated with the CCYW's school reform ideas. The committee campaigned to preserve the standard school day, but it rejected Ruiz's emphasis on racial integration. By 1943, military mobilization forced California districts to start "double sessions," sending one set of students to a school in the morning and a separate set to the same school in the afternoon. The CCYW investigated the impact of these double sessions, finding that shortened school days increased "truancy which eventually leads to delinquency." In a 1944 letter to Governor Warren, the committee unanimously condemned double sessions because "these are days in which youth need full-time constructive activity and leadership." However, the CCYW chairman refused Ruiz's request to investigate several discrimination cases in LA public schools. Eight months after issuing his statement to save the school day, the chairman wrote to Ruiz that all "items on racial or nationality discrimination in California schools will be referred to the State Department of Education and the appropriate legislative committee." Disillusioned with the CCYW, Ruiz formed the first Latin American lobbying organization in

1945. After the war, he would redirect his efforts for language learning toward the new purpose of desegregating "Mexican schools."[74]

Manuel Ruiz was one of several Angelinos who lobbied Earl Warren to consider school integration a decade before Warren wrote the unanimous opinion in Brown v. Board of Education. In 1944, months after the governor's wartime youth committee decided not to comment publicly on racial discrimination in schools, Ruiz recalled that the CCYW had "received the desegregation measure favorably." In fact, Warren's education policies as Supreme Court chief justice drew from the lessons he learned during California's wartime language debates. Nisei Angelinos challenged him to reconsider his position on language and national allegiance. Warren had won the 1942 gubernatorial campaign as a prominent advocate for internment. Before the WRA administered its loyalty oath, Warren used race to justify questioning the patriotism of Japanese Americans:

> When we are dealing with the Caucasian race we have methods that will test the loyalty of them, and we believe that we can, in dealing with the Germans and the Italians, arrive at some fairly sound conclusion because of our knowledge of the way they live in the community. . . . But when we deal with the Japanese we are in an entirely different field and we cannot form any opinion that we believe to be sound. Their method of living, their language, make for this difficulty.[75]

John Aiso was already organizing the MIS Language School when he read California attorney general Warren's statements. Aiso had voted for him by absentee ballot, and now he disagreed with Warren's pledge that Nisei should never return to the Golden State. Aiso appealed for support to Herbert Wenig, the classmate who had competed in the national oratorical contest in Aiso's place and won the championship. During the 1942 campaign, sixteen years after he had replaced Aiso, Wenig served as the lead lawyer in Warren's office. Aiso asked the friend he had coached to a title to tell the attorney general to tamp down the rhetoric. Mentioning his secret work on the MIS Language School, Aiso tried to convince Warren that Nisei could use the Japanese language to prove their American patriotism. As he remembered in 1970:

> I wrote him a letter saying that I thought, at heart, he was a very religious man. I wanted him to know that some of us so-called "Japs" were in the United States Army. I felt that after the war was over he would change his mind and let us come back. I never heard directly from him, but I

did get a letter from my high school debating partner. . . . I got a letter from Herb saying, "The Attorney General acknowledges your letter and thanks you." I am not sure whether [when he got to the Supreme Court] the Chief Justice [Warren] remembered that incident or not.[76]

In his memoirs, Warren expressed regret for supporting internment. As he watched the return of the Japanese American citizens whom he had evacuated, the then–California governor embraced racial integration. The language-learning projects of Manuel Ruiz and John Aiso had persuaded Warren that students of color could make many contributions in California schools. Once the war ended, language instruction became a key component of the state's early desegregation debate.

4 | LANGUAGE AND THE LEGAL CASE FOR SCHOOL DESEGREGATION, 1945–1953

In December 1945, Marie Hughes, the LA County specialist in minority group education, hosted a conference on intergroup relations for the Los Angeles County superintendent of schools. Four months after atomic bombs ended World War II, educators from Pasadena to Compton met to consider intercultural education and the postwar problem of racial equality. Diana Selig and Zoë Burkholder have argued that whereas tolerance education was popular in classrooms across the country between the two world wars, by 1945, teachers' attention was turning toward a new emphasis on school desegregation. When Hughes had assumed her position in 1940, after nineteen years in New Mexico schools, she was shocked to see so many segregated schools. She coordinated the 1945 conference with the Office of Inter-American Affairs, which did not shy away from discussing discrimination. The conference report proposed to end school segregation because "the pattern of 'island neighborhoods' . . . is familiar to all who know Los Angeles County." Hughes identified all minority groups subject to segregation, including Japanese Americans, but she made specific suggestions for the most excluded students, Mexican-origin Angelinos. The conference report advocated for merging Anglo and Mexican American middle schoolers into one building, even if the classes remained segregated, so they could "make adjustments" to each other before high school. It also recommended eight steps to "build competence in intergroup education," telling teachers to "attack directly the myth of racial superiority through discussion and reading." Many Angelino educators could no longer tolerate segregated schools. Unlike teachers across the country, Hughes and her colleagues believed that language instruction could address the problem. After the war, LA teachers, students, parents, and judges used language learning to make the legal case for integration.[1]

That summer, Marie Hughes was the final witness for the plaintiff in *Mendez v. Westminster*, a case before the U.S. district court for California's Southern District in Los Angeles, the first federal court to rule against school segregation. Historians have celebrated this court-ordered integration of four school districts in Orange County as a precedent for the *Brown v. Board of Education* decision eight years later. Yet closer analysis of Hughes's testimony suggests that the court's conclusions about school segregation derived from more radical questions about language learning. Whereas *Brown* focused on five states that segregated African American native English speakers, the *Mendez* plaintiffs argued that California's "Mexican schools" were particularly ill-equipped to teach English to Spanish speakers. "Children learn a language through hearing it and having a motive, a reason, for using it," Hughes insisted, and "the best way to teach English is to give many opportunities to speak English, to hear it spoken correctly, and have reasons for speaking it." Months later, she echoed these ideas at the LA County conference, telling teachers to study their school community by asking questions such as, "What language is spoken in the home?" Segregated schools left Spanish speakers "forever handicapped," she argued, because "they have no opportunity to learn the language and to become at home with other groups . . . as they move on to high school, they are timid, afraid, confused." The *Mendez* case concerned schools in Orange County, but it was LA County's specialist in minority education who linked language acquisition to desegregation.[2]

The *Mendez* plaintiffs called Hughes as their last witness because her experiences in language instruction portrayed the virtues of integrated schooling. "There is no doubt, in my judgment, that children in the mixed schools . . . learn English much faster and much more expertly than they do in a segregated school," she stated. Hughes stressed the mental stimulation of mixing students who speak different languages in all school situations, including recess and lunch. "Children who speak another language, such as Spanish, when in association with children speaking English have a reason to learn and to speak English," she explained. "Moreover, they hear English spoken, and you cannot learn a language and learn to speak it well without hearing it." Hughes helped make *Mendez* a landmark desegregation lawsuit by arguing that language instruction was central to intergroup education. Her argument linking language learning and civil rights was influential beyond that courtroom. The next year, Paul McCormick, the judge who heard Hughes's testimony in the *Mendez* case, ordered the US territory of Hawaii to reinstate the Japanese-language schools it had banned during World War II.[3]

While scholars stress the significance of language in the *Mendez* decision, the case has rightly found its way into civil rights folklore. Long before Earl Warren authored the majority opinion in *Brown v. Board of Education* as Supreme Court chief justice, he followed the *Mendez* case as governor of California, which prompted him to support the integration of "Mexican" school districts in the southland. Philippa Strum's account of the *Mendez* case shows that language and citizenship mattered more than racial discrimination in this desegregation test case, which ignored educational access for black, Asian, and Native American students. Mark Brilliant's comprehensive history of civil rights for many races in California also emphasizes the importance of *Mendez*, arguing that Governor Warren learned about language discrimination when he met Manuel Ruiz in 1943. After the war, Ruiz became a lobbyist who pushed Warren to desegregate schools four days after the final *Mendez* verdict in 1947.[4]

The *Mendez* ruling benefited Los Angeles's reintegrated Japanese community in several ways as well. Verdicts and legislation for language instruction in the 1940s broadened desegregation debates to include immigrants from around the world. These efforts introduced early arguments about bilingual education as a civil rights issue. Framing school integration in the context of language learning encouraged both Mexican and Japanese Angelinos to take public stands against discrimination after World War II in ways that most would not have done during the Americanization era. The desegregation of Mexican-origin students and the reintegration of Japanese-origin students were different issues but both were social justice causes that helped each ethnic group gain acceptance into postwar American society.

Marie Hughes was not the only Angelino who linked language instruction to the national debate over intercultural education. She was one of three hundred LA educators who belonged to the California Elementary School Principals' Association when it printed *Education for Cultural Unity* in 1945. Along with the conference on intergroup relations where Hughes expanded the desegregation defense she had just articulated at the *Mendez* trial, the principals' publication proved that Americanization was no longer the central issue in LA schools after internment and the Zoot Suit Riots. In several of this book's essays, Angelino administrators introduced new ideas about bilingual classrooms and desegregation, illustrating how these language innovations shaped, and were shaped by, racial integration in 1945.[5]

Despite its legacy today, *Mendez v. Westminster* was not simply a school desegregation case when it came to trial in 1945. The historian Gilbert Gonzalez explains that "California courts heard the *Mendez* case in a period of policy shift toward 'intercultural understanding.'" *Education for Cultural Unity* explained this shift by boasting that "the elementary school is doing a real job in promoting democratic feelings toward all races and cultures." While intercultural innovation was the explicit topic of the principals' first postwar volume, it also introduced a new catchphrase to California teachers— bilingualism. That subject was selected by the book's editor, N. D. Myers, the school superintendent in Palos Verdes Estates, a coastal community south of Los Angeles with a history of racial segregation. In addition to soliciting essays from national civil rights leaders of all ethnicities, Myers called for assistance from his former employee Afton Nance, who had left Myers's district after her Japanese students were relocated in 1942. The editor asked Nance for her advice on educating the thousands of Nisei returning from internment. At the same time, Myers conducted his own survey for the purpose of starting bilingual education in LA County. Essays in *Education for Cultural Unity* indicate that language learning and school integration equally influenced Angelinos' ideas of "intercultural understanding."[6]

Myers asked Helen Heffernan along with another LA principal to write the essay "Intercultural Education in the Elementary School." They proposed a curriculum to help students "become understanding, participating, contributing members of a world organized on the basis of social and economic justice and international collaboration." To teach tolerance, they recommended using children's books, folk songs, and art activities from various ethnic groups. Using a range of traditions in the same lesson would teach students that "people are more alike than different" and that "to be different does not mean to be inferior." Yet Heffernan admitted that discrimination still existed. She even seemed to justify segregation based on the language abilities of non-English-speaking immigrants: "In California, there is a large group of children whose first language experience is with another than the English language. In addition to the serious social adjustment these children must make as members of minority groups, they are also confronted with the difficult problem of learning a new language." Heffernan wanted to end "destructive" segregation slowly, "through processes of community education." This gradual approach implied tensions between language learning and school segregation in 1945. Heffernan, the state supervisor of elementary education who had headed the LA Office of Inter-American Affairs during the war, was not sure how students who did not speak English fluently fit into her progressive vision of intercultural education.[7]

Language was just one reason desegregation looked different in Los Angeles than elsewhere in the United States. Myers solicited articles from writers from across the country, including prominent African Americans like Langston Hughes and Alain Locke. However, integration efforts in LA stood out because they brought together more than blacks and whites. One article in *Education for Cultural Unity* featured the Los Angeles Youth Project, which had begun two months after the Zoot Suit Riots as an effort to help Los Angeles avoid the violence of preceding race riots in Detroit and Harlem. With the aid of Manuel Ruiz, the project's Youth Festival Committee united more than eight hundred people from twenty-five neighborhoods to organize an All-Nations Festival in Boyle Heights. The festival featured dancing and storytelling, but "the most interesting and far-reaching was a program in which three minority groups, Mexican, Negro, and Jewish, held a round-table discussion of their common problems." By engaging three racial groups in a common conversation, a curriculum director contended, the LA festival had gone farther than its eastern counterparts in cultivating intergroup understanding.[8]

Other Spanish-speaking activists challenged the relationship between language and Americanization. Anthropologist Ruth Tuck described language as deceptive, because a typical Mexican immigrant "may speak imperfect English, or not at all, but he is familiar with payroll deductions, taxes, and easy payments." Whereas Tuck was skeptical about any Mexican's ability to adjust, even "if he spoke unaccented English," Ernesto Galarza, head of the Bureau of Labor Statistics, argued that multicultural schools were central to success. He told fellow Californians that the value of "the American public school cannot be underestimated in this process of acculturation." Even though segregated schools existed in the Southwest, Galarza insisted that they "never took hold uniformly . . . the American creed of equality of opportunity left many doors unlocked." The federal bureaucrat believed that Tuck's analysis of Spanish speakers' abilities was less concerning than the increasing use of the phrase "Mexican problem." Since many "Mexicans" like him were born in California, Galarza wrote, "it would be just as legitimate to speak of the 'American problem' apropos of the Mexicans." Although Tuck and Galarza disagreed about the need for language instruction, they both believed that prewar versions of Americanization were obsolete.[9]

Nisei Larry Tajiri took a more traditional approach to intercultural education. He cited successful internment camp schools to contradict Galarza's critique of prewar Americanization practices. During the war, Tajiri had been criticized as the editor of *Pacific Citizen*, JACL's national publication, for endorsing internment. He expressed regret in his essay in *Education for Cultural Unity*, but he was proud of the "fact that 30,000 Nisei who went to

California schools were evacuated to un-democratic camps . . . yet still have faith in American democracy." Tajiri targeted ethnic tolerance curricula, along with language, "foreignness," and residential segregation as the biggest "barriers to acculturation." He recalled his struggles to assimilate as a child in suburban Los Angeles in the 1920s, despite belonging to "a growing American-born and English-speaking generation." He had participated in annual Japan Days, performing judo and kendo skills, but his Japanese club was similar to "the Chinese club, the Negro group and the Mexican American." Tajiri lamented that "these organizations were encouraged to hold their own social functions and, in doing so, retarded any impulses among its members for fraternization outside their own racial group." He insisted that separate ethnic celebrations prevented schools from building "bridges of understanding." Just as Japanese evacuees were returning to California, the JACL editor wanted public schools to integrate the traditions of every minority group in their student bodies. He believed foreign-language instruction would delay the processes of Nisei assimilation and reintegration.[10]

N. D. Myers, in contrast, embraced language learning, and he may have been the first to introduce the idea of bilingual education to California educators. In 1945, "bilingual education" referred to English-language instruction for non-native speakers but did not yet include scholarship about the cognitive development of bilingual children. Only two of the ten publications listed in the section of Myers' bibliography entitled "Problems in Bilingualism" came from California teachers. To "stimulate interest in research and experimentation on the bi-lingual curriculum," Myers sent a survey on public attitudes toward bilingualism to sixteen educators, including Helen Heffernan (who had edited some of the articles on bilingualism) and Ruth Ginsburg, a Spanish teacher in Los Angeles who coordinated language workshops with Marie Hughes. Most of Myers's respondents believed the public was ready for bilingual education, but they also shared stories of communities resisting bilingual programs. Myers's survey was subjective and anecdotal but it demonstrated that, like desegregation, language learning was an important part of intercultural education after the war.[11]

The survey results revealed no consensus about what bilingual education should look like. Most respondents told Myers that "facility" in a second language was less important than giving "the minority group pride in its cultural heritage" and "better command of English." Some were skeptical about California's "bi-lingual tradition" and argued against new language programs. Despite the extreme range of perspectives, Myers asked critical questions about bringing bilingual learning to Los Angeles. Who should teach in a bilingual classroom—homeroom teachers, specially trained instructors, or parents? In what grade should the bilingual program start? Most importantly, which languages should be included? Myers understood that this controversial topic moved beyond issues related to language education for minority groups. He pointed out that parents had even agitated against classes in Spanish, German, and French. Anglo administrators weighed these bilingual education questions carefully in 1945. By including this survey, along with articles by Afton Nance and Helen Heffernan, the two teachers who would create California's bilingual education program over the next two decades, Myers made language instruction a central idea in *Education for Cultural Unity*. Across town, in federal court, lawyers and teachers were debating the extent to which school desegregation could promote English learning among immigrant students.[12]

Mendez v. Westminster was the most important decision Paul McCormick wrote in his twenty-seven years on California's Southern District federal court. The Irish Catholic judge was a Progressive teetotaler who had attended mass with Mexican-origin Angelinos for three decades. This made McCormick empathetic to the Méndez family, but before the lawsuit he had assumed that "Mexican" and "Spanish" were mutually unintelligible languages. As McCormick spoke to Gonzalo and Felicitas Méndez, he came to believe that the best way to teach immigrants English was to integrate them into schools with white students. In February 1946, he ruled that education "must be open to all children by unified school association regardless of lineage . . . a paramount requisite in all the American system of public education is social equality." Although this was not as elegantly expressed as Earl Warren's declaration in *Brown v. Board of Education that* "separate educational facilities are inherently unequal," Judge McCormick's opinion raised radical questions about segregation of schools according to language proficiency. The Méndezes and their attorney, David Marcus, changed McCormick's understanding of the Spanish language. As Manuel Ruiz and Marie Hughes wove language learning into their school desegregation demands from 1945 to 1952, LA reformers were building bilingual education into their integration initiatives. The dialogue between the Méndezes and Judge McCormick and the correspondence between Ruiz and Governor Warren suggest that language learning shaped the earliest civil rights victories in California.[13]

David Marcus had faced language and discrimination issues himself. The son of a Jewish immigrant, he had encountered anti-Semitism at the University of Southern California Law School in the 1920s. Marcus married a Mexican immigrant, and they taught their children to speak Spanish as well as English. His daughters attended Pasadena public schools and were "introduced to society" at the 1952 Las Damas Pan Americanas Debutante Ball. Marcus specialized in immigration and criminal law, and he had represented the Mexican consulate after its Spanish-language schools closed in the 1930s. He was familiar with civil rights litigation before the Méndezes hired him, having won the Southern District court's first desegregation lawsuit in 1944 that led to the integration of swimming pools in San Bernardino County. When Marcus first met Gonzalo Méndez, he told his client that California's Education Codes allowed for racial discrimination, and explained that since segregation by race was legal, he would use language education to make his case for integrating the Orange County schools.[14]

The lawyer's most effective trial questions addressed language learning. They came in his cross-examination of a school superintendent who had written a master's thesis titled "Segregation of Mexican School Children in Southern California." Marcus challenged the administrator's claim that Spanish-speaking students had a "bilingual handicap" requiring separate instruction. He asked why Mexican Americans were segregated for language lessons but Japanese and Filipino immigrants were integrated into white classes, and was incredulous when the superintendent said bilingual children were "retarded." Marcus responded that children who speak both Spanish and English have "more comprehensive knowledge, at least linguistically speaking," than monolingual students, and the educator agreed that older children who learned a fourth or fifth language could excel academically. In noting the paradox of calling multilingual students "handicapped," Marcus made language instruction central to his cross-examination.[15]

Marcus's logic eventually persuaded McCormick that speaking Spanish was not a handicap. The judge's Irish Catholic identity had colored his sense of racial differences at the first pretrial hearing, when the lawyers had discussed what terms they could use in questioning. McCormick denied Marcus's request to refer to segregated students as children of "Anglo Saxon descent" and "Mexican descent" because these categories did not account for "Celtic children" like himself. The judge insisted on the terms "English-speaking" and "Spanish-speaking," and he interrupted when Marcus called white students "Anglo." In response, the plaintiff asked the judge if bilingual Mexican students still counted as "Spanish-speaking." McCormick considered the question before responding that "Spanish speaking pupils . . . are not efficient in English," to which Marcus insisted that his clients' children spoke English fluently. This double discussion of language, in terms of proficiency and identity, moved McCormick to reconsider this terminology. At the outset, however, he was willing to reason that segregation by language ability was acceptable even if dividing students by race was not. This meant Marcus's clearest path to victory was proving that Mexican students were fluent English speakers who deserved equal education.[16]

The Méndezes proved their English fluency in court. At the pretrial hearing, McCormick had revealed uncertainty about race and language when he said "a person may be of Spanish descent or origin, ancestry, and yet speak English perfectly as far as grammatical expression is concerned and as far as knowledge of the language is concerned, but yet they do have an accent." So when Gonzalo Méndez took the stand, Marcus asked him to explain why "Spanish-speaking" was an incomplete identifier. After a recess, the judge took over the questioning and asked the Mexican American witness if his wife, a Puerto Rican native, spoke English:

> A [Méndez]: She speaks English a little like me, with a little broken accent or dialect. . . .
>
> Q [McCormick]: Well, of course, that would be natural. That would apply not only to the Mexican people. Any person of Latin or Slavic or Teutonic origin, or perhaps of other origin, would naturally have some. It might be an accent or a brogue . . . I don't mean the accent. I mean the ability to express one's thoughts in words in the English language.
>
> A: She can carry on a good conversation in English. . . .
>
> Q: Well, did you and she have any difficulty in understanding each other in what you call your Mexican language and what she would call her Spanish?
>
> A: No, your Honor. We have no difficulty, although she claims that they talk a better Spanish in her country than my country, but it is all the same Spanish.
>
> Q: You mean it is fundamentally and basically a derivation of the Spanish language?
>
> A: Yes.[17]

The judge's belief that there was a "Mexican language" separate from Spanish seems shocking in retrospect. Nevertheless, McCormick learned from his mistake and gained respect for the plaintiffs. Marcus must have sensed the significance of this exchange because he called Felicitas Méndez to the stand next. When the defense asked if it could stipulate that she would verify her husband's testimony, Marcus said he had mainly called on her so that McCormick could hear her speak English. The judge admitted that "she seems to have a pretty good knowledge of the vernacular . . . as it should be spoken." Before she stepped down, Felicitas told McCormick how it felt when

Judge Paul McCormick (far left) admits Warren Biscailuz to federal practice. Warren is standing next to his father, Eugene Biscailuz, the sheriff of Los Angeles County. *Courtesy of Los Angeles Daily News Negatives, Negative #39778, Department of Special Collections, Charles E. Young Research Library, University of California, Los Angeles.*

the school board denied her children's request to register at the white school. "We got kind of sore," Felicitas said. "We always tell our children they are Americans, and I feel I am American myself, and so is my husband, and we thought they shouldn't be segregated like that, they shouldn't be treated the way they are." This testimony about language and citizenship seemed to shift McCormick's sense of the main issues under litigation. His questioning turned from the plaintiffs to the defense witnesses, specifically the superintendent who described the "bilingual handicap." If Mexican children had no exposure to English in a Spanish-speaking home, the judge asked, shouldn't they go to school with English-speaking students to learn the language? McCormick's conversations with the Méndezes about language and patriotism led to what were for 1946 fairly radical conclusions about desegregation.[18]

After opening his legal opinion by asserting that English proficiency was "the only tenable ground upon which segregation practices . . . can be defended," the judge disproved this argument. By the trial's end, McCormick had been persuaded that segregation impeded language acquisition. "The evidence clearly shows that Spanish-speaking children are retarded in learning English by lack of exposure to its use because of segregation," he wrote.

He did rule that separate classes could be allowed for some students with "foreign language handicaps," but only if there was a "credible examination" of language use by ability only—not by race. However, McCormick added, "such methods of evaluating language knowledge are illusory and are not conducive to the inculcation and enjoyment of civil rights." The judge's hesitation about fair language tests may have emerged after Gonzalo and Felicitas Méndez showed him how much he had to learn about "Spanish speakers." His decision also indicated the extent to which the nation's first school integration ruling in federal court hinged on language ability.[19]

Language played a different role in the desegregation of Los Angeles schools, which were more diverse than Orange County districts like Westminster. Segregated "Mexican schools" still existed in East LA in 1939, where six of the fourteen eastside elementary schools had an estimated 80 percent Spanish surname enrollment compared to less than 35 percent at the other eight schools. Under such conditions, it was not surprising that in the 1930s roughly half of Mexican Angelinos dropped out of school between the ages of fourteen and sixteen. During World War II, teachers like Elis Tipton introduced integration agendas that used language programs to produce positive learning environments. Discrimination continued after the war, but Manuel Ruiz turned school integration into a political agenda. Ruiz shelved the language-learning programs he had promoted during the war and focused on a different kind of "language," the text of the California Education Code that legalized school segregation. Ruiz's lobbying eventually persuaded Governor Warren to sign legislation revising the Education Code in 1947, making integration a central aspect of the postwar bilingual education agenda.[20]

Elis Tipton, principal of San Dimas Elementary School in eastern LA County, promoted the possibilities of desegregation in her contribution to *Education for Cultural Unity*. She celebrated the San Dimas Intercultural Program, her collaboration with Spanish-speaking youth in a town of 2,700 citrus farmers, 20 percent of whom were of Mexican heritage. Initially the segregated Mexican classes had met in a small frame building behind the main elementary school, but the schools shared a playground, where "ever-growing tension manifested itself in frequent fighting" after 1937. Mexican Americans who reached seventh grade went to the white middle school, where they benefited from better classrooms while suffering from heightened racial prejudices. In 1940, a group of seventh and eighth graders who had been Tipton's "star students" in elementary school determined to desegregate her school. They formed an intercultural club that included every Mexican

American middle schooler and "as many other children as cared to join." Segregation was "abandoned" when school opened in the fall of 1943, the principal reported, and "the expected storm of protest did not occur." By working with their white classmates, Mexican American students made integration a reality in three years.[21]

The intercultural club's language initiatives strengthened integration. When it looked like "adult prejudice could quickly undo all the good work the school might accomplish," the community organized an adult club called Americans All that offered monthly meetings with Mexican-themed potluck suppers, movies, and lectures in Spanish and English. San Dimas started an integrated summer school in 1942 with music, dance, and Spanish classes for all ages. The adult classes culminated in a dinner for 150 guests, including the LA County school superintendent and Jerry Voorhis, a San Dimas educator who served in Congress for five terms until Richard Nixon defeated him. There were no complaints when Tipton's school desegregated in 1943 in part because the Americans All parents had met Mexican students who "spoke English exceptionally well." Yet Tipton still had to address "the language handicap of the Spanish-speaking children," who made up 45 percent of the school. In 1944, Tipton secured funds from the Office of Inter-American Affairs to hire two Mexican Americans to teach English to Mexican immigrant students. She also started a bilingual story hour for Spanish-speaking preschool students, who came with "an eagerness to learn never exhibited by our Mexican American children." Thus, one of LA County's early integration initiatives grew out of a language-learning experiment.[22]

Meanwhile, Mexican Angelinos were spearheading a statewide desegregation campaign focused on legislative language. Governor Warren signed a law repealing the remaining segregation statutes from the California Education Code weeks after the Ninth Circuit Court upheld McCormick's *Mendez* decision in 1947. This was the culmination of a two-year campaign by Manuel Ruiz. Five years after the East LA lawyer had failed to secure a separate Pan-American school of Spanish-language instruction, he celebrated a law that ensured equal education for the Spanish-speaking students in his neighborhood. His correspondence with state senators and assemblymen illustrated how Mexican educators shifted their attention from Americanization to integration and subsequently shaped postwar attitudes about bilingual education.[23]

Ruiz turned to desegregation because he had been disappointed by the slow progress of the California Committee for Youth in Wartime in advocating for change. When the California superintendent of public instruction gave the committee no more than vague promises of an integration law, Ruiz

Manuel Ruiz (far right) appears before the Los Angeles Board of Supervisors with other members of the California Committee on Youth in Wartime in 1942. *Courtesy of Department of Special Collections, Los Angeles Public Library.*

announced he was forming the first Mexican American lobbying organization in US history. He fostered new relationships with the governor and East LA's representatives in Sacramento, Democratic Assemblyman William Rosenthal and Republican Senator Jack Tenney, who chaired the state's Fact-Finding Committee on Un-American Activities. When he persuaded both the Jewish liberal and California's leading anti-Communist to endorse limited forms of integration, this marked a major change in political tactics. While many Mexican Angelinos had promoted Spanish-language schools as part of the war effort before 1945, by the 1950s the majority believed that bilingual education was a civil right.[24]

Rather than demanding full integration, Ruiz limited his goal to repealing Section 8003, "which authorizes school districts in California to segregate children of Indian, Chinese, Japanese, and Mongolian origin." He argued that some districts labeled Mexican Americans "Indian" to justify sending them to separate schools. When Rosenthal proposed a compromise—removing

"Indian" from the text—Ruiz carefully considered his priorities. Was he willing to allow Chinese and Japanese Americans to remain segregated so long as Mexican students could attend white schools? If he continued to press for full integration, what response would he get from Earl Warren, who had endorsed Japanese internment three years earlier? What did Section 8003 mean by "Indian," anyway? In the end he decided he was less concerned with the segregation of black students in South Central LA, or the reintegration of Japanese internees than with desegregating the "Mexican schools." Ruiz resolved to focus on Mexican Americans, naming his lobby the National Origins Council of America. Emphasizing indigeneity, the lobbyist began to describe Spanish speakers as Latin Americans and tried to distinguish desegregation from race by focusing on language and equality.[25]

In his first press release, Ruiz said his main concern was to integrate Spanish-speaking students. He only addressed discrimination affecting "Latin American pupils 'on the grounds that they may have some Indian blood.'" The report listed segregated schools across the southland, where "Mexican-American pupils in many instances have been required to attend school in dilapidated structures, far from their homes." Ruiz highlighted El Monte in eastern LA County, where there were five elementary schools, "but pupils of Latin American extraction are required to use a tumbledown building." These unequal facilities may have explained why a quarter of the city's elementary schoolers were Spanish-speaking, but only 3 percent of El Monte High School was of Mexican descent. Despite discrimination in LA County towns like El Monte, Ruiz conceded that "the Los Angeles city school system has not practiced segregation except in isolated instances."[26]

Ruiz's political calculus was accurate. Lawmakers found the idea of limited integration for only Mexican students more palatable than complete desegregation. When Ruiz wrote to William Rosenthal in 1945, the assemblyman was eager to please one of his most active constituents in East LA but he resisted full repeal of Section 8003. Instead, he simply deleted the offending label "Indian" and revised Section 8003 to say that "any school district may establish separate schools for children of Chinese, Japanese, or Mongolian parentage." Rather than hold out for repeal, Ruiz decided to accept this limited revision, although he lamented in his reply to Rosenthal that "one can't very well carry on a crusade" for a bill that treated Asian American children as second-class citizens.[27]

Ruiz spent two months playing with the text of the legislation, trying to classify Mexican and Indian students in language that was "more creative and in keeping with the popular sentiment of Western Hemispheric Brotherhood." The final draft Rosenthal submitted to the legislature banned "separate schools for children who are descendants of natives of any of the other countries of North America, Central America or South America." Instead of emphasizing the exclusion of Chinese and Japanese children, the new bill highlighted the expanded access for the Latin American community. Ruiz stressed the bill's international implications in a letter to the assembly education committee, reasoning that integration was critical at a time "when the nations of the earth" were negotiating the United Nations Charter in San Francisco. Ruiz even wrote a letter in Spanish to Mexico's UN delegation, urging them to make the short trip to the state assembly in Sacramento because "segregation prevents assimilation, and thereby defeats the purpose of this nation's good neighbor policy." The lobbyist thus cited foreign relations as a justification for desegregation after the war.[28]

Ruiz was unable to gain support in the state senate education committee, where a tie vote killed the bill in 1945. He then tried new tactics, appealing directly to school districts, urging voluntary integration. The El Monte school board assured him it would redistrict "without gerrymandering in such a way that certain schools . . . be predominantly Mexican." Ruiz reported that Los Angeles schools were already desegregating, even if he could not convince state senators that Rosenthal's bill held "significance for Inter-American affairs." He told senators that Mexican students were just like earlier European immigrants who had Americanized in the public school "melting pot." Ruiz speculated that "if immigrant Italians, French, or the children of some other national origin had been similarly segregated, the process of assimilation into our national life would have been retarded." He excused the history of Mexican discrimination in California schools, saying that "segregation was originally started because of the language barrier . . . this, however, is no longer necessary and in fact retards their [Mexicans'] education." Ruiz's language policies shifted as political talking points changed from Pan-Americanism during the war to desegregation afterwards, showing he was willing to use language in whatever way would help white Angelinos accept his community.[29]

The senate education committee accepted the limited integration bill on its third presentation in 1947. However, Warren wanted complete desegregation. His aide asked Ruiz why Mexicans cared about a law that only "applies to American Indians, Chinese, Japanese, and Mongolians." Ruiz reminded him that the assembly bill was defeated the day that Mexico's foreign relations minister visited the governor's mansion. Ruiz also wrote to Warren, reminding him of a 1945 encounter when the governor "stated in strong terms that it was [his] belief that Section 8003 of the Education Code ought to be repealed." Just three years after advocating for Japanese internment, Warren wanted to integrate California schools. That made 1947 a key moment in the history of desegregation. While Warren waited for repeal bills to pass both the assembly and the senate, the Ninth Circuit Court of Appeals upheld Judge McCormick's ruling that Westminster School District could not exclude Latin-origin students like Sylvia Méndez.[30]

———————————

As public opinion swung in favor of integrated schools, these civil rights victories helped Marie Hughes build academic support for bilingual education. In December 1945, a few months after she testified in the *Mendez* trial and a week before her conference on intergroup education, she traveled to Texas to attend the First Regional Conference on the Education of Spanish-Speaking People in the Southwest, organized by Professor George I. Sánchez. Like Hughes, Sánchez embraced intercultural education, calling it "the keystone in the structure of cultural relations between the United States and the other American republics." When he proposed creating a monograph series on Mexican American education issues, the attendees elected him editor. Sánchez went on to edit nine volumes from 1946 to 1951. Some of the earliest articles supporting bilingual education appeared in these publications. Marie Hughes made sure that the relationship between language learning and school segregation was also emphasized. By 1951, Hughes and Sánchez saw desegregating schools and reforming language instruction as essential tasks for Spanish-speaking educators.[31]

The 1945 conference addressed language instruction and desegregation independently. Language helped Sánchez redefine so-called Mexicans as "Spanish-speaking people," since the majority of this population was actually American citizens. While he acknowledged that two million people in the Southwest called Spanish "their mother tongue, their vernacular," he also noted that, "In fact, for some the home-language is English; for others a part-English, part-Spanish vernacular is the rule." Sánchez seemed to avoid the situation of Mexican immigrants, but this was not the most pressing issue of the 1945 conference. At that meeting, Hughes and Sánchez signed a petition calling for a socioeconomic survey to measure how each state's "pattern of segregation, isolation, and discrimination" affected Spanish speakers. Such a survey would be particularly useful in California, where Spanish speakers made up 30 percent of elementary school enrollment but less than 8 percent of secondary school students. The conference attendees concluded that the "language handicap" was one of many "other problems," such as adult education and teacher training, facing the Mexican-origin community. In 1945, Hughes and Sánchez did not yet see language and segregation as inseparable elements in improving the education of Spanish speakers.[32]

In a panel that she chaired, Hughes reported that at this point language was not even the primary tool used to integrate the schools. This panel recommended five remedial measures to achieve "complete elimination of the segregated school." "Preparation of reading and language materials" was the final point, coming after such items as understanding "the social and psychological problems involved in minority-group and lower-class status." These steps might keep some students from dropping out of segregated schools, but Hughes also sought more specific reforms, including "such intermediary steps as moving the seventh and eighth grades . . . to the 'Anglo' school, assemblies, play days, picnics, musical participation, and other forms of inter-communication" to allow Anglo and Mexican American students to become comfortable with integration. When she described segregated schools as "a direct impediment to the improvement of our relations with Spanish-speaking people in international affairs," Hughes hinted that integration was more urgently needed than bilingual education. Her hesitation to link language learning to desegregation suggested that the two agendas were not yet connected in 1945.[33]

Six years later, Hughes made that connection the cornerstone of her comments at Sánchez's 1951 Conference on the Education of Spanish-Speaking People in the Southwest. Now the two educators attacked segregation by arguing that it hurt language acquisition. Hughes argued that language instruction provided the best evidence that segregated schools were "educationally unsound and undesirable." She called the idea that Spanish-speaking children could learn English in a classroom without English-speaking peers a "false assumption" because they lacked "a chance to *hear* the language spoken . . . and there is no incentive to speak in English." As she had testified in the *Mendez* case, Hughes maintained in the conference proceedings that children developed language skills by "associating freely with youngsters of their own age on the playground, going to and from school, during the lunch period, and so forth." By 1951 LA's leading minority group educator went one step further, insisting that segregation actually retarded language acquisition. "The wonder," she concluded, "is that so many of our Spanish-speaking people have become bi-lingual."[34]

Along the same lines, Hughes looked at language learning as the best reason to integrate schools. Segregation was as detrimental for Anglo students as it was for minorities, she argued, because it taught both groups "the myth of superiority and inferiority." "English-speaking children very much need to hear another language spoken," she stated, "so that they will recognize that other languages are a part of the reality of the world." Hughes took her argument one step further than she had in the *Mendez* trial, insisting that bilingual classrooms would benefit students of all races. Having come to believe that all children would come out "even better when they attempt to learn another language," Hughes began to link language learning and integration. Progressive educators had finally shifted the desegregation debate away from Americanization and toward immigrant students and bilingual education.[35]

George Sánchez seconded the idea that learning multiple languages benefited all students, saying that segregation by language was "illogical, without foundation in fact, or contrary to sound educational theory." Just as Hughes had done in *Mendez*, Sánchez challenged school districts to prove that low language abilities justified the need for segregated schools. He went beyond Judge McCormick's equivocation about the accuracy of language tests, arguing that such assessments were arbitrary. "What is the standard of English proficiency which governs the point at which segregation begins and ends?" he asked. "Are all English-speaking as well as Spanish-speaking children measured against this standard?" The lack of language tests exposed racial bias as the motivation for segregation, but Sánchez showed that segregation was irrational because policies differed by school district. Why would some districts separate all Spanish speakers while others only segregated elementary schools? What about districts that separated races in different classrooms in the same building? "The very lack of uniformity," Sánchez insisted, "is irrefutable evidence that the educational destinies of these Spanish-name children are being made the butt either of amateurish, or wholly misguided . . . reasoning." By demanding objective language standards to justify segregation, the professor applied academic principles to his integration agenda.[36]

Building on the *Mendez* ruling, Sánchez insisted that desegregated schools required a minimal bilingual education program. He started with the language tests that he and Judge McCormick had agreed upon. Sánchez wanted a narrow exam that "should measure, not English in all its aspects, but *the English which is basic to the school activities of that class.*" This type of screening would single out students who needed extra language lessons. For example, Sánchez objected that speaking drills to change "the child's pronunciation of *thees* to *this*" were irrelevant to using language for instruction. The Texan pointed out that Anglo youth required similar drills in "correcting *payner* to *painter*, or *ya'll* to *you all.*" Sánchez suggested "at the very worst, the Spanish-speaking child needs only to acquire some 600 words in order to do as well in the first grade as his English-speaking fellow students." He believed that most monolingual Spanish children already knew these words in Spanish and, with minimal tutoring, they could keep up with their Anglophone classmates. Rejecting the alleged vocabulary deficiency, the professor argued that language ability was not a valid excuse for segregated Mexican schools.[37]

Sánchez carried the language learning argument to its logical extension in the desegregation debate. He had publicly supported the plaintiffs in the *Mendez* trial in 1945 as well as those in a Texas school integration case in 1948. Yet Sánchez was equivocal when Thurgood Marshall, representing the National Association for the Advancement of Colored People (NAACP), asked him for advice while preparing to argue *Brown v. Board of Education* before the Supreme Court. Sánchez told Marshall that his Texas testimony rejected "the pedagogical soundness of segregation that is based on the 'language handicap' excuse." He questioned whether linking language and integration would help African Americans in the way it had Mexican Americans. Marshall followed Sánchez's advice. Rather than discussing language ability, he used the doll experiments of Kenneth and Mamie Clark and data from multiple school districts to show that segregated schools provided inherently unequal education.[38]

While Marie Hughes was fighting to promote Mexican American integration initiatives in courtrooms and conferences in the early postwar years, another former teacher from LA County was fighting for integration of another ethnic group. Throughout 1945, the federal WRA closed internment camps and allowed Japanese evacuees to resettle in cities across America. The day before David Marcus filed *Mendez v. Westminster* in federal district court, the WRA director sent camp education materials to California's superintendent of public instruction to guide local "school officials dealing with the adjustment problem that will prevail with the return of these children to normal school work." Three months later, at the final commencement ceremonies of Manzanar High School, the camp's Buddhist minister and Catholic priest delivered the baccalaureate in Japanese and English, respectively. Language education did not factor into that evening's speeches about the reintegration of Issei, Nisei, and Sansei (third-generation) students into mainstream American society. As evacuees reflected on their incarceration experiences, California educators like Afton Nance insisted that inclusion and assimilation were more urgent priorities than language instruction.[39]

Nance offered a practical perspective on Nisei reintegration. She wrote "The Return of the Nisei" for N. D. Myers, her former supervisor, when he was editing *Education for Cultural Unity.* Myers asked Nance to author this essay because he knew that she had kept in touch with the internees she had once taught in Palos Verdes Estates. Now a rural schools supervisor in Riverside County, Nance urged "California educators to take a position of leadership in the reintegration" of the Nisei because it was teachers who had Americanized them in the first place. Nance was reiterating a reintegration plan she had first proposed in a speech to southern California principals in Ontario, in San Bernardino County.[40]

In that speech, Nance argued that evacuated students had suffered few if any assimilation setbacks in internment camp schools. She praised their "strong academic records" and was even pleased by the "somewhat greater participation" in student government and class activities that had been available to Nisei internees in their segregated schools. Nance also insisted that the Americanized Japanese students deserved most of the credit for creating strong learning environments. She stated there was "almost a desperate clinging to American ways, and letters from children in the centers to former playmates and teachers show they turn with longing to the life they knew 'on the outside.'" For Nance, it was a foregone conclusion that Japanese Americans had the right to return to California. Dismissing calls to delay reintegration, she devoted her talk to a specific question: "How will they [Nisei children] be accepted when they return to California schools?"[41]

Nance expected only minor problems in reintegrating the returning students. Acknowledging that "individual cases of maladjustment . . . may be expected, even aggressive behavior, as the pattern of camp life has tended to break down parental control," she advocated that teachers should treat a difficult Nisei like any struggling student, keeping in mind that three years of incarceration for "a whole people, accused of no crime," would affect children of all races. "In most cases the Tomis and the Kazues have come in, taken their places in the schoolroom, and waited their turns 'up to bat,'" Nance noted. "The schools on the whole have done a good job of making democracy work." Yet she insisted that lingering anti-Japanese prejudice created a "need for principals and teachers as community leaders" to support reintegration. In her vision of postwar reform, "Opposition to the return of the Japanese American group will not come from schools, but from our adult groups. We, as educators, have an obligation to be informed, . . . [to] make the streets of California towns and villages safe and pleasant places for young Melvin Shiramizu, whose father died for the principles of democracy taught in some schools."[42]

Nance suggested several ways to combat anti-Japanese sentiments through school programs, but she was more passionate about promoting democracy. "We must make real for these young Americans of Japanese ancestry the faith that we gave them" before the war, she said, referring to her past students in LA County. "Most of us have stood at the flag salute with these Nisei boys and girls—we have held out the promise of 'liberty and justice for all.'" Nance was also proud that her classes integrated Anglo and Mexican-origin students alongside the Nisei, boasting that "before the evacuation these children were daily being taught in the schools that democracy meant freedom and justice for all, regardless of color, race or creed." She believed reintegrating the Nisei was part of the larger desegregation project occurring across California after the *Mendez* trial that summer. Schools had to make integration successful, Nance argued, because "until the streets of California towns and villages are safe and pleasant places for Melvin Shiramizu, they are *not* safe for Rudy Garcia, for Tommy Holland, colored, or for any white child." The English teacher did not discuss language instruction in the context of Nisei reintegration, but she vowed that reincorporating Nisei children after four years of internment was integral to school desegregation after the war.[43]

Nisei writer Mary Oyama shared Nance's view. Oyama had spent the war with her husband and son at Santa Anita Assembly Center in Los Angeles then Heart Mountain Relocation Camp in Wyoming. She wrote about her family's return to Los Angeles in *Common Ground*, a liberal journal that invited authors of color to address intolerance and build "mutual understanding resulting from a common citizenship." The journal published Oyama's essay, "A Nisei Report from Home," then a year later printed articles by progressives like Langston Hughes and Carey McWilliams, who used his column to praise *Education for Cultural Unity* as "one of the best handbooks yet issued in the field of intercultural education." Oyama may not have seen Nance's "Return of the Nisei" article, but she agreed that Nisei reintegration would reshape education in California. She used her son's language experiences to give the ultimate endorsement for desegregation.[44]

In Oyama's multiracial neighborhood, school was the epicenter for Nisei reintegration. Upon the Oyama family's return to Los Angeles, white friends met them at Union Station and drove them home, where they greeted "our Negro American friend Jean, who had been living in our house the years we had been away." In contrast to his parents' pleasant reunions, Oyama's son was too young to remember any neighbors. Seven-year-old Rickey went to a school where the principal knew many Nisei in Los Angeles and had visited Japan before the war, but the students were uncomfortable with their new classmate. Rickey complained that students didn't know if he was Chinese or Japanese. Mexican Americans called him "Chino" (Chinese). Oyama explained how Rickey used his English language ability to assert his identity on the playground:

> He told his fellow pupils that if he were Chinese he'd speak Chinese, wouldn't he, and if he were Japanese he'd speak Japanese. . . . Later, when someone would inadvertently let out a "Chino," Eddie Olivas, his loyal Mexican American friend, would jump to his defense. "Ricky's a good guy! If he wuz Chinese he'd be in China. If he wuz a Jap, he'd be

in Japan. But he's *here*—see? *So what!*" . . . The children learned soon enough by Rickey's speech and actions that he was just as American as any of them.[45]

Whereas language instruction was a critical component of Mary Hughes's support for school desegregation, language acquisition played a modest role in Mary Oyama's integration outlook. She worried when new neighbors were reluctant to socialize, but her husband learned that they had just moved from Puerto Rico and "could not speak good English" yet. After exchanging plants and pet food, the families became friends. Oyama's article concluded by quoting Dillon Myer, the WRA superintendent, who maintained that internment "has helped the Nisei to discover America and America to discover the Nisei." Oyama also endorsed Afton Nance's agenda to make Nisei reintegration a platform to end racial prejudice in California schools, but she did not promote foreign-language instruction with the vigor of Mexican American activists. However, Angelino efforts in Japan and in the Hawaiian territory made important links between Japanese-language learning and school integration in the postwar civil rights movement.[46]

———————

While educators planned the reintegration of interned children into LA schools, General Douglas MacArthur looked to veteran linguists as he oversaw the military occupation of Japan from 1945 to 1951. MacArthur consulted white and Nisei Angelinos who had experience in language education as he developed a school system for occupied Japan. He relied on graduates of the Military Intelligence Service Language School to teach soldiers the nuances of Japanese society. MIS officers' postwar work achieved two breakthroughs for the Japanese American community back in Los Angeles. By helping MacArthur reform schools in Japan, they improved international relations after the war. MIS language work also persuaded many Anglo GIs that Nisei volunteers were patriotic Americans. The stories of Helen Heffernan as well as John Aiso and other MIS officers illustrate the important role that language instruction played in the US occupation of Japan.

MacArthur asked Helen Heffernan to supervise the elementary schools in occupied Japan. She was an interesting choice because she did not have much experience with Nisei students before the war, when she had headed California's Division of Elementary Education. Her work with the Friends of the Mexicans in the 1920s had prepared her to head the Office of Inter-American Affairs during World War II. She had worked with Spanish-speaking Angelinos in her first two jobs, but she had spent little time with Nisei students in California before she flew to Japan in 1945. Unlike Nance and other LA principals who had brought books and blankets to the Santa Anita Assembly Center and received death threats as a consequence, Heffernan had not publicly opposed internment. In Tokyo, she faced new challenges "in overcoming hostilities and suspicions, in securing facilities, and in coping with language barriers and military regulations." Heffernan worked with Japanese educators to rewrite children's stories and books on child development. She also brought an exhibition of California children's art to display in a bombed-out department store in Tokyo. She wanted to be remembered as someone who "worked in Japan not as a conqueror, but as one who sought to turn their educational system away from militarism, Shintoism, and racial hatred."[47]

Heffernan may have learned about these qualities of Japanese education from a fellow Californian, MIS Language School director John Aiso. He had begun to speak about an American occupation of Japan twenty months before the emperor surrendered. In November 1943, Aiso sat on the International Problems after the War panel with Vice President Henry Wallace. The army used Aiso's address, "The Postwar Reconstruction of Japan," to test public reaction to many policies that MacArthur implemented after 1945. To spread democracy, Aiso argued, "Japan's military might must and will be destroyed, but the peace-loving elements of her society must be given opportunity for normal life and growth." Noting that Japan's imperial system relied on an "insane militarism" that threatened American security, Aiso insisted that "no republican form of government could function successfully until such time as the populous [sic] has been trained for allegiance to concepts (such as embodied in our Constitution) rather than allegiance to ruling personalities." Many of Aiso's proposals for legal, agricultural, and tax reforms in order to develop a civil society became part of Japan's new constitution during the US occupation.[48]

For policymakers who heard the speech, including Helen Heffernan, the most important reform was education, which Aiso called "the greatest factor in social reconstruction." Based on his experiences teaching English in Tokyo and Japanese in Minnesota, he wanted to replace Japan's prewar school system, which he described as a vehicle "to train useful subjects of the Emperor, not so much a quest for truth." Aiso's education agenda gave Heffernan and MacArthur two paradoxical tasks. On one hand, Aiso maintained that "this wall of intellectual isolation must be battered down and the Japanese given opportunity to engage in the free commerce of ideas." At the same time, stopping censorship did not mean an absence of US intervention. Instead, channeling Franklin Roosevelt's vision of an active government, Aiso insisted that the Japanese "are entitled to freedom from want, equal opportunities of earning a livelihood" and "freedom from fear, fear of oppression and discriminatory treatment from the white man." He hoped that the lessons he had learned studying Japanese in Los Angeles and Tokyo would help Heffernan create schools that would foster those freedoms.[49]

As Aiso tried to improve life for children in Japan, his former MIS students accomplished much to improve the Nisei image in America. Appreciation for the MIS Language School had begun long before the occupation, with Aiso's prescient 1943 speech. Since he was speaking at a public panel, Aiso had worn civilian clothes to keep the school a military secret. The host, however, had introduced him as an American of Japanese ancestry who "is perform-ing specially [sic] important service" and whose views on postwar Japan were "too often overlooked." The next year, Aiso was promoted to lieutenant colonel, becoming the highest-ranking Nisei officer during the war. The school's student population peaked in October 1945, two months after the bombing of Hiroshima and Nagasaki, when the military needed even more translators for the occupation of Japan. In 1946, before the MIS moved to Monterey, California, to begin training students in Korean and Russian, General MacArthur asked Aiso to join him in Japan. To purge the Japanese government of its most threatening imperial officials, MacArthur had to rely on the investigations and opinions of Japanese Americans. These Nisei officers, many of them Angelinos like John Aiso, became genuine war heroes because of the language skills they had acquired at the secret MIS Language School.[50]

Many MIS alumni won military decorations during the war, including five Silver Stars, fifty Bronze Stars, and fifteen Purple Hearts. One Silver Star went to Kenji Yasui, who owned an import-export company in Los Angeles. Yasui was a Kibei who went to college in Tokyo and took on a dangerous mission in Burma behind enemy lines. After swimming to an island full of Japanese soldiers, he pretended to be a Japanese officer. "Japan has lost the war," Yasui told them in their native language. "Lay down your weapons and follow me." Two soldiers blew themselves up with hand grenades and a third tried to kill him. Kenji continued the ruse, barking out orders to swim across the river and surrender. "Afterwards he learned the Japanese had twenty rounds each and had a bead on him when he came ashore," recalled a former State Department language officer in Tokyo. "Only because he started shouting military commands in Japanese did they hold fire." Yasui earned the nickname "little Sergeant York" (after a World War I hero) and, like John Aiso, he won the Legion of Merit. When MIS records were declas-sified in 1973, Aiso's former students learned that Harry Truman had called them "our human secret weapons" and that, according to MacArthur's chief of intelligence, "the 6,000 Niseis shortened the Pacific war by two years."[51]

These honors did not mean that Nisei linguists felt accepted in the US military. Upon graduating from the MIS Language School, each officer was assigned to a separate army combat unit so that every mission had a translator. Many white soldiers were uncomfortable working with the Nisei. MIS alums "may have been the only soldiers in history to have bodyguards to protect us from our own forces in combat zones so we would not be mistaken for the enemy," Aiso explained. Nisei soldiers provided invaluable services by interrogating prisoners and translating captured battle plans. Yet their training in Japanese language and culture made some GIs suspicious about their ultimate loyalties. The combat records of MIS linguists indicate that all language experiences, positive and negative, prepared Nisei soldiers for the problems they would face in postwar Los Angeles.[52]

MIS Language School alumnus James Oda of North Hollywood hinted that discrimination hurt the military more than the Nisei linguists. He was among the first fourteen Angelinos who responded to an MIS recruiting flyer in the Manzanar mess hall in December 1942, and Aiso appointed him instructor of propaganda writing the next spring. In a 1982 article, Oda criticized the US Navy for rejecting the army's MIS model of recruiting Japanese Americans and instead admitting only white students to its language school. The navy viewed Nisei officers as security risks unfit to interrogate prisoners, and it credited white officers for breaking Japan's diplomatic code, called Magic or Murasaki, before Pearl Harbor. Oda admitted that US cryptanalysts had solved most of Magic, but not all of it, by 1940, before Japanese Americans could join the navy. "It makes one wonder how fast a team of competent Nisei linguists could have cracked the Japanese enemy code if given a chance," he stated. "The problem of deciphering Magic was child's play as compared to the cryptographic method of the Japanese Army." Oda could not make public comments until 1982 because the MIS remained classified during the Korean and Vietnam Wars. The silence about Nisei intelligence work illustrates how Cold War diplomacy stifled public support for patriotic language-learning programs.[53]

Nisei linguists were also effective at interrogating prisoners of war. Aiso, Oda, and other instructors had trained the linguists to treat Japanese captives "as individual human beings . . . rather than as animals or fanatical enemy soldiers." Angelino Karl Yoneda kept records from the Office of War Intelligence in India, where he wrote literature to lure soldiers away from the Imperial Army. The propaganda appealed to hungry Japanese troops with photographs of American rice and canned corn alongside soy sauce and chopsticks. "You are like rats in a trap with no place to flee," Yoneda wrote in Japanese. "Here is hot rice to fill your stomach. Sashimi and pickles." Other propaganda included surrender passes that sympathized with potential

Nisei linguists at Fort Snelling, Minnesota. *Courtesy of Minnesota Historical Society.*

defectors. "You have only two fates," the passes read. "Annihilation . . . Or good treatment behind the Allied lines. Think it over. Ghosts in Yasukuni cannot help Japan. Death without meaning is only for fools." These passes proved that MIS officers knew many Japanese men believed that they would meet their family and fellow soldiers in Yasukuni (heaven). The passes "never used the word 'surrender' in Japanese because we did not want to humiliate them," Yoneda explained. "We always used a phrase such as . . . 'We will not reveal your name. We will protect your life with honor.'" Nisei linguists hoped their familiarity with Japanese culture would put the prisoners at ease and lead to effective interrogation.[54]

Many MIS veterans had fond memories of the enemy soldiers they met. When Tad Ichinokuchi was assigned to the court-martial of Tomoyuki Yamashita, the Imperial Japanese Army general who had conquered Malaya and Singapore in 1941 and 1942, he befriended the general's interpreter by lending him a Japanese-English dictionary so that he could translate testimony in prison each evening. "He's quite a nice fellow and I often try to bring him a cigarette while we talk of Japan," Ichinokuchi wrote. The Angelino was also curious about the cultures of Yamashita's victims. He was moved by eyewitness accounts of the "Tiger of Malaya's" conquest because "testimony given by a Filipino in his native Tagalog tongue is certainly a beautiful piece of oratory." As a translator, he regretted that "when interpreted by a slow stuttering interpreter, who pronounces his t's with a hissing 'ssh' sound, the testimony loses the shade of its colorful eloquence" in the original Tagalog. For Ichinokuchi, participating in interrogations and military trials signified the power of learning a foreign language.[55]

Ichinokuchi balanced his interest in Japan with his American loyalties. His court-martial records reveal an assimilated Angelino full of good-humored fascination with his heritage country. "The whole thing is just like a Hollywood movie," Tad told a friend from Los Angeles. "First tears and sobs and then horror and laughter. . . . This is your Manila Correspondent, Tad Ichinokuchi, signing off." Ichinokuchi had grown up on a ranch in Norwalk, in rural LA County, where he picked strawberries with Issei, Nisei, and Mexican laborers. He had two childhood idols: Takeichi Nishi, the Japanese equestrian show jumper who won a gold medal at the Los Angeles Olympics in 1932, and John Aiso. Although Nishi became a lieutenant in the Japanese Imperial Army, he remained popular in the United States. When Aiso's linguists discovered that he was commanding tanks at the Battle of Iwo Jima in 1945, they broadcast thirty-six consecutive nightly appeals to Nishi to surrender. Ichinokuchi once traded a month's rations of US beer for "a kilo of rice and a can of Del Monte brand sardines." The sardines were an American product, but the Nisei was desperate for sashimi and rice, although he was "too dumb to know that cooking rice in your helmet could take the temper out of the metal." These anecdotes demonstrate the complexities of the MIS linguists' outlook toward America and Japan and the lessons about language they learned during the war and the occupation of Japan.[56]

Many Americans knew bilingual Nisei were vital to postwar peace. In 1947, MacArthur invited Roger Baldwin, founder of the American Civil Liberties Union (ACLU), to survey the state of civil liberties in occupied Japan. Baldwin reported that Nisei "constitute a bridge between Americans and Japanese [that is] invaluable in the process of democratization" echoing the "world friendship" agenda that Angelino educators of all ethnicities had espoused before the war. The ACLU director had parochial assumptions of nationalism, insisting that all Asians believed America was the stronger nation, and that "the Nisei play upon the Japanese attitude of looking up to America, accentuated now by the Occupation." Baldwin highlighted their language skills as essential to MacArthur's mission. "The Nisei are, of course, exceedingly valuable aides to the U.S. authorities. Their bilingual abilities open jobs as interpreters, translators, and censors," he boasted. Noting high demand for "educated bilingual Nisei residents" in postwar Japan, Baldwin was amazed at their American patriotism, even in their parents' homeland. "One has only to glance through the special Occupation telephone directory in Tokyo for American officials, sprinkled liberally with Japanese names, to appreciate the importance of Nisei service."[57]

This did not mean that America rewarded all Nisei who lived in postwar Japan. In fact, the United States stripped US citizenship from about five thousand Nisei simply for voting in the Japanese election that approved MacArthur's occupation government. "They thought they were doing something to promote 'Americanism,'" Baldwin lamented. "Scores were grief-stricken when the U.S. consul to whom they applied for U.S. papers told them the cost of their enthusiasm." Baldwin was more outraged by the restrictions placed on the Nisei who had participated in public education. "I met young Japanese American women who had taught school in Japan during the war," he said, "only to discover when they came to claim their U.S. citizenship that those in public school jobs had lost it while those in private school jobs kept it." Baldwin sent the JACL to help Nisei in this predicament. A single ad in Tokyo's English-language daily, *The Nippon Times*, drew thousands of responses. The ACLU and JACL took these citizenship restrictions seriously and, just as they had done in recent amicus briefs for *Mendez v. Westminster*, the groups used language education cases to expose the injustice. Defending schoolteachers in enemy nations fit the ACLU mission, but it is also easy to understand American uneasiness about reinstating citizenship. The US government gave expatriate Nisei who taught in Japan's state schools the same status as the Tule Lake internees who refused to sign loyalty oaths. Despite their service in internment camps and overseas, Nisei language instructors remained targets of loyalty attacks at the dawn of the Cold War.[58]

While John Aiso and Nisei linguists set up a new school system in occupied Japan, thousands of Japanese Americans were preparing for their postwar return to the Pacific coast. The former evacuees focused on reintegrating their children into existing schools rather than demanding racial desegregation. The Nisei did not lobby for legislation as Manuel Ruiz did, but Japanese-language schools did open promptly after the war. The officials who approved the rapid rebirth of language education were Paul McCormick and Earl Warren. The judge who wrote the *Mendez v. Westminster* decision and the governor who repealed the racialized Education Codes appreciated Japanese-language schools because of their prior work with Angelinos like Ruiz, Felicitas Méndez, and John Aiso. The postwar decisions of McCormick and Warren reveal that California's leading legal minds applied national debates over desegregation to Japanese-language schools, and their graduates, in Los Angeles.

Mendez v. Westminster addressed Mexican American segregation, but some Japanese Angelinos joined the integration effort. The JACL wrote an amicus brief, arguing that the prejudiced testimony of the Garden Grove school superintendent threatened all students of color because, "if appellants can justify discrimination on the basis of ancestry only, then who can tell what minority group will be next." Relying on a war reference, they reasoned that "if we learned one lesson from the horrors of Nazism, it is that no minority group, and in fact, no person is safe, once the State . . . can arbitrarily discriminate against any person or group." That the JACL compared school segregation to the Holocaust after World War II suggests Japanese Angelinos remembered their own internment experiences during their neighbors' desegregation lawsuit. One of those families was the Munemitsus, who leased their forty-acre farm in Westminster before relocating to an internment camp. Their tenants, Gonzalo and Felicitas Méndez, helped them maintain ownership. Profits from farming asparagus also gave the Méndezes enough resources to hire an attorney and sue the Westminster school board over its segregation practices. When the Munemitsus returned in 1946, they allowed the Méndezes to remain on the farm to finish the harvest and let their children complete their first year at an integrated school. Perhaps the Munemitsus' kindness ultimately benefited all Japanese Americans because it enabled Felicitas Méndez to meet Paul McCormick at the trial. Two years after Felicitas's testimony taught the judge that "Mexican" and "Spanish" were the same language, McCormick removed the wartime ban on Japanese-language schools.[59]

In 1948, McCormick was one of three federal judges who heard *Mo Hock Ke Lok Po v. Stainback*, a case concerning Chinese-language instruction, segregation, and ethnic minorities. In this lawsuit, two Chinese teachers challenged a 1943 law passed by the Hawaiian Legislature after the attacks on Pearl Harbor that closed the island's Japanese- and Chinese-language schools. Hawaiian Nisei were not interned, but their Japanese school buildings were "permanently abandoned" and "voluntarily turned over to the government." When three Chinese schools sued to resume language instruction after the war, they were fortunate to face two judges who had written rulings in favor of integration and ethnic minorities. Since Hawaii was still a territory, the case was heard in California, where McCormick and a Southern District federal court colleague were joined by Judge William Denman from the

Ninth Circuit Court. The appellate court's most liberal member, Denman had dissented from the majority opinion in *Korematsu v. United States*, which found Japanese internment to be constitutional. When his colleagues upheld the *Mendez* decision with a ruling that was more moderate than McCormick's initial finding, a disappointed Denman wrote a concurring opinion insisting that any form of racial discrimination was unconstitutional. JACL attorneys must have been thrilled when Denman joined McCormick in Los Angeles to deliberate Hawaii's language school law. Sure enough, the two judges who had most favored desegregating Mexican schools two years earlier reinstated Japanese-language schools in 1948.[60]

The *Mo Hock Ke Lok Po* ruling applied language-acquisition principles that McCormick and Denman had learned in the *Mendez* trial. Just as one Orange County school superintendent had tried to justify segregation by arguing that it accommodated the "bilingual handicap" of Spanish-speaking students, the Hawaii legislature asserted that the "use of foreign languages by children of average intelligence . . . definitely detract from their ability to properly understand and assimilate their normal studies in the English language." Remembering the Méndez lawyer's response that students who spoke more languages benefited intellectually, the LA judges were impressed that many children in Hawaii tended to "frame their thoughts and to express them in three distinct languages": English, their heritage language, and pidgin, or "an extension of the lingua franca of the China, South Asiatic, and Malayan coast cities in which the foreign residents conduct their . . . relations with the lesser educated resident nationals." McCormick and Denman treated all these vernaculars with the same respect they had shown when Felicitas Méndez had expressed her pride in American values in two languages.[61]

McCormick and Denman tied their local case to the national foreign policy debate ongoing in the 1948 presidential campaign. That summer Earl Warren was nominated as the Republican Party vice-presidential candidate. Cold War politics were central to the campaign, given that President Truman had ordered the Berlin Airlift in June 1948 and General MacArthur, who was overseeing the occupation of Japan, had competed with Warren for the Republican nomination. In their ruling, the judges wrote that foreign-language schools benefited American diplomacy:

> We do not agree with the defendants that such a denial to . . . such a large proportion of children of the constitutional right to secure a foreign language for them is warranted to secure the elimination of the harm it seeks to avoid for those of lesser ability. It is for the brighter ones that there is the greater gain . . . not only in personal mental

growth and satisfaction and in increased business opportunities but, now, in opportunities in service to his government's need of foreign language experts.[62]

Denman used similar logic of promoting American security and prosperity when he wrote to Warren urging repeal of the California Education Codes. The judge urged the governor to end school segregation a month after he voted on *Mendez* in the Ninth Circuit Court. He emphasized diplomacy when he told Warren that "everyone who has any knowledge of the vigilance of the Latin American Embassies in Washington knows that within a month every ambassador will have been informed of the *Westminster*" case. As he campaigned for the Republican ticket in 1948, international diplomacy drove Warren to support local efforts for foreign-language learning and school desegregation.[63]

The judges in the *Mendez* and *Mo Hock Ke Lok Po* cases were among many Angelinos who influenced Earl Warren's thinking in ways that led him to conclude that "separate educational facilities are inherently unequal" in his 1954 *Brown v. Board of Education* opinion. Manuel Ruiz spent two years lobbying the governor to revise California's Education Codes. Syndicated columnist Drew Pearson reported that shortly before Warren signed the repeal of Section 8003, he told a state senator, "I personally do not see how we can carry out the spirit of the United Nations if we deny fundamental rights to our Latin American neighbors."[64] Warren's position on desegregation was also inspired by another Japanese-language instructor. In his final year as governor, Warren appointed John Aiso to the Los Angeles Municipal Court. The founder of the MIS Language School became the first Japanese American judge outside of Hawaii. The two had never met before 1952, but the governor may have remembered the letter that Aiso sent Warren when he was promoting internment during his first gubernatorial campaign. President Eisenhower appointed Warren as chief justice in 1953, and the chief justice later invited Aiso to have lunch in his chambers at the Supreme Court. The two judges born in Los Angeles developed a close relationship, and Warren met with groups of reserve officers from Southern California every time Aiso brought them to Washington, D.C. In a 1970 oral history, Aiso said that he did not expect Warren to express regret for his wartime internment campaign. Yet he also believed that the chief justice's opinions on cases like *Brown v. Board of Education* represented Warren's efforts to right a wrong. In oratory as eloquent as his salutatorian speech at Hollywood High's 1926 graduation, Aiso insisted that he was not the only Japanese Angelino who had influenced Earl Warren:

Judge John Fujio Aiso. *Courtesy of Hollywood High School Library.*

I have not brought [Warren's internment advocacy] up with him directly. Recently, there have been attacks on him by the Sansei [third-generation], who were demanding a public retraction. They have picketed him when he has appeared publicly. I have written him. I said, "If there's anything I can do, I'd be happy to do so." He has replied that he is grateful for my offer. He looked at it this way, "Those were war days, and in hindsight, I was in error. But the bell has been rung, and what has been rung cannot be unrung." . . . I have often wondered whether this experience of the Chief Justice has not had an influence upon him in his outlook towards civil rights. I have always found him a man that grew in stature with new responsibilities. If, in an indirect way, this experience led to the opportunity of taking a new look when he was free of direct political pressures, then I think the Nisei have in that way also had a minor role in the future destiny of our country.[65]

Aiso's statement illustrates his belief that the chief justice who overturned the doctrine of "separate but equal" was impressed by the six thousand officers who studied Japanese at the MIS Language School Aiso had created. Those patriotic Nisei were not nearly as radical as Mexican American students who walked out of their high school in a protest for better bilingual education in 1968. Yet their wartime experiences established a connection between language education and racial integration that escalated in the 1960s.

5 | BILINGUAL EDUCATION AS POLITICAL MOBILIZATION, 1954–1967

In 1963, Sal Castro got his first full-time job, as a social science teacher in the Los Angeles Unified School District (LAUSD), founded two years earlier. The assignment at downtown Belmont High School was a homecoming in more ways than one, even though Castro was not a Belmont alumnus. Born in East LA thirty years earlier, the US Army veteran had grown up in downtown Los Angeles, graduated from a nearby Catholic school, and done his student teaching at Belmont. The school was four miles west of Roosevelt High, across the Los Angeles River from Boyle Heights, where Mexican and Japanese students had created the World Friendship Club before World War II. Two decades later, 65 percent of Belmont's students were Mexican American, but Castro was one of just three Spanish speakers on the faculty, an ability he had honed visiting his father in Mazatlán as a child. Students were quickly drawn to Castro's charismatic leadership and organizing tactics, which incorporated Mexican language and culture into school activities. Events in his first, and only, semester at Belmont inspired five years of enthusiastic student activism that culminated in the "Blowouts" of 1968, when thousands of Mexican American students would walk out of seven high schools in East LA to demand bilingual education.[1]

Castro quickly confronted many injustices that the majority of the Mexican American students at Belmont suffered. He noticed that no Mexican Americans were in the advanced English class or on the student council. Castro recruited his own candidates, but the faculty sponsor disqualified each Mexican American application even though the students' grades were

Sal Castro with students at Lincoln High School, March 1968. *Courtesy of Los Angeles Times Photographic Archives, Department of Special Collections, Charles E. Young Research Library, University of California, Los Angeles.*

high enough to stand for election. After Castro persuaded the vice principal to reinstate the students' eligibility, he organized them into an ethnic ticket, which they named the Tortilla Movement. The young teacher crossed the administration's line at the assembly where all the candidates gave their campaign speeches. Castro had advised the students to end their addresses with a sentence in Spanish, asking classmates "por favor, voten por mí" [please vote for me]. Because students were not allowed to speak in foreign languages at Belmont assemblies, the principal stopped the assembly after the first Tortilla Movement speech. She suspended Castro the next day, and the district soon transferred him to Lincoln High in East LA, where he would organize student walkouts in 1968. While these walkouts placed Castro at the center of the Chicano civil rights movement, his leadership of students had begun five years earlier when he had challenged Belmont's language ban.[2]

Most scholars of the 1968 Blowouts are social scientists who have analyzed the growth of Chicano grassroots organizing without considering the wider context of language education. In *Speaking American* I emphasize events like the Tortilla Movement's Spanish speeches to illustrate how language learning inspired political activism in LA schools. Just as LA educators had promoted programs like the Home Teacher Act to facilitate Americanization in the Progressive Era, Anglo and Mexican Angelinos used language learning to launch broader civil rights campaigns at the local, state, and national levels in the 1960s. Although Japanese Americans were less vocal in these debates, the campaigns still included a more diverse set of voices than during the postwar era, when lawyers made legal arguments for desegregation and bilingual education. Some Anglo administrators in Los Angeles extended the traditions of liberal reformers, proposing new classes in English as a Second Language (ESL) and sending teachers to Spanish-language boot camp to better serve their limited-English students. Language instruction reforms were even more radical by 1968, when thousands of students marched off their campuses. By that time the Chicano movement was in full swing, and Mexican American youths who demanded Spanish-speaking teachers with an appreciation for Mexican American culture, were opposed by reactionary politicians who believed bilingual education could expand California's conservative constituency. Increasingly ambitious programs inspired a new generation of activists to organize radically different political agendas around similar language-learning ideas. A culture clash emerged when Chicano students realized their efforts to make Spanish-language instruction central to their identity as ethnic minorities could not coexist with conservative campaigns to confine bilingual education to existing English-only assimilation courses that restricted and racialized access to American citizenship.[3]

Meanwhile, other Angelinos were using language education to fight for civil rights. While Sal Castro endorsed new ideas about bilingual/bicultural curricula in East LA, Afton Nance confronted the Bracero labor program as she worked to reform rural schools. Just as she had supported her Nisei former students while they were interned at Manzanar, Nance devoted herself to the children of braceros, migrant farmworkers from Mexico who came to the United States as temporary contract laborers from 1942 to 1964. In 1948 Nance moved to Sacramento, where she teamed with another former LA County educator, Helen Heffernan, to design California's first ESL program to improve the schooling of migrant children. After promoting projects in both Japanese- and Spanish-language instruction during the war, these women brought an even more progressive approach to their work in rural schools. Introduced in 1963, Their ESL program implemented ideas about racial and linguistic integration that progressives had advocated for in *Mendez v. Westminster* two decades earlier. A more radical vision of language instruction came from Patricia Heffernan Cabrera, a teacher education specialist at the University of Southern California (USC), who established the Rural-Migrant Teacher Corps in 1968. This program immersed LA County teachers in the language and culture of the migrant communities they served, signaling that a new generation of Anglo administrators had embraced an empathetic form of language instruction. Whereas Helen Heffernan had developed ESL classes to help migrant children learn English, Patricia Heffernan Cabrera insisted that the burden of language acquisition lay primarily on Anglo teachers who had to communicate with students in Spanish.

After World War II, Afton Nance advocated on behalf of Mexican Ameri- can youth just as she had fought for the rights of Nisei evacuees during the war. While Nance kept in touch with former Nisei students after they returned from Manzanar, her new job as rural schools supervisor in Riverside County introduced her to migrant families from Mexico. She developed a "model intercultural program" in Riverside schools, which emphasized the benefits of racial integration. The Riverside program impressed Helen Heffernan, who subsequently hired Nance as a curriculum consultant for the California Department of Education in 1948. For her part Nance admired Heffernan's work to restructure elementary schools in occupied Japan and also learned about her new supervisor's previous work at the Los Angeles Office of Inter- American Affairs.[4]

Nance's first efforts with the Mexican American community echoed her previous language-learning activism. She was still in touch with the American Friends Service Committee, which had opposed Japanese internment in World War II and, in 1956, sponsored a survey about the educational needs of Spanish-speaking farmworker families who took their children out of school to work in the fields. In one county, church volunteers set up a school bus outside the migrant camps and offered "make-up" classes to the child laborers. Though this resembled La Escuelita, San Bernardino County's roving rural classroom that in 1928 had offered language instruction to migrant workers, there was a key difference. Thirty years later, the instructors in the church bus were credentialed teachers who spoke fluent Spanish. Nance's allies believed that "teachers with a speaking knowledge of Spanish and experience in teaching bi-lingual children are a great asset to school for seasonal farm workers." In 1960, Nance researched the Migrant Citizenship Education Project, which taught itinerant workers how to apply for naturalization and how to protect their status as citizens. Whereas in the Americanization era, the emphasis had been on assimilation through learning English, in the early civil rights era, Nance's inquiries suggested she hoped bilingual education could help immigrants initiate their own pathways to citizenship.[5]

Nance also studied the challenges of migrant education. At the California gathering called Conference on Families Who Follow the Crops in 1960, she outlined a list of proposals to offer continuing education and special high school programs for migrants. In 1961, the Governor's Advisory Committee on Children and Youth funded her proposal "Study of the Education of Children of Migratory Workers." For this study, Nance surveyed superintendents across the Central Valley and visited six migrant school centers. She defined a "migrant child" as a student "whose parents work as seasonal agricultural laborers and who attends at least two schools in different districts during the school year." Seeing the poor condition of schools in migrant camps gave her more empathy for the academic challenges bracero children faced.[6]

Nance's survey covered a wide range of topics and included interview questions for migrant students as well as teachers and administrators. She asked about "the nature and extent of the retardation" of migrant children. In contrast to earlier studies of "retardation," however, Nance's questions implied that she would not accept inequality for migrant students. Instead, she asked rural superintendents how they were meeting bracero children's specific needs, including those for language instruction. In addition, she solicited ideas about what rural schools might need, either from her Sacramento office or from federal legislation. Nance believed her onsite visits to six migrant school centers were particularly important. She interviewed each school's superintendent, attendance clerk, nurse, teachers, and middle school students. The survey ended with writing prompts for bracero children such as, "The school which helped me most." Just as she had urged Nisei students to send letters from internment camps, the former English teacher wanted migrant children to articulate their educational struggles and demands through the written word.[7]

———————

Nance's study culminated in a collaboration with Helen Heffernan to establish California's first ESL program. They introduced their ESL vision at San Jose State College in 1963, several months before LAUSD transferred Sal Castro for urging students to speak Spanish in their campaign speeches. Their report laid out three critical points for bilingual education that would also become central to Castro's Chicano movement a few years later. First, they endorsed new language acquisition techniques that scholars had developed after the war. Second, adopting arguments from *Mendez v. Westminster*, they insisted that racially integrated classrooms would help immigrants gain English fluency. Finally, embracing the notion that children were better students when they took pride in their heritage, they urged language instructors to study and appreciate the culture of Spanish-speaking peoples. These fundamental ideas, which Nance and Heffernan expressed for the first time at California's inaugural ESL conference, ultimately provided the pedagogical and political arguments behind both the East LA Blowouts and the federal Bilingual Education Act of 1968.[8]

The conference framed ESL experiments as part of the civil rights struggle for migrant students. In Santa Clara County, schools designed social science lessons about the diverse populations that had settled the agricultural areas around San Jose. Nance invited a Mexican American activist to lecture on the organizing campaigns of César Chávez and the Community Service Organization. Instructors planned field trips to the canneries in Monterey as well as units about the immigrant groups who had come from Japan, Hawaii, and Mexico. ESL teachers called for "a special library" of children's books in many languages along with a range of "oral communication" activities for subjects from reading and writing to art and music. The conference called for teacher training in linguistics and debated the "impact of television on the Mexican-American child." Heffernan led two discussions—"The Dropout Problem and the Elementary School" and "A Good Educational Program for Spanish-Speaking Children"—that considered opposing views about the nature of effective ESL programs.[9]

The ESL teachers themselves declared their intentions to implement several changes. One teacher said she had felt "helpless when a non-English speaking child would come to my room," but the panels prepared her to identify the "handicaps" that challenged ESL students. She praised reformers for experimenting with ESL, noting that it was "safer to prohibit the speaking of Spanish on the school grounds and in the school than to take the imaginative step of teaching both English and Spanish." Another instructor intended to organize classes into groups with two Anglo students for each Mexican American classmate because "this ratio will provide a grouping which encourages the use of English." At the same time, these integrated, majority-Anglo classes would still teach an "understanding of the minority culture," because "the Mexican-American child should be proud of his heritage." This teacher hoped that teaching ESL would help students "feel proud of their native language and determined to maintain fluency in it." If students' self-esteem could improve by learning their parents' language, ESL classes could empower migrant children to succeed in school.[10]

Ideas from the attendees at the first conference pushed Nance to further modify her program. In 1966, she invited Heffernan to give the keynote speech at a conference on Mexican American children in Ontario, in San Bernardino County. The supervisor spoke of language education as a tool for Cold War diplomacy. Heffernan advocated for ideas she had learned at the inaugural conference of the new organization TESOL (Teaching of English to Speakers of Other Languages), held in 1964. "From this group comes our brightest hope of developing truly bilingual people to help us meet our problems of international relations more effectively," she stated. Heffernan listed an array of language experiments such as tutoring in language arts and reading; stocking school libraries with Spanish-language books, films, and audio tapes; and "study trips to widen the horizons of children—in the immediate community for the younger children, further afield for the older ones." Heffernan had taught English to Spanish-speaking children for decades, but now she wanted them also to "attain literacy in their own language." She embraced these new theories because she believed that bilingual education could improve the lives of Mexican American children and the migrant communities they came from.[11]

Heffernan was excited about new language programs in Los Angeles and the threads beginning to connect these programs to larger social and economic issues. LAUSD had just published a 213-page manual, *Background Information Related to the Mexican-American Child*, to help teachers avoid stereotyping Spanish speakers. This manual, she argued, marked "a change of attitude, an acceptance of social responsibility on a national, state and local level." Heffernan noted that most Mexican American children still struggled in school because they came from poor families with inadequate housing and medical care. "The problems are not all educational," she emphasized, "but education must be a social conscience, a self-renewing stimulus for the society it serves." The supervisor expressed her social conscience by concluding her keynote with an eight-point plan that came from the Mexican American Parents Conference at Lincoln High, where Sal Castro was teaching in 1966. The demands included hiring more Mexican American faculty and adding an administrative office in East LA, but the first two points addressed language. Mexican parents wanted counselors who could "speak Spanish in order to communicate adequately with the families of the students they counsel." They also wanted a "new and powerful emphasis on teaching Spanish along with English to Mexican-American students, at all grade levels so that the natural asset of being bilingual can be exploited." These demands likely originated with Castro, who had worked as a volunteer counselor for Spanish-speaking parents. Hearing his frustrations, Heffernan endorsed Castro's practical plans calling for bilingual teachers as well as his broader vision to instill ethnic pride in bilingual students.[12]

After the keynote address, Nance moderated a discussion titled "How Can the Promise Be Realized," on how educators could turn these demands into practical realities. Three of the four speakers on her panel worked in LA city schools. One taught at an Eastside junior high that fed students into Roosevelt and Lincoln High Schools. The other two panelists came from Malabar Street Elementary School in Boyle Heights, which had more than one thousand Mexican American students between the ages of three and eight, two-thirds of whom spoke Spanish at home. When asked about poverty and community attitudes toward education, the panelists stressed language learning. The Malabar principal's primary concern was "diagnosing what the learning difficulties are in order to develop a creative, dynamic, and appropriate program for language competency." The school had started several projects to help students achieve English competency by third grade. It purchased portable microphones "to record on tape the confusion of Spanish-English, the vocabulary, the flexibility and complexity of language development." While the principal preached the benefits of technology, Malabar's preschool teacher stressed the importance of parent participation. In contrast to Progressive Era reformers, who encouraged Anglo home teachers to show mothers the proper way to raise children, he reported that parents "holding the teachers in such high esteem has helped to create a feeling of 'hands off' on the part of our Mexican-American community." By communicating to families in Spanish, he recruited fifteen parents to visit his class, with seven mothers attending regularly. The volunteers provided assistance but, more importantly, the Malabar teacher insisted, by coming into the classroom parents showed children they valued education. He knew that, in a bilingual family, actions could speak louder than words.[13]

After Nance's panel, the attendees broke into groups to observe and discuss demonstration lessons by ESL teachers from across southern California. Some lessons led to debates about the latest linguistic principles. Virginia Dominguez, a consultant for non-English speakers in LA's East Elementary District, introduced the attendees to words her pupils did not know and urged them to create their own sentences. Dominguez stressed "pattern practice, substitution drills and other activities that help the child to understand and use a given language structure." A first-grade teacher said she supplemented textbooks with "study trips, the language approach to reading, and activities planned to build pride in the heritage from Mexico and Spain." She urged teachers to invite parents to school activities, make home visits (with "a Spanish-speaking companion if necessary"), and offer adult evening classes to improve parents' English skills. These strategies merged academic ideas that bilingual education advocates had endorsed in *Mendez v. Westminster* with the family engagement approach of Nora Sterry's neighborhood schools in the 1920s. Fusing generations of scholarship and activism, LA educators ultimately embraced language instruction in harmony with a new era of Mexican American organizing in the 1960s.[14]

Many teachers brought ideas from Nance's 1966 conference back to their classrooms in East LA, but one Angelino reframed Nance and Heffernan's ESL program as a force for social justice. Shortly after the 1966 conference, Patricia Heffernan Cabrera took over the ESL program at USC. In short order Cabrera created a curriculum that extended her "classroom" from USC's LA campus to California's Central Valley and the Mexican border. In 1968, she offered her first summer camp in high intensity language training. Against the backdrop of the East LA Blowouts, Cabrera was creating the Rural-Migrant Teacher Corps (RMTC), which she envisioned as a domestic version of John Kennedy's Peace Corps.[15]

Cabrera's intense RMTC curriculum differed from older administrators' approach to teacher training. Like the Peace Corps, the RMTC was a two-year program in which teachers would immerse themselves in a migrant community. Unlike Heffernan's ESL workshop, where teachers listened to guest speakers, Cabrera's candidates completed six weeks of high intensity language training. Cabrera linked language to poverty, arguing that "teachers who speak to the migrant poor in middle class terms are, literally, speaking a foreign language and actually impose barriers to learning." The RMTC trained teachers, in Spanish, to "provide creative yet pragmatic responses to the bilingual education needs of culturally alienated Mexican-Americans who suffer the compound problems of migrancy and poverty. . . . They become catalysts of change who bridge the gap between school and community, and introduce members of disadvantaged minorities to concepts of parent participation in school and community life." Reformers like Nance and Heffernan had long promoted learning English as a path out of poverty. Cabrera's program was more radical because she wanted teachers to learn Spanish.[16]

Cabrera also created curricula to celebrate Mexican culture and language in the 1960s. Her high intensity language training was an "experiment to teach specified basic patterns of Spanish in the contextual vocabulary of home and school to non-Spanish speaking teachers who will be teaching

Mexican-American children." She argued that, "if the child's cultural and linguistic orientation is different from the teacher's orientation, it is the irrevocable responsibility of the teacher to reach and teach the child . . . as he functions in his language community." Based on this premise, the heart of her program was five weeks of "Saturation-Immersion in the Spanish Language" at a Franciscan retreat in Three Rivers, California, bordering Sequoia National Park. English-speaking visitors were admitted to this secluded spot only once a week, ensuring that RMTC candidates were forced to speak Spanish around the clock for more than a month. They returned to LA County for a final week of training, continuing Spanish classes in the mornings and spending afternoons in Mexican American communities, "to apply language patterns in real situations." This approach to language was more progressive than Heffernan's ESL program, but it focused on Anglo teachers who did not speak Spanish rather than recruiting Mexican American teachers who were already bilingual. Later, Cabrera proposed to develop "bilingual teachers with a sensitivity to differences between cultures" and she called for a hundred thousand Spanish-speaking teachers by 1970. By preparing a cohort of Anglo and Mexican American teachers competent in Spanish, the RMTC expanded language learning to give migrant children a sense of belonging they had not felt in earlier LA education experiments.[17]

While Patricia Heffernan Cabrera and Afton Nance were launching ESL experiments across rural California, in LA, Mexican Angelinos were debating different bilingual education agendas. Hilario "Larry" Peña, who supervised foreign-language instruction in LA high schools from 1959 to 1968, struggled to start classes in Spanish and Japanese with a limited budget. Other Mexican American teachers supported Sal Castro's bilingual education demands at annual retreats in the Malibu Mountains. However, the two teachers who ran for the Los Angeles school board said little about language on the campaign trail. Ralph Poblano, a member of the Belmont High faculty when Castro was transferred for telling students to speak in Spanish at the assembly, did not demand bilingual classes until after he lost the election of 1965. Julian Nava used the same silent strategy two years later, when he became the first Mexican Angelino elected to a citywide office since the 1880s. Nava's decision not to emphasize language instruction likely helped him to win support across ethnic groups in 1967. It also reflected the lack of consensus about bilingual education among Mexican Americans. While educators with political ambitions avoided controversial debates about language learning, classroom teachers like Castro were collaborating with students who believed that bilingual education was a cause worthy of a school walkout.

As the city's Mexican American population grew in the 1960s, Spanish classes became more prominent. At the same time, LA's stable Japanese American student body expressed less interest in language classes than in other academic subjects. The school district's biannual magazine index illustrates these trends. From 1955 to 1967, the number of Spanish publications—including a translated edition of *Life*—nearly doubled from six classroom sets to eleven, more than any other language. During that decade, Japanese American teachers contributed to the magazine selection committees for the science and art departments, but never for foreign languages, a committee that consistently included three or four Spanish-speaking teachers. Hilario Peña left the magazine committee in 1959 when he became the first Latino language supervisor for the LA schools. He had an ambitious agenda for his tenure, including serving on the Mexican American Ad Hoc Education Committee and creating classes in Japanese at three schools. Neither program was permanent, however, and funding restrictions limited the growth of Peña's Japanese and ESL experiments. By the time he stepped down as language supervisor in 1968, the broad idea of bilingual education had been narrowly defined as Spanish language learning.[18]

Even though Japanese Angelinos were not as vocal about language instruction as they had been in previous generations, Peña promoted several new programs for that community. In 1963, he added Japanese-language classes to the curriculum. Three hundred students volunteered to take Japanese at three high schools across Los Angeles, from downtown to the San Fernando Valley. One Westside school, Venice High, sent an Anglo teacher to a summer institute in New Jersey that was as rigorous as Patricia Heffernan Cabrera's RMTC. The teacher lived in a dormitory and ate with his Japanese instructors, who forbade students from speaking English. Cabrera's colleagues at USC also helped to supervise Venice High's Japanese-language experiment from 1963 to 1965, but there is no record of Japanese classes after that.[19]

In contrast to the three hundred students taking Japanese, thousands of students were requesting Spanish language courses. Peña's biggest burden came in 1965, when LAUSD required foreign-language instruction in the junior high schools. This mandate, deriving from a 1961 state law, presented Peña with two challenges. First, while California now required extra courses, it allocated no funding for language textbooks, which would cost at least $5 million per year. In addition, the language coordinator would have to double the number of teachers he supervised, from 125 to 250, without extra pay.

Still, Peña did his best to promote foreign-language classes and faculty. He required all sixth graders to take Spanish because he had greater access to Spanish teachers and materials. Peña defended the new requirement, calling the 1960s an age in which "international radio and television have brought foreign languages and cultures into the living-room. Suddenly, we have been catapulted into a world that requires communication between people of different cultures." In the last year of LAUSD's Japanese program, the language supervisor offered Spanish to all junior high school students. The school district focused on Spanish instruction as Mexican Angelinos made bolder demands for bilingual education.[20]

However, withholding funding was one of many ways the school district delayed the universal Spanish program. Teacher credentialing requirements prevented Peña from hiring 125 extra Spanish instructors. This was frustrating because his phone had not stopped ringing since the initial call for teachers, and "many of the calls have resulted in new teachers for the district, but some of them have only proved to be headaches." He compromised by asking Spanish-speaking entertainers to make movies and songs that revealed "the value of a bi-lingual society." Instead of more permanent faculty, Peña settled for using these tapes, along with "traveling Spanish teachers" who made periodic classroom visits. He agreed to exempt some students from the language requirement, including "those who have Spanish proficiency beyond the level being taught, mentally retarded students, and youngsters with physical handicaps," an exemption that he claimed affected less than 4 percent of the city's junior high students. He hoped that the use of television and specialized training would help the new Spanish program survive with half the number of teachers it needed. Yet Mexican Angelinos were skeptical that these tactics could accomplish the bilingual education goals that Patricia Heffernan Cabrera had articulated.[21]

Despite Peña's pledge to hire more Spanish teachers in the future, he never got the funding to do so. In 1966, the LA school board secured a one-year exemption from the foreign-language mandate. "We have the books, records, and filmstrips we need for this program but we simply don't have the money to hire the teachers," Peña's supervisor explained after the first year of universal Spanish instruction. The exemption saved the school district less than $900,000, but it prevented Peña from expanding the Spanish program to seventh graders. A year later, when the school board requested another exemption, LAUSD tried to dismantle the sixth-grade program as well. This time, the California Board of Education blocked the attempt to make all language classes electives. Yet in April 1968, a month after the Blowouts, LAUSD again sought a language exemption. Despite Peña's best efforts, he could not meet the state mandate for Spanish-language instruction in seventh and eighth grades.[22]

———————

Peña's struggles as foreign-language supervisor rallied many Mexican American students and teachers to action. They often debated bilingual education at the annual Chicano Youth Leadership Conference (CYLC), which began meeting at Camp Hess Kramer, a Jewish summer camp in the Malibu Mountains, in 1963. Sal Castro volunteered as a counselor for the CYLC retreat held on Palm Sunday weekend. Conference organizers invited about 100–150 outstanding students to participate in leadership activities and group discussions about the challenges of growing up in East LA. Although these students excelled academically, even the brightest youths "faced discrimination in the schools and lack of encouragement from their teachers," Castro recalled. "I found that they only saw the surface of the problems and didn't know what to do about them." Castro knew that these students were focused on getting a college education, but he believed that they could only become leaders by recognizing and discussing the injustices they observed at Eastside high schools like Lincoln and Roosevelt. While acknowledging that their coursework was important, Castro encouraged campers to consider how their schools had created a "lack of self-esteem and even an inferiority complex." He prompted students to challenge standard curricula by asking questions like, "Would the teaching of Spanish in the elementary grades be of particular significance?" and "Do you feel that speaking two languages is a hindrance or an asset?" This line of inquiry suggested to students that their identity, "instead of the problem, . . . became the solution." Indeed, some students who organized the Blowouts believed the ethnic pride they exuded in 1968 came from Castro's questions about language learning at Camp Hess Kramer in 1963. "This is where I got my voice," recalled one Roosevelt student who attended the inaugural CYLC. "This is where my passion for justice was born in me. It changed my whole life."[23]

Castro later celebrated the CYLC as the event that inspired students to organize the Chicano movement in Los Angeles. In 1963, the first retreat was called the Spanish-Speaking Youth Leadership Conference. Students later renamed it the Chicano Youth Leadership Conference to note solidarity with the broader Mexican American struggle for civil rights, that began with César Chávez's farmworker strikes in California's Central Valley and became known as the Chicano movement. The location of the retreat was just as important as the conference's name. Castro's students were not the only Spanish speakers who discussed language instruction at the Jewish summer camp overlooking the Pacific Coast Highway. Camp Hess Kramer also hosted other meetings for Mexican educators in the 1960s that shaped the pedagogical and political debates about bilingual education policy.[24]

Adult members of the LAUSD Mexican American Ad Hoc Education Committee also used the Jewish facility to plan their political agenda. In 1963, months after Castro mobilized students at the first CYLC, the older generation was upset that the ad hoc committee had failed to include any Mexican American testimony in its yearlong hearings about equal educational opportunity. In response, the school board appointed Hilario Peña and Ralph Poblano to the committee. However, when the committee submitted fifteen proposals for Mexican American achievement awards, the school board said it was too late for review. Such bureaucracy did not surprise Peña and Poblano, but it pushed them to recommend extensive reforms. In hosting Mexican American Ad Hoc Education Committee meetings and CYLC student retreats, Camp Hess Kramer became a site where student organizers and elite educators debated policies and tactics in the 1960s—and bilingual education was the most controversial topic.[25]

The most contentious debate at Camp Hess Kramer came when the ad hoc committee met with Max Rafferty, who championed conservatism as state superintendent of public instruction from 1962 to 1970. At first, Rafferty had supported bilingual education as a strategy to recruit Mexican Americans to the Republican Party, but his view changed as he faced opposition from liberal educators in Los Angeles. In 1963, 150 Mexican American educators, politicians, and housewives welcomed the state's newly elected school superintendent to Malibu. Rafferty advised them "to rid themselves of the 'bugaboo' of inferiority complex and assert their rights in the community." Rafferty's coarse language did not amuse audience members like Ralph Poblano, who was at the time Castro's colleague at Belmont High. Poblano dismissed Rafferty's remarks, criticizing him for giving a "politician's canned speech" that contained "too many promises and not enough results." Hilario Peña echoed Poblano's critique, as did a Spanish teacher he supervised at Van Nuys High School. Rafferty responded that the Department of Education had hired two Mexican Americans who did not link bilingual education and self-esteem. The appointment of two token officials did not nearly satisfy the ad hoc committee's demand that California's most vocal conservative initiate robust language instruction.[26]

Rafferty's attempt to win Mexican American support for his limited bilingual education agenda failed. He had not met many Spanish speakers as a student at Beverly Hills High School or as superintendent of the affluent La Cañada school district in the San Gabriel Valley. However, as Natalia

Mehlman Petrzela has shown, Rafferty did make good-faith efforts to educate Mexican Americans who were classified as limited English speakers. In 1965, he visited Mexicali schools with a member of the Mexican Ministry of Education, began a textbook exchange program, and suggested transferring teachers between California and Mexico. Yet Mexican Angelinos knew that using Spanish-language textbooks in Beverly Hills school district science and social studies classes was not as ambitious as the ESL classes that Afton Nance had introduced in poor communities two years earlier. Spanish speakers were suspicious when Rafferty tapped Eugene Gonzales to head the state superintendent's Los Angeles office. In 1964, Ralph Poblano was cautiously optimistic when Gonzales "made a plea for bilingual Mexican-Americans to participate in a special teacher training language program." Yet Mexican American educators turned against Gonzales after the 1968 Blowouts, when he backed his boss's dismissal of Eastside protesters and told teachers to prevent students from taking a stand. In "highly urbanized areas, such as Los Angeles," Gonzales lamented, teachers displayed "adherence to vocal if not militant groups not at all worried about whether Juanito or Jane receive instruction commensurate with ability or potential." As students' language demands intensified, Rafferty's policies grew more reactionary. He had experimented with transnational teacher training in Mexico in his first term as superintendent, but by 1968 most Mexican Americans believed that his support for bilingual education ideas was insincere.[27]

Instead, Mexican Angelinos focused on local language reform efforts. In 1964, the *Los Angeles Times* interviewed Mexican educators who supported LAUSD's new language policies. Hilario Peña praised the school board for permitting Spanish at assemblies after Castro's incident at Belmont High. He also explained the new state and federal policy of "compensatory education," which included ESL programs for remedial assistance to children with special needs. "In arguing for the need for 'compensatory education' for minors of Mexican descent who may need it, we do not want, in any way, to give the impression that we feel that their culture or language are inferior," Peña said. His statement was cautious because it was difficult to develop a language program. Peña wanted Spanish instruction, but he did not want new classes to divide ESL pupils from their classmates, further segregating Mexican American students. One Spanish teacher that he supervised articulated this view by analyzing the educational success of Japanese American students, who turned language challenges into assets by "finding personal dignity and worth in their ethnical and cultural backgrounds." Drawing on the Nisei example, this teacher advised Mexican American students to "sacrifice immediate ethnical integration and assimilation by concentrating in excelling in education and the professions." That approach may have worked for many Japanese Angelinos, but such moderate reforms did not satisfy activists like Sal Castro. In the late 1960s, Mexican educators took these language policy debates into local political elections.[28]

Mexican Angelinos made fewer comparisons to their Japanese counterparts in the 1960s than the previous generation had done. Instead, as the civil rights movement drew more national attention, the Eastside Mexican community began to compare their living conditions with the black experience in South Los Angeles. This was especially true after 1963, when LA liberals launched an integration lawsuit, *Crawford v. Los Angeles Board of Education,* that challenged the racial disparity between the all-white South Gate High and the all-black Jordan High. Unlike in *Mendez,* when the segregation issue had hinged on language learning, the plaintiffs in the *Crawford* suit were native speakers of English.[29]

Mexican American educators struggled to make their voices heard in local elections as well. The school board campaigns of Ralph Poblano and Julian Nava reveal how the changing political landscape influenced bilingual education measures. Seeking a multiethnic coalition large enough to win the election, both candidates tried to downplay their views on "Mexican issues" like language learning and focus instead on broader educational concerns.

Despite his efforts to stress policies that would benefit both the Mexican and African American communities in LAUSD, Ralph Poblano did not reach enough black voters in his 1965 school board race. Poblano had taught for seven years, including a stint with Sal Castro at Belmont High, a downtown high school that was more diverse than Mexican schools on the Eastside or black schools in South Central Los Angeles. This "wide experience in minority group problems" drew the attention of a black assemblyman from South LA, who asked him to draft a bill that would offer high school dropouts cultural opportunities, like tickets to museums or the movies. Aware that more than 30 percent of Mexican Angelinos were high school dropouts, Poblano believed this was an issue on which he and black politicians could unite. The assemblyman agreed, and he endorsed Poblano for the school board, a seat that no Mexican Angelino had ever held. However, California's Negro Political Action Association supported a black candidate who defeated Poblano.[30]

Ironically, the most prominent advocate of Poblano's education bill during the school board election was Max Rafferty, whom Poblano had attacked at Camp Hess Kramer two years earlier. Now Poblano hoped Rafferty's public praise for the legislation would help his campaign. A week before the election, he agreed to head the Superintendent's Advisory Committee on Mexican American Affairs. In return, Rafferty wrote an op-ed in the *Los Angeles Times*, "The Forgotten Minority Is Rising," which framed Mexican American issues such as compensatory education within a "pulling themselves up by their own bootstraps" narrative. Rafferty praised Poblano (and his own associate, Eugene Gonzales) as "young, tough, and realistic, this new breed of Mexican-American. They don't weep crocodile tears over their misfortunes, and they're out to get a good, solid section of the American Dream for themselves." Closing his endorsement with a reference to "amigos" like Poblano, Rafferty revealed colorful conservative views that did not help Poblano win the school board election. They did, however, persuade him to make language instruction a higher priority.[31]

Specifically, Poblano's agenda shifted from school dropout rates to new ideas about language instruction. During the campaign, he had only hinted that language learning affected school success. "The Mexican-American children are two years behind the Negro children here, and the Negro children are two years behind the Caucasians," Poblano exclaimed in the final debate. He said "bilingualism and culture" were the main reasons Spanish-speaking youngsters completed on average only 8.6 years of school while blacks completed 10.5 years and white Angelinos finished 12.1 years. After the election, the *Los Angeles Times* printed a story about the election assembly at Belmont that was terminated when a candidate spoke Spanish. Poblano had not spoken out either when Belmont High transferred Castro or during the school board election. Yet after his defeat, a frustrated Poblano reported that the school had not changed its assembly policy as promised. He wrote a public letter urging the school district to remove its unofficial foreign-language ban "in a 'muy pronto' fashion. This kind of thing cannot be taken lightly and is nothing more than a slap in the face of the total Mexican American community and to Mrs. Lopez Mateos, wife of the President of Mexico, who recently spoke in Spanish to the entire student body at Lincoln High School." By the end of 1965, Poblano identified himself as a "research specialist" working on California's compensatory education bill, the program that helped Hilario Peña launch ESL and bilingual education classes. Rather than discussing the school dropout bill he had written for a mixed-race electorate, Poblano focused on bilingual education and other issues affecting the Mexican American students at Belmont High.[32]

After his election defeat, Poblano made progress on bilingual education. When Rafferty honored him the next month for his work in educating Spanish-speaking people, Rafferty credited Poblano "with helping to pioneer, research and write California's first compensatory education bill." Then Poblano advocated that when his bill became law the next month, "The money should be spent on reading programs, counseling, accurate testing programs that really test bilingual students, and a program of letting schools know what's happening in the home and the parents what is going on in the schools." Poblano's law paved the way for the city's first attempt at bilingual education two years later. In 1967, the Standard Oral English program targeted Mexican and African American high schoolers, teaching "the prevailing dialect in the larger community" to help them succeed in job interviews. The same fall, Helen Heffernan's ESL program opened at five Eastside junior highs and four predominantly Mexican American high schools. The school district touted both vocational programs, but Chicanos like Sal Castro still demanded language classes that empowered students' self-identity rather than remedial training for working-class jobs. As a teacher, Poblano appealed to both constituencies: while advocating for bilingual education, he was proud of passing his compensatory education law.[33]

Two years after Poblano's defeat, Julian Nava became just the second Mexican Angelino elected to citywide office in the twentieth century when he won the 1967 school board race. The history professor at suburban Valley State College surprised the city's establishment when he upset a two-time incumbent, gaining 53 percent of the vote in the runoff election. One columnist predicted that the thirty-nine-year-old Nava, whose good looks and charisma carried well over the television, would become a political power in Los Angeles because it was "second only to Mexico City in numbers of people of Mexican descent." However, Nava placed his political ambitions above ethnic loyalties, alienating himself from Sal Castro and Eastside activists a year before the Blowouts. This split came about during the 1967 campaign when, in contrast to Poblano, Nava chose to deemphasize language instruction. This decision probably helped him win support across ethnic groups, but it also prevented him from becoming a leading spokesman for the plight of minorities struggling in LA schools.[34]

His Spanish ability aided Nava in teaching Latin American history and diplomacy at Valley State, but he insisted he did not want to run as an ethnic candidate. His 1967 campaign rhetoric echoed the stories he had written when he was editor of the Roosevelt High *Rough Rider*. Back in 1945, in a profile of Nava as Boys' League president, the student newspaper reported that "Julian Nava is a typical, clean cut American boy. . . . He likes all kinds of people." Above the story, a classmate drew a cartoon titled "United We

Stand." At the center of the picture stood a short, mustachioed Mexican in a sombrero surrounded by tasteful stereotypes of Russian, Chinese, English, and American men. The cartoon accompanied a column supporting the creation of the United Nations, then being formed in San Francisco. Nava enlisted in the navy for the final months of the war before returning home to East Los Angeles Junior College, where he studied Latin American history with Dr. Helen Bailey Miller, the teacher who had founded Roosevelt High's World Friendship Club in 1931. After becoming student body president at his junior college, Nava was admitted to Pomona College where, Miller said, he "became an ironic sort of celebrity: the first Latin-American student in the Latin-American studies course." Nava continued to study his heritage in graduate school at Harvard, which led to visiting lecturer posts in Puerto Rico, Venezuela, and Spain. Despite having held such prestigious positions, Nava romanticized his humble Boyle Heights roots in his school board race. The neighborhood was predominantly Mexican by 1967, but he remembered Roosevelt High during the war, when "we had a whole United Nations—Oriental, Mexican-American, Jewish—and I dated, fought, played, studied with everyone." In the citywide campaign, he emphasized this multiethnic mixing over the Spanish-language skills that had made him a successful academic. As he had two decades earlier, Nava the candidate presented himself as a "clean cut American boy" who would represent Mexican, Jewish, and Japanese Angelinos on the school board.[35]

In East LA, Nava's Mexican ancestry made him a more attractive mainstream candidate than any of the three opponents who would have challenged him for the Chicano vote. If all four Mexican Angelinos had entered the race against a sitting school board member in an off-year election, low voter turnout would have made it difficult for such a crowded field to force a runoff. However, the Los Angeles Times reported that the city's "Mexican-American community leaders, in an unusual burst of togetherness, have decided that a community convention is the only practical way" to find a consensus candidate to challenge the conservative incumbent. Every Mexican American organization met at Casa del Mexicano, a converted church in East LA, where "the campaigning was fierce and sometimes abrasive." On the fourth ballot, Nava secured the two-thirds majority required for endorsement, but the other Spanish-speaking candidates refused to support the winner. One rival did not endorse Nava until after he had secured victory, when the failed candidate reminded Nava to focus on "his task to help the neglected Mexican-American child." Nevertheless, Nava believed an ethnic campaign would have backfired. "To be supported because I am Mexican-American would only perpetuate what I am fighting to overcome—a race-against-race approach to school politics," he said before the runoff. After his election, that philosophy meant placing universal issues like federal funding and teacher training above Mexican Americans' interest in bilingual education.[36]

Language learning did not become an issue in the runoff because the press focused on the contrast between Nava and his incumbent opponent, Charles Smoot. Whereas Nava "came up through rough-and-tumble Roosevelt High," Smoot had gone to private schools outside Washington, D.C., and was proud of his conservative record. The grandson of the Republican senator who co-authored the Hawley-Smoot Tariff during the Depression, Smoot sought advice from a reactionary who wanted to bring white supremacist Citizens' Councils from the South to California.[37] These shades of segregation made Nava's personal story more attractive to liberal Angelinos of every ethnicity in the civil rights era. Assuming that Spanish-speaking leaders would help him lock up the Eastside vote, the telegenic academic spent much of the campaign speaking at wealthy women's clubs in West LA and suburban San Fernando Valley. Upon winning 53 percent of the vote, he insisted that "this was not a minority victory, we had support throughout the city." Helen Bailey Miller, Nava's junior college professor, pointed out that emphasizing a multiethnic coalition allowed Nava to paper over the feuding factions in East LA that refused to endorse him. Dr. Miller said that, although some Mexican Americans still resented him for leaving Boyle Heights to join the faculty at Valley State, she did not because "he often comes here to the junior college to speak and has been a very great influence on the Mexican-American students. His constant theme is upgrade, upgrade." After Nava's victory, a five-page profile in the *Los Angeles Times* stressed his multiethnic coalition: "Women cheered and men cried, and the whole glorious American faith in political unpredictability was validated. There was joy in Northridge, where Nava now lives. There was bedlam in Boyle Heights, where he came from. . . . Julian Nava sits as symbol, symptom of change, promise of political things to come. The largest minority group in California (some two million people), heretofore famous for going separate or divisive ways, has an official voice."[38] Nava's victory celebration united Spanish-speaking Angelinos temporarily, but he could not rally the community behind his reform agenda.

Once elected, Nava struggled to find his voice as the lone Mexican American member of the school board. After campaigning on the moderate messages of more school funding and racial unity, he hesitated to take progressive positions on issues like bilingual education, even as he found himself sitting on more panels about "minority group tensions." During his first year in office, Nava attended a "reaction panel" that explored how Los Angeles was improving "Negro education" after the 1965 Watts Riot, and he

Julian Nava inspects a school building. *Courtesy of Julian Nava Collection, Department of Special Collections, Oviatt Library, California State University, Northridge.*

spent a weekend at Camp Hess Kramer, where he met Mexican American leaders who were angry that Lyndon Johnson had not invited them to the White House. These meetings lacked the passion that Sal Castro's students had brought to the same campground at the annual CYLC. Even though he was a scholar of Latin American history who focused on foreign leaders and the language of racial politics at home, Nava neglected bilingual education because he knew it did not appeal to the eclectic constituency he had built.[39]

Although Nava made bold statements, his modest agenda frustrated Sal Castro's students. For example, Nava criticized a Republican proposal to split the LA school district into ten small districts as a way to delay integration.

"It would create poor districts and rich districts, majority and minority group districts," Nava said, calling it "an American version of South African apartheid." Yet, while the professor supported desegregation, he did not demand school busing. Like bilingual education, racial integration was an area in which Nava tried to hedge his comments and delay decisions. During the 1967 campaign, he argued that "we are in the middle of a true revolution in education." When CYLC students started a revolution at five Eastside schools a year later, however, Nava was torn between the Mexican American community's demands and the Anglo establishment's expectations of moderate reform. Writing during the week of the Blowouts, one *Los Angeles Times* columnist endorsed a Spanish-language pamphlet from the League of Women Voters instructing Mexican Americans how to register to vote. After praising politicians like Nava for seeking change through the democratic process, the writer told students to stop their walkouts: "And you chicos from Roosevelt High, instead of demonstrating, why don't you distribute the pamphlets to your parents and neighbors? If they vote, it will make a whole different future for you." Nava's strategy endeared him to the liberal establishment at the *Los Angeles Times* but alienated his old neighbors in Boyle Heights—including the student protesters at his alma mater.[40]

As the *Los Angeles Times* column indicated, Roosevelt High School provides a good case study for the Blowouts. Although the protests started at two other schools, Roosevelt was the Eastside school that drew the most attention from the press, the police, and the school board. Julian Nava's former high school captured the range of student opinions about one of the largest school strikes in US history. Several Blowout organizers came from Roosevelt, but only 6 percent of the student body admitted to walking out. When Nava came to campus to address student concerns, the *Rough Rider* newspaper complained that protesters did not speak for all 2,870 Roosevelt students. *Rough Rider* stories from 1966 and 1967 demonstrate that not all students shared the revolutionary spirit before the 1968 Blowouts. Yet students who were inclined toward activism demanded bilingual classes for non-English speakers. *Rough Rider* stories reveal how language instruction proposals prepared Eastside students to organize for broader social reform in 1968.[41]

Roosevelt High students' resistance to the walkouts reflected the school's racial makeup in the 1960s. Despite having a racially diverse student population, Roosevelt's campus reflected the types of segregation that complicated language education in LA County. Using racial classifications that were common in the 1960s, the *Rough Rider* reported that whereas only 19 percent of LA students had Spanish surnames in 1967, Roosevelt was 80 percent "Spanish." The school's white population had dropped to 3 percent, and now 7 percent was "Negro." There were fewer than three hundred "Orientals" left but, as they had before internment, Japanese Americans were still elected to student government. The *Rough Rider* journalist remarked that, although the school was only 10 percent Asian, "superficially, it seems Roosevelt has a higher Oriental population." Mexican Americans actually won more student body elections, however. One teacher remembers that the student body president in 1967, Castulo de la Rocha, decided to "run for office because all the Japanese were winning." Student leaders like de la Rocha and his predecessor, Don Nakanishi, held moderate views about race and language even though they joked about living in an "undesirable" barrio. Unlike Castro's Tortilla Movement at Belmont or his Blowout organizers at Lincoln, these Mexican and Japanese student leaders embraced Americanization over language learning.[42]

The *Los Angeles Times* featured de la Rocha and Nakanishi in a 1967 article challenging the perception that all youths of the civil rights era were radical reformers. "They call them the silent activists," the story began. "They want to change the world—as do their more vocal counterparts, the ones who sit-in, sing, picket, speak, campaign and march. But they want to change it just a little at a time." The reporter interviewed both Roosevelt student body presidents, along with private school students from "comfortable, tree-lined suburbs," at a United Way retreat in the Malibu Mountains. Close to Camp Hess Kramer, where Sal Castro was recruiting their classmates to organize a mass protest, the silent activists brainstormed moderate reforms. Articulating modest improvements was easier for Japanese students than for Mexican students. De la Rocha, for example, only offered a vague goal of running for office after college. He did not discuss details because he worried that peers would say "that I'm a gringado. Gringoized. Americanized. Man, they're right. I'm Americanized." Even though he was unwilling to be identified with Chicano classmates who walked out of school, de la Rocha still won schoolwide election a year before the Blowouts.[43]

Social stigmas did not affect Nakanishi, who volunteered at UCLA Medical Center, earned a scholarship to Yale, and planned to return to East LA as a doctor to practice at clinics "where poor people can get care." At Roosevelt, he ran for office on a message of racial unity. "A school like any other organized group must be united, with each member having pride in being a part of the group," he wrote in the *Rough Rider*. "The group may be divided into various interest or nationality groups but must feel a definite spirit for remaining together." Like Julian Nava, Nakanishi had a knack for finding multiethnic consensus that came from his Boyle Heights background and its language diversity. When he was a young boy, a neighbor had often taken him to the nearby synagogue, where Nakanishi used the playground while his Jewish friend studied Hebrew. Many of his school friends were Mexican American and, as Nakanishi later said, "what makes me into an Asian American was getting an identity as a Chicano first." While campaigning for student body president, he went to Roosevelt's ESL classes and gave speeches in English, Spanish, and Japanese. Nakanishi undoubtedly recognized the power of language learning as an organizing tool.[44]

Issues of immigration and citizenship interested the *Rough Rider* reporters. In 1967, the newspaper covered the graduation ceremony of immigrants who had passed their citizenship tests at the LA City Adult School. The ceremony featured flag-waving activities that resembled the LA Diploma Plan's approach to naturalization in 1915. Rather than interviews with some of the 1,800 immigrants from seventy countries (from Japan to Iran to El Salvador) participating in the ceremony, the story featured the graduation speaker, California's Republican lieutenant governor who had worked for Vice President Richard Nixon. In 1966, student Jesus Perez defended Americanization in a column urging Roosevelt students to resist "dual patriotism." Perez equated patriotism with school spirit—students should transfer their loyalties from grammar school to junior high and then to senior high school. "We must remember, however, that this is not our Mexico, nor our Japan, nor any other country of the world where we came from," he wrote, concluding that only in America could students "realize our ideals." While the *Rough Rider* seemed to endorse traditional views about assimilation, these articles prompted other Roosevelt students to think about citizenship—and how they might want to make naturalization easier or harder.[45]

These generally moderate students took liberal positions on language education, however. Due to recent reforms by Afton Nance and Helen Heffernan, Roosevelt offered ESL classes for non-English speakers (NES). Although the NES students were new to Los Angeles and the American school system, they approached education enthusiastically. In 1966, NES class president Yoshio Okimura began corresponding with a sister school in Nara, Japan. Then in 1967, the *Rough Rider* published two articles by NES students in Spanish, with English translations. The first had a message of general inspiration. "Youth of Roosevelt," the column concluded, "our destiny is clear today, to save those who study in our school, . . . for the benefit of all society." In the second translated article, NES president Antonio García discussed problems with President Lyndon Johnson's Great Society programs, specifically a lack of access to good education and good jobs. García called on Spanish speakers to follow the black civil rights model by drawing attention to their own discrimination "because the president of the United States doesn't demonstrate too much interest in Latin Americans." In two languages, he predicted that school desegregation would become the Chicano movement's next major project. "Discrimination is a very hard situation for the Mexican as well as for the Negro but through the year we'll get rid of it," García pledged. "Education is a problem which we can solve." With these Spanish-language articles, English learners swayed some Roosevelt students. The NES president demonstrated the benefits of bilingual education to the students who would demand its expansion the next year.[46]

In two April Fool's editions, the *Rough Rider* satirized students' growing interest in activism. Many of the prank stories addressed provocative topics like lynching, assassination, LSD, and teachers who sold marijuana. The 1967 issue showed little sensitivity toward Japanese American stereotypes. The feature story reported that math teacher Ronald Hirosawa had staged a coup, sending the principal to Tokyo. Having replaced the entire faculty "with loyal 'Buddahead' teachers," the article continued, "full power should be in the grasp of that Slant-eyed mastermind YELLOW-FINGER (Mr. Hirosawa)." Playing on the idea of Black Power, the story ended with Hirosawa's assassination, when he was "heard screaming YELLOW POWER and We Shall Overcome." The 1966 April Fool's issue also referenced racial protest. It joked that Roosevelt radicals were forming two new groups, the W.E.B. DuBois Club and the John Birch Society, and that students were ready to stage sit-ins until the school stopped sending hall monitors on "controversial 'sweeps'" after the tardy bell. Another front-page story reported that the school board had canceled Easter break. The *Rough Rider* imagined a new movement called REV (Restore Easter Vacation) and a mass meeting held to draft a petition. According to the story, REV spread from Roosevelt to six high schools across East LA and downtown, where students vowed to take off Easter, "with or without the blessing of the school board." The reporter who conjured up this fake story could not know that students at many of the same schools would actually walk out of class just two years later. Both April Fool's editions indicated that students of all ethnicities could envision scenarios in which the civil rights protests of the 1960s—from the Deep South to Sal Castro's Tortilla Movement—would find their way into the schools of East LA. Three weeks before the *Rough Rider* published its next April Fool's issue in 1968, thousands of Eastside students staged one of the largest high school protests the country had ever seen.[47]

6 | THE BILINGUAL EDUCATION ACT AND THE EAST LA BLOWOUTS, 1968–1970

In a year full of violence and protest, the 1968 Blowouts made Mexican American students front-page news. From March 5 to March 12, according to the *Los Angeles Times*, East LA saw "a week-and-a-half of walkouts, speeches, sporadic lawbreaking, arrests, demands, picketing, sympathy demonstrations, sit-ins, police tactical alerts and emergency sessions of the school board." Thousands of students protested the fact that Eastside schools were the only campuses in Los Angeles that still practiced corporal punishment and that the schools were failing to educate Mexican Americans, whose dropout rate was double that of black students. Student organizers asked Sal Castro to represent their interests to the press and the school board. The teacher who had been transferred in 1964 for urging students to speak Spanish in an assembly remained true to the language principles he had discussed at five annual Chicano Youth Leadership Conferences. In interviews with the *Los Angeles Times* during the Blowouts, Castro made bilingual education a protest priority.[1]

The media focused on language education because Castro and his students believed it was necessary for Mexican Americans' academic and emotional success. "Many Mexican-American kids come to school with pretty good ability in English, but the teacher's attitude compounds the language factor and actually turns it into a handicap," Castro told the *Los Angeles Times* a week after the walkouts. "The kid feels the school is not his friend, that he is in an alien situation." LAUSD had created a new Urban Affairs Office, but Castro was not convinced that it could recruit minority counselors, implement compensatory programs in language instruction, and hire Spanish-speakers as teacher aides. "A crash program was needed five years ago," he concluded, "but there has been none." Castro pressed for language reforms at the peak of the protests because they were the most concrete steps schools could take to improve Eastside students' self-esteem.[2]

The Blowout leaders demanded not only better language instruction but a full slate of reforms. After submitting their formal demands to the school board in person, the students saw their list published on the front page of the Sunday *Los Angeles Times.* Eight of the thirty-eight demands addressed bicultural education. The first demand was that no student or teacher be disciplined for walking out, followed by a demand for "compulsory bilingual and bicultural education in all East Los Angeles schools, with teachers and administrators to receive training in speaking Spanish and Mexican cultural heritage." The newspaper labeled some demands "frivolous," such as replacing grades with a pass-fail system and renaming schools after Mexican heroes, but most of the requests were quite serious. The students wanted school counselors to speak Spanish, textbooks "to show Mexican contributions to society," libraries to be stocked with more materials in Spanish, and standardized tests, "which often mistake a language problem with lack of intelligence," to be rewritten. The most extreme demands were that new faculty should "live in the community where they teach," that Spanish-speaking parents should be hired as teacher's aides, and that cafeterias "should have more Mexican dishes and mothers should be allowed to help prepare the food." In sum, the students walked out to improve all aspects of Eastside schools, from academics to materials to racial awareness. The one idea that unified all of these ambitious demands was bilingual education.[3]

Two months before the Blowouts, on January 2, 1968, Lyndon Johnson had signed the Bilingual Education Act (BEA). Most scholars discuss the federal law and the student protest as two separate issues. In many ways, however, the walkouts shaped, and were shaped by, the BEA and its implementation. Democrats and Republicans in Sacramento and Washington had collaborated on this law. They consulted Mexican Angelinos like Julian Nava, who had approved the text, but delays in funding the bilingual programs drove Eastsiders to protest. Administrative inaction pushed Chicano students to prioritize bilingual education in their list of Blowout demands. Rather than providing comprehensive instruction, the LAUSD school board offered piecemeal programs in an attempt to placate the angry students. These compromises did not incorporate crucial elements of bilingual education. Yet the failures of the BEA and the Blowouts were intertwined, and students and teachers from East LA shaped the politics of language learning at the local, state, and federal levels.

Shortly after the BEA introduced the first federal definition of "bilingual education" in 1968, Angelinos proposed alternatives. Many Anglos pictured a classroom in which teachers would simply speak a sentence in Spanish then write the same line in English on the blackboard. *Los Angeles Times* reporter Ruben Salazar wrote that "truly bilingual programs . . . should be the teaching of both languages on an equal basis." As LA educators applied for language instruction grants and students staged walkouts, their local efforts gained national notice. In 1973, the US Office of Education amended its earlier definition of bilingual education to reflect the version promoted by Mexican Angelinos: "the use of two languages, one of which is English, as mediums of instruction for the same pupil population in a well-organized program which encompasses part or all of the curriculum and includes the study of the history and culture associated with the mother tongue." Teaching ethnic history and culture to build self-esteem meant that the new definition of "bilingual education" finally met demands put forth during the Blowouts. During the 1968 protests, LA officials, teachers, and students had struggled to redefine language learning. Their efforts indicate that Angelinos of color viewed language instruction as an opportunity to fight for a vision of US citizenship that embraced non-Anglo cultures and idioms.[4]

In addition to teachers and students, elected officials from both parties tried to claim language learning as part of their agenda. Governor Ronald Reagan signed a bilingual education bill in California six months before the BEA became law. Senate Bill (SB) 53, allowing the use of foreign languages for instruction in California schools, was part of a strategy to secure the Spanish-speaking vote for a new Republican majority. SB 53 provided a road map for the BEA as the latter was being written in late 1967. Historian Gareth Davies credits SB 53 for persuading the Mexican American Political Association (MAPA) not to campaign for the Democratic opponent in 1970, when Reagan won reelection. Reagan was one of several conservatives from the Southwest, including Senator Barry Goldwater of Arizona and Congressman George H. W. Bush of Texas, who supported bilingual education for their Chicano constituents. However, Davies also argues that Republicans responded with less enthusiasm to MAPA's more specific demands to appoint Latinos to public office and host a White House conference on the problems of Spanish speakers. Just as Reagan faced resistance when he tried to work with language activists on the California legislation, Senator Ralph Yarborough, the Texas Democrat who authored the BEA, had to field demands from both conservatives and liberals as he wrote the federal bill. Angelinos had strong feelings about the texts of these measures because they believed that bilingual education could reshape the meaning of American citizenship—and who had access to it.[5]

LA activists pushed Reagan to make his state initiative a stronger first step for bilingual education than Johnson's federal law. The legislation ended a ninety-five-year-old mandate in California's Education Code requiring schools to conduct all instruction exclusively in English. Historian Natalia Mehlman Petrzela argues that, although the BEA authorized federal funding for bilingual programs, SB 53 was a bolder law because the state bill identified the "inherent benefit of Spanish fluency and recognized an inextricable link between language and culture on which the 1968 version of the BEA remained silent." SB 53 encouraged efforts to add a bilingual-bicultural component to the curriculum in every subject. It also advocated for language instruction courses that integrated non-English and English speakers, declaring that "the native language of all students should be respected and utilized . . . and the bilingual ability should be viewed as a distinct asset." While he wanted to appeal to Spanish-speaking voters, Reagan worried that this element of the bill might alienate extreme conservatives. In 1968, a La Mirada man who supported the presidential campaign of George Wallace, the Alabama segregationist, told the *Los Angeles Times* that Reagan's bilingual education bill was "plotted by the Communist Party." Politicians from both parties courted Mexican voters, just as Reagan had done with SB 53, when they asked Congress to bring the BEA debate to Los Angeles in late 1967.[6]

Angelinos actively engaged in drafting both laws. Ed Roybal, California's first Mexican American US congressman since 1879, figured prominently in the process. In 1966, he joined President Johnson and Texas Senator Yarborough on a trip to Mexico, where the trio first discussed the BEA. The president recalled his first year teaching at a segregated Mexican American school in South Texas, telling Roybal and Yarborough that "the students were bright but just did not know the language." Yarborough eventually wrote the final draft of the BEA, but many LA officials had also authored their own versions. Roybal, a Boyle Heights native who had belonged to Roosevelt High's World Friendship Club in 1932, was not the first Angelino to endorse bilingual education in Congress. In 1967, Democrat James Corman, of the San Fernando Valley, introduced the first House bill to offer federal funds for bilingual programs, including "instruction of Spanish as the native language and English as a second language—and the development of programs designed to impart to Spanish-speaking students understanding and pride in their ancestral culture." Months after Corman's Bilingual American Educational Act, and similar bills by Democrats George Brown of Monterey Park and

Gus Hawkins of South LA had been debated, Roybal submitted his own resolution. His Bilingual Educational Opportunity Act promised "millions of non-English-speaking elementary and secondary school children a better chance to realize their full educational aspirations." By late 1967, almost every LA Democrat in Washington had written his own bilingual education bill.[7]

As a cosponsor of the impending legislation, Roybal asked Yarborough to hold one of the three subcommittee hearings on the BEA in Los Angeles. The LA hearing was held in June 1967, one month after Reagan signed SB 53 in Sacramento, and California politicians from both parties supported the legislation. Republican Senator George Murphy, the first Hollywood star elected to statewide office, called the "language problem" the main reason half the Spanish-speaking students in California dropped out of school by the eighth grade. Representative Corman testified that "Mexican-Americans have been victims of one of the cruelest forms of discrimination. . . . Spanish is forbidden to them and they are required to struggle along as best they can in English, a language understood dimly by most and not at all by many." Even though some LA-area schools were trying bilingual experiments, Corman pointed out federal funding would "expand and improve the programs." Roybal reported the "tragic record" in higher education, pointing out that only 10 percent of the twenty thousand Mexican-origin Californians of college age were enrolled in the state's public universities. Senator Thomas Kuchel, an Orange County Republican who was on Yarborough's subcommittee but could not attend the hearings, sent a statement: "We must treat the ability to speak Spanish and other languages as an asset. . . . The United States can no longer pretend that it can communicate with other people with but one tongue." Kuchel sent the letter while he was in the midst of a primary challenge against Max Rafferty, California's reactionary superintendent of public instruction who had tried to make bilingual education a conservative program. Officials on both sides of the aisle eagerly endorsed the BEA at the Los Angeles hearing.[8]

LA's leading Mexican educators, however, demanded better legislation. Julian Nava testified at the Senate hearings two weeks after winning his first school board election. Since "local tax sources cannot or will not assume" the costs of new programs, Nava explained, federal funding was essential to implement bilingual education plans. The Senate subcommittee was eager to include the history professor in its hearings before his first school board meeting in 1967. After the 1968 Blowouts, lawmakers listened to other Latino voices as well. When the California assembly convened an education hearing at Roosevelt High School in Boyle Heights, it invited Sal Castro to speak. Castro, who had been arrested then suspended from his teaching position after the student walkouts, had been reinstated only days earlier. Unhappy with the funding for language instruction provided under both the state and federal laws, the Lincoln High teacher vowed to investigate "where bilingual education is really being conducted on an effective basis." Both federal and state bilingual education hearings were held in LA only weeks after Nava's school board election in 1967 and Castro's teaching reinstatement in 1968. The simultaneity of the BEA hearings and the Blowouts helped Mexican Angelinos use language learning to remain engaged at the elite level of federal legislation as well as in the grassroots politics of protest.[9]

The federal bill that emerged from these hearings incorporated Angelinos' competing definitions of language learning. "Bilingual education," as defined in the appendix to the BEA, was "instruction in two languages and the use of those *two languages* as mediums of instruction for any part or all of the school curriculum" (emphasis in original). The bill distinguished between the purpose and practice of language learning. Its goal was to help immigrant children "develop greater competence in English, to become more proficient in the use of two languages, and to profit from increased educational opportunity." The law also stressed that students would benefit from learning in their heritage language as they mastered English. "The mother tongue, [is] used as the medium of instruction before the child's command of English is sufficient to carry the whole load of his education. . . . The literacy thus achieved in the non-English tongue, if further developed, should result in a more liberally educated adult." The BEA's expansive explanations echoed the range of issues raised by LA lawmakers at the 1967 hearings as well as the goals students had articulated during the 1968 Blowouts.[10]

The Bilingual Education Act that President Johnson signed on January 2, 1968, authorized $7.5 million in grants for the 1969–70 school year. The grants were to fund the development of teacher training for "new and imaginative" language projects. The BEA funding would support teachers to learn "the history and culture associated with their languages," sponsor efforts "to establish closer cooperation between the school and the home," and fund programs "designed for dropouts or potential dropouts having need of bilingual programs." More than three hundred school districts submitted proposals, but Johnson's administration approved only sixty-five grants totaling $5 million, leaving $2.5 million in federal coffers. More than a third of the grants went to schools in California, and LA County alone won grants for six bilingual education projects—nearly 10 percent of the national total—supplying $475,000 to reach more than 1,800 Portuguese- and Spanish-speaking students. Across the country, 90 percent of the grants went to Spanish-language programs. The only Japanese bilingual program to win federal funding was located in Hawaii, which had reinstated language schools after Judge McCormick's ruling in 1948. The BEA provided a start, but funding for bilingual education programs in Japanese, Spanish, and many other languages in LA County was still very inadequate.[11]

Mexican American educators lobbied for more BEA money for LA schools. Between the passage of the BEA on January 2, 1968, and the Blowouts that March, the Los Angeles Teachers Association (LATA) turned bilingual education into an organizing tool. In December 1967, when it was clear Johnson would sign the BEA, LATA approached the school board to decide how it should implement the law in Los Angeles. New board member Julian Nava asked for faculty opinions about funding priorities: supplies and materials, evaluation methods, in-service training, or hiring Spanish-speaking teacher's aides. In January, responses from teachers "anxious to take action immediately" led to a "mass meeting for all teachers interested in bilingual education." On March 1, LATA sponsored a "School Community Talk-In" at Lincoln High, where Sal Castro's students were plotting to lead a walkout five days later. The union endorsed the hiring of more Spanish-speaking counselors and a state law that would "authorize school districts to purchase paperback bi-lingual texts . . . [and] to bring more foreign bi-lingual teachers into the district." In East LA, Mexican American teachers were organizing for the funding of bilingual education experiments with almost as much passion as their students were planning the walkouts.[12]

In contrast to those lobbying for liberal interests, Republicans struggled to persuade Mexican Americans that conservative bilingual education policies were more effective. This became an issue for Beverly Hills High alumnus Max Rafferty when he challenged Thomas Kuchel, who had already endorsed the BEA, in the US Senate primary in 1968. Rafferty referenced Ronald Reagan's SB 53 in front of eight hundred teachers at the Nuevas Vistas (New Horizons) conference at the Biltmore Hotel in downtown LA. Worried about finding enough Spanish speakers who were qualified to teach bilingual education classes, the state superintendent accepted the federal plan to grant $5 million to bilingual education rather than the $7.5 million that had been authorized. Yet he also admitted he could do little more than urge Anglo teachers to study Spanish at summer workshops because "$5 million, spread through fifty states, is not nearly enough to ease the situation." While Rafferty insisted that "the purpose of bilingual instruction is not to perpetuate the student's Spanish, but to teach him English," he also added that "everyone ought to be able to speak more than one language." His mixed message—endorsing bilingual education but only as a tool to teach English—made Mexican Angelinos suspicious. The purpose of Nuevas Vistas was to "send educators back to their school better prepared to reach the bilingual or Spanish-speaking student in an effort to stem the dropout rate." However, the Biltmore conference was chaired by Rafferty's appointee Eugene Gonzales, who had dismissed the "senseless . . . pickets, demonstrations, and walkouts" and told teachers to focus on educating *"the mythical tortilla eater,* the sleepy giant now flexing his muscles" in East LA. The next year, when Reagan addressed the third annual Nuevas Vistas conference at the Biltmore, Chicano college students set fires and caused other "disturbances" to protest the governor who had signed SB 53. Republican plans to begin bilingual education in California were not sufficient to capture the Mexican American vote. In the end, neither SB 53 nor the BEA resulted in the hiring of more bilingual teachers in East LA or addressed the demands of Mexican Angelinos. Ultimately, this factor became one of the main causes of the student walkouts in 1968.[13]

The Blowouts began two months after Johnson signed the BEA. From March 5 to 12, 1968, students staged walkouts at seven high schools in East LA, risking arrest by organizing rallies outside school district offices. Thousands of students protested many injustices in Eastside schools, from corporal punishment to racial segregation to the omission of Mexican culture in predominantly Mexican American schools. With attention already on cultural education due to passage of SB 53 and the BEA, the lack of curricula on Mexican culture was the most measurable problem on this list. As schools impatiently awaited federal funding for bilingual instruction, language learning informed local coverage of the walkouts. While the *Los Angeles Times* speculated that the Blowouts would bring on a revolution in bilingual education, the Roosevelt High *Rough Rider* featured more diverse views about the role of Spanish instruction in Eastside schools. Spirited debates in both newspapers suggest that language demands made bilingual education central to the Blowouts and the emerging Chicano movement in 1968.

Although the *Los Angeles Times* printed mixed reactions to the Blowouts, the most positive coverage emphasized language learning. One editorial supported student complaints about Eastside schools but also argued that those problems could "never be solved by strikes, boycotts and demonstrations." Yet it praised students for keeping the walkouts, "for the most part, non-violent." Most importantly, the editorial linked language ability to both student activism and educational solutions, observing that "young Mexican-Americans themselves are crying for the education tools that will keep them from becoming the victims of a kind of apartheid via language." Another *Los Angeles Times* reporter, who had profiled Roosevelt High's "silent activists" a year earlier, now featured the "Brown Power" generation. She called the Blowouts the "beginning of a revolution—the Mexican-American revolution of 1968." Like these stories in the *Los Angeles Times*, most accounts that addressed language learning supported the Blowouts. These opinions encouraged Eastside students to make bilingual education central to their reform campaign.[14]

According to Castro, the opening of the Blowouts was both chaotic and carefully orchestrated. He had planted the idea in students' minds one year earlier, at Camp Hess Kramer in March 1967. Many had graduated that spring, but they still met at the Piranya Coffee House, where Castro suggested "a mass action in the schools." When students asked about protesting that fall, Castro advised, "Don't walk out. Organize." He advised them to develop a list of demands they could present to the school board before considering a walkout, but the students were impatient. When the Garfield High principal canceled a student performance in March 1968, students walked out the next Tuesday. On Wednesday, nearly five thousand students walked out of class at Lincoln, Roosevelt, and Wilson High Schools. The Roosevelt principal was not surprised; he had seen walkout leaflets circulating on campus a week earlier. In fact, the principal was more shocked by the police, who called a tactical alert at 2 P.M. and "broke up groups of students gathered in front of the school, taking several into custody." One Roosevelt student's arrest was the top story on the evening news. The walkout had attracted attention, but the public did not yet understand the purpose of the protest.[15]

Castro urged students to mobilize as many participants as possible before stating their demands. He led the Lincoln protesters on a two-mile march to the school district's East LA office, where he spoke to administrators over a loudspeaker. Castro announced that students would return to class once the school board agreed to a public meeting with walkout leaders at Lincoln High. Students called another walkout for the next day, inviting local newspaper reporters and TV crews to a rally at Hazard Park. Thousands of students did walk out, but the majority just went home. The cops and Castro had different estimates, but some four hundred to seven hundred students met at the park on a rainy Friday morning. Julian Nava and Ralph Richardson, the latter a white school board member, also gathered with the students outside, along with Congressman Ed Roybal, who had flown back from Washington when the Blowouts began. Richardson was willing to talk about Eastside school conditions, telling students that, "to the extent that you have dramatized the problems, you have me." On Castro's advice, however, the students refused to list specific issues until the full school board was assembled in the Lincoln gymnasium.[16]

Walkout rally at Hazard Park, March 8, 1968. *Left to right:* school board members Ralph Richardson and Julian Nava; unknown; Congressman Ed Roybal; Lincoln High student Robert Rodriguez (on megaphone); and Garfield High student Harry Gamboa. *Courtesy of Los Angeles Times Photographic Archives, Department of Special Collections, Charles E. Young Research Library, University of California, Los Angeles.*

The students' silence did not stop reporters from speculating about the Blowout organizers' agenda—and bilingual education was their first guess. A *Los Angeles Times* article about the Eastside's embarrassingly high school dropout rate ran under the headline "Language Is Key Factor." The school board had made little progress with improving the dropout rate since its study of minority problems in 1963, when it announced "an effort to put Spanish-speaking, culturally-trained teachers into Mexican-American schools." Five years later, only 122 of the Eastside's 1,675 elementary schoolteachers were "Mexican-American and represent[ed] nearly all the teachers with Spanish-speaking ability." While the district offered remedial reading and English classes to "almost everyone who needs it," it did not have enough bilingual teachers to carry out this curriculum. As a result, 90 percent of the remedial classes were already overcrowded, and the school district had not allocated any funding for additional teachers. Regardless of money, the *Los Angeles Times* concluded, "the district says it could not find the number of personnel, particularly Spanish-speaking teachers, counselors, and administrators." For example, it offered Spanish classes "on a voluntary basis for teachers who work in predominantly Mexican-American schools," but claimed it would be too costly to make these classes compulsory. These were not the answers that students wanted to hear, but at least the Blowouts had forced a deeper, more public conversation about bilingual education.[17]

Before protesters officially publicized their demands, students' rhetoric identified language as a key element of their generation's Chicano identity. A *Los Angeles Times* reporter noticed many signs in Spanish reading "'Viva La Raza.' (*Raza* translates as 'race,' but it is used in a sense of 'our people.')" Student organizers tried to "show the country a new type of Mexican-American: one proud of his language, his culture, his raza, ready to take his share of U.S. prosperity." They were angry that, despite Nava's election, the school board had failed to fund bilingual education for nearly a decade. Students said they needed "more bilingual instruction, more Mexican cultural heritage in curricula and textbooks, smaller class sizes, firing of insensitive teachers, updated industrial arts program, replace old buildings, more students' rights, more liberal dress code and Mexican-oriented cafeteria menus." This list later proved accurate, despite Castro's call for secrecy. As predicted, 20 percent of the demanded reforms would involve language learning.[18]

The school that got the most attention during the walkout was Lincoln High, where Sal Castro was organizing the student protests. I, however, focus on Roosevelt High School, Nava's alma mater, where students and teachers were more divided about the Blowouts and had more nuanced debates about the movement's objectives. Roosevelt students evaluated the pros and cons of the walkout and its list of demands, and fewer protesters decided to walk out. This produced a broader range of politically motivated accounts about the Blowouts. For example, whereas the Roosevelt principal told the *Los Angeles Times* that on March 6 about four hundred to five hundred students protested (10–15 percent of the student population), Castro claimed that Roosevelt's walkout rate was 60 percent (around two thousand students). The *Rough Rider*, a student newspaper subject to administration approval, reported only 6 percent participation (two hundred students). The dispute over the walkout statistic suggests that Roosevelt's principal, alumni, student government, and school newspaper were all highly invested in minimizing the extent of student activism. While the Blowouts meant different things to each of these groups, Eastside Angelinos all agreed on two larger goals: demanding bilingual education and proving that they were engaged US citizens ready to fight for their civil rights.[19]

Many students who had not attended Castro's Chicano Youth Leadership Conferences participated in the walkout at Roosevelt. Even students who stayed in class initiated a dialogue with their protesting peers. By the fourth day, the *Rough Rider* reported, "90% of the student body began to voice their opinions on all the action." After initially disapproving of the demonstrations, student council leaders later joined the walkout delegation. This meant that African American and Japanese American peers accompanied Chicano organizers. Their participation did not make the Blowouts a multiethnic movement, but they did contribute outside voices to ensuing discussions about bilingual and bicultural education.[20]

Two months later, the black student council president and a Japanese classmate attended a citywide meeting about race relations in school curricula. They agreed with the majority view that "Afro-American, Mexican-American, Japanese-American, and other minorities of our society were overlooked in our textbooks . . . making it appear that they contributed little, if anything, to the development of this nation." Roosevelt leaders would not have advocated for "including minority contributions in the textbooks" two years earlier, but by 1968 the student council president had embraced one of the Chicano protesters' top demands. The *Rough Rider* captured this conversion by asking and answering a series of questions about the tumultuous events: "Was and is all the bad publicity worth anything? Were the police too rough with the participants of the walk-out? Why aren't parents using their influence to help us get the things we need? There are both positive and negative aspects to the demonstrations. . . . Whatever the outcome, one thing is clear: Roosevelt students are NOT apathetic."[21]

This activism alarmed some Roosevelt teachers and inspired others. When forty-five faculty members requested a transfer after the Blowouts, students suspected that their teachers did not trust them. More than 2,200 Roosevelt students signed a petition protesting the school board's handling of the walkouts, including the decision to leave dissatisfied teachers in Eastside schools. The Blowouts gave hope to many Spanish speakers who had given up on fighting for change. "We feel disturbed and ashamed that these kids are carrying out our fight," said Ray Ceniceroz, a Garfield High teacher. "We should have been fighting for these things as teachers and as a community. Apparently we have been using the wrong weapon. These kids found a new weapon—a new monster—the walkout. . . . I'm just sorry we [teachers] didn't walk out."[22]

The Blowouts also impressed Julian Nava. "This is BC and AD," he told the superintendent of schools as they toured Roosevelt High. "The schools will not be the same hereafter." However, his Eastside visit did not satisfy students who demanded concrete actions. One argued that it was not enough for Nava simply to visit his alma mater and reference a "Brown Power" revolution: *"Dr. Nava came to 'LOOK' over our school, took one look at our gym, turned around and reported the new gym is beautiful. But, did our Dr. Nava look at all our school? Did he notice our crowded classrooms, lousy food, closed restrooms?"* (emphasis in original). Still, Nava fought for more school funding. The politician did not fix toilets when he visited his alma mater, but he did speak from the heart. "The way the walkouts have been conducted made me feel proud, for you have done this in a way not to hurt the school," he said at the March 8 assembly. At the rally, Nava dismissed a *Los Angeles Times* reporter's question about student violence. "I still think this thing is fully controllable and is positive and constructive," he said. "As long as we keep up the dialog, things should remain all right." The media left out the rest of his assembly speech, in which the Valley State professor tried to lower students' expectations. He said their unnamed demands would cost a lot of money, and that he had already gone to Sacramento to ask for funds that did not exist. Still, he convinced his colleagues to convene a school board meeting at Lincoln High in response to student requests.[23]

Bilingual education played a prominent role in the discussion when the school board came to Sal Castro's campus on March 26, three weeks after the Blowouts began. Students, community members, and reporters filled all 1,100 seats in Lincoln's auditorium for more than two hours. Although the school board wanted to speak directly to the walkout organizers from each school, the students all asked to be represented by Castro and other adults. After arguing that the school district needed to hire more Mexican American administrators, Castro and his colleagues turned to language-related concerns. The Chicano activists asked to make bilingual-bicultural education mandatory for the first three grades of elementary school. They also insisted on hiring more Mexican American teachers. When Julian Nava explained that the school district was going to spend $1 million that summer to train Anglo teachers in Spanish and Mexican culture, the activists answered that they should spend the money on training new Chicano teachers instead. The racial identity of the teachers selected for language training escalated tensions in the Lincoln auditorium. Even as LA schools applied for more BEA funds, Chicano students demanded a different bilingual education agenda.[24]

Many Eastside students did not support the entire Blowout agenda, but there was consensus on the eight demands about bilingual education. The *Rough Rider* disapproved of the protesters' thirty-eight reforms, saying "it's always easier to criticize and debase rather than to complain and present

Wilson High School student Peter Rodriguez speaks at a school board meeting, March 12, 1968. Student walkout leaders refused to state their demands until the school board members agreed to meet at Lincoln High School, which they did on March 26. *Courtesy of Department of Special Collections, Los Angeles Public Library.*

possible solutions." Roosevelt's student council created an official Solutions Committee, which presented twelve more specific requests to the school board. Bilingual education was first on this agenda, and a third of the demands addressed language learning. Admitting that many Roosevelt students had a "reading problem related to their particular culture and or bi-cultural backgrounds," the Solutions Committee called for replacing two reading teachers with bilingual teacher's aides. It addressed the high dropout rate by adding more counselors and an attendance officer, "preferably one who is able to communicate in Spanish." Other additions to the Blowout demands included suggestions that a new intelligence test "should be devised to test bi-lingual students" and that all Roosevelt High staff, from teachers to the principal, should have "on-campus opportunities to study Conversational Spanish." Building off of the Blowout demands, the Roosevelt Solutions Committee articulated a practical approach to bilingual education.[25]

The *Rough Rider* continued reporting this story longer than the *Los Angeles Times* did, and eventually the students received elaborate, if paradoxical, responses from the school board. Some two thousand school district employees were already taking conversational Spanish classes, it reported, and district "policy provides extra pay for bi-lingual personnel." The district had also addressed the dropout rate by hiring a Mexican American professor to teach Spanish so that all attendance officers could achieve fluency. However, the school board questioned the assumption that bilingual education should be compulsory: "It is highly desirable to provide some degree of bi-lingual and cultural education to Spanish surname students. It is now possible to offer bi-lingual instruction when 'educationally advantageous to the pupils,' . . . [But] not all Spanish surname students are Mexican-American, and vast differences of opinion are found in the Spanish surname community regarding the extent of bi-lingual and cultural instruction." It is true that Mexican-origin Angelinos' opinions on bilingual education were as diverse as their individual experiences and language abilities. However, the school board's statement seemed to contradict the policies it had just promoted, causing students to question the sincerity of its responses. This uncertainty lingered over the summer, as Castro continued to appear on the front pages of the *Los Angeles Times* and the Roosevelt *Rough Rider*. As news coverage shifted from Eastside campuses to Los Angeles Superior Court and school board conference rooms, bilingual education remained a rallying cry for Eastside students after the Blowouts.[26]

The Blowouts lasted only one week, but the issues students raised during these demonstrations dominated public education debates for more than a year. The story shifted from the streets to courtrooms and board rooms when an LA County grand jury indicted Castro, along with the editor of *La Raza* newspaper and eleven local college students, for organizing the walkouts and disrupting school routine. The arrests of the "East LA Thirteen," on felony charges of conspiracy to disturb the peace, made Castro the public spokesman for the Chicano students who had walked out of English-only classes in segregated schools. Citing the felony charges, school officials tried to remove Castro from his teaching position, launching a weeklong sit-in before the school board allowed the teacher to return to his post at Lincoln High. Castro's arrest and the school board sit-in drew even more passionate debates about language learning curricula than the initial walkouts had done. These legal victories gave Castro the confidence to campaign for bilingual education as the key to school reform.[27]

Castro's arrest on Saturday, June 1, underscored the cultural and political polarization underlying the Blowouts in 1968. One week earlier, Castro had been at a reception for César Chávez at Julian Nava's home in Northridge, where he had learned that the LA County grand jury was planning to charge him and twelve other Chicano adults for conspiracy to disturb the peace. The district attorney was a Republican standing for reelection on June 4, and he used Castro's arrest, on the weekend before the primary, to prove that he was a "law and order" conservative like his party's presidential nominee, Richard Nixon. His action reminded suburban voters of the Blowouts, a time when white teachers felt "threatened, school property was destroyed, and law enforcement officers, called to quell the disturbances, were assaulted with rocks and bottles." Conspiracy charges allowed the district attorney to elevate the crime of disturbing the peace from a misdemeanor to a felony. To grab more attention, the prosecutor set bail for each alleged conspirator at $10,000, more than twice the standard bail amount for assault with a deadly weapon. Since Castro was arrested on the weekend, he could not post bail until the following Monday. Thus, Castro began his week meeting the organizer who fasted for farmworker rights and ended it being arrested by a conservative prosecutor for political purposes. The arrest made Castro the unofficial voice for Chicano youths at a time when students were celebrating active protests as a means of achieving an ambitious agenda that included bilingual education.[28]

The Chicano community rallied around Castro after his weekend in jail. When Castro reported to school on Tuesday morning, the Lincoln High principal told him to leave campus because teachers under felony indictment could not work in a classroom. In response, Eastside students and parents organized the Educational Issues Coordinating Committee (EICC). As its first act, the EICC asked the school board to reinstate Castro, but the board upheld the principal's ban in a closed meeting. Outraged by this secrecy, the EICC leader argued that the school board did not understand Castro's symbolic importance to the Mexican American community. "We believe in teachers who give our students . . . a new image of success through education," said the EICC head. "He is an example of devotion and courage to stand up like a man." In solidarity, the EICC planned a picket in front of Lincoln High on the first day of school in September 1968. Students did not participate, but many gathered at the edge of campus to watch some one hundred demonstrators, who continued to march daily for two weeks. When the picket finally ended to avoid violence, the EICC sent forty students, parents, and clergy to occupy the school board chambers after a public meeting in October. The sit-in succeeded after seven days.[29]

Members of the Educational Issues Coordinating Committee demonstrate in front of Lincoln High School, September 1968. *Courtesy of Department of Special Collections, Los Angeles Public Library.*

During that week, Castro's supporters used their language and culture to express the goals of the budding Chicano civil rights movement. After refusing a compromise—the school board president had offered to form a committee to study teacher transfer policies—the activists settled into the chamber for the weekend. On the blackboard, they renamed the room "The Free and Liberated Board of Chicano Education." The sit-in participants ranged from twenty-five to seventy people, and several parents brought the protesters tamales, tacos, and chorizo burritos, Castro recalled, giving "the board room . . . the beautiful aroma of a Mexican restaurant." A mariachi band serenaded the group on Saturday, and on Sunday an Episcopalian priest said mass for the Catholic Chicanos, using bits of tortillas to give Communion. When school board meetings resumed on Monday, the chamber filled to its capacity of two hundred seats, with protesters frequently interrupting the proceedings with slogans like "Sal is for you—are you for him?" The EICC head hoped to end the sit-in on Tuesday, but rank-and-file members voted to remain in the chambers until the school board made a decision.

On Wednesday the board did not reinstate Castro, but it authorized the arrest of thirty-five protesters who tried to continue the sit-in that night. By Thursday, the uproar became so heated that the school board reversed course, reinstating Castro at Lincoln High rather than transferring him to another school, as some board members had suggested. The protesters were proud to bring back to Lincoln High a teacher who would celebrate the Mexican music and food that had fueled the sit-ins.[30]

The reversal angered reactionary Angelinos. Eight housewives from suburban Westchester and Playa del Rey came to the board meeting a week later to stage a seventeen-hour "sleep-in" to mock minority activism. At the four Chicano activist schools, about a quarter of the faculty requested transfers out of the Eastside. While admitting that predominantly Mexican American schools were substandard, these Anglo teachers blamed the students for the shortcomings. One of Castro's colleagues at Lincoln articulated this view in the faculty newsletter. "Absenteeism is his culture, his way of life," the teacher wrote. "Always mañana, maybe he will get an education—mañana, when it comes to repairing his home, controlling child birth, planning for tomorrow, he is passive." Simultaneously, the Blowouts also emboldened Chicano students to respond to intolerant teachers. This racist article motivated more protesters to picket outside Lincoln High. The EICC sent new picketers to urge the forty teachers who asked for transfers to stay in East LA. At Roosevelt High, students were angered when they learned that 45 of the school's 150 teachers had requested transfers. There was so much suspicion about the faculty's attitudes toward Chicano students that the *Rough Rider* printed an anonymous letter from a teacher, apologizing for underestimating the aptitude and work ethic of Mexican Americans.[31]

The sit-ins confirmed Castro's role as spokesman of the LA Chicano movement. When Castro was finally reinstated at Lincoln, the *Los Angeles Times* plastered his photo on the front page, above the fold. An editorial dramatized the school board's vote to reinstate Castro after six hours of deliberation, when the teacher was "greeted with cheers from an overflow audience of some 300 persons who then emotionally embraced Castro and carried him on their shoulders from the chambers." Three days later, the *Times* wrote a more measured editorial that considered Castro from positive and negative perspectives. He was "rated a good teacher," supported by "both moderates and militants in the Mexican-American community. Most significantly he is a symbol for many of the fight by Mexican-Americans for better education." However, other Eastside parents and teachers argued that "his actions have contributed to an undercutting of their professionalism and authority in the classroom." The controversy surrounding Castro captivated the newspaper, attracting more coverage of school segregation and bilingual education after the Blowouts.[32]

Ironically, Castro's indictment improved his public image. The East LA Thirteen case went through so many suits and countersuits that it involved almost forty Los Angeles Superior Court judges and lasted more than two years. In 1970, California's Second Appellate Court finally cleared Castro of all charges. The vindication of a contrarian who stood up for Mexican American students resembled the opinion in the *Mendez v. Westminster* case. Although Castro hired a Chicano attorney, he was also represented by the ACLU, which assigned the same lawyer who had filed amicus briefs in the *Mendez* suit two decades earlier. Abraham Lincoln "A. L." Wirin filed two legal actions that were unprecedented in a California criminal case. Claiming that his clients were denied equal protection, he asked the LA Superior Court to stop the district attorney from prosecuting the East LA Thirteen. Wirin also petitioned the court to set aside any indictment for organizing a peaceful protest since prosecution for peaceful protest violated Castro's constitutional right to freedom of speech. Wirin blamed Castro's indictment on racial bias, providing evidence that, in the last decade, only 1 percent of the potential grand jurors selected by Superior Court judges had Spanish surnames. Whereas Wirin's amicus brief against the Westminster School District in 1946 contributed to the nation's first federal court ruling against school segregation, his trial work on behalf of the East LA Thirteen would determine whether Castro and his colleagues would have to register as felons for the rest of their lives. As with the *Mendez* case, however, Mexican Angelinos used the East LA Thirteen legal proceedings to press judges to confront their biases about race and education. When the case finally made its way to the Second Appellate Court, that court found no violations in the Superior Court grand jury selection process, but the district attorney decided to drop all charges against Castro and the East LA Thirteen.[33]

Through his leadership in the Blowouts, and the school board sit-ins, Castro created a public platform for Chicano education. While suspended from his teaching position, he traveled to Washington, D.C., as an educational consultant to the US Justice Department, then visited California State University, Long Beach, where he was a keynote speaker at La Semana de La Raza alongside César Chávez. At these two appearances, Castro articulated a plan to give Chicano students dignity and self-worth. He did not initially emphasize language learning, but when public officials, school administrators, and reporters demanded a specific agenda, language learning became a useful topic to address. When he was first reinstated at Lincoln High on October 3, 1968, Castro did not emphasize bilingual education. Yet the more he spoke, the more he stressed language learning, and six months after the Blowouts, he formally endorsed bilingual education.[34]

Castro linked language learning to larger socioeconomic issues after the 1969 CYLC, the first conference after the walkouts. Two of the speakers there used bilingual education to explain the problems of poverty and segregation. One was Marcos De León, a former Spanish teacher who had criticized Sal Castro's Tortilla Movement assembly in 1963. Now a community coordinator for the school district, De León urged students to embrace English as a path out of poverty. "Remember that that which is Gringo is just as important as that which is Chicano," he said. "Accept and respect the bicultural concept. . . . You'll never get away from the barrio, because it is an extension of you." Meanwhile, the western director of the US Commission on Civil Rights worried that emphasizing language education would hinder school integration. "I only hope that bilingual education does not become another way of segregating the Chicano kid. . . . The way for the Spanish language to gain status is for everyone to take bilingual education, and not only Chicanos." Castro took these concerns to other audiences after the camp. The *Los Angeles Times* applauded him for addressing bilingualism at a presidential commission on welfare in East LA. Castro's charisma helped him turn a hearing on poverty programs into a referendum on the school district's "lack of an effective bilingual teaching approach." The absence of bilingual education raised dropout rates in Eastside schools, he argued. "Charging that many teachers are unaware and badly trained to cope with the needs of the bilingual child, Castro said heatedly, . . . 'From 9 in the morning until 3 in the afternoon, our kids are dying by the thousands in our classrooms.'" After the Blowouts brought attention to poor, segregated schools in East LA, the CYLC speakers debated whether bilingual education could improve those schools. Castro's own statements both praised and criticized the relationship between language learning and social justice, but he continued to speak about bilingual education because it remained a polarizing subject after the Blowouts.[35]

By a year after the sit-ins, bilingual instruction had become the core of Castro's reform campaign. In a 1969 speech to one hundred people in Van Nuys, he questioned why "we force pupils to quit speaking Spanish in the lower grades and then make them learn it in the eighth grade. If we had bilingual education by the eighth grade our kids would be bilingual and by the ninth grade they would be ready for a third language." Castro also linked language to dignity and self-worth. He criticized classrooms where youths were "ashamed of speaking Spanish and the accomplishments of their Mexican forebears are hidden from them by textbook writers who use

'Spanish' as a euphemism for 'Mexican.'" He proposed a new interpretation of bicultural education, which also revised the way California history was taught to emphasize Mexican contributions. Castro called out textbooks that said Spanish explorers were the first "civilized" people to settle California, insisting that Mexicans had not only founded California but had also created the first university in North America "long before the people came from England in little boats." Romanticizing Mexican history challenged the standard Anglocentric narrative. "It is a racist concept to teach that Columbus discovered America," he argued. "They discovered each other." These were bold claims for a bicultural curriculum, but Castro knew the Blowouts had built momentum for reform. "The only way to go is bilingual education," he told the suburban audience. "It has to happen."[36]

In a 1969 interview, Castro argued that language policies were central to the struggles of Chicano students. "Education in the barrio doesn't free the mind of the *chicano*," he said. "It imprisons his mind." Reporting that the school board still defended paddling students who spoke Spanish, Castro claimed that bilingual education would give Mexican students more self-confidence. "We are teaching these kids with psychological guns pointed at their heads," Castro lamented. "If a kid speaks in Spanish, he is criticized. If a kid has a Mexican accent, he is ridiculed. If a kid talks back, in any language, he is arrested. If a kid wants to leave school, he is forced back. We have gun point education. The school is a prison." Bringing bilingual education into such conditions presented a major challenge. Yet Castro's radical rhetoric brought the voices of the East LA Blowouts into the policy debates that followed the BEA.[37]

Lyndon Johnson signed the BEA in January 1968, just as he kicked off his short-lived reelection campaign. Even before the Blowouts that spring, politicians from both parties had recognized that the growing Hispanic vote was crucial to electoral success. As campaign rhetoric escalated, Republicans embraced bilingual education while Democrats demurred. Liberal Angelinos, however, continued to take action that favored desegregation and language accommodations while California conservatives, led by President Richard Nixon, hid their hesitation about bilingual instruction behind promises they did not keep.

LA Democrats were dubious about bilingual education even as their Washington allies wrote the BEA. Discussions took place across the city in various formats, including meetings, conferences, and panels that liberals organized in the aftermath of the Blowouts. In the summer of 1968, the

FDR-Sunset Democratic Club asked, "Will Anglo-American Education Survive in East LA?" That winter, the Valley Interfaith Commission addressed the complicated situation by cosponsoring a four-part series called "Crisis in Education: Who Needs It?" The first session, "Who's Running the Schools?" included panelists from the school district, the teachers' union, the Black Student Union, and the EICC, the Chicano group that had helped organize the Blowouts. The second panel, "Are We Teaching Students What They Need to Know?" included the supervisor of bilingual education in LA schools. The final panel asked, "What Should the Change Be? Who Are the Change-Makers?" The next spring, in Sacramento, a state assemblyman from Rialto created a "Joint Committee on Bilingual Education to study problems of education for persons speaking two languages." The topics of these panels suggest that, although they were unsure of the wisdom of bilingual education, Los Angeles liberals were determined to reform schooling for students who had suffered racial and language discrimination.[38]

One local Democrat sought federal funding to end educational discrimination. While serving on the school board in 1968, Julian Nava secured several grants for teacher training at Valley State College. Like Sal Castro, Nava lamented the lack of qualified bilingual and nonwhite teachers in Los Angeles. As students walked out of Eastside schools, Nava's suburban college received nearly $100,000 to prepare teachers for bilingual education and classrooms of disadvantaged children. Valley State won another $67,500 for Nava's proposal to "assist teachers of minority pupils." Nava proposed sending forty-five teachers to a seven-week course in Northridge called "Contributions of Minority Groups to US History." Emphasizing the history of Mexican Americans and African Americans, the summer seminar included such luminaries as Congressman Roybal, immigration historian John Higham, and an Occidental professor whose 1959 essay "Problems of Mexican-American Youth" was the first to report the alarming prevalence of discrimination in Eastside schools. This seminar did not address language learning issues directly, but it shared with bilingual education the goal of maintaining students' cultural identities. Nava's codirector concluded that the program would "strengthen teacher background in the history of minority groups so that teachers can help pupils better understand their heritage and problems." Neither grant accommodated the East LA protesters' demands for language acquisition, but they illustrate that Nava's goals coincided with some of Sal Castro's demands.[39]

LA conservatives also catered to Chicano constituents by advocating for bilingual education. Just as Max Rafferty promised limited language instruction in his Senate campaign, Richard Nixon made a moderate play for endorsement by Mexican Americans. Hours before nominating Nixon for president at its 1968 national convention in Miami, the Republican Party added to its platform "modern instructional techniques such as educational television and voluntary bilingual education." These calls for voluntary action did not go as far as efforts by the Democrats Nava, Roybal, or Lyndon Johnson, but after Nixon's election Republicans also tried to secure federal funding for language innovations in LA schools. Republican Senator George Murphy, the former Hollywood star, crossed the aisle to co-sponsor the BEA. When the House voted to eliminate the $5 million that President Johnson had earmarked for bilingual education, Murphy asked the Senate Appropriations Committee to restore the funds. Murphy called the BEA one of his proudest political moments, but he had to fight for the bill even after it became law.[40]

Senator Murphy must have been happy when President Nixon appointed Robert Finch as Secretary of Health, Education, and Welfare (HEW) in 1969. A Pasadena lawyer who had managed Nixon's 1960 presidential campaign, Finch was elected California's lieutenant governor in 1966, receiving more votes than the state's new governor, Ronald Reagan. During his time in Sacramento, he had viewed Reagan's bilingual education bill as smart politics. Finch declared that 1968 would be "the last election that will be won by the un-black, the un-poor and the un-young." The Roosevelt High School *Rough Rider* reported on Lieutenant Governor Finch's speech to immigrants who passed the citizenship test in the LA Adult School. When he joined Nixon's cabinet in 1969, Finch hired a liberal Californian, Democrat Leon Panetta, to write the memo clarifying the provisions of the recently passed BEA. The actions he took in Washington were influenced by his work with Ronald Reagan in passing SB 53 in Sacramento two years earlier.[41]

A month after becoming HEW secretary, Finch tried to continue Reagan's approach, promising "substantial expansion of federal aid to bilingual education." This pledge came on the same day that Miguel Montes, a San Fernando professor whom Reagan had appointed to the state board of education, said that "existing education programs for Mexican Americans are woefully inadequate." Finch assured the superintendent of LA schools that he would hire "an outstanding educator in the Spanish-speaking community" as special assistant. Three months later, despite Finch's assurances, the Nixon administration rejected the LA school district's $500,000 grant proposal for bilingual education. George Murphy promptly wrote a letter to HEW Secretary Finch. Noting that the grant application "was developed with full community participation," the senator asked his fellow Angelino to reconsider the proposal so that Spanish-speaking kids could "get the kind of first-class education they deserve, and urgently need." With Murphy's intervention,

LA's $500,000 grant request got more attention—first from the *Los Angeles Times*, then from Finch and Nixon. Republican reluctance to fund similar grants became another roadblock for bilingual education after 1968.[42]

The *Los Angeles Times* wrote several editorials endorsing bilingual education in 1969. "Will Congress this year again fail to provide sufficient financial support for bilingual teaching programs in US schools?" it asked in January. The paper praised the BEA for authorizing $30 million for language education but wondered why Congress had allocated only a quarter of that money. The *Times* cited Senator Murphy's statistic that half of California's Mexican American children dropped out of school by eighth grade, partly due to a "lack of instruction in their native tongue." It applauded LA schools for "making an increasing effort at bilingual teaching" by expanding Spanish instruction to more than five thousand students. Yet that program, funded by local money, reached only a fraction of the city's Spanish-speaking students. One solution was to increase the number of qualified bilingual teachers, and the *Los Angeles Times* endorsed a Ford Foundation grant for $325,000 to add language training programs, but this too was only a drop in the bucket. In May, the *Times* again asked why Congress had distributed only $7.5 million of the allocated funds when the US Office of Education had received more than three hundred proposals, totaling $47 million in spending requests. Reminding readers that LA's own Robert Finch had promised "prompt, massive upgrading" of bilingual education when Nixon appointed him HEW secretary, the paper reported that the school district was one of seventy-seven finalists for a federal bilingual education grant. For Nixon and Finch to live up to their words, the *Los Angeles Times* concluded, Congress needed "to provide the means for expanding educational opportunity by breaking the language barrier." Despite the earlier promises of conservative power brokers in Washington, journalists and Chicano activists realized they could not count on action. Instead, they kept campaigning for bilingual education at individual schools, continuing a grassroots tradition of LA educators that dated from the first settlement house teachers in 1903 to the Blowouts of 1968.[43]

Ruben Salazar, the *Los Angeles Times*'s top Latino reporter, continued writing about bilingual education after the Blowouts. He had covered Sal Castro's 1964 transfer for advising students to speak Spanish in a school assembly, but after that Salazar had left the country to serve as a foreign correspondent in Vietnam and Mexico. When he returned in 1969, Salazar's connection to Castro provided the respected reporter with access to militant youths and the Chicano movement. Salazar surprised his colleagues when he left the newspaper to become news director at KMEX, LA's Spanish-language television station. He explained that he moved from the prominent mainstream newspaper to community television because "I wanted to really communicate with the people about whom I had been writing for so long, the Mexican-American community, directly and in their language." Meanwhile, he continued to comment on bilingual education in guest columns for the *Los Angeles Times*. He addressed President Nixon's veto of the BEA in the last column he wrote before he was killed by LA County sheriff's deputies at the Chicano Moratorium march against the Vietnam War in 1970. Salazar's stories about language learning and about Sal Castro reinforced the political significance of bilingual education after the Blowouts.[44]

Salazar asserted that the best bilingual education programs taught academic content in both languages. He lauded a Laredo, Texas, elementary school where the Pledge of Allegiance was recited in both English and Spanish. Praising Laredo's concurrent language instruction in academic classes, the reporter criticized LA schools, where "limited bilingual programs are geared to helping Spanish-speaking students make the transition into English instruction as soon as possible." Borrowing terminology from education scholars, he wrote, "Spanish is used as a tool only until the children are proficient enough in English to use it exclusively in classes. No attempt is made to improve the quality of the children's Spanish, much less make Spanish an educational tool." Salazar identified two steps to win local support so that "both Anglos and Mexican-Americans could benefit from bilingual education." First, the school district would have to define Spanish as "a blessing which should be developed by the Mexican-American child and shared with his Anglo fellow student." Second, schools would need more bilingual teachers who could carry out programs similar to Laredo's two-way approach. This was a far cry from LA's current grant proposals, which Salazar said were "concerned entirely with English-as-a-second-language instruction," rather than bilingualism. Still, he stressed that LA schools had one of the nation's top eleven programs for disadvantaged youth. Yet the city's bilingual education classes could become even better if they added academic instruction in Spanish. Salazar believed that Chicanos could achieve these changes if they applied the tactics used by LA activists from Nora Sterry and her neighborhood schools to the students who participated in the Blowouts.[45]

Although he was in Mexico during the 1968 protests, Salazar wanted to write about student activism in LA. In 1969, he reported that Roosevelt High had suspended its chapter of United Mexican American Students (UMAS), after some of its leaders participated in the Blowouts the previous year. UMAS had broken its club constitution by working with chapters at other schools, sponsoring a sit-in that had been presented to school administration as a speak-in, and failing to keep "outsiders" off campus. The principal criticized the club's three faculty sponsors who blamed the violations on individual students rather than UMAS. He stated he would reinstate UMAS only if it accepted a new faculty sponsor, Carmen Terrazas. Terrazas had written a letter to the *Los Angeles Times* implying that UMAS "perpetuates racism" and that "the majority of teachers at Roosevelt feel strongly that UMAS disrupts the educational process." Club president Mario Esparza was insulted by the principal's proposal because "an enemy of UMAS is being named as faculty sponsor so she can control our organization and destroy it." A year after the Blowouts, students who had joined the walkouts were still creating (and confronting) controversies.[46]

Roosevelt students used UMAS to carry on the agenda of the Blowouts. The summer after the walkouts, UMAS president Mario Esparza met Chicano student leaders at an Upward Bound program. Just as Castro had coordinated the CYLC, this network helped form new UMAS chapters at every high school that had joined the protest. In 1969, Esparza planned to invite guest speakers, "make educational opportunities known to Mexican Americans, and organize strong school leadership." To underscore the influence of the Blowouts on UMAS, Esparza responded with an op-ed piece when the *Rough Rider* debated the question, "What Good Were the Walkouts?" He refuted a fellow student's lament that television cameras had made Roosevelt High look like a campus of "rioting students without a cause," arguing that, because of the walkout, "attention was focused on the problems overlooked for years" by the school board. Listing problems like dropout rates and the lack of Mexican American history instruction, Esparza explained that "the walkout was the only weapon the students and the community could use to express their desire to be heard and to make sure they would not be neglected as they had been in the past." By 1969, the walkout had already accomplished several changes at Roosevelt. Esparza celebrated that the school had hired more Mexican American teachers and had added classes about the "contributions of Mexican-Americans in the southwest." The Blowouts did not bring bilingual education to all Eastside schools, but the rise of UMAS chapters revealed how educational opportunities for Chicano students were expanding after the spring of 1968.[47]

In addition to reporting on UMAS students in 1969, two of the final stories Salazar wrote covered Sal Castro and the BEA. Although Salazar had been working abroad during the Blowouts, he had first learned about LA's language controversies in 1964, when the school district transferred Castro for encouraging student council candidates to speak in Spanish at an assembly.

In 1969, Salazar attended a solidarity rally in which eight hundred Castro supporters marched from Olvera Street to the school board offices to protest an imminent decision to transfer Castro out of East LA. The march began with a mariachi performance at the Old Plaza and ended with speakers from the Mexican American Education Commission who were upset that the school district had removed Castro from Lincoln High School while the board was reviewing the decision. The reporter recognized that Castro's leadership in the Blowouts and the school board sit-ins made him a spokesman for the Chicano movement.[48]

In 1970, two months before he was killed, Salazar celebrated Castro as an activist at the same time as Superior Court judges were reaching their final verdict in the East LA Thirteen case. In June, the reporter credited Castro for emphasizing issues like bilingual education in a list of demands to the school board. Salazar's article quoted Julian Nava, the only board member who supported reinstating Castro on every vote. Nava claimed that Castro had "been singled out for harassment and persecution" for his "telling criticism and disclosures of the ineffectiveness of Los Angeles schools." Salazar reported that Castro's case was endorsed by Congressmen Ed Roybal and George Brown, the liberal Angelinos who had proposed their own bilingual education bills a year before the Blowouts. In July, in one of the final columns he wrote before his death, Salazar praised the judges who ruled that there was insufficient evidence to convict the East LA Thirteen of conspiracy. While his headline, "A Beautiful Sight: The System Working the Way It Should," captured the moral victory of Castro's acquittal, it did not explain the latest setback for bilingual education in Los Angeles.[49]

Salazar stumbled across the true limits on language instruction in his final column, published the day before local deputies killed him at an antiwar protest. The article reported on a debate between Democratic senators and Vice President Spiro Agnew about government spending on a range of federal programs, but Salazar insisted that education was the key to economic success for Chicanos. Senator Walter Mondale confirmed this point: "We found that the best way to get television cameras out of this room and reporters to leave is to hold a hearing on Mexican-American education," Mondale said. "There doesn't seem to be any interest. Yet this is the second largest minority in America." Salazar interrupted his business story to report that President Nixon had struck bilingual education from the 1970–71 education budget. Congress overrode the veto, but Nixon's veto confirmed Salazar's suspicion that, while politicians loved to talk about language, they were reluctant to implement education policies that were "truly bilingual." Such compromises had not prevented the US Army from hiring Japanese Angelinos to establish the Military Intelligence Service Language School during World War II, nor would it stop LA educators from future efforts to advance language learning at the local, state, and federal levels. It was, instead, another reminder that many LA citizens of every stripe—from students to teachers to reporters—would work tirelessly to promote language instruction that would help students of all colors succeed in American society.[50]

7 | ENGLISH-ONLY POLITICS AND THE RISE OF LANGUAGE IMMERSION, 1971–1998

Linguistics scholar S. I. Hayakawa became a reactionary hero when, as president of San Francisco State College in 1968, he shut down a student strike for racial justice. That event launched the administrator's rapid rise in conservative politics, culminating when he became the first Japanese American Republican ever elected to the US Senate in 1976. As a senator, Hayakawa founded the first national organization to make English the official language of the United States and introduced the English Language Amendment (ELA) on the Senate floor in 1981.

Fittingly, Hayakawa used data from the Los Angeles school district to make the case for his language amendment. The senator spent four days reading one academic paper into the *Congressional Record*: "Bilingual Education: A Non-conforming View," written by Dr. Robert Rossier, a teacher and counselor who had worked with minority students in LA schools for decades. He believed that students learned English best in English-only classrooms, and he bemoaned the lack of "evidence to answer the question, 'Are bilingual programs, with all of the additional expense and disruption that they cause in the schools, doing a better job of teaching English than the educational programs they replaced?'" Rossier praised a Harvard professor who called bilingual education "a bad cause of liberals" because it blamed economic and educational inequality primarily on language. This argument funneled federal funds to language instruction, while limiting resources to improve schools and job opportunities in Spanish-speaking areas. To Rossier, it seemed illogical for liberals to support bilingual policies that put "disadvantaged, mostly Hispanic children . . . in programs that segregated the children from their black and white peers." Rossier argued that Mexican American activists supported bilingual education only because it created job opportunities for Spanish speakers and political patronage for elected leaders. Fourteen years after Lyndon Johnson signed the Bilingual Education Act, California's first Japanese American senator used data from the LA Unified School District (LAUSD) to accuse Hispanic leaders of manipulating bilingual programs for personal benefit.[1]

Rossier's report also described many examples of LAUSD expanding bilingual education for mysterious reasons. He alleged that the school district repeatedly suppressed research showing that alternative curricula might be superior to bilingual programs. This included Rossier's own 1968 study of 150 immigrants who had graduated from four LA high schools that offered a "special English program." A 1975 study in the San Fernando Valley found that a majority of Spanish-speaking parents and students would prefer English-only instruction over bilingual classes. Rossier implied that the school board had stopped initiating studies comparing bilingual and English-only classes because it did not want to produce research that would cause it to lose federal funding for BEA programs. Rossier also singled out board member Julian Nava, lamenting that "while he [Nava] spoke eloquently of the great benefit these programs would have for thousands of language minority students, he failed to mention how these programs would benefit him personally." Rossier claimed that Nava supported the BEA only because the school district placed some of his own books on the bilingual program's recommended reading lists and because he arranged for a friend to earn an administrative salary as a bilingual education consultant. These unproven allegations tainted LAUSD's language projects on the floor of the US Senate.[2]

Rossier's report was a change in tone from how most Angelinos had discussed bilingual education before Hayakawa's ELA proposal. Since 1900, LA immigrants had increasingly used language learning as a means to gain acceptance into American society, culminating with the BEA in 1968. After the civil rights legislation—and the East LA Blowouts two months later— conservatives began a backlash campaign that stretched from Sacramento to Washington. Rossier wrote one of the most reactionary papers against bilingual education, but it was part of a broader effort by both opponents and advocates of bilingual education to approach language learning with academic rigor. While Hayakawa used Rossier's research to win support for his ELA, another linguistics professor, Russell Campbell at UCLA, launched an equally audacious experiment when he opened the nation's first language immersion school in Culver City, a Westside suburb bordering Santa Monica.

The juxtaposition of English-only policies and a creative approach to language learning indicates that Los Angeles remained a hotbed for original language projects even after the Blowouts and the BEA. Opposing visions about the relationship between English acquisition and access to civic participation continued to make language learning a lightning rod issue for LA politicians, educators, and students after 1968.

In chapter 7 I trace the origins of the contradictory programs that continued to attract national attention to the language experiments launched in Los Angeles. Just as Angelinos had developed new interpretations of bilingual education before 1968, LA educators redefined language immersion in many different ways after the BEA was signed. Campbell introduced immersion as an Anglocentric alternative to bilingual education in 1971; rather than teaching English to Spanish speakers in Culver City, he would do the opposite: teach Spanish to English-speaking students only. Two decades later, after Hayakawa's ELA campaign nearly crippled bilingual education, LA liberals endorsed "two-way immersion," arguing that English speakers and Spanish speakers should learn each other's languages and could do so best if they were in the same classroom. California voters threatened both immersion models in 1998 when they passed Proposition 227, an English-only initiative that banned permanent bilingual education programs in the state. Ironically, English-only advocates endorsed "structured English immersion" as an alternative to prepare limited-English students for monolingual education. Yet the vague wording of Proposition 227 allowed "two-way immersion" schools to welcome students from traditional bilingual education programs. The colorful characters who conceived of these projects made Los Angeles the hub of increasingly polarized debates that threw language learning and immersion schools into a new culture clash over questions of citizenship, education, and ethnic identity.

While California lawmakers shaped the national debate over language learning after the BEA passed in 1968, LA educators launched multiple language projects. Some federally funded projects pioneered new approaches to language immersion while others took public school students to Catholic churches and former internment camps for bilingual classes. Activists adopted a broad view of language instruction as part of a larger project to honor the heritages, histories, and cultures of racial minorities who felt marginalized by traditional school curricula. Several proposals in 1968 supported a range of political positions. Some used language programs to support revolutionary ideas from the Blowouts, which drove conservatives to oppose all forms of bilingual education in the growing "culture wars" of the 1970s.

The Asian American community did not demand bilingual education, but two Japanese radicals incorporated language learning into a reform agenda. George Kiriyama and Warren Furutani were young educators who had watched the East LA Blowouts in 1968. The unrest inspired both men to develop their own list of demands. They believed the nation had to remember the pain of wartime internment in order to overcome racial discrimination. They also agreed that one way to preserve these memories was by teaching children Japanese. Two decades later, Kiriyama and Furutani would both reverse their position and win election to the LA school board. In the aftermath of the 1968 protests, however, they used internment memories as a reason to teach Japanese.

George Kiriyama lived through the full range of educational experiences available to Nisei Angelinos in the twentieth century. Raised in a Japanese enclave in West LA, he attended Sawtelle Boulevard Elementary School, where his principal was Nora Sterry until she died in 1940 and the Japanese community renamed the school after the "neighborhood school" reformer. In 1942, George joined his family in Manzanar, where he loved to play softball but also learned judo and kendo. When his father refused to sign the loyalty oath a year later, the Kiriyamas were sent to Tule Lake, and George attended a private Japanese-language school because his father planned to take him back to Japan after the war. Yet his mother insisted that the family return to Los Angeles in 1945, and George's language skills led to a successful teaching career in the LA school system. An Air Force veteran who served in the Korean War, Kiriyama captured the contradictions of post-internment life. He was an assimilated US citizen, but his father's wartime suspicions pushed him to insist that future generations continue to learn Japanese in LA schools.[3]

Kiriyama began teaching middle and high school social studies in 1964 in West LA, and he added Japanese-language courses in 1966, two years before the BEA. In 1968, months after the Blowouts, he wrote the curriculum for, and taught, America's Intercultural Heritage, the first multicultural course in California schools. He believed that assigning students to interview friends and report on classmates' cultures "brings out things that they'll never learn in a regular course." Thanks to LAUSD's new voluntary busing program, the Nisei teacher's class was about half black, a quarter Jewish, and a quarter Mexican, with a few students "of Chinese or Japanese descent." He invited speakers from each ethnic group and told them "to pull no punches" about life as a minority. Kiriyama connected his class to current events with audio recordings of Martin Luther King's speeches, played the day after King was killed in Memphis that spring. He even assigned students to ask their friends what they thought of Japanese Americans ("gardener" was the first word associated with

Japanese of all ages). By insisting on studying the experiences of minority groups, Kiriyama supported the principles that had guided Afton Nance and Sal Castro in earlier efforts to bring bilingual education to LA schools.[4]

In addition to coordinating LA's earliest experiments in voluntary busing, Kiriyama also oversaw bilingual education. He chaired the school district's Bilingual Japanese Fluency Exam for teachers from 1976 to 1985, and he authored several resource manuals to accompany Asian American teaching kits, filmstrips, and cassette tapes. He was an innovative instructor, replacing traditional tests with committee reports in which small groups of students would present the history of individual ethnic groups. In 1978, the school district offered the class Kiriyama designed, America's Intercultural Heritage, to bilingual education students in five languages. Kiriyama also supervised a relatively large number of Japanese-language instructors. By 1984, Los Angeles schools had 119,000 students who spoke only Spanish and just 374 students who spoke only Japanese. Yet the school district had seventy-nine Japanese teachers, one for every five non-English-speaking Japanese student, while the Spanish-speaking ratio was one teacher for every seventeen students. Three-fourths of the city's Japanese teachers were adult volunteers, which confirmed the Japanese community's desire to preserve its heritage language. George Kiriyama's language-learning experiences, from Tule Lake's underground school in 1944 to his Westside classrooms in 1984, made him a community leader.[5]

Warren Furutani had more inflammatory views on language and internment. Furutani was a Yonsei (fourth-generation) American, born in 1947 at the beginning of the baby boom. Born after World War II, Furutani never experienced incarceration, but his parents met in an internment camp, a fact that gave him deep pride in his Japanese ancestry. While Kiriyama had military and corporate jobs for a decade before becoming a teacher in 1964, Furutani joined the LA office of the Japanese American Citizens League at age twenty-two. He was even prouder of his regular column in *Gidra*, a radical monthly newspaper created by UCLA students in 1969 that became the local voice of the Asian American movement. Furutani's first column warned readers not to call him "Tabo," the moniker for his Japanese name, Tadashi. His writings were stream-of-consciousness commentaries on all manner of slights to his race. He was deeply offended when Richard Nixon's running mate called a Nisei reporter a "fat Jap" during the 1968 campaign. The internment camps had been the ultimate insult, and Furutani fought to keep memories of the camps alive. His pilgrimage campaigns used Japanese American history and language to address generational questions of identity, indignation, and ethnic pride.[6]

In 1969, Furutani planned the first annual pilgrimage to Manzanar, a ceremonial visit to raise public awareness that the US government had interned American citizens during World War II. Most of the pilgrims were Yonsei and Sansei (third-generation) who barely remembered internment, so he invited Sue Kunitomi Embrey to describe her Manzanar experiences. Embrey was a Nisei who had attended Kohei Shimano's Japanese school in Little Tokyo before the war, and she served as an assistant teacher in Manzanar schools during the war. Embrey's public memories of internment at the 1969 pilgrimage made the network news. When the LA Department of Water and Power deeded the Manzanar cemetery to the JACL in 1970, Furutani called Embrey. They formed the Manzanar Committee: Embrey organized the annual pilgrimages, and Furutani lobbied to make the former camp a historical landmark. When the head of the California Department of Parks and Recreation refused to approve a plaque describing internment, Furutani called him a racist and a bigot. In 1973 the state erected the plaque, whose inscription concluded, "May the injustices and humiliation suffered here as a result of hysteria, racism and economic exploitation never emerge again." The Manzanar pilgrimages instituted by Furutani and Embrey galvanized a new generation of Japanese Americans to preserve their ethnic history and language in LA schools.[7]

While studying internment linked younger generations to their past, Yonsei like Furutani used language learning to look to the future. In 1970, Furutani listed short-range goals for social change, many of which related to language. The first two goals were to bring ESL classes to Chinatown and to support youth programs in Little Tokyo. He also reported on the Asian-American Tutorial Project, in which twenty-five UCLA students went to a downtown park to offer ESL workshops to more than two hundred Chinese-speaking children, helping them acquire conversational English. Believing language instruction could launch a new social movement, Furutani couched his optimism in the logic of economics and foreign diplomacy:

> The Japanese language in America will live on because the young people are developing a pride in their culture and heritage. Many of the public schools, colleges, and universities are teaching Asian languages, and they are not being taught as academic or intellectual subjects, but as a practical means of communication. Also with this emphasis on international relations, Japan and China are two world powers to be reckoned with. News and information which can be read in its native language will be more noteworthy than information which passes through government controlled news agencies.[8]

Although Furutani and Kiriyama came from different generations, they both believed that internment shaped the postwar decisions of all Japanese Americans. They also agreed that language education was an opportunity for the Nisei, Sansei, and Yonsei to embrace their identity and succeed in school. While Kiriyama continued to supervise all Japanese-language teachers in LA city schools, Furutani became a student advisor and community liaison at the UCLA Asian American Studies Center in 1972. Two decades later, they would become the first two Japanese Americans elected to the LAUSD school board.

While Kiriyama and Furutani promoted Japanese language instruction to preserve cultural memory for the next generation of Angelinos of Japanese descent, the city's first bilingual program after President Johnson signed the BEA aimed to teach adult Spanish speakers skills for immediate use. Unwilling to wait for federal funding, Mexican Angelinos started their own programs, such as the Adult Experimental School, in Catholic churches. The school board embraced this private enterprise and promoted language instruction in independently run adult schools. These developments pulled the discussion away from the scholarly view that bilingual education meant academic instruction in both languages. Eastsiders boasted that their grassroots curriculum covered "more than instruction in two languages—it employs the development of new roles, new perceptions, and new attitudes." This pronouncement echoed the optimism of Nora Sterry's "neighborhood schools," which linked language to vocational training in the 1920s. As their predecessors had done, these adult educators called their school the "first of its kind in the nation." The school renewed the longstanding debate about language learning. While Spanish speakers attending the Adult Experimental School wanted to celebrate their Mexican heritage, supervisors shared Nora Sterry's goal to "maintain the American way of life." Comparing LA's first post-BEA language experiment with earlier Americanization efforts suggests that the school district saw "bilingual" education as a way to placate community members.[9]

Some Mexican activists planned their own bilingual programs before the school district was ready for implementation. In February 1968, as Sal Castro's students staged teach-ins before the Blowouts, a former teacher opened a Latin American study center for Spanish-speaking adults at a Catholic church across town in the northern San Fernando Valley. Six weeks after the walkouts, the principal of Roosevelt High's adult school approved a sister site, the Eastside Bilingual Study Center. Adults could get education credit for taking bilingual classes at a Catholic church six blocks away from Roosevelt. The

East Los Angeles Pastors' and Priests' Committee presented this model to Julian Nava's Adult Education Committee at the school board. Nava allowed the clergy to recruit bilingual teachers and design classes such as Spanish literature and Spanish-American cultural heritage. Nava praised the clergy's efforts but, mindful of student demands during the Blowouts, he insisted that "'community involvement' does not mean 'community control.'" Like Nora Sterry, Nava believed that the school board should set language policy. After the walkouts, however, he conceded that "a bilingual school . . . must be willing to confer with the grass roots people and be willing to listen and to build a program under their guidance."[10]

The school district soon started the Adult Bilingual Experimental School, which stressed culture and careers over language learning. Hilario Peña, the school district's former foreign-language supervisor, promoted "'community center[s]' where adults can renew themselves. . . . These programs help develop community pride, leadership, self realization, and social fabric." LAUSD also offered vocational programs that trained students to work for television stations such as KMEX, the Spanish-language channel. After the Blowouts, the school district named Peña the new principal at Hollenbeck Junior High in Boyle Heights. These efforts did not resolve the Eastside's student dropout problem, but they did indicate that the school district wanted to hire Chicano leaders who had experience teaching bilingual education.[11]

Two principals along with a former Spanish teacher at suburban Reseda High wrote an article about the Adult Bilingual Experimental School. They explained how the school was reaching out to the community, printing 25,000 flyers and asking Eastside priests to distribute them at Sunday services. The flyers advertised adult classes "taught in Spanish . . . for personal development, for improvement, for advancement of the economic status . . . and to serve as an example to the younger generation." Several church parishes provided bus transportation to the nightly classes, helping many students enroll in their first-ever adult education course. Trying to meet community demands for bilingual education before BEA funding and bilingual curricula were available posed huge challenges for the Adult Experimental School. In the first year, the authors explained, "teachers have struggled heroically to provide their own materials by translating existing texts or writing their own lessons in Spanish."[12]

––––––––––––––––

The passage of the BEA in 1968 did not mean a uniform vision for bilingual education existed. In the three years after federal funding for language programs became available, Angelinos applied for multiple grants. In East LA, the Malabar Street School sought $500,000 for a "promising pilot project" that relied on bilingual college students and other community members to teach Mexican American elementary schoolers. Meanwhile, in Culver City on LA's west side, UCLA professor Russell Campbell proposed an immersion school that would teach all academic subjects in Spanish, but to Anglo students only. Both programs promoted Spanish instruction, but the ethnic groups they targeted drove their teaching methods in different policy directions.[13]

In 1969, the Malabar project enlisted Eastside residents who embraced Chicano culture and American education to implement new elementary school programs. The project involved "bilingual college students as research assistants, an emphasis on teacher attitudes toward the cultural background of Mexican American children, [and] intensive parent participation in school activities." This approach appeared to work. Only 1 percent of first graders could read English proficiently before the Malabar project began, but by 1968–69 that figure had grown to 37 percent. There were various theories to explain this success. One *Los Angeles Times* reporter stressed the role of the Eastside college students, featuring photos of bilingual teacher's aides playing with students during recess. Her story started with an anecdote about a psychology major at California State University, Los Angeles, who was helping a student in a third-grade classroom spell a word by having him trace the letters in the air and on paper. "If the youngsters have difficulty understanding English," the article concluded, "teacher aides can communicate with them in Spanish." In the summer of 1970, grant funding enabled sixty-three bilingual college students to work as classroom aides at Malabar, where they taught reading, writing, and arithmetic. That year, the Malabar project was named "one of the top eleven education programs for disadvantaged youth in the nation."[14]

Bilingual teacher's aides were not the only factor in Malabar's success according to one of the project's founders, Felix Castro. The basic problem for Mexican American students, he argued, "is not the bilingual bit. . . . Education will continue to fail these children unless there is an environment at school that is truly receptive to these kids and a belief that they are normal, healthy human beings who have the whole spectrum of intelligence." Bilingual teachers could be supportive, but faculty attitudes about students' ethnic origins were just as important. Castro was proud that Malabar offered after-school laboratories taught by bilingual community members, and especially that, in addition to Spanish, learning lab topics included Mexican folk dance, guitar, art, and Mexican songs. During the school day, Malabar dedicated 80 percent of instruction time to reading and students spent the remaining 20 percent on arithmetic. This approach helped students who stayed at Malabar from kindergarten to third grade improve their reading scores by 700 percent and raise their IQ scores by twenty-eight points. Castro was convinced that combining academics and cultural appreciation contributed to Malabar students' success.[15]

———————————

Across town, in Culver City, a UCLA professor wanted to try teaching Spanish language and culture to Anglo students. A linguist and past president of TESOL (Teachers of English to Speakers of Other Languages), Russell Campbell could not convince either the Los Angeles or Santa Monica school boards to accept his language experiment. Finally, in 1971, Culver City agreed to adapt a program from French-speaking Canada. Six years earlier, when he was studying second language acquisition with Afton Nance and Helen Heffernan in California, Campbell's colleagues in Montreal had created the first immersion education program in North America, recruiting a classroom of English-speaking students to learn from francophone teachers. Placing monolingual children in a setting where they had to speak a foreign language, the Quebec scholars reasoned, would speed their language acquisition. At El Marino School in Culver City, Campbell applied the Montreal model but substituted Spanish for French. Anglophone students learned every academic subject in Spanish with the goal that they would begin to think in Spanish. Children enjoyed the program, even if they did not understand its intentions. One immersion researcher recalled asking a kindergartener about her teacher. "I like Señora Wright," she told him, "but why doesn't she speak English?" Linguists studied the Culver City schools in the 1970s, seeking new insights about language acquisition. Unlike Eastside students, for whom Spanish instruction incorporated validation for their home culture into the classroom, Westside students took Spanish classes to test how fully assimilated Anglos could immerse themselves into a foreign culture.[16]

In 1984, Campbell concluded that El Marino's immersion classes had exceeded expectations. As an experimental program in a good school district, it advertised immersion as a special option that attracted the most academically oriented families and faculty. El Marino hired only teachers who were fluent in Spanish and volunteered to teach the immersion classes. In its first decade, only three teachers left the school, and one of those did so to found her own immersion program. Campbell called the faculty "enthusiastic advocates of immersion education [who] are frequently called on to share their experiences with educators . . . across the country." The administration had little turnover, too. El Marino had two principals in its first eleven years: the first left after writing her doctoral dissertation on language immersion, and the second sent his daughter to the school. Most parents were pleased

with the program they had selected for their children. Some loved the "enthusiastic and dedicated" teachers. Others explained that immersion offered
their children the best chance to learn LA's second most frequently spoken
language: "Knowledge of Spanish in California is very important. . . . After
visiting a classroom one time, I decided this was an excellent opportunity.
I believe that immersion in a foreign language is the best way of learning."[17]

El Marino students learned more than simply Spanish. Campbell compared
how immersion and non-immersion students fared on the California Test of
Basic Skills from 1977 to 1979. Immersion students scored higher than their
peers in every category of reading, math, and language except mechanics
(English spelling, punctuation, and grammar). They were particularly strong
in reading comprehension and language expression. The support of parents
and teachers, one linguist argued, helped students develop "positive attitudes
toward Spanish language and culture and toward foreign language learning
in general." Intercultural acceptance was a side benefit of language immersion, but some affluent families sent their children to El Marino strictly to
improve their academic performance. Campbell did not guarantee fluency
in Spanish, but some parents still preferred his immersion experiment over
a traditional public school.[18]

The success of immersion education revealed more about the economic
and social differences between Culver City and East LA than it did about
language acquisition. While the Malabar School sought federal grants to pay
bilingual college student aides, Westside parents put their own money into
El Marino School by organizing Advocates for Language Learning (ALL), a
parent group that raised money to support the school in many ways. Parent
donations fully funded an adjunct program, supplying every class with a
"native language support provider" so that students could hear two adults
converse in fluent Spanish. ALL also raised money for an exchange program in
which fifth graders spent four weeks living with a host family in Guadalajara,
Mexico, offering children "the opportunity to be part of a Mexican family,
experience school in a foreign country, try new foods, absorb a rich culture,
and see some sights." ALL was proud of the exchange program, calling it the
capstone of immersion education, but some bilingual education advocates
wondered aloud why El Marino School did not send its students across town
to East LA, where Mexican culture was just as vibrant.[19]

Mexican American scholars criticized Campbell's program for failing
to help poor students who needed to learn English as a second language.
Anthropologist Eduardo Hernández-Chávez, director of the Instituto de
Lengua y Cultura near Sacramento, pointed out that immersion schools like
El Marino offered "enrichment or additive bilingualism" in which wealthy

white families gave their children the privilege of learning a second language as "a socially and economically valuable extension of the child's educational repertoire, much like learning to play the piano." In contrast, he described most immigrant education programs as "displacement . . . or subtractive bilingualism." Hernández-Chávez noted that "the overriding objective is to render the student fully proficient in English," but he stressed that traditional bilingual education displaced the immigrants' native language, depriving these students of the cultural benefits of bilingualism that enrichment immersion schools supplied. By excluding ESL students from the nation's first immersion school, Angelinos escalated the cultural divide between Spanish speakers and English speakers.[20]

When immersion advocates became aware of these criticisms, they began a series of gradual adjustments to their language programs. They agreed with the critical analysis of one-way programs that required all students to be monolingual English speakers, turning language admissions criteria into a justification for virtually excluding an entire ethnic group of children. In 1985, California funded a desegregation project at five schools that agreed to pilot two-way immersion programs. According to the Center for Applied Linguistics, two-way immersion programs "integrate language minority and language majority students in the same classroom with the goal of academic excellence and bilingual proficiency for both student groups." Russell Campbell concurred that teaching both languages to both groups of children, in the same classroom, would increase students' appreciation for their classmates' languages and cultures. Between teaching terms in Westwood, the linguist developed curricula to train English teachers in Egypt and oversaw four language schools in China. After retiring from UCLA in 1991, Campbell turned his attention to two-way immersion in a time of racial strife. He opened a two-way Korean program at a school in Koreatown—the site of race riots in the wake of the Rodney King police beating. Meanwhile, Campbell's original school project continued to grow. In 1992, two decades after El Marino became the nation's first language immersion school, it added a Japanese program. Yet even as Culver City embraced Japanese-language teachers, Campbell clashed with a Japanese American senator who advocated for English-only instruction.[21]

After passage of the BEA, the number of bilingual education students in LA schools exploded to one hundred thousand by 1976.[22] A culture war erupted across the city as Angelinos of every ethnicity—and every political persuasion—shared provocative reactions to this curriculum shift. Mexican

Americans in East LA expressed concerns about the Westside's "one-way" immersion programs, and some conservative Anglos responded to Eastsiders' complaints by asking why Spanish speakers did not learn English as quickly as Japanese students did. These comparisons in school board meetings and letters to the editor drew Japanese-language instruction into the bilingual education debate. Although Japanese classes had not attracted controversy since World War II, when they had been banned from LA schools, by 1980 the Japanese language had once again become part of the local culture war over the relationship between bilingual education and American citizenship.

While both sides of the language debate tried to use Japanese instruction to make their points, Los Angeles schools had a very small Japanese-language program in the late 1970s. Spanish speakers were the large majority in 1976, but there were only 156 Spanish teachers to reach 87,000 students—so 40 percent of that student population did not receive bilingual education. There were faculty shortages for the next four most commonly spoken languages (Korean, Cantonese, Tagalog, and Vietnamese), but their teacher-student ratios were much better than those in the Spanish classes. Although Japanese speakers were only the sixth-largest language cohort in LA schools, this group had the largest number of teachers with forty-five Japanese instructors. The school district's Bilingual-ESL Services Branch set aside $43,000 to purchase the Asian Cultural Kits designed by George Kiriyama. In 1978, LAUSD spent $2.3 million for bilingual education at forty schools, including a Japanese program at Kiriyama's alma mater, Nora Sterry Elementary. The school board continued its relatively robust program in Japanese instruction while 35,000 Mexican Angelinos could not obtain bilingual education. This disparity was not lost on a number of citizens who wrote letters comparing Japanese American and Mexican American students in order to argue against bilingual education.[23]

The school board received letters from Angelinos on both sides of the debate. Some local citizens portrayed bilingual education as an attack on democracy and citizenship. "America is supposed to be a Melting Pot, not the land of special interests," Greg Raven wrote in 1978. "Once you decide to conduct classes in other languages, you are not only handicapping these people later on, but you are flying in the face of everything that America has always stood for, and you are spending tax-dollars to do it." Several opponents disparaged Spanish-speaking Angelinos for demanding bilingual education, comparing them with the local Asian community. "Just 'why' must we have added expense to train Spanish teachers?" Mrs. LeGate asked. "Why don't these children know English by school age? We don't have Chinese or Japanese teachers—so why Spanish? No—if they want Spanish culture—let them do as the Japanese and others do—get this training after school hours at their own expense—not the taxpayers." Such critiques by opponents of bilingual education revealed the intersection of language learning with racial prejudice.[24]

In fact, Asian Angelinos were campaigning for more bilingual instruction. By the time Greg Raven and Mrs. LeGate had mailed their letters to the school board in 1978, the board had already approved the Japanese bilingual program at Nora Sterry School, along with three Korean and two Cantonese programs at other schools. That year, the Agape Christian Fellowship also sent the school board a petition signed by twenty-nine Asian students demanding courses in Korean, Vietnamese, and Tagalog at the local branch of California State University. The students also addressed the teaching of English in K–12 schools: "We feel that the best teachers for the bilingual/bicultural programs are people who are of those particular nationalities. . . . We urge you to actively recruit these people as teachers and aides. Many of them have had training in their own countries and would be a valuable asset." They suggested clustering non-English speakers in several magnet schools so that Asian students could form a large enough cohort to justify hiring teachers in certain languages. Even as many Asian Angelinos argued for more language learning, however, California's Japanese American senator was campaigning to make English the nation's official language.[25]

———————

Shortly after Californians elected Samuel "S. I." Hayakawa to the US Senate in 1977, he launched the most comprehensive attack on bilingual education since the BEA had been enacted. Hayakawa's campaign for an English-only amendment to the Constitution was one of the most divisive episodes of his only term on Capitol Hill. Before founding the lobbying group US English, Hayakawa had been a linguist whose liberal outlook led him to condemn "slogans of fear and race hatred" in his 1949 book, *Language in Thought and Action.* His political views had changed by 1968 when he served as president at San Francisco State College and a strike was organized by students representing the Black Panthers and the Third World Liberation Front, a Pan-Asian group. Once he occupied a position of power himself, the academic became concerned with the potential for language to provoke popular challenges to authority. After having critiqued Hitler's linguistic totalitarianism during the war, Hayakawa flashed fascist tendencies of his own, unplugging loudspeakers at a rally where student protesters demanded ethnic studies courses. The San Francisco State strike happened the same year as the East LA Blowouts, and the demands of both groups of activists were similar. Hayakawa hesitantly approved the nation's first College of Ethnic Studies, but he also planned for a political career where he could undo many of the changes that minority students had made happen.[26]

Hayakawa was an accomplished academic like John Aiso, but the two California Nisei had vastly different language backgrounds. Although Hayakawa studied the semantics of language, he could not speak Japanese. During World War II, when Aiso postponed his legal career to volunteer for the army and oversee Japanese instruction at the MIS Language School, Hayakawa was an instructor at the Armour Institute of Technology in Chicago. Since he resided outside of the West Coast military zone, he was not sent to an internment camp. Furthermore, as a Canadian citizen, he did not have to register for the US military draft. While John Aiso was appointed to a judgeship after his distinguished wartime service, Hayakawa's scholarly career blossomed because he was able to avoid the war entirely. These experiences gave the two Nisei leaders different views of how language learning could influence an individual's participation in public service.

Hayakawa's support for Republican proposals to restrict immigration eventually evolved into advocacy for English-only programs. In 1969, a year after the San Francisco State strike, he denigrated the importance of Japanese American history by questioning Sansei activism to preserve the memory of internment camps. This led to an interethnic clash at the JACL meeting at the Disneyland Hotel in Orange County, California's conservative bastion. Hayakawa told JACL members that internment would never happen again, and he admonished the Sansei generation for organizing its first Manzanar pilgrimage. Some seventy-five Sansei radicals drove from LA to Anaheim to protest Hayakawa's appearance before the JACL. Students reported that police threatened to arrest a Sansei photographer for sitting in the lobby of the Disneyland Hotel. The students challenged Hayakawa's failure to mention internment when he described the Nisei generation as "one of the greatest stories in the history of immigration." Hayakawa's anti-immigration, assimilationist agenda indicated why he was more comfortable wearing his Scottish tam-o'-shanter cap than he was speaking Japanese. Just as the reactionary linguist dismissed the Sansei desire to remember internment in 1969, he would scorn the demand for bilingual education a decade later.[27]

As a senator, Hayakawa supported conservative immigration policies reminiscent of the Bracero Program. He sponsored legislation that, like the wartime worker program, brought cheap labor to the Southwest, but he did not protect voting rights for immigrant US citizens. In 1979, he partnered with Arizona's Barry Goldwater to propose a guest worker bill that would grant six-month visas to Mexican nationals looking for work in the Southwest. Hayakawa met with Mexico's president twice to discuss the bill, arguing that

S. I. Hayakawa waves his tam-o'-shanter from the back of a train during the US Senate election of 1976. *Courtesy of Los Angeles Times Photographic Archives, Department of Special Collections, Charles E. Young Research Library, University of California, Los Angeles.*

it was "substantially different" than the exploitative Bracero Program and calling his version the Compañeros Program. The Senate did not pass the bill in three attempts, even after Hayakawa renamed it the US-Mexico Good Neighbor Act. These failures forced the senator to change his legislative tactics. Abandoning the Compañeros Program, he tried to remake immigration policy by focusing on foreign languages.[28]

Hayakawa developed his language emphasis in 1981 when he introduced a bill to amend the Voting Rights Act of 1965 by repealing the requirement to print bilingual election ballots. This bill also fell short, but simply by presenting it, Hayakawa had articulated a new language policy. In addition to costing California $1.2 million, he argued, bilingual ballots were inefficient because some families with Japanese surnames, such as Hayakawa and his Anglo wife, only spoke English. On the Senate floor, he stressed that he was a semanticist who understood that newcomers needed to learn English. "If I decide not to learn your language and you decide not to learn mine, . . . both our cultures are impoverished," he declared. "Our Nation has been enriched because our immigrants have eliminated communications barriers with the use of a common language—English." While noting the contributions of immigrants, Hayakawa mobilized their efforts in the service of his English-only campaign.[29]

Three months later, in May 1981, Hayakawa introduced a constitutional amendment to make English the nation's official language. If ratified by Congress and three-fourths of the states, his English Language Amendment would have abolished bilingual election materials, replaced native-language courses in academic subjects with extra instruction in English for non-native speakers, and "end[ed] the false promise being made to new immigrants that English is unnecessary." The ELA provoked liberals because it was a clear assault on the Voting Rights Act and the Bilingual Education Act. Six months later, he cosponsored an amendment to the BEA, requiring all bilingual students to take "an intensive course of English instruction." The bill limited bilingual programs to one year, and it allowed new students to skip bilingual classes even if they were not able to read English at grade level. These actions angered Angelinos who believed that bilingual education helped immigrants and the society into which they were incorporated.[30]

Hayakawa argued that he was simply applying the conservative principle that government should not be involved in issues like bilingual education. The senator insisted that the ELA would not prevent public schools from offering instruction in other languages to English speakers. He also distinguished between private schools and federally funded bilingual education, saying that, "Yiddish schools, Hispanic schools, Japanese and Chinese schools are perfectly all right insofar as their support by local communities, but not by the taxpayer." Hayakawa denied any ties to the term "English-only." From the Senate floor, he declared that "nothing I say in this amendment encouraging the use of an official language in the United States is intended to discourage the study of all languages around the world." However, the linguistics scholar did not believe in bilingual nations, either. "Bilingualism for the individual is fine, but not for a country," he explained. Hayakawa had rational fiscal concerns, but the ELA led to a debate about bilingual education across the nation. Some of the most vocal advocates on both sides of the issue were centered in Los Angeles.[31]

The senator from San Francisco targeted LA schools for creating allegedly corrupt language projects. When Hayakawa reintroduced the ELA in 1982, he emphasized potentially fraudulent practices in LAUSD by reading Robert Rossier's paper, "Bilingual Education: A Non-Conforming View," into the *Congressional Record*. Whereas the Los Angeles school board celebrated its expansion of bilingual education, Rossier questioned the reliability of LAUSD's data. The teacher and counselor argued that the number of bilingual students in LA schools had slowly crept up from 13,000 in 1968 to 23,000 in 1977 and 29,000 in 1979. Although the district's Bilingual-ESL Services Branch agreed with the 1968 numbers, it reported four times as many bilingual students by 1973 (56,000), and another doubling to 100,000 students by 1978. Refusing to accept that this rapid expansion may have been a result of the BEA in 1968, he stressed that the superintendent had not explained the disparity between his statistic of 29,000 students and the district's claim of 100,000 bilingual students. The introduction of new language proficiency tests supported Rossier's claim that LAUSD viewed bilingual education as a "growth industry." In 1976, LAUSD adopted San Diego's assessment tool, the Bilingual Inventory of Natural Language, which immediately increased the number of low-English-speaking (LES) students. At one junior high school, the new test raised the number of LES students from 150 to 208—an increase Rossier found suspicious because only half of those students were taking bilingual classes. He concluded that school officials had selected a test that would reclassify capable students as LES speakers "to support their demands for expansion of and increased funding for the district's bilingual education program and not because they were interested in accurately addressing the English language proficiency." By reading Rossier's report on the Senate floor over four days, Hayakawa used LAUSD's data to undermine liberal efforts to turn bilingual education into a tool to make federal immigration and citizenship policies more inclusive.[32]

Conservative LA politicians argued that the ELA constituted good public policy. A state senator from Long Beach submitted his own resolution to make English the official language of California. Citing controversy over Canada's decision to become a bilingual nation, the Republican insisted that Californians should "fear that the extensive use of foreign languages could encourage separatist governments" like the provincial government of Quebec. In Orange County, Tustin's mayor endorsed Hayakawa's amendment and criticized bilingual services, arguing that "we have moved too far in accommodating the short-range convenience of new immigrants to the detriment of the long-range well-being of those same new immigrants." Even

ELA opponents acknowledged the appeal of the legislation. Democrat Alan Cranston, California's senior senator, said he had received 101 letters about the amendment—and only one opposed it. This support made sense to Lance Izumi, a summer intern in Hayakawa's office who was studying how to attack opponents of the ELA. "Proponents of bilingualism expressed their usual indignation over the administration's 'lack of compassion' and 'insensitivity,'" said Izumi, who had recently graduated from Gardena High School, which served one of the largest Japanese student populations in Los Angeles. "The problem with the rhetoric of bilingualism's advocates is that it completely avoids the inherent problems that bilingualism causes," Izumi continued. Hayakawa went further than his intern, replacing Izumi's indignation with pity for bilingualism advocates. "We are being dishonest with linguistic minority groups if we tell them they can take full part in American life without learning the English language," he insisted. By contrasting immigrant aspirations with the realities of language learning, Hayakawa hoped the ELA would be seen as a practical solution to problems regarding education and border control. However, while many LA Republicans supported his campaign, even more Democrats opposed it.[33]

Liberal officeholders worried that the ELA would lead to more restrictive immigration policies. In the California state senate, LA Democrats gave varying explanations for their votes against the Long Beach Republican's "official English" resolution. Joe Montoya of Whittier called it "a statement of dumbness and reaction." Alan Sieroty of San Gabriel Valley tied it to questions of border control and foreign policy. "This resolution is going to be interpreted as a narrowing of our commitment to open our gates, to open our hearts, to people from all over this world," he said, warning that it would tell "those who do not speak English that they are second-class citizens." Congressman Ed Roybal of East LA attacked Hayakawa in an American Legion debate. The former Spanish Club president at Roosevelt High confronted two conservative myths about bilingual education. Citing longstanding language-learning programs in Europe, Canada, and Israel, Roybal refuted the claim that bilingual education was a new experiment. He insisted that, contrary to reactionary fears of cultural separatism, bilingual learning actually helped children assimilate into American life. Roybal challenged Hayakawa further, questioning whether English-only classrooms were successful. "Educators have compared this method of teaching English to children as similar to that of teaching children to swim by throwing them into deep water," he said. "Some children learn, but for the majority it is a traumatic experience." These images alerted voters that Hayakawa's amendment would disrupt not only federal immigration policy but also daily life in Los Angeles.[34]

LA liberals inspired Senator Hayakawa to make some of his strongest attacks on bilingual education. In response to Roybal's criticisms, Hayakawa asked how Congress had raised federal spending from the $15 million authorized by the 1968 BEA to $500 million a decade later. In 1981, weeks before introducing the ELA on Capitol Hill, Hayakawa spoke to high school journalists in Culver City. Aides warned that there would be "large numbers of Hispanic students—they may get hostile." They told the senator to expect questions like, "Why are you discriminating against Hispanics?" and "People should have a right to speak the language of their homeland." Yet Hayakawa did not hold back. He was angry that California had to pay $2 million to print multilingual ballots, and he did not like Jimmy Carter's new requirement that foreign-born students would be taught academic subjects in their native languages. He disagreed with the activists who said that "by learning English, by becoming part of the mainstream of American life . . . that you are rejecting your heritage." Some Culver City students were shocked when he said, "The thing that scares me is that by the year 2000, there may be enough Hispanics to make Spanish an official language." By ignoring his advisors' instructions not to engage with hostile Hispanic students during his Culver City speech, Hayakawa made the ELA a divisive issue even before he read it into the Senate record.[35]

Although the Senate did not ratify Hayakawa's proposed ELA, his plan to make English the nation's official language had success at the state level. After retiring from the Senate in 1983, Hayakawa founded US English, a lobbying organization focused on making English the official national language. Thirty states have done so, including California, which passed Proposition 63 with 73 percent of the vote in 1986. The public had lost faith in bilingual education less than two decades after the BEA passed. There was greater interest in a different idea: immersion schools. While it was still a small-scale experiment in the 1980s, language immersion became central in the debates leading up to the passage of Proposition 227 in 1998, when California voters banned permanent bilingual education programs.[36]

During the debate over Hayakawa's amendment in 1981, the bilingual education and English-only movements both used immersion to justify their respective causes. While immersion schools were largely successful, their accomplishments could be attributed to one of two things: monolingual classes, or instruction in a non-English language. Experts warned that approaches to immersion education were too diverse to determine which side was right. "Does it work?" asked a consultant at the Center for Applied

Linguistics, which supported research in immersion education. "A better question might be, 'Does what work'?" Questions like these helped immersion programs emerge as a distinct alternative to both English-only and bilingual education.[37]

By 1980, the growing popularity of language immersion caused scholars to question the concept of bilingual education. When the *Los Angeles Times* ran a two-day feature on the subject, nobody could agree on a definition. "You have a lot of birds of different colors flying under the banner of bilingual education," said Reynaldo Macías, an East LA native who was assistant director for reading and language studies at the US Department of Education. This made it difficult for Russell Campbell to research the best form of language instruction. The UCLA linguist admitted he "would be hard put to come up with [findings] that said, 'Here are some things we know, based on reliable research.'" That fact strengthened his support for Culver City's Spanish Immersion Program, for which he had ample data proving student achievement. It also made it easier for English-only advocates to attack bilingual education.[38]

The high rates of failure in LA schools showed that bilingual students needed more teacher attention than English-speaking students to succeed academically. LA schools had 100,000 Latino students who tested as low English proficient but only 980 teachers who were qualified to teach Spanish-speaking students. The *Los Angeles Times* reported that, although the school district had granted waivers to 2,300 teachers who pledged to study Spanish while they taught, an additional 2,000 bilingual teachers were still needed to reach Culver City's student-teacher ratio of twenty to one. The front-page stories illustrated that bilingual education was both essential and understaffed in LAUSD schools. The approach also lacked a lobbying organization. The *Los Angeles Times* interviewed Russell Campbell as a supporter of bilingual education, but he often highlighted the benefits of language immersion instead. Without a pure advocate from academia, Spanish speakers could not stop the newspaper from writing headlines like "Bilingual Education: Even Experts Are Confused." As immersion schools grew in popularity, they weakened the case for bilingual education.[39]

Campbell's equivocation about the efficacy of bilingual education was partially biased by his campaigns for language immersion funding. He stressed that, while some studies found that bilingual education was successful, he had read others "casting great doubts." He was even less certain about calls to cut language instruction. The *Los Angeles Times* cited one study which concluded that many failing students who spoke English and Spanish with equal proficiency would be better off in English-only classes.

Campbell warned officials to consider this reform with "great care" because "most teachers tend to teach those who are quickest to respond and leave the other children behind." He was even more skeptical about new Carter administration regulations that capped a student's time in bilingual instruction at three years—a time frame that neither side accepted. English-only experts argued that schools should "transition" immigrants into the mainstream curriculum in one year, while bilingual educators insisted that students should maintain their native languages permanently. Campbell defended language instruction, arguing that bilingual citizens benefited American society. "This emphasis on 'transition' means we will systematically eradicate foreign languages in elementary school, then spend millions to try to develop these same skills in high school and college," he said. "That doesn't make much sense." This unequivocal endorsement of language learning made it difficult for conservatives to use Campbell's immersion experiments as evidence in their English-only campaign, although that did not stop them from trying.[40]

Hayakawa's position on immersion schools evolved as he advanced the ELA. In 1968 he had visited the Montreal school that inspired Campbell's Culver City project. Afterwards he declared that "vigorous attempts should be made to persuade English-speaking Quebecers to speak French, and an equally vigorous attempt should be made to get French-speaking Quebecois to speak English." However, he changed his position after francophone politicians proposed to separate Quebec from anglophone Canada. The province never seceded but, twelve years after his visit, Hayakawa insisted that Montreal's immersion schools were a symbol of separatism: "If you are beginning to use language as a means of cultural assertion—my culture against yours . . . and think to yourself 'I'm protecting my culture as opposed to your culture by refusing to speak to you in your own language,' then you're ceasing to use language as a means of communication. This is what happened in Quebec." Blaming the French language for Quebecois separatism helped Hayakawa make a case for the ELA. By extension, the senator questioned the national loyalties of language immersion advocates.[41]

Hayakawa's LA colleagues also manipulated immersion experiments to find evidence against bilingual education. When Senator Hayakawa read the second part of Robert Rossier's paper on the Senate floor, he cited a study by Andrew Cohen, who had joined Campbell at UCLA and in the Culver City immersion project in 1972. As a doctoral student at Stanford, Cohen had studied the bilingual instruction at a school in northern California, concluding that "the preliminary results . . . are highly supportive of bilingual/bicultural schooling" as leading to student progress in both English and Spanish. A decade later, Hayakawa used Cohen's data to show that students in English-only classes scored higher than bilingual education students. Cohen did not disagree, but he countered that the Bay Area school struggled because bilingual education was less effective than immersion education. He pointed out that, whereas bilingual classrooms shifted between two languages, immersion teachers spoke only in the target language, "even if a parent, or even if the principal, came into the classroom." Cohen added that, rather than part-time instruction in two languages, "the Culver City program was not watered down—it was pure immersion for immersion's sake." Campbell's colleague clearly did not support English-only instruction, but Hayakawa appropriated Cohen's research as evidence to bash bilingual education and promote the ELA.[42]

––––––––––––––

Immersion experiments remained central to all sides of the language debate in the 1990s. In 1991, three LA County districts introduced "two-way immersion" classes that taught Spanish speakers and English speakers together with blocks of instruction in each language. The next year, Culver City opened a second immersion program in Japanese. These projects demonstrated that Angelinos remained pioneers in language instruction at the end of the twentieth century. Yet they lived alongside many English-only advocates who viewed immersion programs as a means to advance their own cause. One Angelino loved reading about Culver City's new Japanese program in the *Los Angeles Times*, but his 1992 letter to the editor also asked how "foreign students arriving in local districts can take advantage of this method with English as the language of immersion, instead of bilingual education." This question politicized immersion experiments before 1998, the year Proposition 227 was approved. The dynamic between immersion schools and English-only laws captures the legacy of language learning in Los Angeles. Activists used the city's newest linguistic experiment to advocate two diametrically opposed approaches to language learning.[43]

The LAUSD school board promoted new immersion programs in a continuation of its support for bilingual education throughout the 1990s. In particular, Mexican and Japanese Americans on the school board argued that instruction in heritage languages raised enrollment and funding. Warren Furutani became the first Asian Angelino elected to the school board in 1987, fifteen years after he had founded the Manzanar Committee to educate the public about Japanese internment. In 1992, when the mayor called out Latino sixth graders for drawing "Japan-bashing" images, Furutani brought seaweed and rice cakes to their South LA school to promote racial tolerance. When he stepped down after two terms on the board, Furutani's seat was claimed by George Kiriyama, the Tule Lake survivor who had introduced ethnic studies to LA schools in 1968. Both Japanese Angelinos supported bilingual education, but the policy's biggest advocate was board member Vicky Castro. A Roosevelt High alumna who had helped organize the 1968 Blowouts, Castro was elected to the school board in 1993 on a ticket promoting a bicultural curriculum. At Roosevelt she had offered her car to help college students pull down a chain-link fence during the walkouts; later, she spent two decades as a math teacher and junior high principal, frequently watching East LA schools lose vital funding. In 1996, she celebrated LA schools for sending 26,000 students (just 8.7 percent of the Spanish-speaking school population) from the bilingual program into mainstream classes. When Proposition 227 stopped what she viewed as successful bilingual education programs in 1998, Castro sought new ways to improve the education of English learners, leading to more innovations in language immersion.[44]

Two decades after the Culver City experiment started, immersion schools had expanded in numbers and in philosophical approach. In 1991, the US Department of Education funded seventeen model schools across the country, five of them in LA County. These schools practiced two-way immersion. Unlike Culver City's first "one-way" class in 1971, designed to provide students of privilege with additive bilingualism, two-way programs put Spanish and English speakers in the same classroom, and alternated instruction between the two languages, to serve dual purposes. As Anglophones were immersed in Spanish, Spanish-speaking students could learn academic content in their native language, and vice versa. Integrating Anglo and Latino students would also teach both groups to respect each other's cultures and give them opportunities to strengthen both languages as they played at recess. Santa Monica's two-way immersion program occupied two-thirds of Edison Elementary School by 1991, and two years later the LAUSD school board approved two-way immersion at four schools from the West Valley to South LA. Already the site of seven Spanish immersion classes, Culver City embraced two-way immersion in 1992 when it added a Japanese immersion program, the first in California. These programs, along with similar courses at schools in Long Beach and Artesia, received $166,000 in federal funding to pay for tutors, books, and bilingual social workers.[45]

Many of the traditions that Japanese schools had brought to Los Angeles before World War II carried into Culver City's two-way program. The school board had selected Japanese as the second language for immersion for several reasons. Five percent of Culver City residents had Japanese ancestry, and many of them enrolled their children in the program. The assistant superintendent added that white families were drawn to the program due to Japan's "importance as a dominant business language in the Pacific Rim and Southern California." The administrator hired Japanese-born Naomi Kawano to teach a combined class of kindergarten, first, and second graders. Following the two-way model, Kawano spoke Japanese for 90 percent of the school day, during lessons in math, science, and Japanese, before switching to a forty-minute period of English language arts. By second grade, students had practiced writing in all three Japanese alphabets—hiragana, katakana, and kanji. Although they could not necessarily speak Japanese, parents played an active role in the school. They built *taiko* drums for after-school enrichment courses and organized fundraisers to send students on two-week exchange trips to Kaizuka, Japan. These trips resembled the Nisei study tours and ethnic celebrations of the 1930s, but now it was white parents who wanted their children to acquire both cultural and linguistic knowledge. One mother said that "people think we're crazy" for enrolling her son in Japanese immersion, but doing so "seemed like a way to provide a challenge, enrichment, and offer him opportunities for the future." By 1994, the immersion classes were overcrowded and Culver City moved both immersion programs to a larger elementary school campus.[46]

Students supported Spanish immersion for various reasons. Culver City students stressed the academic value of their language abilities. An eighth grader boasted that she read *Don Quixote* and wrote a book report, all in Spanish. Alumni also used their immersion experiences after college. Several of them spent a year studying French at the University of Bordeaux. One woman returned to Los Angeles as an international marketing consultant. Another was confident she could regain Spanish fluency after her year in France. "I was fluent by the third grade," she said. "Spanish is a native language for me. I don't have to translate 'a shoe is zapato.' I look at the thing and think 'zapato.'" In the nation's first immersion school, students learned foreign languages to expand their intellectual curiosity and career choices, not to avoid dropping out before graduation.[47]

Whereas Anglo parents were happy that their children could translate for them on trips to Argentina, Mexican Angelinos hoped that two-way immersion could teach students to respect other cultures. By 1990, Santa Monica's immersion program embodied the vision of racial integration that legal desegregation efforts had failed to achieve. After five years, the student body at the immersion school had shifted from 88 percent Latino to 61 percent Latino, 30 percent white, and 9 percent African American. The immersion program attracted families from outside the school district, ranging from affluent areas like Pacific Palisades to working-class neighborhoods like Inglewood. To the bilingual faculty, this socioeconomic diversity mattered more than whether immigrants learned English. "When they come here, and realize the teacher is speaking Spanish, they realize it's good [to know Spanish], it's not just for the busboy," one teacher explained. Another Santa Monica teacher marveled at how much language instruction had changed since she had started teaching in the 1960s. "I was one of those teachers in Texas who punished kids [for] speaking Spanish," she said. "I look back and shudder." Immersion was not simply an effective way to learn a new language; it also showed immigrant children that their heritage culture and language were welcome in America.[48]

Yet many Angelinos remained skeptical of language immersion. Although the Japanese program in Culver City was popular, some residents questioned the consequences of alternative public education. In a letter to the *Los Angeles Times*, Sandy Hack criticized Culver City for allowing immersion students to benefit from lower student-teacher ratios and extra classroom aides. Hack also postulated that immersion classes "may encourage a trend toward segregating schoolchildren by ethnic group," asking why the school board did not add new programs in Ukrainian, Hebrew, or Korean. Anglo parents were more resistant in the West Valley, where the majority of immersion students were Spanish speakers. The LAUSD's Language Academy head for the Valley believed that Anglo parents hesitated "because they panic when their children enter first grade and learn to read in Spanish before English." She argued that, while the advantages for Spanish speakers were obvious now, English-speaking students would reap benefits from immersion classes later in life. Further, she challenged Hack's segregation charge, insisting that two-way immersion programs opened new forms of intercultural communication. "We hoped busing would create better understanding [among] students of diverse backgrounds, but it didn't really," she said. "This program succeeds in doing that." In the 1990s, liberal Angelinos hoped that language immersion would solve the racial segregation problems that had persisted after school busing and bilingual education.[49]

––––––––––

LA reactionaries also embraced language immersion, but solely as a path to English-only instruction. In 1995, when the California Board of Education loosened its commitment to native-language instruction, southern California school districts developed "immersion" courses that placed Spanish speakers in English-only classrooms. The first structured English immersion classes were organized in Westminster, Orange County, where fifty years earlier Gonzalo and Felicitas Méndez had fought to desegregate schools. English-only advocates in greater Los Angeles launched a grassroots campaign reminiscent of the 1968 Blowouts—but on the other end of the political spectrum. Their leader was Alice Callaghan, a minister who had founded Las Familias del Pueblo, a storefront community center for migrant sweatshop workers and their families. During the Proposition 227 campaign of 1998, the *Los Angeles Times* labeled Las Familias' single-room headquarters "ground zero of the latest hot-button initiative to confront Californians: a roomful of chattering children ruled by a no-nonsense Episcopal priest on the urine-scented fringe of Los Angeles's skid row." Callaghan and her colleagues often clashed with Vicky Castro, the Roosevelt High alumna who now represented both East LA and downtown (including Skid Row) on the school board. Heading into the twenty-first century, their debates defined LAUSD's approach to language learning—which resembled earlier struggles over Americanization, citizenship, and the dilemma that all ethnic groups faced over whether or not to provide formal instruction in their native language.[50]

Callaghan's campaign against bilingual education began in 1995. She recruited seventy immigrant families to sign a petition requesting English-language instruction for their Spanish-speaking children at the Ninth Street School. When the petition was ignored, Callaghan coordinated a boycott that pulled children out of school until they were released from the city's bilingual program. During the boycott, which involved 20 percent of the school's population, protesting students attended English-only classes at Las Familias del Pueblo. With this activism, Callaghan continued the tradition of white women demanding language reform in LA schools. As Progressive-era home teachers had done before her, she persuaded many immigrant workers to embrace English-only instruction. "We want our children to be taught in English . . . that's why we came to the United States," said Jovita Ruiz, a Mexican immigrant with a daughter in second grade. "If not, better to keep her in my country. There she can learn Spanish." The boycott lasted two weeks, drawing more news coverage each day. In a populist appeal to her foreign-born constituents, Callaghan criticized bilingual education supporters as elitists who were privileged to be US-born and literate in English. "They're lawyers. They're businesspeople. They're saying the children of garment workers should be learning to read and write Spanish." This charge of class prejudice caught the attention of Vicky Castro and the school board, which defended the benefits of bilingual education.[51]

When Castro questioned Callaghan's claims, the priest mobilized her base. Protesters insisted that the Ninth Street principal meet with Callaghan at Las Familias del Pueblo on Skid Row, but Castro asserted that school officials had already met with Callaghan to explain the theories behind LA's bilingual program. "They are getting a response from us, it's just not the response they want," Castro said. "It's a real disservice to their own children to keep them out of school." She tried to assuage concerns by explaining that English instruction was included in the bilingual curriculum. Meanwhile, the principal pointed out that fewer than five parents had filed formal requests to move their children from bilingual to English-only classes. This response only convinced Callaghan that LA educators would resist any efforts to restrict foreign languages. Once the petition and the boycott had failed, she brainstormed more radical ways to ensure English-only instruction, including a statewide ballot initiative. "There is no other way on God's earth, I am absolutely convinced, that the bilingual program will ever change in Los Angeles, ever," she said. "There is so much invested in the system." Callaghan's clash with Castro in 1996 led her to promote a grassroots movement for Proposition 227 two years later.[52]

The priest inspired Ron Unz to sponsor the initiative. Unz, a Jewish businessman in Silicon Valley, had challenged Governor Pete Wilson in the 1994 Republican primary. He had grown up in North Hollywood and was heartened that garment workers in downtown Los Angeles would organize against bilingual education. After the boycott, he asked Callaghan to help him draft Proposition 227, which he named "English for the Children" to honor the Skid Row families who had boycotted school. Opponents argued that the name appealed "fraudulently to the immigrant hunger for English by depicting existing education programs as anti-English." Regardless, the provocative title turned the 1998 election into a referendum over whether immigrants had to learn English in order to gain acceptance into American society.[53]

Although most Mexican Americans opposed Unz's initiative, several prominent Latino teachers embraced it. Jaime Escalante, the math teacher at Garfield High in East LA whose advanced placement calculus class inspired the 1987 film *Stand and Deliver*, agreed to be honorary chairman of "English for the Children." On the opposite side, a UCLA Chicano studies professor who contested the English-only initiative argued that Spanish speakers had endorsed it only because they associated bilingual instruction with the poor conditions of LA schools. "Parents are kind of glossing over the complexities of bilingual education and are in part voting because they think something needs to be different in education in general," he said. Other Mexican Americans were more blunt. One student at East Los Angeles College explained, "If you're in this country, you should learn to speak the language first. . . . Go out to somewhere in Nebraska and you're not going to see any sign in Spanish or Japanese." This was the majority opinion in 1998 when, after a two-year campaign by Callaghan and Unz, 61 percent of Californians voted for Proposition 227. Thirty years after Lyndon Johnson had authorized federal funding for bilingual education, this legislation banned those pioneering programs from California schools.[54]

Despite their clear-cut victory, English-only advocates struggled to enforce Proposition 227. Their opponents defended bilingual education by any means necessary, including protesting in the streets and exploiting loopholes in the text of the measure. These efforts allowed veterans of the East LA Blowouts to redefine "bilingual education" for a new generation. They also led Eastside activists to embrace language immersion programs in relatively affluent school districts. While Proposition 227 was intended to end instruction in languages other than English, it actually produced new experiments in LA County. As the twentieth century concluded, LA schools experienced a confluence of innovative projects in English-only, bilingual, and two-way immersion instruction.

Proposition 227 mapped a simple path to English-only education. Asserting that English was America's "national public language" and that immigrants believed their children had to learn English to "fully participate in the American Dream," it mandated that "all children in California public schools shall be taught English by being taught in English." Traditional bilingual education was replaced with a one-year program of "Structured English Immersion," which was the inverse of the Culver City model: instead of speaking only Spanish, structured English immersion classes would be "nearly all . . . in English but . . . designed for children who are learning the language." Unz and Callaghan embraced the label after a *Los Angeles Times* poll found that 21 percent of Californians who supported Proposition 227 believed immersion was superior to bilingual instruction. However, the ballot measure allowed bilingual education to continue on a limited basis. Dissatisfied parents could apply for a waiver to remove their children from Structured English Immersion and place them in traditional bilingual programs. In line with the measure's assertion that children should learn English as early as possible, however, waivers were not available to students who were under age ten or not fluent in English. This restricted bilingual education to upper-elementary students who were already assimilated. English-only advocates hoped the measure would transform language instruction, but school districts across the state avoided enforcing Proposition 227.[55]

The LAUSD school board resisted implementing Proposition 227 because liberals across California resisted the legislation as robustly as Callaghan defended it. Five hundred students walked out of classes at Belmont and Roosevelt High Schools, two schools that had participated in the Blowouts thirty years earlier. A Honduran immigrant who learned English over two

Marchers in Oakland protest two initiatives on the ballot in California in 1998—Proposition 227, intended to replace bilingual education, and Proposition 226, limiting unions' ability to collect money from members for use in political campaigns. Across the state, opponents of the two propositions tried to link them together by portraying them as joint attacks on working-class people and immigrants. *Courtesy of David Bacon.*

years was skeptical about structured immersion: "I don't know where I would be if I didn't have those classes," he said in defense of bilingual education. "It's ridiculous for them to think everyone is going to make it in just one year." Some one thousand LA teachers signed pledges opposing Proposition 227, arguing that there was no single best approach for all English learners. The LAUSD school board accepted the pledge and tried to work around the initiative as the 1998–99 school year began in September 1998.[56]

Vicky Castro led school board efforts to loosen restrictions on bilingual education. In 1998, one month after Proposition 227 passed, she became the LAUSD school board's new president. While the initiative ordered nonnative speakers into Structured English Immersion classes ("Model A"), the district created another alternative. Defying the English-only measure, "Model B" allowed schools to teach non-English-speaking students in their native language for up to 49 percent of the school day. Castro justified "Model B" by arguing that spending 51 percent of class time in English satisfied Proposition 227's mandate for "overwhelmingly" English instruction. Ron Unz questioned Castro's interpretation, insisting that the initiative required lessons to be "nearly all" in English. LA educators who viewed Proposition 227 as a threat to the civil rights and personal dignity of non-English speakers resisted the initiative in creative ways.[57]

English-only advocates vowed retribution against the LAUSD school board. Unz warned that if the district allowed bilingual education teachers to spend up to 30 percent of the day speaking Spanish, English for the Children would file personal lawsuits against Castro and her colleagues. Alice Callaghan was more concerned about "Model B," Castro's call for only 51 percent English instruction. She insisted that this flouted the new initiative and was simply a strategy to continue California's "failed 30-year 'bilingual' educational experiment." Callaghan also complained that the state Board of Education issued loose guidelines for parental waivers, ignoring the limitations specified in Proposition 227. Indeed, Oxnard schools (located northwest of LA County) had collected 1,700 signed waivers before the school year had even begun. The Skid Row organizer was also disappointed that most LA schools did not adopt the successful Structured English Immersion models that two schools had implemented. Threatening more lawsuits against schools that defied Proposition 227, Callaghan pledged to keep fighting for English-only instruction into the next century.[58]

Some school officials accepted all waivers to avoid enforcing Proposition 227, but others directed their efforts to implementing Structured English Immersion. In 1997, as voters were debating the initiative, the *Los Angeles Times* editorial board examined the pros and cons of both language approaches. A recent newspaper poll had found that 80 percent of Californians wanted schools to teach in English. The editorial admitted that "bilingual education is big business," with $400 million spent on teachers and materials in Spanish and other languages, but it pointed out that the state still needed 20,000 more bilingual teachers to reach 1.4 million English learners. The *Los Angeles Times* empathized with citizens who wondered why bilingual teachers received $5,000 bonuses even though many of their students did not matriculate into mainstream classes before completing seven years of bilingual education. Although the newspaper pushed LAUSD schools to lower the target transfer rate from five to three years, the editors were not ready to accept the Proposition 227 mandate that schools replace bilingual instruction with English immersion techniques. Whereas Callaghan praised Westminster schools for eliminating bilingual education in 1997, *Los Angeles Times* reporters challenged the district to demonstrate how much English its Spanish-speaking and Vietnamese-speaking students would learn during the immersion experiment. Meanwhile, the Orange County school district wanted to help immigrant children from Asia and Latin America to learn

English. It won a temporary waiver in federal court to hire part-time bilingual teacher's aides to help design immersion programs for the district's increasingly diverse student population. The *Los Angeles Times* editorial and the federal court waivers indicate that evaluations of the language abilities of immigrant students from Mexico, Vietnam, and other nations significantly influenced civic discourse after the passage of Proposition 227.[59]

An editorial in the *Los Angeles Times* argued that racial integration was a better way for immigrants to learn English. Without dismissing Westminster's English-only experiment, the editors argued that two-way immersion was a more effective form of language instruction. "The program works best when children who speak a language other than English learn side by side with children who speak English fluently," the editor stated. "Each learns in both languages, taught by teachers who are fluent in both." Yet this solution was not feasible, because California schools struggled to achieve a balance of English speakers and English learners, and because there were not nearly enough bilingual teachers to meet increasing demand. Although two-way immersion would be better than the current "hodgepodge of approaches" to bilingual instruction, the editorial endorsed the status quo over the complete elimination of bilingual education. An LA County supervisor who had moved to the United States from Mexico before the BEA was enacted was quoted as saying that she had learned nothing in her first days as a student in English-only classes; she estimated that the absence of bilingual education cost her three years of classroom time, putting her at an avoidable disadvantage. Ultimately, the *Los Angeles Times* supported two-way immersion because that approach was backed with evidence that Westminster's English-only experiment did not yet have. Having examined Russell Campbell's Korean-English immersion program, the editors raved that bilingual third-graders in that program excelled at standardized tests. The Korean (and English-speaking) students scored higher than the national average in reading tests and more than double the average for native speakers in LA schools. These data proved that two-way immersion programs strengthened students' English literacy. The editorial illustrated that LA's two most recent experiments, English-only and language immersion programs, remained inextricably linked as the "city of the future" moved into the twenty-first century.[60]

The clash between Vicky Castro and Alice Callaghan continued the tradition of LA educators arguing over language instruction. They were not the first female reformers whose local activism shaped a national debate about the role of language in public education. Two-way immersion schools and English-only classes created curricula that articulated competing visions of immigration, assimilation, and citizenship. To the dismay of both sides, the contest did not have a clear victor, even though California's 1998 election seemed to mark one of the biggest victories for English-only advocates in US history. California voters passed the English-only initiative with a 61 percent majority, but language instruction reemerged in two-way immersion classes that aimed to achieve the unrealized goals of earlier bilingual education experiments. Just as activists in previous generations had debated the best tactics to fight for Americanization and desegregation programs, grassroots organizers after 1998 determined when and in what context to emphasize Proposition 227's bilingual education ban versus its innovation in structured English immersion. At the same time, Mexican and Japanese Angelinos enrolled in two-way immersion schools that found new ways for non-Anglo groups to celebrate their ethnic identities in the twenty-first century. Both campaigns were part of a long history of Los Angeles immigrants creating language programs to gain acceptance into American society.

EPILOGUE
REMAKING LANGUAGE AND CITIZENSHIP
IN THE TWENTY-FIRST CENTURY

For more than a century, Los Angeles schools have used language learning programs to express local attitudes about federal immigration policy. Most of these methods favored an expansive approach in which women and immigrants pushed the school district to implement language experiments that assimilated racial minorities. In 1924, when Congress passed the National Origins Act, which instituted quotas to restrict newcomers by nationality, Angelinos offered Americanization programs like home teachers and neighborhood schools. During World War II, when Japanese-language instruction was prohibited in internment camps, Nisei Angelinos managed to escape incarceration by volunteering to learn Japanese as members of the Military Intelligence Service. Three years after Lyndon Johnson eliminated quotas by signing the Immigration Act of 1965, predominantly Mexican Angelino students walked out of seven high schools to demand more Spanish-speaking teachers according to the provisions of the newly passed Bilingual Education Act of 1968. Yet these innovations were accompanied by reactionary projects that used language instruction to exclude from the civic benefits of public schools Angelinos considered nonwhite. This backlash culminated in 1998, when California voters approved Proposition 227, banning most forms of bilingual education in the state. The historian Eric Avila argues that this "English-only" initiative, along with the Rodney King riots of 1992 and the anti-immigrant Proposition 187 of 1994, represented the racialized state of California at the turn of the twenty-first century. Proposition 227 did not end the fight over bilingual education—it only strengthened opposition to English-only policies in a political environment of increasingly hostile rhetoric over questions about assimilation, immigration, and what it means to be an American.[1]

Angelinos of all ethnicities continue to view language learning as a means by which their city can influence the national mood about immigration and American identity. This is most evident in LA's many iterations of language immersion classes. When the nation's first immersion school introduced its new Japanese program in 1992, a reporter opened her *Los Angeles Times* story by joking that Culver City alone could change national standards of language acquisition: "If someone who speaks two languages is bilingual, what do you call someone who speaks one language? Answer: An American. Culver City schools will be doing their best to change that perception of Americans."[2] Twenty-first-century debates over immersion schools reveal that immigrants still envision language experiments as racial and ethnic projects expressing the notion that US citizenship is earned by actions and deeds rather than by mastery of the English language. Many of the colorful characters who participated in these experiments came to Culver City in 2011 to celebrate the fortieth anniversary of language immersion in the United States. The rapid expansion of two-way immersion emboldened LA teachers and legislators to repeal Proposition 227 with a landslide victory in November 2016. Californians made a statement in voting to restore foreign-language instruction by a 73 percent majority on the same day that Americans elected a president who promised to build a wall along the Mexican border and ban Muslim refugees. This backlash against English-only programs has resurfaced in an era when immigration policy is tied to questions of national security and racialized conceptions of citizenship. While their immersion ideas have been largely welcome in Los Angeles since 1998, educators have also had to defend themselves against charges of disloyalty. As immigrants have argued about new immersion experiments in the wake of Proposition 227, they have envisioned a society in Los Angeles that is more inclusive than in other parts of America because of the unique language innovations the city has created.

As they did in the past, LA's language experiments have helped teachers and local leaders shape perceptions of immigrants. Like many advocates throughout the twentieth century, the grassroots organizers on both sides of the Proposition 227 campaign were women who sought to uplift the city's Spanish-speaking communities. Just as Amanda Chase and Helen Heffernan had created language courses after working in schools near the original Pueblo de Los Angeles, Alice Callaghan introduced different forms of immersion classes. Callaghan, an Episcopal priest who assisted Latino garment work-ers in downtown LA, had collaborated with Ron Unz, the author of the English-only initiative, before and after 1998. Her main counterpart was Shelly Spiegel-Coleman, a veteran bilingual education teacher in LA County who had criticized Proposition 227 since its passage. For two decades, these organizers had endorsed immersion programs that took opposite approaches to native language instruction. Callaghan and Spiegel-Coleman articulated their opinions about Proposition 227 on the Sunday *Los Angeles Times* op-ed page in 2010, but their views neglected the experiences of Mexican-origin Angelinos. Sal Castro, the East LA teacher who led the 1968 Blowouts, pro-vided that ethnic perspective when he wrote about Proposition 227 in 2011, two years before his death.

In his 2011 *testimonio*, Sal Castro showed less faith in the power of language learning than he had displayed in the 1968 Blowouts. Castro opposed the English-only initiative of 1998, but he was also disappointed that bilingual education had not improved Chicano students' self-confidence as he had anticipated it would three decades earlier. "I didn't like Prop 227, because it originated from the same racists who had promoted Prop 187" (which established a citizenship screening system and barred illegal immigrants from non-emergency public services) the teacher recalled. "On the other hand, I was not a supporter of the way bilingual ed had evolved in the schools. . . . So I didn't shed too many tears when Prop 227 passed." In the 1970s, the LA school district paid Castro to write bilingual lessons about the history of Mexicans in California to give Spanish speakers "a balanced, positive, and secure identity that would work against any feelings of inferiority or identity crisis." In 2011, Castro complained that those materials were not in use, and that teachers were not building children's pride in their heritage, their language, and their status as US immigrants: "The focus of bilingual ed programs became centered on language and marginalized the cultural component. . . . The fact was that even what passed as bilingual ed was problematic, in my opinion. . . . Many teachers got into the program not because they were committed to it but because they received an extra salary stipend. Many of these teachers didn't even know Spanish or didn't even bother to learn it."[3]

Castro's memoir reflected his disenchantment with bilingual education. This issue, which during the Blowouts received so much attention from all parties—including Castro and his students—appeared on only three pages of his *testimonio*. He expressed doubt that Proposition 227's Structured English Immersion program would improve students' self-esteem. "The student might learn English faster this way," he concluded, "but if in the process there is no support of his cultural heritage, the kid will be stripped not only of his family language but of his family culture. The result will be an insecure child who feels inadequate." The *testimonio* suggested that Castro supported a combination of language and cultural instruction that gave children confidence about their heritage language and identity while also teaching them English. It also offered insights into why Chicano activists like Castro could never support Structured English Immersion—even if the woman who proposed the English-only experiment defied xenophobic stereotypes by living with Latino garment workers a short car ride away in downtown LA.[4]

Whereas Castro stressed students' self-esteem and cultural identity, Alice Callaghan emphasized that schools needed to teach children English literacy. In her 2010 *Los Angeles Times* editorial, she celebrated the success of academic English instruction at Las Familias del Pueblo, which had left its storefront community center for a larger facility on Skid Row, where it ran a two-classroom charter school for kindergarteners and first graders. Each year since Proposition 227 passed, this school has offered Structured English Immersion annually to forty students who thereby attended school 198 days a year, twenty-five more days than most LA schools offered. Callaghan noted that most of these students had moved on to second grade at an award-winning elementary school on the Westside that offered free bus transportation to more than a thousand students living all across the city. She believed that Structured English Immersion was the key to their success. "Teaching English by teaching in English was the necessary first step in helping these students achieve academic literacy," Callaghan declared. "The post–Proposition 227 concern we must now turn to is teaching English learners the complex academic English needed to succeed." By focusing on academic English, the priest stressed that schools should use language instruction for the sole purpose of assimilating immigrants.[5]

Targeting English literacy meant that there was no room in the curriculum for heritage languages (or cultures)—or, according to Sal Castro, for potentially bolstering students' self-esteem. Callaghan criticized teachers who approached Structured English Immersion as another form of bilingual education. She accused one school of counting hundreds of American-born students as "English learners" in order to receive an extra $5,000 in federal funding. Declaring this evidence that some teachers exploited language instruction for private gain, the priest made two more personal attacks against "the 25-year failed program of transitional bilingual education." She dismissed Castro's claims about bilingual education, arguing that "schools' primary job isn't to promote home language and heritage cultures, but rather to teach academic competence in English so students can flourish scholastically." Callaghan also compared the conversations she overheard between toddlers and Anglo mothers at a park in affluent San Marino to much shorter dialogues she listened to at parks in East LA. By blaming Spanish-speaking families for failing to teach their children enough vocabulary in either language, Callaghan concluded that the city's largest non-Anglo community had failed to take advantage of public schools as places to become assimilated and literate in English.[6]

Other educators questioned Callaghan's claim that English-only instruction was the best way for non-native speakers to achieve academic success. Some one thousand LA teachers signed petitions opposing Proposition 227, arguing that there was no single best approach for all English learners. The leader of those teachers was Shelly Spiegel-Coleman, who had spent her entire career in language instruction. Her first teaching job was at El Rancho school district in the San Gabriel Valley, where she worked in one of the first schools funded by the 1968 Bilingual Education Act. After running a bilingual school for the United Farm Workers union in Delano, she worked at the LA County Office of Education, coordinating the Bilingual Teacher Training Program. As president of the California Association for Bilingual Education, Spiegel-Coleman spent two decades testifying before legislatures in Sacramento and Washington while writing language instruction legislation. In 1998, however, her efforts failed to stop the passage of Proposition 227. After the election, she formed Californians Together, a coalition of parents, teachers, and civil rights groups focused on school reform for English learners. In that capacity, the bilingual education expert determined that dual language immersion was the best option under the English-only initiative.[7]

In 2010, Spiegel-Coleman and Callaghan wrote opposing editorials, printed on the same page in the Sunday *Los Angeles Times*. The bilingual education advocate attacked Proposition 227: "Instead of nurturing the promise of our English-learner children, California's adherence to an 'English-only' teaching policy has left most of them in a linguistic no man's land, with inadequate English skills and undeveloped skills in their home languages." Spiegel-Coleman proceeded to provide evidence of Proposition 227's failure with data from LAUSD, where 97 percent of English learners were in English-only classrooms. Following the 1998 vote, the percentage of third-grade English learners who could read proficiently fell from 14 percent in 2002 to 11 percent in 2009. The promising literacy rate at Callaghan's English-only charter school had not carried over to neighboring schools in the LAUSD.[8]

Spiegel-Coleman believed that two-way language immersion was an effective method that Proposition 227 permitted. She praised the Glendale school district in LA County for encouraging parents to opt out of English-only instruction. In Glendale, the school board advised all students to learn at least one language other than English, offering Japanese, Spanish, and four other languages, with instruction beginning in kindergarten. While acknowledging that there were many effective ways to educate English learners, Spiegel-Coleman promoted one approach above others: "One type of bilingual program—dual language immersion—teaches in two languages to all students, both English learners and English-only speakers. When well implemented, these programs have consistently produced the highest academic outcomes, the best English proficiency and the lowest dropout rates. All that, with the added bonus that students come out with mastery of and literacy in two languages." She could point to a successful example across town in Culver City, which had introduced two-way immersion in 1992. After Proposition 227, immersion schools like El Marino increasingly attracted interest from immigrant communities. Bilingual education advocates who had once been wary of the Westside school now saw dual immersion as the best alternative to English-only instruction.[9]

Spiegel-Coleman visited Culver City in 2011 to speak at a symposium celebrating the fortieth anniversary of the nation's first language immersion school. Earlier that week, the *Los Angeles Times* had published a front-page article about language learning—thirteen years after the passage of Proposition 227. "Bilingual education has basically become a dirty word, but dual-language programs seem to have this cachet that people are glomming onto," explained a spokesman from the Center for Applied Linguistics in the article. "They are successful for English-language learners. And white, middle-class parents want these programs to give their children an edge in the increasingly globalized world." The symposium brought together advocates of traditional bilingual education (namely teachers of largely poor, non-Anglo immigrants who did not speak English as a primary language) with affluent Anglo parents who wanted their children to experience different cultures. Between 1998 and 2011 the number of two-way immersion schools in California had nearly tripled, to 224—giving the Golden State about a quarter of such programs nationally. Indeed, topics related to dual-language immersion programs dominated the Culver City symposium. Following an introduction by the Center for Applied Linguistics director of foreign-language education, half of the breakout panels discussed this subject.[10]

The symposium's keynote speaker demonstrated the continuing influence of Angelinos in the national debate about bilingual education. After a *taiko* drumming performance by El Marino's Japanese immersion students, the audience heard from Judy Chu, the first Chinese American woman ever elected to Congress, representing Monterey Park east of Los Angeles. Chu explained that she first entered politics in 1985, when the Monterey Park city council passed English-only laws banning Chinese street signs from the nation's most concentrated Chinese American municipality. Once elected to Congress in 2009, Chu's first official act was to introduce the Global Languages Early Education (GLEE) bill to fund foreign-language instruction from pre-school to eighth grade. She chose to fund pre-kindergarten and elementary schools because "starting young is shown to have the best success at creating bilingual students and increasing academic achievement amongst English Language Learners." The congresswoman wanted GLEE to become part of a new Elementary and Secondary Education Act, the same law that had incorporated Lyndon Johnson's BEA in 1968. However, the new education act stalled after Republicans reclaimed a majority in Congress in the 2010 midterm elections. Despite that setback, Chu continued to speak out for immigration reform. In 2015, she condemned the mayor of Roanoke, Virginia, for using 1940s wartime internment to justify banning Syrian refugees, lamenting that "the false admiration for the failed and embarrassing policy of Japanese internment is just one example of how extreme the rhetoric around Syrian refugees has become." Just as Nisei Angelinos in John Aiso's MIS Language School had studied Japanese to show their American patriotism during World War II, Judy Chu lobbied for language education to help newly targeted ethnic groups disprove prejudicial labels and earn the rights of US citizens.[11]

In 2015, Chu voted to reauthorize the Elementary and Secondary Education Act as Barack Obama's Every Student Succeeds Act. She called the law an improvement over George W. Bush's No Child Left Behind Act, but as chair of the Asian Pacific American Caucus she also had concerns about it. Chu praised Obama's plan requiring that states identify schools where subgroups (like English learners) were struggling. Yet she could not persuade Congress to authorize division of ethnic subgroups by nationality. This meant that all Asian Americans and Pacific Islanders (AAPI) constituted a single ethnicity. "I have worked to combat the so-called 'model minority myth,' which leads people to believe that AAPI students are all high-achieving and successful," she said, noting that the AAPI community incorporates forty-eight ethnic groups that speak more than one hundred languages. "When AAPI data is not disaggregated by ethnic subgroups, this diversity in experience and success is often masked. As a result, many AAPI students fail to receive resources that would help them succeed." In 2015, four years after Chu celebrated dual immersion at Culver City's symposium, she continued to correct public opinion about Japanese internment, the model minority myth, and the importance of language learning.[12]

On the local level, Chinese American reformers were engaged in more extreme fights over language innovations. Jay Chen, president of the

Hacienda–La Puente school board in eastern LA County, was invited to the Culver City symposium for a panel called Advocacy: Fostering Positive Attitudes towards Bilingualism. At the time, Chen was facing a recall election for approving the use of the Confucius Classroom Mandarin program, an initiative funded by the government of the People's Republic of China that included a $30,000 annual subsidy along with textbooks and CDs prepared by China's International Language Council. The recall drive was supported by the school district's former superintendent. "The Chinese government is paying the bill, providing the books, and they wanted to supply the teachers," the seventy-three-year-old explained. "The culture would be only the grand and glorious nature of the People's Republic of China—that's propaganda and it has no place in the classroom." Other school districts had adopted the Confucius Classroom, and Chen suspected that the recall might have been triggered by the fact that three of the five school board members were Asian Americans. In the Hacienda–La Puente district, one of the most racially and ethnically diverse in California, Anglo retirees focused their protest on the language curriculum. In the end, however, they abandoned the recall effort after four months, and the Chinese American incumbents won reelection.[13]

The recall raised Chen's political profile. He pointed out that public schools from Oregon to Rhode Island used the Confucius Classroom program because there was no evidence of Communist propaganda in it. "These classes are not about politics; they don't teach anything about Communism or Chinese forms of government," he said. "I don't see anything sinister about using books from China, practically everything we use is made in China." This ironic aspect of the recall attracted attention from national media like *The Daily Show with Jon Stewart*. It sent correspondent Aasif Mandvi to Hacienda Heights, where he found an elderly woman who claimed the program would brainwash young children. Mandvi agreed satirically: "It's simple. In the same way that anyone learning German becomes a Nazi or anyone learning French becomes an asshole, learning Chinese has only one outcome." *The Daily Show* captured the comedic contradictions of angry conservatives. As many previous language-learning fights in Los Angeles had done, this debate brought Jay Chen's policies to national attention.[14]

Chen capitalized on his newfound fame to run for Congress a year after the recall. The Harvard graduate was thirty-four years old, an officer in the Naval Reserve, and fluent in Mandarin and Spanish. Yet he faced anti-Chinese rhetoric that exceeded anything in the previous recall campaign. Opponents tore down posters outside his Fullerton headquarters and replaced them with signs that read "Vote for the American" and "Is Jay Chen a Closet Commie?" A disbarred attorney from Costa Mesa replied to one of Chen's campaign emails by declaring, "I'd never vote for a slant-eyed gook. Asians are trying to take over out [sic] country, so why would I want to vote for a slope. Fuck off and die. I hope you get cancer of the eyes." Chen carried the district's LA precincts, but Orange County voters helped the Republican incumbent win reelection. Aasif Mandvi's segment indicated that the educated, liberal audience who tuned into the *Daily Show* accepted Chen's activism in public life, but reactionary voters used his language school project to make racist attacks challenging the national loyalty of a Chinese Angelino running for Congress.[15]

California voters reaffirmed the legitimacy of foreign-language instruction in the 2016 election, even as Donald Trump exploited xenophobic fears about immigrants to win the Electoral College and the presidency. While 62 percent of Californians voted against the presidential candidate who promised to build a wall along the Mexican border, 73 percent voted in favor of Proposition 58, the California Non-English Languages Allowed in Public Education Act. This initiative repealed Proposition 227, allowing schools once again to offer multiple language programs, including bilingual education. The new measure's lead author was state senator Ricardo Lara, whose LA district stretched from Long Beach to Huntington Park. He attacked the status quo, calling English-only requirements "linguistic tyranny, where we [politicians] decide what language our kids are going to learn." The decisive margin of approval for Proposition 58 supported Lara's claim that, since 1998, Spanish speakers had felt persecuted by the Proposition 227 mandate of "nearly all English instruction." They were angry that less than 5 percent of California public schools offered multilingual programs in 2016, even though 1.4 million students were English learners—80 percent of them monolingual Spanish speakers. The battle to repeal Proposition 227 had actually begun in 2014 (before any presidential candidate had entered the 2016 primaries) when Lara wrote a senate bill that would allow families "to choose a language acquisition program that best suits their child." The 2014 floor fight in the California senate suggested that, whereas xenophobes still dismissed bilingual education with intolerant rhetoric, Spanish speakers were still using language learning to create a political culture in which most Californians would treat non-English speakers with dignity and respect.[16]

The legislature passed Proposition 58 by a wide margin, but the bill still inspired impassioned comments on both sides of the language education debate. Lara, the author of the multilingual education measure, was an LAUSD alumnus who remembered resenting Proposition 227's landslide victory as a college student in 1998. "There was a lot of shame cast on us,"

Lara recalled eighteen years later. "There was a clear sentiment that we were somehow different and un-American because we were Spanish speakers." Lara's most poignant appeal on behalf of the proposal was that English-only instruction hurt the self-esteem of non-English speakers. He also relied on economic evidence, arguing that "children who participate in multilingual programs not only outperform their peers, they also have higher earning potential when they enter the workforce." Most scholars agreed with Lara's academic and emotional arguments. A sociolinguist at Florida International University wrote that opposition to bilingual education was based on four myths: that Latinos in the United States do not want to learn English; that speaking Spanish at school detracts from learning English; that children will be able to learn Spanish adequately at home; and that Spanish is taking over American schools. The academic refuted all four myths, comparing them to the anti-German hysteria that had led some states to outlaw German-language schools during World War I. Californians endorsed these conclusions in 2016 with their votes on Proposition 58 and in the presidential election.[17]

Facing those lopsided margins, California conservatives in 2016 remained divided over language instruction because many of their constituents wanted reform. The state senate's Republican leader lived in Diamond Bar, a city in eastern LA County between the Orange County border and Jay Chen's diverse Hacienda–La Puente school district. The GOP leader would not fully endorse bilingual education, but he supported Proposition 58 because it gave school districts local control. In contrast, eight Republicans outside LA County vigorously opposed the language-learning initiative. One senator said bilingual classrooms would produce graduates "who are functionally illiterate in two languages," while another pledged he would never "take the chance that a single child's life will be compromised in any way by a lack of fluency in English." Those remarks lacked the hyperbole of Ron Unz, the author of Proposition 227, who disputed the premise of the repeal effort. "The proposal is totally ridiculous and demonstrates that Sen. Lara has never bothered to investigate the issue," Unz told the *Los Angeles Times*. "The academic performance of over a million immigrant students roughly doubled in the four years following the passage of Proposition 227." Unz defended English-only instruction with the same ferocity as Lara used to denounce it. This time, however, the local electorate agreed with the Latino legislator from Los Angeles. While the nation elected a president who promised extreme vetting of nonwhite immigrants, Angelinos were instrumental in restoring non-English-language instruction in California schools.[18]

In *Speaking American* I chronicle the long, unique relationship between the politics of language in Los Angeles and debates over federal immigration policy. Early in the twentieth century, before LA city schools had merged to form the LAUSD in 1961, school districts across the county tried to use language instruction as a means to assimilate immigrants into American society, teaching them vocabulary suited for careers in manual labor. Unlike policies over voting rights or naturalization restrictions, however, language education became a malleable entity over which immigrants believed they shared equal ownership with civic leaders. For more than a century, school districts and the county's Mexican and Japanese communities proposed language experiments that shaped, and were shaped by, national events like the National Origins Act of 1924, Japanese internment, and the Bilingual Education Act of 1968. In some cases, Progressive and liberal Anglos worked with immigrants to design language programs that promoted integration into the city's daily life. I have argued that, after the school district introduced English-only curricula at moments when the government was cracking down on immigrant rights at local and national levels, Mexican and Japanese Angelinos looked to their heritage language teachers to lead the resistance against programs that threatened to limit their access to American citizenship and equal education. These efforts explained the emotional debates surrounding Proposition 227 (the English-only initiative) in 1998 and its repeal in 2016.

Although the 2016 election marked a significant split between local and national agendas in Los Angeles, Angelinos have a history of laughing about the diversity of languages in their city. One example is a humorous story about famous Jewish émigrés who escaped the Holocaust and settled in Los Angeles. Otto Preminger fled Austria in 1935 and became a successful Hollywood director. He was playing cards at a country club with two other émigrés, who suddenly started speaking in Hungarian. Preminger interjected, "Wait a minute! This is Los Angeles. This is the United States. We've come here from Europe, we've found physical safety here, this great city has welcomed us, we've found work in the motion picture industries and the universities and you're sitting there speaking Hungarian. This is Los Angeles. Speak German!"[19]

This anecdote conveys the complex ways in which immigrants have used language to mark their identity as foreign-born Americans. The filmmaker and his Jewish colleagues were grateful that America offered them opportunities to remake their careers in Hollywood and became loyal to their adopted country. Their ultimate response to the anti-Semitic terrorism Germany instigated in the 1930s was to play a leisurely game of cards in Los Angeles—while speaking German (or Hungarian). The story is funny because it challenges the assumption that learning to speak English is central to becoming an American. Japanese Angelinos made similar statements by founding the

Military Intelligence Service Language School during World War II, and so did Mexican Angelinos when they celebrated the repeal of English-only requirements in 2016. In each of these cases, language education empowered ethnic minorities to advance their own ideas about what it means to be an American. Telling friends to speak German (or Japanese or Spanish) is not simply a punch line to a joke. For more than a century, immigrants in Los Angeles have introduced innovative language education to demonstrate that there are many different ways to "speak American."

NOTES

ABBREVIATIONS

CCIH Records Records of the California Department of Industrial Relations, Division of Immigration and Housing, Bancroft Library

CEB *Community Exchange Bulletin*

CSRC Bilingual Education Papers, Chicano Studies Research Center, UCLA

LASJ *Los Angeles School Journal*

LAT *Los Angeles Times*

LAUSD Records Los Angeles Unified School District Board of Education Records, Special Collections, Young Research Library, UCLA

Manzanar WRC Records Manzanar War Relocation Center Records, Special Collections, Young Research Library, UCLA

SRR Survey of Race Relations, Hoover Institution, Stanford University

UCLA University of California, Los Angeles

INTRODUCTION

1. Gareth Davies, "The Great Society after Johnson: The Case of Bilingual Education," *Journal of American History* 88, no. 4 (2002), 1405–29; Mario García and Sal Castro, *Blowout! Sal Castro and the Chicano Struggle for Educational Justice* (Chapel Hill: University of North Carolina Press, 2011).

2. James Sparrow, *Warfare State: World War II Americans and the Age of Big Government* (New York: Oxford University Press, 2011), 3.

3. For more on the idea of immigration as a "process of negotiation" built on relationships, see Kathleen Neils Conzen et al., "The Invention of Ethnicity: A Perspective from the U.S.A.," *Journal of American Ethnic History* 12, no. 1 (1992), 4–41.

4. Natalia Molina, *How Race Is Made in America: Immigration, Citizenship, and the Historical Power of Racial Scripts* (Berkeley: University of California Press, 2014); Vicki Ruiz, "Dead Ends or Gold Mines? Using Missionary Records in Mexican American Women's History," in *Unequal Sisters: A Multicultural Reader in U.S. Women's History*, 2nd ed., ed. Vicki Ruiz and Ellen DuBois (New York: Routledge, 1994), 298; Henry Yu, *Thinking Orientals: Migration, Contact, and Exoticism in Modern America* (New York: Oxford University Press, 2001), 9.

5. Woodrow Wilson introduced "the great melting-pot" in a campaign speech during the 1912 presidential election. Wilson, *The New Freedom: A Call for the Emancipation of the Generous Energies of a People* (New York: Doubleday, 1913), 97.

6. James Barrett, "Americanization from the Bottom Up: Immigration and the Remaking of the American Working Class in the United States, 1880–1930," *Journal of American History* 79 (December 1992), 996–98; Conzen et al., "Invention of Ethnicity"; Shelley Lee, "Cosmopolitan Identities: Japanese Americans in Seattle and the Pacific Rim, 1900–1942" (PhD diss., Stanford University, 2005), 10–11; David Hollinger, *Postethnic America: Beyond Multiculturalism* (New York: Basic Books, 1995). See also John Higham, *Strangers in the Land: Patterns of American Nativism, 1860–1925* (New Brunswick, N.J.: Rutgers University Press, 1955), 262.

7. Jeffrey Mirel, *Patriotic Pluralism: Americanization Education and European Immigrants* (Cambridge, Mass.: Harvard University Press, 2010); Diana Selig, *Americans All: The Cultural Gifts Movement* (Cambridge, Mass.: Harvard University Press, 2008); Zoë Burkholder, *Color in the Classroom: How American Schools Taught Race, 1900–1954* (New York: Oxford University Press, 2011); Frank Van Nuys, *Americanizing the West: Race, Immigrants, and Citizenship, 1890–1930* (Lawrence: University Press of Kansas, 2002); Yoon Pak, *Wherever I Go, I Will Always Be a Loyal American: Schooling Seattle's Japanese American Schoolchildren during World War II* (New York: Routledge/Falmer, 2002). All these works build off John Higham's original study of Americanization as a nativist movement, *Strangers in the Land*.

8. Carey McWilliams, *Brothers under the Skin*, rev. ed. (Boston: Little, Brown, 1951), 49. The National Origins Act set miniscule quotas for Asian countries (one hundred per nation), but it did not apply to countries in the Western Hemisphere, so immigration from countries in Latin America and the Caribbean increased without regulation after 1924.

9. Mark Brilliant, *The Color of America Has Changed: How Racial Diversity Shaped Civil Rights Reform in California, 1941–1978* (New York: Oxford University Press, 2010), 3–4; Natalia Mehlman Petrzela, *Classroom Wars: Language, Sex, and the Creation of Modern Political Culture* (New York: Oxford University Press, 2015). Also see Daniel HoSang, *Racial Propositions: Ballot Initiatives and the Making of Postwar California* (Berkeley: University of California Press, 2010); Scott Kurashige, *The Shifting Grounds of Race: Black and Japanese Americans in the Making of Multiethnic*

Los Angeles (Princeton, N.J.: Princeton University Press, 2008); Shana Bernstein, *Bridges of Reform: Interracial Civil Rights Activism in Twentieth-Century Los Angeles* (New York: Oxford University Press, 2011).

10. Linda Bosniak, *The Citizen and the Alien* (Princeton, N.J.: Princeton University Press, 2006). According to Bosniak, "citizenship is treated as the highest measure of social and political inclusion" (p. 3).

11. Stephen May, *Language and Minority Rights: Ethnicity, Nationalism, and the Politics of Language* (Harlow, Essex, UK: Longman, 2001), 129; Burkholder, *Color in the Classroom*; Petrzela, *Classroom Wars*; Benedict Anderson, *Imagined Communities: Reflections on the Origin and Spread of Nationalism* (London: Verso, 1983); Eugen Weber, *Peasants into Frenchmen: The Modernization of Rural France, 1870–1914* (Stanford, Calif.: Stanford University Press, 1976). Other Europeanists who address language instruction in the context of nation-building include Eric Hobsbawm and Terence Ranger, eds., *The Invention of Tradition* (Cambridge: Cambridge University Press, 1983); and Patrice Higonnet, "The Politics of Linguistic Terrorism and Grammatical Hegemony during the French Revolution," *Social History* 5 (1980), 41–69. Scholarship of language instruction outside Europe includes Mary Kay Vaughan, *Cultural Politics in Revolution: Teachers, Peasants, and Schools in Mexico, 1930–1930* (Tucson: University of Arizona Press, 1997) and Hiraku Shimoda, "Tongues-Tied: The Making of a 'National Language' and the Discovery of Dialects in Meiji Japan," *American Historical Review* 115, no. 3 (2010).

12. George J. Sánchez, *Becoming Mexican American: Ethnicity, Culture, and Identity in Chicano Los Angeles, 1900–1945* (New York: Oxford University Press, 1993), 88; Reginald Bell, *Public School Education of Second-Generation Japanese in California* (Stanford, Calif.: Stanford University Press, 1935), 379; Edward Strong, *The Second-Generation Japanese Problem* (Stanford, Calif.: Stanford University Press, 1934), 68–69; Mrs. Pierce and Mrs. Dorsey Discuss Matters before the Principals' Club," *Los Angeles School Journal* 6 (February 12, 1923), 59 (hereafter *LASJ*).

13. Mark Wild, *Street Meeting: Multiethnic Neighborhoods in Early Twentieth-Century Los Angeles* (Berkeley: University of California Press, 2005); Allison Varzally, *Making a Non-white America: Californians Coloring Outside Ethnic Lines, 1925–1955* (Berkeley: University of California Press, 2008); Kathleen Weiler, *Democracy and Schooling in California: The Legacy of Helen Heffernan and Corinne Seeds* (New York: Palgrave Macmillan, 2011); Judith Raftery, *Land of Fair Promise: Politics and Reform in Los Angeles Schools, 1885–1941* (Stanford, Calif.: Stanford University Press, 1992).

14. Randolph Bourne, "Trans-National America," *Atlantic Monthly* 118 (1916), 86–97, http://www.theatlantic.com/magazine/archive/1916/07/trans-national-america/304838/.

15. Sánchez, *Becoming Mexican American*. Other studies of Americanization in Los Angeles during the Progressive Era include Sánchez, "'Go after the Women': wAmericanization and the Mexican Immigrant Woman, 1915–29," in Ruiz and DuBois, *Unequal Sisters*, 284–97; and Lawrence Culver, "Closing America's Playground: Los Angeles and the History of Our Parks and Recreation Crisis," *History News Network*, accessed April 11, 2011, http://www.hnn.us/articles/138310.html. Other scholars have

also compared past ethnic attitudes toward citizenship. In her history of public health in Los Angeles, for example, Natalia Molina found that county officials used the discourse of health to racialize Mexican and Japanese immigrants, creating a hierarchy that energized and legitimized racism. Molina, *Fit to Be Citizens? Public Health and Race in Los Angeles, 1879–1939* (Berkeley: University of California Press, 2006).

16. Eiichiro Azuma, *Between Two Empires: Race, History, and Transnationalism in Japanese America* (New York: Oxford University Press, 2005), 145. Other binational border histories include Kelly Lytle Hernández, *Migra! A History of the U.S. Border Patrol* (Berkeley: University of California Press, 2010). For more on the Nisei, see Lon Kurashige, *Japanese American Celebration and Conflict: A History of Ethnic Identity and Festival, 1934–1990* (Berkeley: University of California Press, 2002); Yuji Ichioka, *Before Internment: Essays in Prewar Japanese American History*, ed. Gordon Chang and Eiichiro Azuma (Stanford, Calif.: Stanford University Press, 2006).

CHAPTER 1

1. Mary Gibson, "Schools for the Whole Family," *The Survey* 56, no. 5 (June 1, 1926), 300; Portillo quoted in Gertrude Ford, "A Home Teacher Graduation," *Community Exchange Bulletin* 4, no. 4 (1926), 19 (hereafter *CEB*).
2. Diane Wood, "Immigrant Mothers, Female Reformers, and Women Teachers: The California Home Teachers Act of 1915" (PhD diss., Stanford University, 1996), 5; quotation from "Education for Everybody: The California Plan," *The Survey* 56, no. 5 (June 1, 1926), 297.
3. Jane Addams introduced the term "city housekeeping" in "The Modern City and the Municipal Franchise for Women," reprinted in *The Concise History of Woman's Suffrage*, ed. Mari Jo Buhle and Paul Buhle (Urbana: University of Illinois Press, 1978), 371.
4. "The College Settlement (formerly Casa de Castelar)" in *Handbook of Settlements*, ed. Robert Woods and Albert Kennedy (New York: Russell Sage Foundation, 1911), 11–12; Louise Cooperider, "History of the Americanization Department in the Los Angeles City Schools" (master's thesis, University of Southern California, 1934), 112; George Jackson, "A History of the Adult Education Program in the Los Angeles Public Schools" (PhD diss., UCLA, 1957), 36–37.
5. Amanda Mathews, *The Hieroglyphics of Love: Stories of Sonora Town & Old Mexico* (Los Angeles: Artemisia Bindery, 1906), 72–82.
6. Mathews, *Hieroglyphics of Love*, 72–82.
7. Ethel Richardson, "Program Reports of the Assistant Superintendent of Public Instruction," April 1, 1921, Carton 92, Folder 11, Records of the California Department of Industrial Relations, Division of Immigration and Housing, Bancroft Library, University of California, Berkeley (hereafter CCIH Records); Wood, "Immigrant Mothers, Female Reformers," 33; Amanda M. Chase, "Working Plans for the Home Teacher," in *The Home Teacher: The Act, with a Working Plan and Forty Lessons in English* (Sacramento: Commission of Immigration and Housing of California, State Printing Office, 1916), 7–9.

8. Chase, "Working Plans for the Home Teacher," 9–12.

9. Chase, quoted in Wood, "Immigrant Mothers, Female Reformers," 57; Chase, "Ninth Lesson," in *Primer for Foreign-Speaking Women, Part I* (Sacramento: Commission of Immigration and Housing of California, 1918), 15; "Home Teaching Experiences II, by Amanda Mathews Chase, Amelia St. School," *LASJ* 5 (November 14, 1921), 5.

10. Cooperider, "History of the Americanization Department," 58, 116; Raftery, *Land of Fair Promise*, 77; Baughman, "Elementary Education for Adults," *Annals of the American Academy of Political and Social Science* 93 (January 1921), 163–68.

11. Baughman, "Elementary Education for Adults," 161, 163, 165.

12. Although sixteen of the articles focused on "the Japanese question" in California, eight writers, including Aronovici, joined Baughman in commenting about national questions of assimilation. Aronovici was also one of four authors who addressed Mexican immigration. "Present-Day Immigration with Special Reference to the Japanese," special issue, *Annals of the American Academy of Political and Social Science* 93 (January 1921), 93, x.

13. Mary Gibson to Henry Norton, August 8, 1919, Norton to Gibson, October 7, 1919, and Gibson to Simon Lubin, November 10, 1919, Carton 1, Folders 15–16, CCIH Records; Profile of Carol Aronovici, 1931, Box 3, Folder 27, University of California Extension School Records, Bancroft Library.

14. Carol Aronovici, "Americanization," *Annals of the American Academy of Political and Social Science* 93 (January 1921), 134–38; Baughman, "Elementary Education for Adults," 161–62.

15. Mary Gibson to Henry Norton, August 8, 1919, Norton to Gibson, October 7, 1919, and Gibson to Simon Lubin, November 10, 1919. Gibson was the educational commissioner who insisted on hiring Collier. She was also the author of the California Home Teacher Act in 1915. For more on Collier, see Kenneth Philp, *John Collier's Crusade for Indian Reform, 1920–1954* (Tucson: University of Arizona Press, 1977).

16. Yu, *Thinking Orientals*, 40–41; Ruiz and DuBois, *Unequal Sisters*, 298.

17. Annie Callaghan, "A Community Organization I Have Known" (blue book exam written for Economics 89 course, University of California, Southern Branch), July 9, 1920, Carton 93, Folder 8, CCIH Records.

18. Druzilla Mackey, "A Community Organization I Have Known" (blue book exam for Economics 89), July 9, 1920, Carton 93, Folder 11, CCIH Records.

19. Cooperider, "History of the Americanization Department," 56–58; Mackey, "Impresiones de México," *CEB* 4, no. 1 (1925), 28–31; Gilbert G. Gonzalez, *Labor and Community: Mexican Citrus Worker Villages in a Southern California County, 1900–1950* (Urbana: University of Illinois Press, 1994), 122–32. Mackey also published *An Easy English Book for the Foreign Born* (Dansville, N.Y.: Owen, 1922).

20. Natalie Loewenthal and R. Tate, "An Immigrant I Have Known" (blue book exam for Economics 52), July 9, 1920, Carton 93, Folders 5 and 7, CCIH Records; Mary Lanigan, "Second Generation Mexicans in Belvedere" (master's thesis, University of Southern California, 1932), 39–42.

21. Flora Smith, "Cottage Classes," *CEB* 4, no. 2 (1926), 16–17. Flora Smith, the Americanization director, was so proud of her classes that she invited the Mexican consul to take a tour. Smith argued that "Americanization is the encouragement of decent living." Quoted in Cooperider, "History of the Americanization Department," 12.

22. Margaret Holdsworth, "A Community Organization I Have Known" (blue book exam for Economics 89), July 9, 1920, Carton 93, Folder 10, CCIH Records; Gretchen Tuthill, "Study of the Japanese in the City of Los Angeles" (master's thesis, University of Southern California, 1924), 39–41.

23. Holdsworth, "A Community Organization I Have Known"; Grace Palmer, "Escuelita," *CEB* 5, no. 2 (1926), 37.

24. The most detailed statistical studies of immigrants' academic performance included Merton Hill, *The Development of an Americanization Program* (Ontario, Calif.: Board of Trustees of the Chaffey Union High School, 1928); Ellen McAnulty, "Achievement and Intelligence Test Results for Mexican Children Attending Los Angeles City Schools," *Los Angeles Educational Research Bulletin* 11 (March 1932); Bell, *Public School Education*; and Strong, *Second-Generation Japanese Problem*.

25. William Smith, "Oriental vs. Mexican Children in School (interview with Miss James)," n.d., No. 327, Box 35, Survey of Race Relations, Hoover Institution, Stanford University (hereafter SRR); Paula Fass, *Outside In: Minorities and the Transformation of American Education* (New York: Oxford University Press, 1989), 45–46. While Nisei earned higher grades in academic classes, Anglo-Americans continued to score the highest on IQ exams.

26. Hill, *Development of an Americanization Program*, preface, 6, 13–15, 52–55, 62–64, 82–83. Hill calculated "index of ability" by direct comparisons of Mexican Americans' and Anglo-Americans' scores on tests of vocabulary and language acquisition (in both English and Spanish). He gave students tests designed by the Educational Research division of LA city schools. In a 1932 survey of 1,240 Mexican-origin children, the LA school district found that the average Mexican IQ was nine points below the control group of 1,074 Anglo-American children, in part due to the language handicap. Although the Mexican children's reading comprehension scores were on par with their IQ measures and grade placements, the school district concluded that the average Mexican child was "found to be chronologically retarded one full year." McAnulty, "Achievement and Intelligence Test Results for Mexican Children," 91–92.

27. Bell, *Public School Education*, 32–62. Bell's data about "educational progress" and academic success of US-born Japanese came from Los Angeles junior and senior high schools.

28. Bell, 35; Hill, *Development of an Americanization Program*, 95; William Petersen, "Success Story, Japanese-American Style," *New York Times Magazine*, January 9, 1966, 20–21.

29. Stories in *La Opinión* included "50 colegios mexicanos en California del Sur," November 12, 1927, 1; "La escuela 'México,' de Belvedere," February 17, 1927, 2; "Grave disputa en Belvedere: la escuela 'México,' en peligro de desaparecer," July 31, 1927, 1; "Ocho escuelas mexicanas en Los Angeles: informe del Departamento Educativo

del Consulado," September 1, 1929, 1; "Tres escuelas para educar 80,000 niños," October 12, 1930, 1; James Cameron, "The History of Mexican Public Education in Los Angeles, 1910–1930" (master's thesis, University of Southern California, 1976), 39, 179–80. For more on education reform in postrevolutionary Mexico, see Vaughan, *Cultural Politics in Revolution*.

30. Manuel Gamio, *The Life Story of the Mexican Immigrant* (New York: Dover, [1931] 1971), 205–8, 55–58, 237–42, 50–52, 109–11. The claim that Mexican immigrants in Los Angeles were more likely to speak English than their counterparts in other cities was confirmed by labor organizer Bert Corona who, upon moving to LA from El Paso in 1936 was told that "here it's best not to speak Spanish. It's best if they don't know you're Mexican. They treat you better." Mario García, *Memories of Chicano History: The Life and Narrative of Bert Corona* (Berkeley: University of California Press, 1994), 68–73.

31. "Mrs. Pierce and Mrs. Dorsey Discuss Matters before the Principals' Club," *LASJ* 6 (February 12, 1923), 59.

32. Koyoshi Uono, "The Factors Affecting the Geographical Aggregation and Dispersion of the Japanese Residences in the City of Los Angeles" (master's thesis, University of Southern California, 1927), 110–30; Sue Kunitomi Embrey, interview by Arthur Hansen and David Hacker, August 24, 1973, interview no. 1366, California State University, Fullerton, Oral History Program, 102; Diana Bahr, *The Unquiet Nisei: An Oral History of the Life of Sue Kunitomi Embrey* (New York: Palgrave Macmillan, 2007), 13; Tamiko Tanaka, "The Japanese Language School in Relation to Assimilation" (master's thesis, University of Southern California, 1933), 34, 39; Fumiko Fukuoka, "Mutual Life and Aid among the Japanese in Southern California with Special Reference to Los Angeles" (master's thesis, University of Southern California, 1937), 69–70.

33. Embrey interview by Hansen and Hacker, 102; Tanaka, 56–58; Toyotomi Morimoto, "Language and Heritage Maintenance of Immigrants: Japanese Language Schools in California, 1903–1941" (PhD diss., UCLA, 1989), 68, 80–93; quotation from Shimano on 87. Morimoto explains that in *Farrington v. Tokushige* (1927) the Supreme Court overturned a language education ban imposed in Hawaii, and this decision annulled the California Private School Control Law.

34. Kiichi Kanzaki, *California and the Japanese* (San Francisco: R and E Research Associates, [1921] 1971), 20–21.

35. Quotation from Tanaka, "Japanese Language School in Relation to Assimilation," 51; Morimoto, "Language and Heritage Maintenance," 8.

36. William Smith, "Takeuchi: The Life History As a Social Document," August 14, 1924, no. 86, Box 25, SRR, 13; Stories about Aiso in the *Los Angeles Times* (hereafter *LAT*) included "Boy Orator on Way East," May 30, 1926, 4; "Oratory Champion Arrives Home," June 16, 1926, A1; "John Aiso to Visit Japan: American-Born Oriental Who Gave Wenig Chance to Win Oratorical Honors Holds High Record," October 28, 1926, A11.

37. "John Aiso to Visit Japan"; Aiso, "As Japan Sees America," *LAT*, July 31, 1927, B4.

CHAPTER 2

1. Roosevelt quoted in Shafer, "Naturalization," *LASJ* 2 (March 23, 1919), 465–66; *LASJ* 5 (November 14, 1921), 11; Shafer, "Americanization," *LASJ* 2 (September 16, 1918), 34. Shafer cited another ceremony in addition to the one at the Amelia Street School.

2. "Citizens Made As They Wait: Los Angeles' First Social Center Launched," *LAT*, September 12, 1911, section II, 1.

3. "School News," *LASJ* 1 (December 1917), 34; Shimano quoted in Ichioka, *Before Internment*, 20; recollection of Amelia Street School in Embrey, interview by Hansen and Hacker, 102. Also see Cameron, "History of Mexican Public Education," and Gilbert G. Gonzalez, "The System of Public Education and Its Function within the Chicano Communities, 1920–1930" (PhD diss., UCLA, 1974).

4. Mae M. Ngai, "The Architecture of Race in American Immigration Law: A Reexamination of the Immigration Act of 1924," *Journal of American History* 86, no. 1 (1999), 67–92; Ngai, *Impossible Subjects: Illegal Aliens and the Making of Modern America* (Princeton, N.J.: Princeton University Press, 2004); Natalia Molina, "'In a Race All Their Own': The Quest to Make Mexicans Ineligible for U.S. Citizenship," *Pacific Historical Review* 79, no. 2 (2010), 167–201; Molina, *How Race Is Made in America*.

5. "Teacher Raps Race Division," *LAT*, April 6, 1931, A2; "Little Mexico Honors Its Heroine," *LAT*, November 14, 1924, A1–A2; "Patriotic Program Featured," *LAT*, December 4, 1927, C33; William Deverell, "Ugly Reactions to a 1924 Los Angeles Plague Outbreak Offer a Lesson for Fight against SARS," *LAT*, April 24, 2003, B17. Also see Deverell, *Whitewashed Adobe: The Rise of Los Angeles and the Remaking of Its Mexican Past* (Berkeley: University of California Press, 2004), 172–206.

6. Preface to Asbury Bagwell, "The Los Angeles Diploma Plan of Naturalizing the Alien" (master's thesis, University of Southern California, 1929), n.p.

7. Harry Shafer, "Naturalization," *LASJ* 2 (March 23, 1919), 465–66; Bagwell, "Los Angeles Diploma Plan," 147–52; General Circular No. 14, Los Angeles School District, Office of the Superintendent, *LASJ* 5 (November 14, 1921), 11; Shafer, "Americanization," *LASJ* 2 (September 16, 1918), 34.

8. Bagwell, "Los Angeles Diploma Plan," 104–7; Jackson, "History of the Adult Education Program," 48–49.

9. Jackson, " History of the Adult Education Program," 49–50; "Citizens Made As They Wait," *LAT*, September 12, 1911.

10. Superintendent Francis's Annual Report for 1914, quoted in Jackson, "History of the Adult Education Program," 50–52; "Pleas to Keep Guiding Hand: Macy-street School Patrons Miss Teacher-friend," *LAT*, September 21, 1915, 9.

11. Bagwell, "Los Angeles Diploma Plan," 106–16, 140, 142–46. Even though Sterry and Kelso were the key advocates of the citizenship course, the administrator of Macy Street Evening School in 1912 was L. J. White. Bagwell, 122–23.

12. Bagwell, "Los Angeles Diploma Plan," 82, 108; Bagwell, "Local Courses Boon to Aliens," *LAT*, August 21, 1927, B2.

13. Nora Sterry, "The Neighborhood School," *California Quarterly of Secondary Education* 2 (January 1927), 117; quotation in Florence Mount, "The Neighborhood School," *LASJ* 10 (March 21, 1927), 11, 26–29.

14. Sterry, "Neighborhood School," 118–23.

15. Ruby Baughman, "A Foreword on the Year's Work in Americanization," *LASJ* 2 (September 2, 1918), 12–14; Baughman, "Elementary Education for Adults," *Annals of the American Academy of Political and Social Science* 93.

16. Carol Aronovici, "Americanization," *Annals of the American Academy of Political and Social Science* 93 (January, 1921), 134–38; Mary Cox, "Americanization and Foreign Language Study," *LASJ* 3 (October 20, 1919), 5–6. *LASJ* promoted "Language Games" on the facing page 4.

17. Bagwell, "Los Angeles Diploma Plan," 115.

18. Bagwell, "Local Courses Boon to Aliens"; Bagwell, "Los Angeles Diploma Plan," 117–23.

19. All quotations from Bagwell, "Local Courses Boon to Aliens"; see also Bagwell, "Los Angeles Diploma Plan," 1, 82, 108.

20. Bagwell, "Los Angeles Diploma Plan," 39–40, 122–36; William Bell, "What the Los Angeles Schools Have Done for the Alien Seeking Citizenship Training," *LASJ* 5 (October 10, 1921), 5; Molina, "'In a Race All Their Own,'" 181–82. Bagwell stated that LA Americanization classes had students from 46 different nationalities, and that 2.5 percent of students were Japanese. No Asian immigrants took citizenship classes; those students came from only 24, mostly European, nationalities.

21. Kelso was fortunate that the School of Citizenship opened the year before the stock market crash. Jackson, "History of the Adult Education Program," 107; Bagwell, "Los Angeles Diploma Plan," 114–22; Wood, "Immigrant Mothers, Female Reformers," 79–113.

22. Emory Bogardus, *Essentials of Americanization* (Los Angeles: University of Southern California Press, 1919), 273–74. The quotation about higher standards for citizenship comes from Bagwell, "Los Angeles Diploma Plan," 122–36;

23. Jane Sedgwick, "My Impressions of a Few Mexican Homes in the Macy Street District," *LASJ* 10 (March 21, 1927), 28–29.

24. Nora Sterry, *The International Cook Book of The Elementary Principals' Club of Los Angeles, Cal.: A Collection of Choice Recipes from Foreign Lands* (Los Angeles: Citizen Print Shop, 1930), contents page. George J. Sánchez explores Angelinos' attempts at culinary assimilation in *Becoming Mexican American*, 97–107.

25. For more on "bridges of understanding" from the Japanese national perspective, see Azuma, *Between Two Empires*, 145.

26. "School News," *LASJ* 1 (December 1917), 34; Shimano quoted in Ichioka, *Before Internment*, 20; Embrey interview by Hansen and Hacker, 106. Rafu Daiichi Gakuen was LA's first Japanese-language school, founded by Kohei Shimano.

27. California Council for the Humanities, "History of Miss Oliver and the Oliver Clubs," accessed November 11, 2016, http://www.discovernikkei.org/en/nikkeialbum/albums/84/?view=list.

28. Ichioka, *Before Internment*, 59–64.

29. Ichioka, *Before Internment*, 27–33; Azuma, *Between Two Empires*, 138–39, 145–51.

30. Tad Ichinokuchi, "John Aiso and the MIS" in *John Aiso and the MIS: Japanese-American Soldiers in the Military Intelligence Service, World War II*, ed. Tad Ichinokuchi (Los Angeles: Military Intelligence Service Club of Southern California, 1988), 7–9.

31. Ichinokuchi, *John Aiso and the MIS*, 7–9; John Aiso, "As Japan Sees America," *LAT*, July 31, 1927, B4.

32. Merton Hill, "Conference of 'Friends of the Mexicans,'" *Pomona College Magazine* 17, no. 2 (1928), 1. For more on the Friends of the Mexicans conferences, see Matt García, *A World of Its Own: Race, Labor, and Citrus in the Making of Greater Los Angeles, 1900–1970* (Chapel Hill: University of North Carolina Press, 2001), 109–16.

33. "The College and the International Mind," *Pomona College Magazine* 16 (1928); "Mexican Educators to Be Entertained," *LASJ* 11 (May 14, 1928), 13–14. For analysis of the San Gabriel Mission Play and "fantasy heritage," see Deverell, *Whitewashed Adobe*, 207–49.

34. "Friends of the Mexicans," *CEB* 8, no. 2 (1929), 35–37.

35. Shafer, "1928 'Friends of the Mexicans' Conference," *CEB* 7, no. 4 (1929), 9–10; James Batten, letter to the editor, *CEB* 6, no. 1 (1927), 41.

36. Vaughan, *Cultural Politics in Revolution*, 7; quotation from Batten, "Friends of the Mexicans," *CEB* 4, no. 2 (1926), 23.

37. Alberto Rembao, "What Should Be Done for Juan Garcia?" *Pomona College Magazine* 17, no. 3 (1929), 145–48.

38. Joyce Hirohata and Paul Hirohata, eds., *Nisei Voices: Japanese American Students of the 1930s—Then & Now* (Oakland: Hirohata Design, 2004). Joyce Hirohata updated her grandfather's original publication, *Orations and Essays by the Japanese Second Generation of America*.

39. Azuma explains the "Issei pioneer thesis" in "The Politics of Transnational History Making: Japanese Immigrants on the Western 'Frontier,' 1927–1941," *Journal of American History* 89, no. 4 (2003), 1405–7; quotation from Shiro Fujioka, "English Translation of a Message from the Secretary of the Los Angeles Japanese Association," in Hirohata and Hirohata, *Nisei Voices*, 246; Kay Sugahara, "Japanese American Citizens League's Message in *Orations and Essays* in 1935," ibid., 250.

40. Toshito Satow, "The Consul of Japan's Recommendation Published in *Orations and Essays* in 1932 and 1935," in Hirohata and Hirohata, *Nisei Voices*, 249; State Superintendent Vierling Kersey, "Foreword in the 1932 and 1935 Editions," in Hirohata and Hirohata, 248.

41. Aiso, "Lincoln's Devotion to the Constitution," in Hirohata and Hirohata, 191–93; Aiso, "As Japan Sees America," *LAT*, July 31, 1927, B4.

42. Aiso, "Lincoln's Devotion"; Ichinokuchi, "John Aiso and the MIS," 5.

43. Aiso, "Lincoln's Devotion"; "As Japan Sees America," B4.

44. Mark Wild describes "internationalism studies" in "'So Many Children at Once and So Many Kinds': Schools and Ethno-racial Boundaries in Early Twentieth-Century Los Angeles," *Western Historical Quarterly* 33, no. 4 (2002): 453–76. Also see Burkholder, *Color in the Classroom*; Selig, *Americans All*.

45. Emma Raybold, "Brotherization," Mary Foster, "Teaching Brotherhoodness," and Alice Wells, "The Pan-Pacific Association for Mutual Understanding," all in *LASJ* 8 (November 2, 1925), 10–23. This "Education for World Relationships" issue of *LASJ*

also included articles titled "Modern Foreign Language Study" and "The League of Nations."

46. Raybold, "Brotherization," 19; "The Federation of World Friendship Clubs," *LASJ* 10 (March 21, 1927), 76; "Our Contributors: 'Mexican Education' Issue," *LASJ* 11 (May 14, 1928), 12. Also see Cameron, "History of Mexican Public Education," and Gonzalez, "System of Public Education."

47. The results of the 1926 survey appear in Wild, "'So Many Children,'" 457; "World Friendship Club Organized in 1931," *Rough Rider*, April 26, 1935, 1; Arthur Takemoto, "Fireside Chat," *Rough Rider*, November 2, 1939, 2; "Hugh Acevedo Elected to Vice Presidency," *Rough Rider*, June 7, 1935, 4; "Albert Teplitz to Preside at World Friendship Aud," *Rough Rider*, November 8, 1934, 1. I thank Joseph Zanki Sr., retired Roosevelt High School history teacher, for sharing old volumes of the *Rough Rider*.

48. "Friendship Club Receives Books from Spain," *Rough Rider*, November 17, 1933, 1; "Spanish Club Presents Aud: Pan American Day Is Theme for Assembly," *Rough Rider*, April 20, 1933, 1; "Peace Club Plans Play: Pan American Day Is to Be Celebrated in Conjunction with Spanish Club," *Rough Rider*, April 5, 1935, 1; "Pan-American Day Observed," *Rough Rider*, April 12, 1935, 2 (from Zanki collection).

49. "Spanish Club to Hold Tilt" and "14 Optimists Given Honor," *Rough Rider*, January 10, 1935, 1; "Friendship Club Holds Meeting," *Rough Rider*, January 31, 1935, 1; "Peace Day Costume Parade," *Roosevelt Round Up* (yearbook), 1940, 45–46; "Peace Club Hosts Armistice Day," *Rough Rider*, November 15, 1934, 4; "World Friendship Clubs Gathered at Poly High," November 2, 1939, 1 (from Zanki collection).

50. "Peace Club in Charge of Assembly," *Rough Rider*, May 17, 1935, 1; "Rooseveltian Delegates Attend World Friendship Convention," *Rough Rider*, May 18, 1934, 1; "World Friendship Clubs of L.A. Discuss Peace," *Rough Rider*, October 26, 1939, 3; "Lieut.-Governor Patterson Gives Speech at Aud," *Rough Rider*, December 14, 1939, 3 (from Zanki collection).

51. Zevi Gutfreund, "Immigrant Education and Race: Alternative Approaches to 'Americanization' in Los Angeles, 1910–1940," *History of Education Quarterly* 57, no. 1 (2017), 7–8.

52. "Mrs. Bailey Gives Talk," *Rough Rider*, October 27, 1933, 4; "Peace Club Meets Today," *Rough Rider*, October 11, 1934, 4 (from Zanki collection).

53. "Nippon Club Hears Talk," *Rough Rider*, March 15, 1935, 1; "World Friendship Students Hear Miss Eby Talk of European Tour," *Rough Rider*, October 5, 1939, 1 (from Zanki collection).

54. "A. Bagwell Starts New NRA Contest," *Rough Rider*, October 20, 1933, 1; "Mr. A. A. Bagwell to Speak to Aldebarans on Cuban Situation," *Rough Rider*, November 24, 1933, 1; "Mr. A. A. Bagwell Speaker at Social Science Class," *Rough Rider*, June 1, 1934, 1; "Friendship Club Holds Meeting," *Rough Rider*, January 31, 1935, 1; "Teplitz to Lead S'35 Peace Club," *Rough Rider*, February 15, 1935, 1 (from Zanki collection).

55. "Mrs. Bailey Gives Talk," *Rough Rider*, October 27, 1933, 4 (from Zanki collection); "Cancer Claims Life of ELAC's Helen M. Bailey," *LAT*, September 30, 1976, SE4.

CHAPTER 3

1. Embrey interview by Hansen and Hacker, 102; Togo Tanaka, interview by Betty Mitson and David Hacker, May 19, 1973, interview no. 1271, pp. 56–58, California State University, Fullerton, Oral History Program; Morimoto, "Language and Heritage Maintenance of Immigrants," 68, 80–93; air mail to central office of Immigration and Naturalization Service, November 20, 1943, Box 91, Folder 3,Yuji Ichioka Papers, Young Research Library, UCLA.

2. Quotation from Embrey interview by Hansen and Hacker, 105; "Kohei Shimano Death Report"; Lloyd Jensen to Albert del Guercio, May 15, 1944; and FBI notes from arrest on December 7, 1941, all in Ichioka Papers, Box 91, Folder 3, Young Research Library, UCLA.

3. Ichinokuchi, *John Aiso and the MIS*, 16, 44, 193; "Fort Snelling: Breaking the Code," accessed April 1, 2013, http://www.nps.gov/miss/historyculture/langschool.htm.

4. See David Yoo, *Growing Up Nisei: Race, Generation, and Culture among Japanese Americans of California, 1924–49* (Urbana: University of Illinois Press, 1999); Sánchez, *Becoming Mexican American.*

5. Zoë Burkholder, *Color in the Classroom*, 99.

6. Tanaka quoted in Magner White, "Between Two Flags," *Saturday Evening Post*, September 30, 1939, 73–74. Like Afton Nance, Tanaka worked with the American Friends Service Committee campaign against internment. Tanaka interview by Mitson and Hacker, 97.

7. "Tolerance," *Rough Rider*, December 18, 1942, 2 (from Zanki collection).

8. "The Colonel Speaks," *Rough Rider*, March 9, 1942, 2 (from Zanki collection).

9. Murray Rubenstein, "A Tribute to Japanese Students," *Rough Rider*, April 9, 1942, 1 (from Zanki collection).

10. *Rough Rider*, March 19, 1942, 3; "Japanese Students Withdraw from School," *Rough Rider*, April 9, 1942, 1–3; quotation from "Mr. Williams Aids Japanese Students," *Rough Rider*, April 16, 1942, 1; "Why Don't We—," *Rough Rider*, April 16, 1942, 3 (from Zanki collection).

11. Quotation from "Maruki and Soto Head Senior A's," *Rough Rider*, March 12, 1942, 1 (from Zanki collection).

12. Quotations from "Students Await Evacuation Orders," *Rough Rider*, March 19, 1942, 1; "Roosevelt Joins in U.S.O. Drive," *Rough Rider*, March 26, 1942, 3; "Rooseveltians in the Service," *Rough Rider*, April 30, 1942, 4; "Miss Inquisitive," April 9, 1942, 2 (from Zanki collection).

13. Anthony Lehman, *Birthright of Barbed Wire: The Santa Anita Assembly Center for the Japanese* (Los Angeles: Westernlore Press, 1970), 16, 24, 50–51; Tomi Matsumoto to Afton Nance, June 3, 1942, Box 1, Afton Nance Papers, Hirasaki National Resource Center, Japanese American National Museum, Los Angeles.

14. Lehman, *Birthright of Barbed Wire*, 50–51; *Rough Rider*, March 19, 1942, 3 (from Zanki collection). Most graduates came from Los Angeles and San Diego Counties.

15. Lehman, *Birthright of Barbed Wire*, 49–51; Charles Kikuchi, *The Kikuchi Diary: Chronicle from an American Concentration Camp*, ed. John Modell (Urbana: University of Illinois Press, 1973), 82.

16. Palos Verdes Estates was a community with restrictive housing covenants, including "the usual restrictions prohibiting negroes, Asiatics, and people of other than the white or Caucasian race, except in the capacity of domestic servants." Tract 6883 *Protective Restrictions Palos Verdes Estates*, p. 4, California Ephemera, Box 78, Palos Verdes Estates Folder, UCLA Special Collections. I thank Laura Redford for this research.

17. Matsumoto to Nance, May 13, May 26, June 3, and June 30, 1942, Box 1, Nance Papers.

18. Matsumoto to Nance, July 7, May 13, April 25, May 14, May 11, and February 2, 1942, Box 1, Nance Papers.

19. "Pan-Americanism Now?" *LASJ*, February 24, 1941, 15; "Afton Dill Nance Biographical Material," August 18, 1967, Box 2, Nance Papers.

20. McWilliams *North from Mexico*, 212–26. Also see Luis Alvarez, *The Power of the Zoot: Youth Culture and Resistance during World War II* (Berkeley: University of California Press, 2008).

21. Alma Wedberg, "The Teaching of Speech to Mexican Children," *California Journal of Elementary Education* 10, no. 4 (1942), 216–22.

22. Wedberg, "Teaching of Speech to Mexican Children," 216–22. Carlos Blanton describes the "direct method" in *The Strange Career of Bilingual Education in Texas, 1836–1981* (College Station: Texas A&M University Press, 2004).

23. "Suggestions from the Inter-American Conference at USC," January 16, 1941, Box 2, Folder 4, and "Pan Americanism," Box 2, Folder 20, Ruiz Papers; *California Journal of Elementary Education* 10, no. 3 (1942), 130; quotation from *LASJ*, February 9, 1942; "Pan-Americanism Now?" *LASJ*, February 24, 1941, 15, 31.

24. "Maruki and Soto Head Senior A's," *Rough Rider*, March 12, 1942, 1–3; *Rough Rider*, May 14, 1942, 1–2 (from Zanki collection).

25. "Maruki and Soto Head Senior A's," *Rough Rider*, March 12, 1942, 1–3; *Rough Rider*, May 14, 1942, 1–2 (from Zanki collection).

26. Ruiz, grant proposal to World Peace Foundation, June 20, 1940, and Carnegie Endowment for International Peace to Ruiz, June 26, 1940, Box 2, Folder 6, Ruiz Papers. The library proposal was endorsed by the former president of Nicaragua.

27. "Program for Los Angeles, 1942," and Major Sanford to Ruiz, October 2, 1942, Box 2, Folder 9, Ruiz Papers.

28. Dr. Benedict to Dr. Egas, October 5, 1942, Box 2, Folder 9, Ruiz Papers.

29. Russell Peterson to Eduardo Quevedo, June 23, 1942, Edith Condon to Quevedo, July 1, 1942, and Howard Campion to Quevedo, November 5, 1942, Box 1, Folder 10, Eduardo Quevedo Papers, Special Collections, Green Library, Stanford University. Stanford, Calif. Sánchez also discusses Quevedo in *Becoming Mexican American*, 250.

30. Program for Dedication Ceremony," April 13, 1943, and William McGorray to *Parientes y Amigos*, April 1943, Ruiz Papers, Stanford (Box 5, Folder 3).

31. William McGorray to Ruiz, April 7, 1943, and "Progress Report on the Pan American Trade School," April 1943, Box 5, Folder 3; J. Douglas Wilson to Quevedo, July 10, 1943, Box 2, Folder 18, all in Ruiz Papers.

32. Beatrice Griffith, *American Me* (Boston: Houghton Mifflin, 1948), 45; Robin Scott, "The Sleepy Lagoon Case and the Grand Jury Investigation" in *The Mexican-Americans: An Awakening Minority*, ed. Manuel Servín (Beverly Hills: Glencoe Press, 1970), 105–14.

33. Edward Escobar, "Zoot-Suiters and the Cops: Chicano Youth and the Los Angeles Police Department during World War II," in *The War in American Culture: Society and Consciousness during World War II*, ed. Lewis Erenberg and Susan Hirsch (Chicago: University of Chicago Press, 1996), 285–97. Ruiz's Washington ally was Alan Cranston, California's future US senator who headed the Office of War Information's foreign-language division during the war. The Pomona College alum had studied Spanish at the National Autonomous University of Mexico. McWilliams credits Cranston for "bringing about a noticeable change in tone and character of newspaper reporting on the Mexican problem." McWilliams, *North from Mexico*, 231; Cranston to Quevedo, July 15, 1943, Box 1, Folder 11, Quevedo Papers.

34. Escobar, "Zoot-Suiters and the Cops," 290–91; Griffith, *American Me*, 45, 55–59.

35. CCLAY Articles of Incorporation, August 31, 1943, Box 2, Folder 11, Ruiz Papers; Quevedo to Earl Warren, October 26, 1944, Box 1, Folder 12, Quevedo Papers.

36. Ruiz to Dick Connor, August 12, 1942, and Ruiz to David Orozco, August 28, 1942, Box 2, Folder 13, Ruiz Papers; "Convocatoria asemblea general de CCLAY," July 18, 1943, Box 1, Folder 11, Quevedo Papers.

37. Elizabeth Sands to Ruiz, June 10, 1943, and "Los Angeles City and County Schools Workshop for Education of Mexican and Spanish-speaking Pupils," July 6–16, 1943, Box 2, Folder 18, Ruiz Papers; McWilliams, *North from Mexico*, 231. In addition to editing the Spanish-language weekly *El Espectador*, López was lead plaintiff in *Lopez v. Seccombe* a 1943 lawsuit that desegregated swimming pools in San Bernardino. López's lawyer won *Mendez v. Westminster* three years later. Philippa Strum, Mendez v. Westminster: *School Desegregation and Mexican-American Rights* (Lawrence: University of Kansas Press, 2010), 39.

38. Sands to Ruiz, and "Los Angeles City and County Schools Workshop." Ginsburg later became a language supervisor for LA schools. Los Angeles City Schools, *Magazines: 1959–61*, Mary Springer Papers, San Fernando High School Library. Los Angeles Unified School District.

39. "CCLAY Resolution on Juvenile Delinquency," August 27, 1943, Box 3, Folder 15, Ruiz Papers.

40. Thomas James, *Exile Within: The Schooling of Japanese Americans, 1942–1945* (Cambridge, Mass.: Harvard University Press, 1987), 3–8; Richard Drinnon quoted in Yoo, *Growing Up Nisei*, 94.

41. John Armor and Peter Wright, *Manzanar: Commentary by John Hersey, Photographs by Ansel Adams* (New York: Times Books, 1988), x–xii; Bahr, *Unquiet Nisei*, 56. Also see Yoo, *Growing Up Nisei*, 122–23.

42. Yoo, *Growing Up Nisei*, 122; Bahr, *Unquiet Nisei*, 56; James, *Exile Within*, 30.

43. James, *Exile Within*, 37–43.

44. James, *Exile Within*, 61; *Cardinal and Gold*, 1943, Manzanar War Relocation Center Records, Box 59, Folder 2, Special Collections, Young Research Library, UCLA

(hereafter Manzanar WRC Records). Diana Bahr argues that, although some five hundred students graduated from Manzanar High, "many internees believed these students had been deprived by not receiving diplomas from their original schools." Survivors finally received their diplomas in 2004. *Unquiet Nisei*, 168.

45. "Education Section Summary," May 31, 1945, Box 59, Folder 2, Manzanar WRC Records, UCLA.
46. Jeanne Wakatsuki Houston, *Farewell to Manzanar: And Related Readings*, ed. Jeanne Wakatsuki Houston and James Houston (Evanston, Ill.: McDougal Littell, 1998), 68; Paul Kusuda, "December 6," Box 1, Nance Papers.
47. "Education Section Summary," Box 59, Folder 2, Manzanar WRC Records.
48. "Education Section Summary."
49. Paul Kusuda to Afton Nance, May 21, 1942, and January 14, 1944, and "Report on Tutoring Classes," May 22, 1942, Box 1, Nance Papers.
50. "Caucasian Staff Meeting," September 22, 1942, Box 1, Nance Papers.
51. "Caucasian Staff Meeting"; Frank Chuman, "Persistent Idealism," in Hirohata and Hirohata, *Nisei Voices*, 133–34.
52. Kusuda to Nance, October 8, 1942, and July 29, 1942, and "Caucasian Staff Meeting," September 22, 1942, Box 1, Nance Papers. One Anglo-American adult education teacher opined that the internees "should not indulge in self-pity."
53. Kusuda to Nance, August 3, 1942, and August 4, 1942, "Meeting of the Manzanar Citizens' Federation, September 9, 1942, and Kusuda, "December 6 Diary," Box 1, Nance Papers. Also see Houston, *Farewell to Manzanar*, 68.
54. Kusuda to Nance, December 8, 1942, December 12, 1942, and January 20, 1943, Box 1, Nance Papers.
55. Kusuda to Nance, November 26, 1942, and January 23, 1943, Box 1, Nance Papers.
56. Kusuda to Nance, January 23, 1943, Box 1, Nance Papers.
57. Houston, *Farewell to Manzanar*, 75; Brian Hayashi, *Democratizing the Enemy: The Japanese American Internment* (Princeton, N.J.: Princeton University Press, 2004), 144.
58. James, *Exile Within*, 143, 160.
59. James, *Exile Within*, 145–49, quotation on 148. The WRA did not provide Japanese-language schools with teaching materials.
60. James, *Exile Within*, 149–51, quotation on 149.
61. James, *Exile Within*, 151–53.
62. James, *Exile Within*, 151–53.
63. "Recruiting for Army's Language School," November 28, 1942, and December 1, 1942, Box 30, Folder 1, Karl Yoneda Papers, Special Collections, Young Research Library, UCLA; Paul Kusuda, "Personal Recollections of Chicago: 1943–1949," *Asian Wisconsine*, June 2009, accessed April 1, 2013, http://www.asianwisconzine.com/0609PaulKusuda.html. One Anglo-American instructor at Manzanar also went to the MIS Language School. The student paper reported that Paul Kess had studied French and German as a foreign-language major at UCLA, and that he had learned Japanese at Manzanar. *Campus Pepper*, April 20, 1943, 3, Box 59, Folder 4, Manzanar WRC Records.

64. John Weckerling, "Nisei Language Experts," in Ichinokuchi, *John Aiso and the MIS*, 186–89; "Fort Snelling: Breaking the Code," http://www.nps.gov/miss/historyculture/langschool.htm. For more anecdotes about Aiso and others, see James McNaughton, *Nisei Linguists: Japanese Americans in the Military Intelligence Service during World War II* (Washington, D.C.: Department of the Army, 2006).

65. Ichinokuchi, *John Aiso and the MIS*, 16–17.

66. Ichinokuchi, 16, 44; Weckerling, "Nisei Language Experts," 193; "Fort Snelling: Breaking the Code."

67. Weckerling, "Nisei Language Experts," 190–91.

68. Quoted in Shig Kihara, "That Day Will Be Long Remembered," in Ichinokuchi, *John Aiso and the MIS*, 206; see also 12–16.

69. Mark Brilliant also records Ruiz's account in *The Color of America Has Changed*, 82–84.

70. George Hjelte to Manuel Ruiz, February 14, 1942, Box 4, Folder 12; and Robert Kenny to Ruiz, September 27, 1943, Box 4, Folder 1, Ruiz Papers; H. P. Blome to Eduardo Quevedo, Box 1, Folder 11, Quevedo Papers.

71. Manuel Ruiz to Earl Warren, October 7, 1943, Robert McKibben to Ruiz, October 13 and 22, 1943, Kenny to "Mr. Westphal," December 14, 1943, and "Minutes of First Meeting, CCYW," November 1, 1943, all in Box 4, Folder 1, Ruiz Papers.

72. Karl Holton, "Progress Report on the Work of the California Youth Authority," April 20, 1944, and John Carroll to Ruiz, January 7, 1944, Box 4, Folder 1, Ruiz Papers.

73. "To the Governor of the State of California, CCYW," n.d., Box 4, Folder 2, Ruiz Papers.

74. Quotation from McKibben to Ruiz, December 28, 1944; see also McKibben to Warren, April 13, 1944, and "Arguments against Double Sessions in the Schools," December 14, 1943, all in Box 4, Folder 1, Ruiz Papers; airmail to "Evans, Mexity," April 30, 1945, Box 16, Folder 3, Ruiz Papers. Mark Brilliant writes that the CCYW urged Warren to repeal the school segregation law in November 1944 (an action Ruiz takes credit for in his later writings), but the committee quickly dropped its desegregation demand the following month, as McKibben's letter evidences. Brilliant, *Color of America Has Changed*, 82.

75. Earl Warren, "The Question of Loyalty," quoted in Mae Ngai and Jon Gjerde, eds., *Major Problems in American Immigration History: Documents and Essays*, 2nd ed. (Boston: Wadsworth Cengage Learning, 2013), 414.

76. John Fujio Aiso, interview by Marc Landy, August 3, 1970, p. 106, UCLA Oral History Program, 106.

CHAPTER 4

1. Marie Hughes, ed., *The School's Responsibility for the Improvement of Intergroup Relations: Report of Conference, December 20–22, 1945* (Los Angeles County Superintendent of Schools, with Office of Coordinator of Inter-American Affairs, 1946).

2. Hughes, *School's Responsibility for Intergroup Relations*, 12–13, 20–23; Hughes quoted in Strum, Mendez v. Westminster, 116.

3. Hughes quoted in Strum, Mendez v. Westminster, 116.

4. Strum, Mendez v. Westminster; Brilliant, *Color of American Has Changed*, 58–88.

5. Hughes, *School's Responsibility for Intergroup Relations*, 11–13, 20–23. N. D. Myers, ed., *Education for Cultural Unity: Seventeenth Yearbook* (Oakland: California Elementary School Principals' Association, 1945). Carey McWilliams described Hughes as "a tireless and effective worker in the field." McWilliams, "Round-Up," *Common Ground* 7 (Winter 1947), 95–96.

6. Gonzalez quoted in Strum, Mendez v. Westminster, 158; "President's Message," in Myers, *Education for Cultural Unity*. Also see Burkholder, *Color in the Classroom*, and Selig, *Americans All*.

7. Helen Heffernan and Corinne Seeds, "Intercultural Education in the Elementary School," in Myers, *Education for Cultural Unity*, 76, 79, 84.

8. Beulah Dana Bartlett, "A Pattern for Community Cooperation: A Summer Program—Los Angeles Youth Project," in Myers, *Education for Cultural Unity*, 100–102; "Letter to the Los Angeles Community Welfare Federation," August 7, 1943, and "The Los Angeles Youth Project Board," March 14, 1945, and November 22, 1943, Box 4, Folder 12, Ruiz Papers.

9. Ruth Tuck, "Mexican-Americans: A Contributory Culture," in Myers, *Education for Cultural Unity*, 108; Ernesto Galarza, "The Mexican Ethnic Group," *Education for Cultural Unity*, 35. Tuck taught at Redlands College, east of LA County.

10. Larry Tajiri, "Barriers to Acculturation," in Myers *Education for Cultural Unity*, 25–28.

11. Wedberg, "The Teaching of Speech to Mexican Children," *California Journal of Elementary Education* 10, no. 4 (1942), 218; Myers, "Problems in Bilingualism," in *Education for Cultural Unity*, 124; Myers, "Foreign Language Instruction at the Elementary Level," in *Education for Cultural Unity*, 72–75.

12. Myers, "Foreign Language Instruction at the Elementary Level," in *Education for Cultural Unity*, 72–75. Myers did not mention what happened to the Japanese-language schools of his Nisei former students who were just starting to return to southern California. For his bilingual education survey, however, Myers consulted with their former English teacher, Afton Nance, along with Helen Heffernan, who had worked on the education of Spanish speakers at the Office of Inter-American Affairs.

13. Paul McCormick, "Conclusions of the Court," 7–8, United States District Court, Southern District of California, Central Division, February 18, 1946, Box 16, Folder 4, Ruiz Papers; Strum, Mendez v. Westminster, 65–68, 123–33, 151–53; Brilliant, *Color of America Has Changed*, 67.

14. Strum, Mendez v. Westminster, 39–41.

15. Marcus quoted in Strum, Mendez v. Westminster, 82–84, 106–7.

16. McCormick quoted in Strum, Mendez v. Westminster, 66–74.

17. McCormick and Méndez quoted in Strum, Mendez v. Westminster, 74, 101–2.

18. McCormick and Méndez quoted in Strum, Mendez v. Westminster, 102–7.

19. McCormick, "Conclusions of the Court," 7–8, 10; McCormick quoted in Strum, Mendez v. Westminster, 125–26.

20. "Airmail to Evans, Mexity," April 30, 1945, Box 16, Folder 3, Ruiz Papers.
21. Elis Tipton, "The San Dimas Intercultural Program," in Myers, *Education for Cultural Unity*, 94, 95.
22. Tipton, "San Dimas Intercultural Program," 94, 95, 99.
23. Brilliant, *Color of America Has Changed*, 82–83.
24. Ruiz to Warren, October 7, 1943, and McKibben to Ruiz, December 28, 1944, Box 4, Folder 1, Ruiz Papers. Regarding Tenney, see Scott, "The Sleepy Lagoon Case," in Servín, *Mexican-Americans*, 1st ed., 107–9; McWilliams, *North from Mexico*, 231, and Martha Kransdorf, *A Matter of Loyalty: The Los Angeles School Board vs. Frances Eisenberg* (San Francisco: Caddo Gap Press, 1994), 45.
25. "Airmail to Evans, Mexity," April 30, 1945, and Ruiz to Senator Slater, May 15, 1945, Box 16, Folder 3, Ruiz Papers.
26. "Airmail to Evans, Mexity," April 30, and May 14, 1945, "Wire Story, Dateline Los Angeles," and Ezequiel Padilla to Ruiz, June 5, 1945, Box 16, Folder 3, Ruiz Papers.
27. William Rosenthal to Ruiz, January 17, 1945, and Ruiz to Rosenthal, January 20, 1945, Box 16, Folder 3, Ruiz Papers.
28. "Airmail to Evans, Mexity," April 30 and May 14, 1945, "Wire Story, Dateline Los Angeles," and Padilla to Ruiz, June 5, 1945, Box 16, Folder 3, Ruiz Papers.
29. "Airmail to Evans, Mexity," June 20, 1945, Ruiz to El Monte School District Board of Trustees, May 14, 1945, Ruiz to Harold Kingley, May 20, 1945, and Ruiz to Senator Slater, May 15, 1945, Box 16, Folder 3, Ruiz Papers.
30. Ruiz to Warren, October 1, 1945, Ruiz to Beach Vasey, October 8, 1945, Vasey to Ruiz, October 15, 1945, and Ruiz to Warren, October 31, 1945, Box 16, Folder 3, Ruiz Papers.
31. George I. Sánchez, *First Regional Conference on the Education of Spanish-Speaking People in the Southwest*, Occasional Papers of Inter-American Education 1 (Austin: University of Texas Press, 1946), 3.
32. Sánchez, *First Regional Conference*, 7, 12–15.
33. Sánchez, *First Regional Conference*, 14–18. See also Blanton, *Strange Career of Bilingual Education in Texas*.
34. Marie Hughes quoted in Sánchez, *Concerning Segregation of Spanish-Speaking Children in the Public Schools*, Occasional Papers of Inter-American Education 9 (Austin: University of Texas Press, 1951), 50–52.
35. Hughes quoted in Sánchez, *Concerning Segregation*, 52–54.
36. Sánchez, *Concerning Segregation*, 23–31.
37. Sánchez, *Concerning Segregation*, 24, 30.
38. Sánchez quoted in Brilliant, *Color of America Has Changed*, 84–85; Sonya Ramsey, "The Troubled History of American Education after the *Brown* Decision," *American Historian* 11 (February 2017), 36.
39. D[illon]. S. Myer to Superintendents & Principals of Schools, March 1, 1945, Carey McWilliams War Relocation Authority (WRA) Correspondence, Box 7, Folder 8M, Honnold/Mudd Library, Claremont Colleges; "Annual Commencement: Manzanar High School," June 2, 1945, Box 59, Folder 2, Manzanar War Relocation Records.
40. Afton Nance, "The Return of the Nisei," *Education for Cultural Unity*, 65.

41. Nance, "Return of the Nisei," 65–66; Nance, "The Re-Integration of American Children of Japanese Ancestry into the Schools," paper presented at the California Southern Section Principals' Association conference, February 24, 1945, Box 2, Nance Papers.

42. Nance, "Return of the Nisei," 66–68 (Tomi and Kazue are common Japanese names); Nance, "Re-Integration of American Children."

43. Nance, "Return of the Nisei," 66; Nance, "Re-Integration of American Children."

44. Carey McWilliams, "Round-Up," *Common Ground* 7 (Winter 1947), 95–96. For more on Oyama, see Valerie Matsumoto, *City Girls: The Nisei Social World in Los Angeles, 1920–1950* (New York: Oxford University Press, 2014).

45. Mary Oyama, "A Nisei Report from Home," *Common Ground* 6 (Winter 1946), 26–27. Transfers of residence when Japanese families returned did not always go smoothly in Little Tokyo, which was called Bronzeville during the war because many black families moved into evacuated houses. See S. Kurashige, *Shifting Grounds of Race*.

46. Oyama, "Nisei Report from Home," 28.

47. "Helen Heffernan Honor Grove," pp. 10–11, October 1, 1966, Box 2, Nance Papers; Weiler, *Democracy and Schooling in California*.

48. John Aiso, "The Postwar Reconstruction of Japan," in Ichinokuchi, *John Aiso and the MIS*, 19–23.

49. Aiso, "Postwar Reconstruction of Japan," 19–23.

50. Aiso, "Postwar Reconstruction of Japan," 19–23. The MIS Language School is now the Defense Language Institute in Monterey, California, home of the Aiso Library. "Defense Language Institute, Foreign Language Center, accessed April 14, 2018, http://www.dliflc.edu/resources/libraries/.

51. "Field Promotions," in Ichinokuchi, *John Aiso and the MIS*, 195; Charles Hillinger, "The Secrets Come Out for Nisei Soldiers: Japanese-American Role in Military Intelligence Service Finally Told," *LAT*, July 20, 1982, F1–F4; Jordan Steffen, "White House Honors Japanese American WWII Veterans," *LAT*, October 6, 2010, accessed April 14, 2018, http://www.latimes.com/news/nationworld/ nation/la-na-veterans-medal-20101006,0,3141243,print.story. Also see Kelli Nakamura, "'They Are Our Human Secret Weapons': The Military Intelligence Service and the Role of the Japanese-Americans in the Pacific War and in the Occupation of Japan," *The Historian* 70, no. 1 (2008): 54–74.

52. Aiso quoted in Ichinokuchi, *John Aiso and the MIS*, 177.

53. James Oda, "The Exploration of the Magic Code," in Ichinokuchi, *John Aiso and the MIS*, 98–105; "Recruiting for Army's Language School," November 28 and December 1, 1942, Box 30, Folder 1, Yoneda Papers. Also see James Stone, David Shoemaker, and Nicholas Dotti, *Interrogation: World War II, Vietnam, and Iraq* (Washington, D.C.: National Defense Intelligence College Press, 2008), 67–68.

54. Stone, Shoemaker, and Dotti, *Interrogation*, 71–74; No. 11: "Is Your Stomach Empty?" Book "A" issued to Karl Yoneda, Ledo OWI, March 24, 1944; and No. 17: "Surrender Pass No. 1," Ledo OWI, April 1944; and "Propaganda Work in CBI for OWI," February 2, 1946, Boxes 30 and 31, Yoneda Papers; "Yasukuni Jinja Yushukan," accessed

October 5, 2011, http://wgordon.web.wesleyan.edu/kamikaze/museums/yushukan/index.htm.

55. Ichinokuchi, "Court Martial of General Yamashita," in *John Aiso and the MIS*, 142–43. This contrasts with the interrogations by Ali Soufan, a Lebanese-American FBI agent who questioned al-Qaeda captives. Soufan, *The Black Banners: The Inside Story of 9/11 and the War Against al-Qaeda* (New York: W.W. Norton, 2011).

56. Ichinokuchi, "Court Martial of General Yamashita," 142–43, Ichinokuchi, *John Aiso and the MIS*, 1–2, 125–27.

57. Roger Baldwin, "The Nisei in Japan," *Common Ground* 8 (Summer 1948), 27–28.

58. Baldwin, "Nisei in Japan," 24–27. Baldwin acknowledged the Tule Lake internees who refused to sign the loyalty oath, but he said most "disloyals" who "had voluntarily gone back to Japan, now expressed regret" and missed California (p. 25).

59. Strum, Mendez v. Westminster, 36, 133–35, 159–61.

60. Milton Konvitz, "Law Restricting Teaching of Foreign Languages Held Unconstitutional," *Common Ground* 9 (Winter 1949), 99–101; Strum, Mendez v. Westminster, 141–46; Drew Pearson, Washington Merry-Go-Round Column: "California Discrimination," *San Bernardino Sun-Telegram*, May 11, 1947, 30. California Digital Newspaper Collection, accessed April 22, 2018, https://cdnc.ucr.edu/cgi-bin/cdnc?a=d&d=SBS19470511.1.30.

61. Marcus quoted in Strum, Mendez v. Westminster, 82–84, 106–7; "An Act Regulating the Teaching of Languages to Children," n.d., Frank Chuman Papers, UCLA Special Collections (Box 530, Folder 5).

62. "An Act Regulating the Teaching of Languages to Children," Box 530, Folder 5, Chuman Papers, Special Collections, Young Research Library, UCLA.

63. Pearson, "California Discrimination," 30.

64. Pearson, 30.

65. John Aiso, interview by Marc Landy, August 3, 1970, UCLA Oral History Program, 105–8.

CHAPTER 5

1. García and Castro, *Blowout!* 89–95, 337–38.

2. Ruben Salazar, "New School Plan Sees Bilingualism as Asset," *LAT*, February 25, 1964, E2–3; García and Castro, *Blowout!* 95–100. Castro claims that as a new teacher he did not know about the Spanish-language ban at assemblies, but he admits, "even if I had known about this, I would have ignored it."

3. Brilliant, *Color of America Has Changed*, 229–34. In addition to Castro's autobiography, other studies of the Blowouts include Marguerite Marin, *Social Protest in an Urban Barrio: A Study of the Chicano Movement, 1966–1974* (Lanham, Md.: University Press of America, 1991); Dolores Delgado Bernal, "Chicana School Resistance and Grassroots Leadership: Providing an Alternative History of the 1968 East Los Angeles Blowouts" (PhD diss., UCLA, 1997); Henry J. Gutierrez, "The Chicano Education Rights Movement and School Desegregation: Los Angeles, 1962–1970" (PhD diss., University of California, Irvine, 1990); Kaye Briegel, "Chicano Student Militancy: The Los Angeles High School Strike of 1968," in Servín, *Mexican-Americans*, 2nd ed., 215–25.

4. "Afton Dill Nance Biographical Material," August 18, 1967, Box 2, Nance Papers. Riverside's intercultural program drew on the ideas of Allison Davis, the first black professor at the University of Chicago. Nance supported the Bracero Program in a 1961 letter to James Roosevelt, congressman from Los Angeles (and Franklin Roosevelt's eldest son), endorsing Public Law 78, the final two-year extension Congress granted to the Bracero Program. Box 6, Folders 16–17, and Carton 22, Folders 3, 16–26, National Council on Agricultural Life and Labor Records, Bancroft Library, University of California, Berkeley.

5. Dorothy Goble, "Education Today—Self-Sufficiency Tomorrow: Report on the Educational Project for Seasonal Farm Families in Santa Clara County, California, 1955–1960," pp. 2, 8, 13–14, and "Migrant Citizenship Education Project," December 10, 1958, Carton 5, Folders 47 and 46, Florence Wyckoff Papers, Bancroft Library University of California, Berkeley.

6. Nance to Florence Wyckoff, January 20, 1961, "Proposed Study of the Education of Children of Migratory Workers," n.d., Carton 5, Folder 48, Wyckoff Papers.

7. Nance "Proposed Study of the Education of Children of Migratory Workers."

8. Helen Heffernan and Afton Nance, ""Report on Conference on Teaching English as a Second Language," June 24–July 14, 1963, San Jose State College, Carton 26, Folder 25, Wyckoff Papers (hereafter "ESL Conference").

9. Heffernan and Nance, "ESL Conference," 3–11.

10. Heffernan and Nance, "ESL Conference," 9–12.

11. Helen Heffernan, "The Promise of the Future" in Afton Nance and Mary Peters, eds., *Conference on the Education of Spanish-Speaking Children and Youth,"* Ontario, *Calif., March 25–26, 1966,* 5–8.

12. Quotations in Heffernan, "Promise of the Future," 11, 12, 13; García and Castro, *Blowout!* 89–95.

13. Nance, "How Can the Promise Be Realized?" in Nance and Peters, *Conference on the Education of Spanish-Speaking Children,* 16–17.

14. "Reports of Study Sections," in Nance and Peters, *Conference on the Education of Spanish-Speaking Children,* 28–32, 35–37.

15. "High Intensity Language Training," pamphlet, July 22–28, 1968, Box 16, Folder 12, Ruiz Papers.

16. "High Intensity Language Training," 4.

17. "High Intensity Language Training"; anonymous document about the Federal Bilingual Education Act of 1968, Folder 3, Bilingual Education Papers, Chicano Studies Research Center, UCLA (hereafter CSRC).

18. Los Angeles City School Districts Division of Instructional Services, *Magazines,* 1955–67; "Notes and Quotes," in *Short Waves: To All Employees of the Los Angeles City Schools,* October 8, 1959, all in Mary Springer Papers, San Fernando High School Library.

19. "Japanese Will Be Offered at Monroe High," *LAT,* June 12, 1963, E9; "Teacher in Training for Class in Japanese: Venice High One of First Schools to Begin Language Course in Fall," *LAT,* August 8, 1963, K14. By 1950, John Aiso and Japanese educators across California were more focused on immigration reform than on language

instruction. Tats Kushida, "Annual Report," May 1, 1951, Box 2, JACL History Collection, Japanese American National Library, San Francisco.

20. "In the Spotlight: Foreign Language: From Sacramento: A $5–9 Million Price Tag," *Spotlight: A Newsletter for Employees of the Los Angeles City Schools* 1 (May 20, 1964), 2, Springer Papers.

21. "Needed: Foreign Language Teachers," *Spotlight* 2 (March 24, 1965), 2; "Enrollment to Pass 790,000 This Year," *Spotlight* 3 (September 10, 1965), 1–3, Springer Papers; Hilario Peña, " . . . And Answer Given," *LAT*, May 29, 1965, B4.

22. "7th Grade Spanish Exemption Sought," *Spotlight* 3 (May 11, 1966), 1–3; "State Grants Exemption from Language Program," *Spotlight* 4 (April 7, 1967); "Exemption Sought from Foreign Language Requirement," *Spotlight* 5 (April 15, 1968), 2, Springer Papers. On paper the mandate was for all middle schoolers, although it never extended beyond sixth grade.

23. García and Castro, *Blowout!* 104–9, quotations p. 108; Carlos R. Moreno, comments in the program for the Sal Castro and the Chicano Youth Leadership Conference: The Development of Chicana/o Leadership since 1963, symposium at UCLA CSRC, May 26, 2006, p. 9, accessed April 15, 2018, from http://studylib.net/doc/8856165/castro-program-bandw_52606---the-ucla-chicano-studies#; Ruben Salazar, "Youths Study Problems of Mexican-Americans, April 10, 1963," in Salazar, *Border Correspondent: Selected Writings, 1955–1970*, ed. Mario T. García (Berkeley: University of California Press, 1995), 112–13.

24. García and Castro, *Blowout!* 105–6.

25. Salazar, "Latins Urged to Shed Inferiority Complexes: Leaders Told to Assert Rights by Speaker at Conference on Problems of Area Group," *LAT*, October 28, 1963, 30; Salazar, "Problems of Latins Seen as Thing Apart: New Policy for U.S. Spanish-speaking Students Urged, September 16, 1963," in Salazar, *Border Correspondent*, 127–29.

26. Salazar, "Latins Urged to Shed Inferiority Complexes." For more on Max Rafferty, see Zevi Gutfreund, "Standing Up to Sugar Cubes: The Contest over Ethnic Identity in California's Fourth-Grade Mission Curriculum," *Southern California Quarterly* 92, no. 2 (2010), 167–77; and Lisa McGirr, *Suburban Warriors: The Origins of the New American Right* (Princeton, N.J.: Princeton University Press, 2001), 160.

27. Eugene Gonzales cited in Natalia Mehlman Petrzela, "Origins of the Culture Wars: Sex, Language, School, and State in California, 1968–78" (PhD diss., Stanford University, 2009), 80; Salazar, "New School Plan Sees Bilingualism as Asset," E2–3.

28. Salazar, "New School Plan Sees Bilingualism as Asset," E2–3.

29. For the *Crawford* case see Becky Nicolaides, *My Blue Heaven: Life and Politics in the Working-Class Suburbs of Los Angeles, 1920–1965* (Chicago: University of Chicago Press, 2002), 286–307; Josh Sides, *L.A. City Limits: African American Los Angeles from the Great Depression to the Present* (Berkeley: University of California Press, 2003), 158–67; Gutierrez, "Chicano Education Rights Movement and School Desegregation," 106–20. John Caughey, *To Kill a Child's Spirit: The Tragedy of School Segregation in Los Angeles* (Itasca, Ill.: F. E. Peacock, 1973).

30. "Author of Drop-out Bill Cites Aid to Children," *LAT*, January 30, 1963, 4; Salazar, "Civic Leaders Troubled by School Dropouts, October 22, 1962," in Salazar, *Border Correspondent*, 69–72; Carl Greenberg, "Censure of Politicians Stirs Hot Controversy," *LAT*, March 16, 1965, A4; "Dymally Faces Blast by Negro Political Group," *LAT*, February 21, 1965, E11; Ralph Poblano, "Disclaimer," *LAT*, March 23, 1965, A4; "Endorsements for Jones Announced," *LAT*, May 23, 1965, WS3. Poblano's ally was Assemblyman Mervyn Dymally. In the runoff, Poblano endorsed James Jones, the black candidate who had defeated him in the primary.

31. "Poblano Given New Position by Rafferty," *LAT*, March 29, 1965, B12; Max Rafferty, "The Forgotten Minority Is Rising," *LAT*, March 29, 1965, A5.

32. "Board of Education Candidates Attack, Defend School Programs," *LAT*, April 2, 1965, 3; "Valley Dignitaries to Salute Educator," *LAT*, May 13, 1965, SG3; Ralph Poblano, "Ruben Salazar Series Held Highly Laudable," *LAT*, February 29, 1964, B4; "No Education Labeled Bar to Progress," *LAT*, February 11, 1965, A3.

33. "Valley Dignitaries to Salute Educator," SG3; "Language Skills Raise Job Prospects," and "Spanish Class Aids Teachers," *Spotlight: Los Angeles City Schools Employee Newsletter* 5 (October 16, 1967), 2, 4, Springer Papers.

34. "Metropolitan," *LAT*, December 23, 1966, 2; Richard Bergholz, "7 Council Seats; 4 City School Board Posts Up for Election," *LAT*, January 3, 1967, 3; Art Seidenbaum, "The Importance of Being Nava," *LAT*, July 23, 1967, A34; Paul Coates, "The Mexican-Americans—Why They Don't Vote," *LAT*, March 13, 1968, A6.

35. "Life with Julian Nava . . ." and "United We Stand; Divided . . . ," *Rough Rider*, April 5, 1945, 2 (from Zanki collection); "Noneducators Hit as School Board Members," *LAT*, April 21, 1967, C20; "Democratic League to Hear Two Candidates," *LAT*, March 9, 1967, SF6; Seidenbaum, "The Importance of Being Nava."

36. Bergholz, "2 Professors Seeking Minority Endorsement," *LAT*, January 15, 1967, 19; Seidenbaum, "The Importance of Being Nava"; "Democratic Clubs Biased, Guerra Says," *LAT*, February 7, 1967, 20; Manuel Guerra, "'And We All Join Dr. Nava in . . . '" *LAT*, August 5, 1967, B4; Bergholz, "Foes for School Board Seat Provide Contrast," *LAT*, May 7, 1967, G3.

37. Quoted in Bergholz, "Foes for School Board Seat Provide Contrast," G3; Seidenbaum, "The Importance of Being Nava," A34; Jack Smith, "Dr. Nava Calls Self Practical Idealist," *LAT*, June 4, 1967, F4; Greenberg, "Latin Groups in State, N.Y. Forge Voting Link," *LAT*, July 16, 1967, F26. While Nava won 53 percent of the vote, voter turnout was only 25 percent in 1967.

38. Seidenbaum, "The Importance of Being Nava."

39. Jack Jones, "Mexican-American Units Draft List of Complaints," *LAT*, October 6, 1967, A6; "Negro Education Gains but It Has Pitfalls, Professor Says," *LAT*, October 2, 1967, C1.

40. Charles Donaldson, "Plan to Split Schools Is 'Apartheid'—Nava: Harmer's Bill to Create 10 L.A. Districts Would Appeal to Integration Foes, He Says," *LAT*, February 15, 1968, SF1; "Noneducators Hit as School Board Members," *LAT*, April 21, 1967, C20; Paul Coates, "The Mexican-Americans—Why They Don't Vote," *LAT*, March 13, 1968, A6.

41. "State Releases Ethnic, Racial Survey Summarization, Commentary on Results," *Rough Rider*, March 10, 1967, 3 (from Zanki collection).
42. "State Releases Ethnic, Racial Survey Summarization," 3; "The Locker Room," *Rough Rider*, May 24, 1968, 4 (Zanki collection); Joseph Zanki Sr., interview by Zevi Gutfreund, July 20, 2011.
43. Dial Torgerson, "Young Activists Work to Bring Good to Their Communities: They, Too, Want to Change World," *LAT*, June 18, 1967, G1, G7.
44. Torgerson, "Young Activists Work to Bring Good"; "SB Pres. Nakanishi Expresses Opinion," *Rough Rider*, October 21, 1966, 2 (from Zanki collection); Hector Tobar, "Journey Back to East L.A.: Don Nakanishi Believes Cityhood Could Revive Diversity," *LAT*, April 9, 2010, A2.
45. "Robert Finch Talks to 'New Americans': Lieutenant Governor Welcomes Citizens," *Rough Rider*, May 12, 1967, 2; Jesus Perez, "Student Analyzes 'Dual Patriotism,'" *Rough Rider*, March 18, 1966, 2 (both from Zanki collection). For more on Finch, see chapter 6.
46. "Roosevelt 'Adopts' Sister High School," *Rough Rider*, December 16, 1966, 4; "Aproveche para un favorable porvenir," *Rough Rider*, January 13, 1967, 2; Antonio García (translated by Manuel del Real), "Latin Americans' Problems Discussed: NES President Expresses Philosophies," *Rough Rider*, March 1, 1967, 3 (all from Zanki collection).
47. Kenny Watanabe, "Hirosawa to Lead Ted Yellow Guards," *The Freak Press*, April 1, 1967, 1; "DuBois Club Fights Contreras Regime" and "John Birch Society Formed on Campus," *Rough Rider*, April 1, 1966, 3; "Students Protest 'Sweeps': Revolt Staged in 'A' Building," *Rough Rider*, April 1, 1966, 2; "School Board Ousts Vacation; Student REV Movement Begun," *Rough Rider*, April 1, 1966, 1 (all from Zanki collection).

CHAPTER 6

1. Dial Torgerson, "Start of a Revolution? 'Brown Power' Unity Seen behind School Disorders," *LAT*, March 17, 1968, B1; Jack McCurdy, "Language Is Key Factor: East Side Dropout Rate Stressed in School Unrest," *LAT*, March 18, 1968, A6.
2. Torgerson, "Start of a Revolution?" B1; McCurdy, "School Board Yields to Some Student Points in Boycotts," *LAT*, March 12, 1968, 1; García and Castro, *Blowout!* 185–88. Castro downplays the "language factor" in his 2011 *testimonio*. But he says that, unlike other Mexican American faculty, he "didn't give a damn about the rule that only English could be used in school," *Blowout!* 118.
3. McCurdy, "Frivolous to Fundamental: Demands by East Side High School Students Listed," *LAT*, March 17, 1968, 1.
4. Ruben Salazar, "Mexican-American's Dilemma: He's Unfit in Either Language, February 27, 1970," 241–42, and "Bilingual Texas Public School Gains Support, October 13, 1969," 228–31, both in Salazar, *Border Correspondent*; Lawrence Wright, "Bilingual Education: Where the U.S. Stands in Improving the Education of the Non-English Speaking Student," *Race Relations Reporter* 4, no. 17 (1973), 14.
5. Gareth Davies, "The Great Society after Johnson," notes 14–19, 28–29; Natalia Mehlman Petrzela, "Before the Federal Bilingual Education Act," *Peabody Journal of*

Education 85 (2010), 414; "Hearings in L.A. Due on Bilingual Education Bills," *LAT*, June 18, 1967, G1.

6. "Evolution of Important Events in California Bilingual Education Policy," Folder 1, CSRC; Petrzela, "Before the Federal Bilingual Education Act," 413–15; "Hearings in L.A. Due on Bilingual Education Bills"; "Rafferty Sees Gains for Mexican-Americans," *LAT*, May 11, 1968, B1, B10; Kenneth Burt's Blog, "Spanish-Surnamed Citizens for George Wallace in 1968," accessed April 15, 2016, http://kennethburt.com/blog/?p=1778.

7. Rodolfo Acuña, *A Community under Siege: A Chronicle of Chicanos East of the Los Angeles River, 1945–1975*. CSRC Publications Monograph No. 11 (Los Angeles: UCLA, 1984), 150. For President Johnson's experience teaching in a segregated Mexican school, see "LBJ Linked Latinos, Civil Rights in 'Selma' Speech," accessed April 30, 2018, http://www.sandiegouniontribune.com/sdut-lbj-linked-latinos-civil-rights-in-selma-speech-2015mar04-story.html; "Law Proposed to Aid Bilingual Education: Legislation Would Authorize Federal Funds for Instruction in Spanish," *LAT*, March 12, 1967, SF_C6; "Some Provisions of H.R. 8000: Extension of Remarks of Hon. Edward R. Roybal of California in the House of Representatives," in Julian Nava, ed., *Viva La Raza! Readings on Mexican Americans* (New York: Van Nostrand, 1973). 125–26.

8. Acuña, *Community under Siege*, 160; "Hearings in L.A. Due on Bilingual Education Bills"; Bob Rawitch, "Murphy Hits Lack of Bilingual Education at Senate Hearing," *LAT*, June 25, 1967, D8.

9. Rawitch, "Murphy Hits Lack of Bilingual Education at Senate Hearing"; "Crowther Again Skips Hearing on Education in East L.A.," *LAT*, October 5, 1968, B5.

10. Appendix A, Bilingual Education Act, Title VII, Elementary and Secondary Education Act of 1965, As Amended in 1967, Public Law 90-247, January 2, 1968, Folder 4, CSRC.

11. Appendix A, Bilingual Education Act; "Title VII: Proposals Approved for 1969–70," *The Center Forum* 4, no. 1 (1969), 9–10, Folder 4, CSRC.

12. "Bilingual Education Program under Analysis," *LATA Hot Line* 4 (December 4, 1967), 2; "Bi-lingual Education Receives Help," *LATA Hot Line* 4 (December 11, 1967), 1; "LATA Takes Swift Action on Bi-lingual Education," *LATA Hot Line* 4 (January 15, 1968), 1; "Habla Usted Español? Do Your Students Speak Spanish?" *LATA Hot Line* 4 (January 22, 1968), 1; "Problemas: Education in East Los Angeles," *LATA Hot Line* 4 (February 19, 1968), 1; "State Education Conference Concentrates on Needs of Mexican-Americans," *LATA Hot Line* 4 (April 29, 1968), 1, all in Springer Papers.

13. "Rafferty Sees Gains for Mexican-Americans," *LAT*, May 11, 1968, B1, B10; Salazar, "Brown Berets Hail 'La Raza' and Scorn the Establishment, June 16, 1969," in Salazar, *Border Correspondent*, 212–19; Ray Ripton, "Santa Monica Schools Helping Mexican-Americans," *LAT*, November 2, 1969. Gonzales quoted in Petrzela, "Origins of the Culture Wars," 105.

14. "School Boycotts Not the Answer," *LAT*, March 15, 1968, A4; Torgerson, "Start of a Revolution?" *LAT*, March 17, 1968, B1.

15. Torgerson, "Start of a Revolution?" B1; Jack McCurdy, "Student Disorders Erupt at 4 High Schools; Policeman Hurt," *LAT* March 7, 1968, 3; Ken Reich, "Dyer's Test by Fire: Principal Walks Narrow Path in School Walkout," *LAT*, March 14, 1968, B6; Gutierrez, "Chicano Education Rights Movement and School Desegregation," 1–2; García and Castro, *Blowout!* 136–40, 160–61. The principal cancelled the play (*Barefoot in the Park*) for reasons completely unrelated to bilingualism.

16. McCurdy, "Student Disorders Erupt at 4 High Schools," 3; McCurdy, "1,000 Walk Out in School Boycott: Jefferson Teachers Quit Classes; 19 Juveniles, 1 Adult Arrested," *LAT*, March 9, 1968, B1; García and Castro, *Blowout!* 172–77.

17. Torgerson, "Start of a Revolution?" B1; McCurdy, "School Board Yields to Some Student Points in Boycotts," 1; McCurdy, "Language Is Key Factor," A6; McCurdy, "Frivolous to Fundamental: Demands Made by East Side High School Students Listed," *LAT*, March 17, 1968, 1.

18. Torgerson, "Start of a Revolution?" B1; McCurdy, "School Board Yields to Some Student Points in Boycotts," 1; McCurdy, "Student Disorders Erupt at 4 High Schools," 3; McCurdy, "1,000 Walk Out in School Boycott," B1; García and Castro, *Blowout!* 172–77.

19. Reich, "Dyer's Test by Fire," B6; "What Happened?" *Rough Rider*, March 12, 1968, 1 (from Zanki collection).

20. "What Happened?" The black participant was Roosevelt's basketball star, Lenzy Stuart. After leading the school to two straight city titles, he had an athletic scholarship to UCLA, which was about to win its fourth national championship in five years. But coach John Wooden withdrew the offer after he learned of Stuart's leadership in the Blowouts. Joseph Zanki Sr., interview by Zevi Gutfreund, July 20, 2011.

21. "What Happened?"; Cleveland Gillis, "Views of a President," *Rough Rider*, May 17, 1968, 2 (from Zanki collection).

22. "What Happened?"; "Teacher Transfer: A Clarification," *Rough Rider*, April 5, 1968, 1 (from Zanki collection); Torgerson, "Start of a Revolution?" B1; Reich, "Dyer's Test by Fire," B6; McCurdy, "School Board Yields to Some Student Points in Boycotts," 1.

23. Torgerson, "Start of a Revolution?"; quotation in Juan J. Inda, "La comunidad en lucha: The Development of the East Los Angeles High School Blowouts." Paper presented at the 29th Stanford Center for Chicano Research Working Papers Series, Stanford, Calif., March 1990, 15; "Roybal, Nava, Richardson Come to Assembly," *Rough Rider*, March 12, 1968, 1 (from Zanki collection); McCurdy, "1,000 Walk Out in School Boycott," B1.

24. Gutierrez, "Chicano Education Rights Movement and School Desegregation," 81–83. Castro cites Gutierrez in his *testimonio*. He inflates Gutierrez's numbers, however, saying there were 1,200 people (not 1,100) in attendance on March 26, and that the meeting lasted almost four hours (not 2½ hours). García and Castro, *Blowout!* 189–90.

25. "Roosevelt Solutions Committee Complains and Finds Solutions," *Rough Rider*, March 12, 1968, 1 (from Zanki collections).

26. "Board Responds to Walkout Proposals," *Rough Rider*, May 17, 1968, 2 (from Zanki collection).

27. Inda, "La comunidad en lucha," 17–18. The college students belonged to the Brown Berets.

28. García and Castro, *Blowout!* 198–99; "Calderon Reception to Be at Nava Home," *LAT*, May 26, 1968, SF_A3; Ron Einstoss, "13 Indicted in Disorders at 4 L.A. Schools: Arrests Underway," *LAT*, June 2, 1968, D12A; Gene Blake, "Don't Link Law, Order, Ex-Justice Clark Says," *LAT*, October 11, 1968, 31. The district attorney was Evelle Younger, who would become California's attorney general two years later.

29. García and Castro, *Blowout!* 207–16. Castro says there were between one hundred and three hundred picketers. The *Los Angeles Times* reported one hundred picketers. McCurdy, "Latins Urge Reinstatement of Teacher Who Led Walkout," *LAT*, August 30, 1968, B; McCurdy, "Board Upholds Ban on Teacher Indicted in Student Strikes," *LAT*, September 13, 1968, 3; McCurdy," East Side Still Plagued with Hangover from School Boycott," *LAT*, September 15, 1968, EB; McCurdy, "Lincoln High Pickets Protest Absence of Indicted Teacher: No Students or Teachers Participate," *LAT*, September 17, 1968, 3; "Group Conducts Sit-In at School Board Chambers," *LAT*, September 27, 1968, A3. The EICC head was the Reverend Vahac Mardirosian.

30. García and Castro, *Blowout!* 216–20; McCurdy, "Student-Parent Sit-In Continuing on Weekend," *LAT*, September 28, 1968, B1; "School Board Sit-Ins Pass Time Musically," *LAT*, September 29, 1968, A3; McCurdy, "School Board Sit-In Extended," *LAT*, October 1, 1968, 1; McCurdy, "School Board Sit-In to Wind Up Today," *LAT*, October 2, 1968, 3; Mc-Curdy, "Castro Restored to Teaching Job," *LAT*, October 4, 1968, 1. The two front-page stories appeared above the fold.

31. McCurdy, "Board Defeats Move to Void Castro Ruling," *LAT*, October 15, 1968, 3; McCurdy, "Women End School Board Sit-in Protesting Lack of Sit-in Ban," *LAT*, October 16, 1968, 3; McCurdy, "East Side Still Plagued with Hangover from School Boycott"; "Pickets Urge Teachers to Remain at Lincoln," *LAT*, October 23, 1968, B4; "104 RHS Teachers Sign Petition Protesting School Board's Handling of Walkouts," *Rough Rider*, April 5, 1968, 1–2 (from Zanki collection).

32. "Victories for the Dissenters," *LAT*, October 6, 1968, F5; "A New Protest at Lincoln High," *LAT*, October 9, 1968, A4.

33. Ron Einstoss, "ACLU Suit Seeks to Prevent Prosecution of 13 Militants," *LAT*, August 24, 1968, B1; Oscar Acosta, "The East L.A. 13 vs. the L.A. Superior Court," *El Grito* 3 (Winter 1970), 12–18; "Judge Upholds Prosecution of 13 Accused in School Walkouts," *LAT*, November 26, 1968, SG1; Einstoss, "DA's Office Hits Back at Criticism in Sal Castro Case," 3; "Jury Urges Suspension of Any Indicted Student," *LAT*, December 21, 1968, A1; "State Appeal Court Bars Prosecution of Castro on 2 Counts," *LAT*, July 18, 1970, A1. Oscar Acosta, Castro's attorney, stressed that only 1 percent of the grand jury was Mexican American, even though Latinos made up 13 percent of the LA population by 1969—or, as Acosta put it, Mexican Americans were "the largest minority in America's numerically largest county." Acosta, "East L.A. 13 vs. the L.A. Superior Court," 12.

34. McCurdy, "40 Teachers Ask for Transfers after Reinstatement of Castro," *LAT*, October 8, 1968, A1; "Mexican-Americans' Cultural Week Opens Today at College,"

LAT, October 12, 1968, C1; Salazar, "Latin Youths Take a Hard Look at Life," *LAT*, April 13, 1969, D17.

35. Jack Jones, "Welfare System Hit at Hearings in East LA," *LAT*, May 23, 1969, C1. For full accounts of the CYLC speeches, see Philip Montez, "The Psychology of Mexican-American Students," and Marcos De León, "A Theory of Bicultural Education," both in Nava, *Viva La Raza*, 122–24.

36. Charles Donaldson, "Bilingual Education Urged for All Latins," *LAT*, October 10, 1969, SF7. Castro later became disillusioned with bilingual education. See epilogue, note 3.

37. Stan Steiner, "The De-Education Schools," *Center Forum* 4 (September 1969), 6, CSRC.

38. "Bilingual Education," *LAT*, August 15, 1968, WS3; "4 Panels to Discuss Crisis in Education," *LAT*, February 7, 1969, SF10; "Day in Sacramento," *LAT*, March 14, 1969, C4.

39. "Federal Funds Awarded VSC for Teachers," *LAT*, April 7, 1968, SF_A4; "VSC Gets Grant to Assist Teachers of Minority Pupils," *LAT*, March 3, 1968, SF_C1. The Occidental professor was Paul Sheldon. See Salazar, "Civic Leaders Troubled by School Dropouts," 70–71.

40. "Complete Text of GOP Platform," *LAT*, August 5, 1968, 17; "The Nation: Sen. George Murphy," *LAT*, July 2, 1968, A2; Richard Bergholz, "Critics Abate: Once Derided, Murphy Wins Senate Spurs," *LAT*, July 28, 1969, 3.

41. Davies, "Great Society after Johnson," notes 14–19, 28–29; Petrzela, "Before the Federal Bilingual Education Act," 414; "Hearings in L.A. Due on Bilingual Education Bills," *LAT*, June 18, 1967, G1. "Robert Finch Talks to 'New Americans': Lieutenant Governor Welcomes Citizens," *Rough Rider*, May 12, 1967, 2 (from Zanki collection).

42. Vincent Burke, "President Will Seek Expanded Funding for Bilingual Education," *LAT*, February 13, 1969, A1; "Sen. Murphy Urges Aid for School Plan," *LAT*, May 31, 1969, A1.

43. "Breaking the Language Barrier," *LAT*, January 27, 1969, B8: "Overcoming the Language Barrier," *LAT*, May 20, 1969, A8.

44. García, introduction to Salazar, *Border Correspondent*, 25–36; Salazar quoted in "La Voz del Pueblo," *Backstory* podcast entitled "Behind the Bylines: Advocacy Journalism in America," accessed March 23, 2017, http://backstoryradio.org/shows/behind-the-bylines.

45. Salazar, "Bilingual Texas School Gains Public Support, October 13, 1969," in Salazar, *Border Correspondent*, 229–31.

46. Salazar, "UMAS to Be Reinstated at Roosevelt High, April 23, 1969," in Salazar, *Border Correspondent*, 210–11.

47. Mario Esparza and Ricardo Perea, "Contra Corner: What Good Were the Walkouts?," and Karen Balderrama, "The UMAS Affair," *Rough Rider*, October 22, 1968, 1–2 (from Zanki collection).

48. Salazar, "800 Supporters of Sal Castro March on School Board," *LAT*, October 7, 1969, 3. For more on Castro's transfer see García and Castro, *Blowout!* 228.

49. Salazar, "Mexican–American School Walkout Focused on Problem, June 26, 1970," in Salazar, *Border Correspondent*, 263–64; McCurdy, "East Side Still Plagued with Hangover from School Boycott"; Salazar, "A Beautiful Sight: The System Working the Way It Should," *LAT*, July 20, 1970, C7.

50. Salazar, "Mexican-American's Dilemma: He's Unfit in Either Language," and "The Mexican-Americans NEDA Much Better School System," in Salazar, *Border Correspondent*, 241–42 and 267–69, respectively.

CHAPTER 7

1. "Bilingual Education: A Non-Conforming View," Parts I and IV," *128 Congressional Record of the 97th Congress*, September 27 and 30, 1982, S25243, Box 28, S. I. Hayakawa Papers, Hoover Institution, Stanford University, Stanford, Calif.

2. "Bilingual Education," Part IV, S26628.

3. Barbara Koh, "Breaking the Long Silence: Sugi Kiriyama," *LAT*, November 25, 1990, 1; "George Kiriyama: Los Angeles Unified School District Board Member," accessed July 29, 2015, http://www.lausd.k12.ca.us/lausd/board/ kiriyama.html; "History of Nora Sterry Elementary School," accessed July 29, 2015, http://www.sterryelementary.org/ history-of-nora-sterry-elementary.html.

4. "George Kiriyama: Los Angeles Unified School District Board Member"; "Teachers Pioneer Racial Minority Courses: Venture into Unexplored Academic Territory," *LAT*, April 28, 1968, WS1.

5. "George Kiriyama, Los Angeles Unified School District Board Member," 74; "Career Educator," *LAT*, August 22, 2005; LAUSD *Lau* Plan, May 25, 1978, pp. 109–10, Box 560, Los Angeles Unified School District Board of Education Records, Special Collections Young Research Library, UCLA (hereafter LAUSD Records); LAUSD *Lau* Plan Year-End Report, 1984–85, pp. 11, 42, Box 1361, LAUSD Records.

6. Warren Furutani, "The Warren Report: Don't Call Me Tabo," *Gidra* 1 (August 1969), 2; "Text of Speech by Warren Furutani: Asian Americans for Peace Rally, Little Tokyo," *Gidra* 2 (February 1970), 5–8.

7. Embrey, interview by Hansen and Hacker, 152–75.

8. Warren Furutani, "The Warren Report: Changes," *Gidra* 2 (March 1970), 12; Neil Chan, "Tutorial Project," *Gidra* 2 (January 1970), 12–13; Furutani, "Warren Out," *Rafu Shimpo*, April 1, 1970, 1.

9. Salazar, "Mexican-American's Dilemma," in Salazar, *Border Correspondent*, 241–42; Wesley Balbuena, Edward Morton, and Byrl Robinson, "The Adult Bilingual Experimental School," *California Journal of Secondary Education* 44 (May 1969) 225–30.

10. Balbuena, Morton, and Robinson, "Adult Bilingual Experimental School," 225–27; Julian Nava, "Adult Education Is Community Involvement," *California Journal of Secondary Education* 44 (May 1969), 196–98.

11. William Johnston, "Adult Education in Los Angeles," *California Journal of Secondary Education* 44 (May 1969), 199–202; "State Education Conference Concentrates on Needs of Mexican-Americans," *LATA Hot Line* 4 (April 29, 1968), 1, Springer Papers; Ellen Rodman, "Pollution of Mind a Problem," *LAT*, September 8, 1970, H1; "Five Adult Education Centers Opened," *Spotlight*, June 9, 1969, 2, Springer Papers.

12. Balbuena, Morton, and Robinson, "Adult Bilingual Experimental School," 225–30.

13. "Funding Found for Bilingual Project," *LAT*, July 7, 1969, A8.

14. McCurdy, "Intervention by Nixon Aids L.A. School Project," *LAT*, July 6, 1969, B; "Funding Found for Bilingual Project," *LAT*, July 7, 1969, A8; Ellen Rodman, "Malabar Experiment Raises Reading Skills," *LAT*, July 30, 1970, D1.

15. Ray Ripton, "S.M. Schools Helping Mexican-Americans," *LAT*, November 2, 1969, WS1.

16. Wallace Lambert, "An Overview of Issues in Immersion Education," in *Studies on Immersion Education: A Collection for United Stated Educators*, ed. Office of Bilingual Bicultural Education (Sacramento: California State Department of Education, 1984), 8; Andrew Cohen, telephone interview by Zevi Gutfreund, January 4, 2008; Ann Snow interview by Gutfreund, December 6, 2007, Los Angeles; Leslie Evans, "Russell N. Campbell, September 5, 1927–March 30, 2003," UCLA International Institute website, accessed March 29, 2013, http://www.international.ucla.edu/article.asp?parentid=3507. Heffernan, Nance, and Campbell all spoke at the Conference on Understanding and Teaching Mexican-American Children and Youth, Oxnard, Calif., October 16–17, 1964.

17. Russell Campbell, "The Immersion Approach to Foreign Language Teaching," in Office of Bilingual Bicultural Education, *Studies on Immersion Education*, 119, 120.

18. Quotation in Campbell, "Immersion Approach to Foreign Language Teaching," 122; see also Campbell, "Bilingual Education and the English-Speaking Majority," in *Bilingual Program, Policy, and Assessment Issues* (Sacramento: California State Department of Education, 1980), 89.

19. Madeline Erlich, interview by Zevi Gutfreund, December 10, 2007, Culver City; Concepción Valadez, interview by Zevi Gutfreund, January 8, 2008, Los Angeles; Advocates for Language Learning El Marino website, accessed July 31, 2015, http://www.allelmarino.org/.

20. Eduardo Hernández-Chávez, "The Inadequacy of English Immersion Education as an Educational Approach for Language Minority Students in the United States," in Office of Bilingual Bicultural Education, *Studies on Immersion Education*, 151–53.

21. Evans, "Russell N. Campbell"; Donna Christian, Christopher Montone, Kathryn Lindholm, and Isolda Carranza, *Profiles in Two-Way Immersion Education* (McHenry, Ill.: Center for Applied Linguistics and Delta Systems, 1997), 1, 46; Nancy Rhodes and Tara Fortune, "Language Immersion: Yesterday, Today, and Tomorrow," paper presented at Celebrating 40 Years of Language Immersion Education, Southern California Language Symposium, Culver City, Calif., May 13, 2011.

22. This expansion was also driven by the decision in *Lau v. Nichols*. In 1974, the Supreme Court ruled that school districts had to provide non-English speakers "a meaningful opportunity to participate in the educational process." Although *Lau* was filed by a Chinese-American parent against San Francisco Unified School District (not LAUSD), the court's unanimous opinion required all school districts to submit their own "*Lau* Plans" to qualify for bilingual education funding.

23. "Services for NES and LES Pupils, 1976–77," May 26, 1977, LAUSD Records, UCLA (Box 909); "ESEA, Title VII: Bilingual Education Programs," August 7, 1978, LAUSD Records, UCLA (Box 909).

24. Greg Raven to L.A. City Board of Education, November 6, 1978, and Mrs. LeGate to L.A. City Schools, October 23, 1978, both in Box 909, LAUSD Records.

25. "ESEA, Title VII: Bilingual Education Programs," August 7, 1978, and Agape Christian Fellowship to Board of Education, May 1, 1978, both in Box 909, LAUSD Records.

26. S. I. Hayakawa, *Language in Thought and Action* (New York: Harcourt, Brace, 1949); Embrey, interview by Hansen and Hacker, 149; William Wei, *The Asian American Movement* (Philadelphia, Pa.: Temple University Press, 1993); Gerald Haslam and Janice Haslam, *In Thought and Action: The Enigmatic Life of S. I. Hayakawa* (Lincoln: University of Nebraska Press, 2011).

27. Quotation in "S.I. Rips *Gidra!*" *Gidra* 1 (May 1969), 1; "Pigs, Pickets & a Banana," *Gidra* 1 (May 1969), 1.

28. *125 Congressional Record of the 96th Congress*, June 27, 1979, S16863–64, and Hayakawa, "Testimony before Select Commission on Refugees," June 9, 1980, both in Box 23, Hayakawa Papers.

29. *127 Congressional Record of the 97th Congress*, January 6, 1981, S167–68, and Hayakawa to Chairman, February 4, 1982, both in Box 23, Hayakawa Papers.

30. "The Hayakawa Amendment: English—The Official Language," n.d., Box 406-A, Hayakawa Papers; quotation in "Proposed Constitutional Amendment," *126 Congressional Record of the 97th Congress*, April 27, 1981, Box 30, Hayakawa Papers.

31. "The Senator's English," *Wall Street Journal*, May 6, 1981, Box 406-A, Hayakawa Papers; quotation from "Proposed Constitutional Amendment," *126 Congressional Record*, S7444–45, Box 30, Hayakawa Papers; US English website, accessed March 30, 2013, http://www.usenglish.org.

32. "Bilingual Education: A Non-Conforming View," Part IV, *128 Congressional Record*, S26631, Box 28, Hayakawa Papers.

33. "Senate Seeks English as Official Language," *Rafu Shimpo*, September 14, 1981, Box 25, Hayakawa Papers; Tustin's mayor quoted in Diane Kiese, "Hayakawa Proposal Supports English," *Antelope Valley Press*, August 20, 1981, 1, Box 25, Hayakawa Papers; "We All Lose This One," *Gardena Valley News*, October 14, 1981, 1, Box 133, Hayakawa Papers.

34. "Senate Seeks English as Official Language"; Montoya and Sieroty quotations in John Stanton, "State Senate Backs Sen. Hayakawa Plan to Make English Official Language of U.S.," *Peninsula Times-Tribune*, n.d., Box 25, Hayakawa Papers; Edward Roybal, "Should the U.S. Adopt a Bilingual Education Program?" *American Legion*, September 1979, 8, Box 133, Hayakawa Papers.

35. S. I. Hayakawa, "Should the U.S. Adopt a Bilingual Education Program?" *American Legion*, September 1979, 8, Box 133, Hayakawa Papers (Roybal and Hayakawa wrote opposing articles for the same edition); "Speech to California Scholastic Press Association," April 13, 1981, Box 152, Hayakawa Papers; "California's Top Hispanic

Official Challenges Sen. Hayakawa to Bilingual Education Debate," *Rafu Shimpo*, April 16, 1981, 1, Box 170, Hayakawa Papers.

36. May, *Language and Minority Rights*, 205–22; US English website, accessed March 30, 2013, http://www.usenglish.org.

37. William Trombley, "Bilingual Education: Even Experts Are Confused," *LAT*, September 5, 1980, 21.

38. Trombley, "Bitter Fight: Can Bilingual Education Do Its Job?" *LAT*, September 4, 1980, 1.

39. Trombley, "Bilingual Education: Even Experts Are Confused," 1.

40. Trombley, "Bilingual Education: Even Experts Are Confused," 1, 20.

41. S. I. Hayakawa, "English Is Not Social Studies," *Christian Science Monitor*, n.d., 3, Box 133, Hayakawa Papers.

42. "Bilingual Education: A Non-Conforming View, Part II," Box 28, Hayakawa Papers; Andrew Cohen, telephone interview by Zevi Gutfreund, January 4, 2008.

43. William Adrise, "A Different Twist on Language Immersion," *LAT*, September 13, 1992, 8.

44. Bob Williams, "Greenwood Challenges Furutani's Background," *LAT*, April 9, 1987, 1; Stephanie Chavez, "Furutani Takes Tolerance Message to School," *LAT*, May 20, 1992, 3; Jon Garcia and Kim Kowsky, "Kiriyama Wins Seat Vacated by Furutani," *LAT*, April 16, 1995, 3; George Ramos, "Victoria Castro Recalls Her Role in 1968 Chicano 'Blowouts' at Eastside Campuses—and Life Today as a School Board Member," *LAT*, April 17, 1996, accessed May 4, 2018, http://articles.latimes.com/1996-04-17/local/me-62401_1_sal-castro; Amy Pyle, "L.A. Schools Shift 26,000 out of Bilingual Classes," *LAT*, December 3, 1996, 8.

45. Barbara Koh, "Bilingual Immersion Program Teaches Students to Understand Spanish and English—And Something About Each Other," *LAT*, January 31, 1991, 1; Bernice Hirabayashi, "In Any Language, This Program Is Intense Education," *LAT*, August 16, 1992, 1; "Two-Way Language Learning Pays Off," *LAT*, June 13, 1993, 18.

46. Hirabayashi, "In Any Language, This Program Is Intense Education," 1; Carol Chastang, "Language Immersion Programs Involve More Than Memorizing Different Words," *LAT*, February 27, 1994, 12; "Culver City: School Board Proceeds with Plan to Relocate Immersion Programs," *LAT*, March 6, 1994, 10; Advocates for Language Learning El Marino website, accessed August 10, 2015, http://www.allelmarino.org.

47. Hirabayashi, "In Any Language, This Program Is Intense Education," 1; Chastang, "Language Immersion Programs Involve More Than Memorizing Different Words," 12.

48. Koh, "Bilingual Immersion Program Teaches Students to Understand Spanish and English."

49. Sandy Hack, "Ethnic Immersion Program," *LAT*, March 10, 1994, 23; Sue Reilly, "Language Immersion Schooling Draws Praise, Sparks Fears," *LAT*, August 15, 1994, 5.

50. Amy Pyle, "Latino Parents to Boycott School Bilingual Plan," *LAT*, February 13, 1996; Bettina Boxall, "Que Pasa Aqui? Spanish-Speaking Garment Workers and

Their Fervent Advocate Seem an Unlikely Group to Launch the Bid to Virtually End Bilingual Education," *LAT*, April 5, 1998, 1.

51. Pyle, "Latino Parents to Boycott School Bilingual Plan"; Callaghan quoted in Boxall, "Que Pasa Aqui?" 1.

52. Pyle, "Latino Parents to Boycott School Bilingual Plan"; Boxall, "Que Pasa Aqui?"

53. Boxall, "Que Pasa Aqui? 1; Alice Callaghan, "Desperate to Learn English," *New York Times*, August 15, 1997, accessed on March 30, 2013, http://www.onenation.org/1997/081597.html.

54. Jaime Escalante to Ron Unz, October 10, 1997, accessed on March 30, 2013, http://www.onenation.org/escalante.html; Boxall, "Popularity Extends Past Racial Lines: Measure to Virtually End Bilingual Education Has Widespread Support," *LAT*, May 29, 1998, 3.

55. Ron Unz and Gloria Tuchman, "Proposition 227: English Language Education for Children in Public Schools," accessed August 11, 2015, http://www.onenation.org/fulltext.html; poll cited in Boxall, "Popularity Extends Past Racial Lines," 3.

56. James Rainey, "500 Students March against Prop. 227," *LAT*, June 12, 1998, 3; Jocelyn Stewart, "An In-Depth Look at People and Policies Shaping Los Angeles County," *LAT*, June 19, 1998, 2; Nick Anderson, "L.A. Teachers Group Pledges Defiance if Prop. 227 Passes," *LAT*, May 21, 1998, 3.

57. Doug Smith, "Education: Incumbent Ousted after One Term," *LAT*, July 2, 1998; Ron Unz, "Prop. 227 and LAUSD," *LAT*, September 14, 1998; Alice Callaghan, "Bilingual Instruction: Californians Voted for English Immersion, but Many Districts Play Obfuscating Word Games," *LAT*, September 3, 1998, 9.

58. Smith, "Incumbent Ousted after One Term"; Ron Unz, "Prop. 227 and LAUSD," *LAT*, September 14, 1998; Alice Callaghan, "Bilingual Instruction: Californians Voted for English Immersion, but Many Districts Play Obfuscating Word Games," *LAT*, September 3, 1998, 9.

59. "Bilingual Education: A Squandered Opportunity," *LAT*, October 26, 1997, accessed August 11, 2015, http://articles.latimes.com/print/1997/oct/26/opinion/op-46854.

60. "Bilingual Education: A Squandered Opportunity.,

EPILOGUE

1. Eric Avila, "The Historical Antecedents to California's Superdiversity," panel discussion at inaugural conference of the Institute of American Cultures, UCLA Faculty Center, February 28, 2013.

2. Bernice Hirabayashi, "In Any Language, This Program Is Intense Education," *LAT*, August 16, 1992, 1.

3. García and Castro, *Blowout!* 273–75. Personal disappointments colored Castro's opinion. "It also amazed me that I could not have taught bilingual ed., because, as the system was set up, I was not 'qualified' to teach it," he complained. "Spanish-speaking teaching aides did most of the Spanish used in their classes. When you have the aide doing the actual teaching, it's a half-ass program. . . . Instead of eliminating these programs, I would have returned them to the original version of language acquisition and transition with cultural enrichment."

4. García and Castro, *Blowout!* 275.

5. Callaghan, "Quality Counts," *LAT*, July 11, 2010, A33. The Westside school was Brentwood Magnet Elementary.

6. Callaghan, "Quality Counts."

7. James Rainey, "500 Students March against Prop 227," *LAT*, June 12, 1998, 3; Jocelyn Stewart, "An In-Depth Look at People and Policies Shaping Los Angeles County," *LAT*, June 19, 1998, 2; Nick Anderson, "L.A. Teachers Group Pledges Defiance if Prop 227 Passes," *LAT*, May 21, 1998, 3; "Ms. Shelly Spiegel-Coleman," accessed December 24, 2015, http://latinocongreso.org/agenda07.php?bio=215.

8. Laurie Olsen and Shelly Spiegel-Coleman, "A Skill, Not a Weakness," *LAT*, July 11, 2010, A32. For more on reading proficiency, see Patricia Gándara, "In the Aftermath of the Storm: English Learners in the Post-227 Era," *Bilingual Research Journal* 24, nos. 1–2 (2000): 1–13.

9. Olsen and Spiegel-Coleman, "A Skill, Not a Weakness."

10. Quotation in Teresa Watanabe, "New Approach to Bilingual Teaching: Dual-Language Immersion Targets Both Immigrant and Native-Born Students," *LAT*, May 9, 2011, A1; "The ABCs of Dual Language Immersion" and "The Guiding Principles for Dual Language Education," panel discussions at Celebrating 40 Years of Language Immersion Education, Southern California Language Symposium, Culver City, Calif., May 13, 2011.

11. Judy Chu, keynote address at Celebrating 40 Years of Language Immersion; Chu, education website, accessed May 4, 2018, https://chu.house.gov/issues/education; "Rep. Chu Condemns Comparisons to Japanese Internment," accessed December 26, 2015, https://chu.house.gov/press-release/rep-chu-condemns-comparisons-japanese-internment-and-other-xenophobic-rhetoric-around . Chu's predecessor, Hilda Solis, had proposed a similar bill in 2007, the Providing Resources to Improve Dual Language Education (PRIDE) Act, Minutes, November 27, 2007, Box 772, LAUSD Records.

12. "Rep. Chu Sees Opportunity and Disappointment in ESEA Reauthorization," accessed December 26, 2015, https://chu.house.gov/press-release/rep-chu-sees-opportunity-and-disappointment-esea-reauthorization.

13. Thomas Himes, "Opponents of Confucius Classroom Launch Recall Effort in Hacienda–La Puente Unified," *San Gabriel Valley Tribune*, February 14, 2011, accessed April 26, 2018, http://www.sgvtribune.com/general-news/20110214/opponents-of-confucius-classroom-launch-recall-effort-in-hacienda-la-puente-unified; also Advocacy: Fostering Positive Attitudes towards Bilingualism, panel discussion at Celebrating 40 Years of Language Immersion.

14. Chen quoted in Himes, "Opponents of Confucius Classroom Launch Recall Effort;" Ni Ching-Ching, "Education Aid from China Stirs Debate: Some See a Language Program as a Tool for Propaganda, Backers Try to Calm Fears," *LAT*, April 4, 2010, A25; Brandon Ferguson, "More American Than Jay Chen?" *O.C. Weekly* [Orange County], October 25, 2012, accessed May 4, 2018, https://www.ocweekly.com/more-american-than-jay-chen-6424390/; "Socialism Studies: Aasif Mandvi Explores the Communist

Threat as Hacienda Heights Introduces a Chinese Language Program to Middle School Kids," *Daily Show with Jon Stewart*, June 7, 2010, accessed May 4, 2018, http://www.cc.com/video-clips/kir3p5/the-daily-show-with-jon-stewart-socialism-studies.

15. Ferguson, "More American Than Jay Chen?"

16. "California Proposition 58: Non-English Languages Allowed in Public Education (2016)," *Ballotpedia*, accessed May 4, 2018, https://ballotpedia.org/California_Proposition_58,_Non-English_Languages_Allowed_in_Public_Education_(2016); Jazmine Ulloa, "Bilingual Education Has Been Absent from California Public Schools for Almost 20 Years; But That May Soon Change," *LAT*, October 6, 2016, accessed February 12, 2017, http://www.latimes.com/politics/la-pol-ca-proposition-58-bilingual-education-20161012-snap-story.html; Patrick McGreevy, "Senate Supports Asking Voters to Repeal Ban on Bilingual Education," *LAT*, May 27, 2014, accessed December 27, 2015, http://www.latimes.com/local/political/la-me-pc-state-senate-voter-approval-of-bilingual-education-20140527-story.html.

17. Lara quoted in Ulloa, "Bilingual Education Has Been Absent from California Public Schools"; McGreevy, "Senate Supports Asking Voters to Repeal Ban on Bilingual Education;" Philip Carter, "Why This Bilingual Education Ban Should Have Repealed Long Ago," *CNN* news segment, March 4, 2014, , accessed May 4, 2018, https://www.cnn.com/2014/03/04/opinion/carter-bilingual-education/index.html.

18. State senator Mark Wyland (R-Escondido) quoted in McGreevy, "Senate Supports Asking Voters to Repeal Ban on Bilingual Education"; Unz quoted in Patt Morrison, "Should California Reinstate Bilingual Education?" *LAT*, February 28, 2014, accessed May 4, 2018, http://www.latimes.com/opinion/opinion-la/la-ol-california-reinstate-bilingual-education-proposition-227-20140228-story.html.

19. Kenneth Marcus, "*Heimat* and Hybridity: Arnold Schoenberg and Southern California Modernism," *Forum for Inter-American Research* 4, no. 1 (2011), accessed August 26, 2016, http://www.interamerica.de/volume-4-1/marcus/.

BIBLIOGRAPHY

ARCHIVES AND COLLECTIONS

Bancroft Library, University of California, Berkeley
    California Department of Industrial Relations, Division of Immigration and Housing
        Records, 1912–1939
    Florence Wyckoff Papers, 1940–1990 (bulk)
    National Council on Agricultural Life and Labor Records, 1937–1967
Chicano Studies Research Center, University of California, Los Angeles
    Bilingual Education Papers
    Desegregation Collection, 1976–1983
    Julian Nava Papers, 1964–1994
Hirasaki National Resource Center, Japanese American National Museum. Los Angeles
    Afton Dill Nance Papers, 1942–1981
Honnold/Mudd Library of the Claremont Colleges. Claremont, Calif.
    Carey McWilliams War Relocation Authority Correspondence, 1919–1994
Hoover Institution, Stanford University. Stanford, Calif.
    Survey of Race Relations, 1924–1927
    S. I. Hayakawa Papers, 1926–1994
Japanese American Citizens League History Collection, 1923–1995, Japanese American
    National Library. San Francisco, Calif.
Special Collections, Green Library, Stanford University. Stanford, Calif.
    Eduardo Quevedo Papers, 1929–1968
    Manuel Ruiz Papers, 1931–1986
Special Collections, Los Angeles Public Library. Los Angeles, Calif.

Special Collections, Young Research Library, University of California, Los Angeles
    Frank Chuman Papers, 1900–ca. 1993
    Karl Yoneda Papers, 1925–1989 (bulk)
    Los Angeles Daily News Negatives
    Los Angeles Times Photographic Archives
    Los Angeles Unified School District Board of Education Records, 1875–2009
    Manzanar War Relocation Center Records, 1942–1946
    Yuji Ichioka Papers, 1936–2002
Mary Springer Papers, 1900–1990, San Fernando High School Library, Los Angeles Unified School District, Calif.
Joseph Zanki Sr. private collection, 1923–1969, Fountain Valley, Calif.

PERIODICALS CITED

California Journal of Elementary Education
California Quarterly of Secondary Education
Center Forum
Common Ground
Community Exchange Bulletin (California Department of Education, Division of Immigrant Education)
Gidra
Hot Line (Los Angeles Teachers Association)
La Opinión
Los Angeles Educational Research Bulletin
Los Angeles School Journal
Los Angeles Times
Magazines (Los Angeles City School Districts Division of Instructional Services)
New York Times
Pomona College Magazine
Race Relations Reporter
Rafu Shimpo
Rough Rider (Roosevelt High School)
Saturday Evening Post
Spotlight: A Newsletter for Employees of the Los Angeles City Schools
The Survey

INTERVIEWS

Aiso, John Fujio. Interview by Marc Landy. UCLA Oral History Program, UCLA Library Special Collections. August 3, 1970.
———. Interview by James C. McNaughton. In author's possession. October 30, 1987.
Cohen, Andrew. Telephone interview by author. January 4, 2008.
Embrey, Sue Kunitomi. Interview by Arthur Hansen and David Hacker. California State University, Fullerton, Oral History Program, interview no. 1366. August 24, 1973.
Erlich, Madeline. Interview by author. December 10, 2007. Culver City, Calif.

Snow, Ann. Interview by author. California State University, Los Angeles. December 6, 2007.

Tanaka, Togo. Interview by Betty Mitson and David Hacker. California State University, Fullerton, Oral History Program, interview no. 1271. May 19, 1973.

Valadez, Concepción. Interview by author. University of California, Los Angeles. January 8, 2008.

Zanki, Joseph Sr. Interview by author. Fountain Valley, Calif. July 20, 2011.

PUBLISHED SOURCES

Acosta, Oscar. "The East L.A. 13 vs. the L.A. Superior Court." *El Grito* 3, no. 2 (1970): 12–18.

Acuña, Rodolfo. *A Community under Siege: A Chronicle of Chicanos East of the Los Angeles River, 1945–1975.* Chicano Studies Research Center Publications, Monograph No. 11. Los Angeles: UCLA, 1984.

———. *Occupied America: A History of Chicanos.* 2nd ed. New York: Harper & Row, 1980.

Alvarez, Luis. *The Power of the Zoot: Youth Culture and Resistance during World War II.* Berkeley: University of California Press, 2008.

Anderson, Benedict. *Imagined Communities: Reflections on the Origin and Spread of Nationalism.* London: Verso, 1983.

Armor, John, and Peter Wright. *Manzanar: Commentary by John Hersey, Photographs by Ansel Adams.* New York: Times Books, 1988.

Avila, Eric. *Popular Culture in the Age of White Flight: Fear and Fantasy in Suburban Los Angeles.* Berkeley, University of California Press, 2004.

Azuma, Eiichiro. *Between Two Empires: Race, History, and Transnationalism in Japanese America.* New York: Oxford University Press, 2005.

Bagwell, Asbury A. "The Los Angeles Diploma Plan of Naturalizing the Alien: A Comparison of the Los Angeles Diploma Plan with Certain Other American Naturalization Methods in the Light of the Social Process of Assimilation and Socialization." Master's thesis, University of Southern California, 1929.

Bahr, Diana. *The Unquiet Nisei: An Oral History of the Life of Sue Kunitomi Embrey.* New York: Palgrave Macmillan, 2007.

Barrett, James. "Americanization from the Bottom Up: Immigration and the Remaking of the American Working Class in the United States, 1880–1930." *Journal of American History* 79 (December 1992): 996–1020.

Bell, Reginald. *Public School Education of Second-Generation Japanese in California.* Stanford, Calif.: Stanford University Press, 1935.

Bernal, Dolores Delgado. "Chicana School Resistance and Grassroots Leadership: Providing an Alternative History of the 1968 East Los Angeles Blowouts." PhD diss., University of California, Los Angeles, 1997.

Bernstein, Shana. *Bridges of Reform: Interracial Civil Rights Activism in Twentieth-Century Los Angeles.* New York: Oxford University Press, 2011.

Blanton, Carlos Kevin. *The Strange Career of Bilingual Education in Texas, 1836–1981.* College Station: Texas A&M University Press, 2004.

Bogardus, Emory S. *Essentials of Americanization.* Los Angeles: University of Southern California Press, 1919.

Bosniak, Linda. *The Citizen and the Alien: Dilemmas of Contemporary Membership.* Princeton, N.J.: Princeton University Press, 2006.

Bourne, Randolph. "Trans-National America." *Atlantic Monthly* 118 (1916): 86–97, http://www.theatlantic.com/magazine/archive/1916/07/trans-national-america/304838/.

Brilliant, Mark. *The Color of America Has Changed: How Racial Diversity Shaped Civil Rights Reform in California, 1941–1978.* New York: Oxford University Press, 2010.

Burkholder, Zoë. *Color in the Classroom: How American Schools Taught Race, 1900–1954.* New York: Oxford University Press, 2011.

Cameron, James. "The History of Mexican Public Education in Los Angeles, 1910–1930." Master's thesis, University of Southern California, 1976.

Campbell, Russell. "Bilingual Education and the English-Speaking Majority." In *Bilingual Program, Policy, and Assessment Issues.* Sacramento: California State Department of Education, 1980, 89.

Caughey, John. *To Kill a Child's Spirit: The Tragedy of School Segregation in Los Angeles.* Itasca, Ill.: F. E. Peacock, 1973.

Christian, Donna, Christopher Montone, Kathryn Lindholm, and Isolda Carranza. *Profiles in Two-Way Immersion Education.* McHenry, Ill.: Center for Applied Linguistics and Delta Systems, 1997.

Chase, Amanda Mathews. *The Home Teacher: The Act, with a Working Plan and Forty Lessons in English.* Sacramento: Commission of Immigration and Housing of California, 1916.

———. *Primer for Foreign-Speaking Women, Part I.* Sacramento: Commission of Immigration and Housing of California, 1918).

Chu, Judy. Keynote address at Celebrating 40 Years of Language Immersion Education, Southern California Language Symposium, Culver City, Calif., May 13, 2011.

Conzen, Kathleen Neils, David A. Gerber, Ewa Morawska, George E. Pozzetta, and Rudolph J. Vecoli. "The Invention of Ethnicity: A Perspective from the U.S.A." *Journal of American Ethnic History* 12, no. 1 (1992): 4–41.

Cooperider, Louise. "History of the Americanization Department in the Los Angeles City Schools." Master's thesis, University of Southern California, 1934.

Davies, Gareth. "The Great Society after Johnson: The Case of Bilingual Education." *Journal of American History* 88, no. 4 (2002): 1405–29.

Deverell, William. *Whitewashed Adobe: The Rise of Los Angeles and the Remaking of Its Mexican Past.* Berkeley: University of California Press, 2004.

Escobar, Edward. "Zoot-Suiters and the Cops: Chicano Youth and the Los Angeles Police Department during World War II." In *The War in American Culture: Society and Consciousness during World War II,* ed. Lewis Erenberg and Susan Hirsch, 285–97 (Chicago: University of Chicago Press, 1996).

Fass, Paula. *Outside In: Minorities and the Transformation of American Education.* New York: Oxford University Press, 1989.

Fukuoka, Fumiko. "Mutual Life and Aid among the Japanese in Southern California with Special Reference to Los Angeles." Master's thesis, University of Southern California, 1937.

Gamio, Manuel. *The Life Story of the Mexican Immigrant.* 1931. New York: Dover, 1971.

Gándara, Patricia. "In the Aftermath of the Storm: English Learners in the Post-227 Era." *Bilingual Research Journal* 24, nos. 1–2 (2000): 1–13.

García, Eugene. *Teaching and Learning in Two Languages: Bilingualism and Schooling in the United States.* New York, Teachers College Press, 2005.

García, Mario T. *Memories of Chicano History: The Life and Narrative of Bert Corona.* Berkeley: University of California Press, 1994.

García, Mario T., and Sal Castro. *Blowout! Sal Castro and the Chicano Struggle for Educational Justice.* Chapel Hill: University of North Carolina Press, 2011.

García, Matt. *A World of Its Own: Race, Labor, and Citrus in the Making of Greater Los Angeles, 1900–1970.* Chapel Hill: University of North Carolina Press, 2001.

Gonzalez, Gilbert G. *Labor and Community: Mexican Citrus Worker Villages in a Southern California County, 1900–1950.* Urbana: University of Illinois Press, 1994.

———. "The System of Public Education and Its Function within the Chicano Communities, 1920–1930." PhD diss., University of California, Los Angeles, 1974.

Griffith, Beatrice. *American Me.* Boston: Houghton Mifflin, 1948.

Gutfreund, Zevi. "Standing Up to Sugar Cubes: The Contest over Ethnic Identity in California's Fourth-Grade Mission Curriculum." *Southern California Quarterly* 92, no. 2 (2010): 161–97.

———. "Immigrant Education and Race: Alternative Approaches to 'Americanization' in Los Angeles, 1910–1940." *History of Education Quarterly* 57, no. 1 (2017): 1–38.

Gutierrez, Henry J. "The Chicano Education Rights Movement and School Desegregation: Los Angeles, 1962–1970." PhD diss., University of California, Irvine, 1990.

Haslam, Gerald, and Janice Haslam. *In Thought and Action: The Enigmatic Life of S. I. Hayakawa.* Lincoln: University of Nebraska Press, 2011.

Hayakawa, S. I. *Language in Thought and Action.* New York: Harcourt, Brace, 1949.

Hayashi, Brian. *Democratizing the Enemy: The Japanese American Internment.* Princeton, N.J.: Princeton University Press, 2004.

Hernández, Kelly Lytle. *Migra! A History of the U.S. Border Patrol.* Berkeley: University of California Press, 2010.

Higham, John. *Strangers in the Land: Patterns of American Nativism, 1860–1925.* New Brunswick, N.J.: Rutgers University Press, 1955.

Higonnet, Patrice. "The Politics of Linguistic Terrorism and Grammatical Hegemony during the French Revolution." *Social History* 5 (1980): 41–69.

Hill, Merton. *The Development of an Americanization Program.* Ontario, Calif.: Board of Trustees of the Chaffey Union High School, 1928.

Hirohata, Joyce, and Paul Hirohata, eds. *Nisei Voices: Japanese American Students of the 1930s—Then & Now.* Oakland: Hirohata Design. 2004. (Originally *Orations and Essays by the Japanese Second Generation of America,* 1932, 1935.)

Hobsbawm, Eric, and Terence Ranger, eds. *The Invention of Tradition.* Cambridge: Cambridge University Press, 1983.

Hollinger, David. *Postethnic America: Beyond Multiculturalism.* New York: Basic Books, 1995.

HoSang, Daniel. *Racial Propositions: Ballot Initiatives and the Making of Postwar California*. Berkeley: University of California Press, 2010.

Houston, Jeanne Wakatsuki. *Farewell to Manzanar: And Related Readings*, ed. Jeanne Wakatsuki Houston and James Houston. 1973. Evanston, Ill.: McDougal Littell, 1998.

Hughes, Marie, ed. *The School's Responsibility for the Improvement of Intergroup Relations: Report of Conference, December 20–22, 1945*. Los Angeles County Superintendent of Schools, with Office of Coordinator of Inter-American Affairs, 1945.

Ichinokuchi, Tad, ed. *John Aiso and the MIS: Japanese-American Soldiers in the Military Intelligence Service, World War II*. Los Angeles: Military Intelligence Service Club of Southern California, 1988.

Ichioka, Yuji. *Before Internment: Essays in Prewar Japanese American History*, ed. Gordon Chang and Eiichiro Azuma. Stanford, Calif.: Stanford University Press, 2006.

Inda, Juan J. "La comunidad en lucha: The Development of the East Los Angeles High School Blowouts." Paper presented at the 29th Stanford Center for Chicano Research Working Papers Series, Stanford, Calif., March 1990.

Jackson, George. "A History of the Adult Education Program in the Los Angeles Public Schools." PhD diss., University of California, Los Angeles, 1957.

James, Thomas. *Exile Within: The Schooling of Japanese Americans, 1942–1945*. Cambridge, Mass: Harvard University Press, 1987.

Kanzaki, Kiichi. *California and the Japanese*. 1921. San Francisco: R and E Research Associates,1971.

Kikuchi, Charles. *The Kikuchi Diary: Chronicle from an American Concentration Camp*. Ed. John Modell. Urbana: University of Illinois Press, 1973.

Kransdorf, Martha. *A Matter of Loyalty: The Los Angeles School Board vs. Frances Eisenberg*. San Francisco: Caddo Gap Press, 1994.

Kurashige, Lon. *Japanese American Celebration and Conflict: A History of Ethnic Identity and Festival, 1934–1990*. Berkeley: University of California Press, 2002.

Kurashige, Scott. *The Shifting Grounds of Race: Black and Japanese Americans in the Making of Multiethnic Los Angeles*. Princeton, N.J.: Princeton University Press, 2008.

Lanigan, Mary. "Second Generation Mexicans in Belvedere." Master's thesis, University of Southern California, 1932.

Lee, Shelley. "Cosmopolitan Identities: Japanese Americans in Seattle and the Pacific Rim, 1900–1942." PhD diss., Stanford University, 2005.

Lehman, Anthony. *Birthright of Barbed Wire: The Santa Anita Assembly Center for the Japanese*. Los Angeles: Westernlore Press, 1970.

Lozano, Rosina. "*Lenguaje sin fronteras* (Language without Borders): The Spanish Language in New Mexico and California, Politics, Education, and Identity, 1848–1952." PhD diss., University of Southern California, 2011.

Marin, Marguerite. *Social Protest in an Urban Barrio: A Study of the Chicano Movement, 1966–1974*. Lanham, Md.: University Press of America, 1991.

Mathews, Amanda. *The Hieroglyphics of Love: Stories of Sonora Town & Old Mexico*. Los Angeles: Artemisia Bindery, 1906.

Matsumoto, Valerie. *City Girls: The Nisei Social World in Los Angeles, 1920–1950*. New York: Oxford University Press, 2014.

May, Stephen. *Language and Minority Rights: Ethnicity, Nationalism, and the Politics of Language*. Harlow, UK: Longman, 2001.

McGirr, Lisa. *Suburban Warriors: The Origins of the New American Right*. Princeton, N.J.: Princeton University Press, 2001.

McNaughton, James C. *Nisei Linguists: Japanese Americans in the Military Intelligence Service during World War II*. Washington, D.C.: Department of the Army, 2006.

McWilliams, Carey. *Brothers under the Skin*. Rev. ed. Boston: Little, Brown, 1951.

———. *North from Mexico: The Spanish-Speaking People of the United States*. 1949. New York: Greenwood Press, 1990.

Mirel, Jeffrey. *Patriotic Pluralism: Americanization Education and European Immigrants*. Cambridge, Mass.: Harvard University Press, 2010.

Molina, Natalia. *Fit to Be Citizens? Public Health and Race in Los Angeles, 1879–1939*. Berkeley: University of California Press, 2006.

———. *How Race Is Made in America: Immigration, Citizenship, and the Historical Power of Racial Scripts*. Berkeley: University of California Press, 2014.

———. "'In a Race All Their Own': The Quest to Make Mexicans Ineligible for U.S. Citizenship." *Pacific Historical Review* 79, no. 2 (2010): 167–201.

Moreno, Jose, ed. *The Elusive Quest for Equality: 150 Years of Chicano/Chicana Education*. Cambridge, Mass.: Harvard Educational Review, 1999.

Morimoto, Toyotomi. "Language and Heritage Maintenance of Immigrants: Japanese Language Schools in California, 1903–1941." PhD diss., University of California, Los Angeles, 1989.

Myers, N. D., ed. *Education for Cultural Unity: Seventeenth Yearbook*. Oakland: California Elementary School Principals' Association, 1945.

Nakamura, Kelli Y. "'They Are Our Human Secret Weapons': The Military Intelligence Service and the Role of the Japanese-Americans in the Pacific War and in the Occupation of Japan." *The Historian* 70, no. 1 (2008): 54–74.

Nance, Afton D., and Mary Peters, eds. *Conference on the Education of Spanish-speaking Children and Youth, Ontario, Calif., March 25–26, 1966*. Sacramento: California Department of Education, 1966.

Nava, Julian, ed., *Viva La Raza! Readings on Mexican Americans*. New York: Van Nostrand, 1973.

Ngai, Mae M. "The Architecture of Race in American Immigration Law: A Reexamination of the Immigration Act of 1924." *Journal of American History* 86, no. 1 (1999): 67–92.

———. *Impossible Subjects: Illegal Aliens and the Making of Modern America*. Princeton, N.J.: Princeton University Press, 2004.

Ngai, Mae, and Jon Gjerde, eds. *Major Problems in American Immigration History: Documents and Essays*. 2nd ed. Boston: Wadsworth Cengage Learning, 2013.

Nicolaides, Becky. *My Blue Heaven: Life and Politics in the Working-Class Suburbs of Los Angeles, 1920–1965*. Chicago: University of Chicago Press, 2002.

Office of Bilingual Bicultural Education. *Studies on Immersion Education: A Collection for United Stated Educators*. Sacramento: California State Department of Education, 1984.

Omi, Michael, and Howard Winant. *Racial Formation in the United States: From the 1960s to the 1990s*. 2nd ed. New York: Routledge, 1994.

Pak, Yoon. *Wherever I Go, I Will Always Be a Loyal Americans: Schooling Seattle's Japanese American Schoolchildren During World War II.* New York: Routledge/Falmer, 2002.

Petrzela, Natalia Mehlman. "Before the Federal Bilingual Education Act." *Peabody Journal of Education* 85 (2010): 406–24.

———. *Classroom Wars: Language, Sex, and the Creation of Modern Political Culture.* New York: Oxford University Press, 2015.

———. "Origins of the Culture Wars: Sex, Language, School, and State in California, 1968–78." PhD diss., Stanford University, 2009.

Philp, Kenneth. *John Collier's Crusade for Indian Reform, 1920–1954.* Tucson: University of Arizona Press, 1977.

"Present Day Immigration with Special Reference to the Japanese." Special issue, *Annals of the American Academy of Political and Social Science* 93 (January 1921).

Raftery, Judith. *Land of Fair Promise: Politics and Reform in Los Angeles Schools, 1885–1941.* Stanford, Calif.: Stanford University Press, 1992.

Rhodes, Nancy, and Tara Fortune, "Language Immersion: Yesterday, Today, and Tomorrow." Paper presented at Celebrating 40 Years of Language Immersion Education, Southern California Language Symposium, Culver City, Calif., May 13, 2011.

Ruiz, Vicki, and Ellen DuBois, eds. *Unequal Sisters: A Multicultural Reader in U.S. Women's History.* 2nd ed. New York: Routledge, 1994.

Salazar, Ruben. *Border Correspondent: Selected Writings, 1955–1970,* ed. Mario T. García. Berkeley: University of California Press, 1995.

Sánchez, George I. *Concerning Segregation of Spanish-Speaking Children in the Public Schools.* Occasional Papers of Inter-American Education 9. Austin: University of Texas Press, 1951.

———. *First Regional Conference on the Education of Spanish-Speaking People in the Southwest.* Occasional Papers of Inter-American Education 1. Austin: University of Texas Press, 1946.

Sánchez, George J. *Becoming Mexican American: Ethnicity, Culture, and Identity in Chicano Los Angeles, 1900–1945.* New York: Oxford University Press, 1993.

Selig, Diana. *Americans All: The Cultural Gifts Movement.* Cambridge, Mass.: Harvard University Press, 2008.

Servín, Manuel, ed. *The Mexican-Americans: An Awakening Minority.* 1st and 2nd eds. Beverly Hills, Calif.: Glencoe Press, 1970, 1974.

Shimoda, Hiraku. "Tongues-Tied: The Making of a 'National Language' and the Discovery of Dialects in Meiji Japan." *American Historical Review* 115, no. 3 (2010): 714–31.

Sides, Josh. *L.A. City Limits: African American Los Angeles from the Great Depression to the Present.* Berkeley: University of California Press, 2003.

Sparrow, James. *Warfare State: World War II Americans and the Age of Big Government.* New York: Oxford University Press, 2011.

Sterry, Nora. *The International Cook Book of the Elementary Principals' Club of Los Angeles, Cal.: A Collection of Choice Recipes From Foreign Lands.* Los Angeles: Citizen Print Shop, 1930.

———. "The Sociological Basis for the Reorganization of the Macy Street School." Master's thesis, University of Southern California, 1924.

Stone, James, David Shoemaker, and Nicholas Dotti. *Interrogation: World War II, Vietnam, and Iraq.* Washington, D.C.: National Defense Intelligence College Press, 2008.

Strong, Edward K. *The Second-Generation Japanese Problem.* Stanford, Calif.: Stanford University Press, 1934.

Strum, Philippa. Mendez v. Westminster: *School Desegregation and Mexican-American Rights.* Lawrence: University Press of Kansas, 2010.

Tanaka, Tamiko. "The Japanese Language School in Relation to Assimilation." Master's thesis, University of Southern California, 1933.

Thomas, Dorothy Swaine, and Richard Nishimoto. *The Spoilage: Japanese American Evacuation and Resettlement.* Berkeley: University of California Press, 1946.

Tuck, Ruth. *Not with the Fist: Mexican-Americans in a Southwest City.* New York: Harcourt, Brace, 1946.

Tuthill, Gretchen. "Study of the Japanese in the City of Los Angeles." Master's thesis, University of Southern California, 1924.

Uono, Koyoshi. "The Factors Affecting the Geographical Aggregation and Dispersion of the Japanese Residences in the City of Los Angeles." Master's thesis, University of Southern California, 1927.

Van Nuys, Frank. *Americanizing the West: Race, Immigrants, and Citizenship, 1890–1930.* Lawrence: University Press of Kansas. 2002.

Varzally, Allison. *Making a Non-White America: Californians Coloring Outside Ethnic Lines, 1925–1955.* Berkeley: University of California Press, 2008.

Vaughan, Mary Kay. *Cultural Politics in Revolution: Teachers, Peasants, and Schools in Mexico, 1930–1940.* Tucson: University of Arizona Press, 1997.

Weber, Eugen. *Peasants into Frenchmen: The Modernization of Rural France, 1870–1914.* Stanford, Calif.: Stanford University Press, 1976.

Wei, William. *The Asian American Movement.* Philadelphia, Pa.: Temple University Press, 1993.

Weiler, Kathleen. *Democracy and Schooling in California: The Legacy of Helen Heffernan and Corinne Seeds.* New York: Palgrave Macmillan, 2011.

Wild, Mark. "'So Many Children at Once and So Many Kinds': Schools and Ethno-racial Boundaries in Early Twentieth-Century Los Angeles." *Western Historical Quarterly* 33, no. 4 (2002): 453–78.

———. *Street Meeting: Multiethnic Neighborhoods in Early Twentieth-Century Los Angeles.* Berkeley: University of California Press, 2005.

Wood, Diane. "Immigrant Mothers, Female Reformers, and Women Teachers: The California Home Teachers Act of 1915." PhD diss., Stanford University, 1996.

Woods, Robert, and Albert Kennedy, eds. *Handbook of Settlements.* New York: Russell Sage Foundation, 1911.

Yoo, David. *Growing Up Nisei: Race, Generation, and Culture among Japanese Americans of California, 1924–49.* Urbana: University of Illinois Press, 1999.

Yu, Henry. *Thinking Orientals: Migration, Contact, and Exoticism in Modern America.* New York: Oxford University Press, 2001.

INDEX

CPSIA information can be obtained
at www.ICGtesting.com
Printed in the USA
LVHW091612100420
652978LV00003B/44/J

9 780806 161860